W9-CFF-275

Bitter Canaan

BLACK CLASSICS OF SOCIAL SCIENCE

Wilbur H. Watson, Series Editor

This series of classics focuses on major contributions by Black social scientists to understanding human behavior, history, and social change. A basic goal of the series is the reprinting of important theoretical and empirical works now out of print, and which address issues relevant to contemporary social science and policy. In addition to titles originally written as slave protest pamphlets but never widely circulated, this series offers works by twentieth-century figures who have influenced social scientific thought. In the selection of both titles and writers of introductory essays, we attempt to draw attention to points of convergence and divergence among Black American, African, and West-Indian social scientists, ranging from general to specific issues.

Bitter Canaan
The Story of the Negro Republic

Charles S. Johnson

Introductory Essay by
John Stanfield

Transaction Books
New Brunswick (U.S.A.) and Oxford (U.K.)

Copyright © 1987 by Transaction, Inc.
New Brunswick, New Jersey 08903

Library of Congress Catalog Number: 87-1670
ISBN: 0-88738-053-0
Printed in the United States of America

Library of Congress Cataloging in Publication Data

Johnson, Charles Spurgeon, 1893-1956.
  Bitter Canaan.

  (Black classics of social science)
  Includes index.
  1. Liberia—History. 2. Afro-Americans—
Colonization—Liberia. 3. Liberia—Relations—
United States. 4. United States—Relations—
Liberia. 5. Liberia—Economic conditions.
6. Liberia—Social conditions. I. Title.
II. Series
DT631.J59   1987   966.6'2   87-1670
ISBN 0-88738-053-0

Contents

Preface

In 1929, Fisk sociologist Charles Spurgeon Johnson was already a well-known figure in American race relations policy circles. When, late that year, Johnson accepted President Herbert Hoover's invitation to serve as the American representative on the International Commission of Inquiry into the Existence of Slavery and Forced Labor in the Republic of Liberia, little did he know that it would be the threshold to a luminary professional career that would soar to extraordinary heights. Johnson's service on the Commission was also an impetus of an intellectual preoccupation that would hold his attention for nearly twenty years: the writing of *Bitter Canaan*.

When Commissioner Johnson returned to the United States from his seven month-long assignment in Liberia (March to September 1930), he was deeply disturbed. He was thoroughly disgusted with what he saw and heard in what was supposed to be the Canaan land of the Black presence on planet earth, the prime-model bastion of Black self-rule. Johnson was appalled at how the Liberian elite—the Amero-Liberians—who were descendents of Afro-Americans who emigrated from a white America, exploited and generally mistreated native populations. The means through which Amero-Liberians, the neighboring imperialistic European colonial powers, and the United States as reluctant guardian of the nation-state handled Liberia's underdevelopment problems did not sit comfortably with him.

His disgust and his outrage at the Liberian conditions he observed moved him to write *Bitter Canaan*. For almost two decades, *Bitter Canaan* was Johnson's labor of love, created in the "cracks" of a busy career. Johnson considered *Bitter Canaan* his best work, but for reasons to be given, it was never published. *Bitter Canaan* was also Johnson's most unique work. More than any other book-length work he wrote, *Bitter Canaan* displays Johnson's lifelong interest in synthesizing literary and social scientific logics of inquiry. More important, *Bitter Canaan's* moralistic tone and principle concepts offer evidence of Johnson's independent thought from the Chicago School of Sociology and his disbelief in what C. Wright Mills called *abstract empiricism*. *Bitter Canaan* places Johnson firmly in the mainstream of what is now considered humanistic sociology, a label he probably would have been happy with. Regardless of the methodology Johnson used in a particular study, he maintained a sympathetic posture toward the oppressed and a disdain toward oppressors. He never forgot the humanity of his subjects and dedicated his life to describing the conditions through which their humanness was denied through structures of oppression. He also worked tirelessly toward developing a more humane society and world for all, supporting the theory of democracy and encouraging its practice.

The importance of Johnson's *Bitter Canaan* in the history of sociological thought and in the sociology of African development is multifaceted. First, the book is a significant precursor to Walter Rodney's *How Europe Underdeveloped Africa* and the critical sociology of development of the underdevelopment school it represents. Second, *Bitter Canaan* adds a needed dimension to the Rodney thesis. Understandably, Rodney discusses Liberia very little since his focus is on European metropolitan powers and their imperialistic activities in Africa. Johnson's *Bitter Canaan* sheds light on the major American colonial extension into Africa; it brings into clear focus the way American interests (economic, political, and military), a dependent Amero-Liberian elite, and European colonial powers underdeveloped a coastal territory in West Africa.

Although what Johnson comments on may be common knowledge today, in the 1930s and 1940s, that was not the case; particularly not in the context of development of underdevelopment perspective. *Bitter Canaan* must be evaluated in its historical context and when we do so, its significance as a precursor to contemporary critical thinking about African development becomes more than apparent.

Third, the background on how Johnson came to write *Bitter Canaan* and why it was never published is an important question in the sociology of knowledge exemplifying the career dilemmas of pre-World War II Afro-American scholars. Through "great persons" analyses or gossipy exposés that dwell on personality quirks, contributors to the literature in conventional Afro-American sociological thought generally focus on the sociology of published ideas. This dominant perspective has encouraged an avoidance of issues evolving around the racial etiquette of scholarly production. As in other major institutional spheres, racial stratification, maintained through prescribed rites, rituals, and taboos, is a central organizing principle in the world of scholarship.

Specifically, the racial etiquette governing scholastic productivity is a reflection of the patterns of historically-societal racial inequality which have traditionally determined what themes and ideas are acceptable in the realm of traditional scholarship, and what groups are to be given priority in the production and transmission of knowledge. During the pre-World War

II period, for instance, Black scholars who dared to address the issue of caste found their ideas ignored or marginalized. As well, those who were openly hostile to the monopoly held by White philanthropists on educational issues affecting Blacks, and who questioned the role of these persons in furthering the careers of certain (generally submissive) intellectuals, found themselves persecuted, labelled as unreasonable or viewed as intellectual troublemakers. Blacks who were bold enough to question the influences of American foundations in the formation of European colonial policies in Africa were likewise ignored and dismissed. Meanwhile, Black scholars who were more disposed to accommodate the rules of Jim Crow social science, which stressed paradigms of asymmetrical assimilationist and interracial cooperation, had their ideas cited and celebrated and were deemed intellectual leaders.

Sometimes, as can be seen in the example of *Bitter Canaan*, Black social scientists who otherwise had their more accommodated ideas circulated widely in professional circles, were unable to get their less tactful ideas published. These more radical ideas were taboo topics among the White elite and in conservative Black bourgeois circles. Given the persistence of racial stratification in the social sciences and its accompanying racial etiquette, it is imperative that we examine the ideas left in the private papers of Black social scientists not only for their intellectual import but also to gain a sense of historically specific patterns of racial caste relations of scholarly production. The availability of the papers of Charles S. Johnson, E. Franklin Frazier, Carter G. Woodson, and of major pre-World War II funding sources enable us to begin more comprehensive analyses of Afro-American sociological thought from the perspective of the sociology of knowledge.

As a major contribution to the history of American sociological thought, Johnson's *Bitter Canaan* deserves a full critical examination. Guided by the sociology of knowledge, this examination begins with the premise that an intellectual product such as a book cannot be divorced from the life history of its author, the attitudes of its financiers, and the culture of the institutional context in which it is produced. Thus, although textual analysis is a vital and necessary method of unpacking an intellectual product, it is, by no means, a sufficient one. The materialization of a book's contents is a social act that cannot be understood fully without consideration given to the historial milieu, the culture and politics of knowledge production, and the biographical characteristics of the writer.

The lengthy discussion on how *Bitter Canaan* fits into Johnson's sociological thought, presented later in this introductory essay, is meant to demonstrate the need to go beyond the biographical, bibliographical, and personal traditions in the study of Afro-American social scientists and scholars in general. Also, it will correct the often mistaken view that Johnson was merely a carbon copy of Robert E. Park and the Chicago School. A close reading of Johnson will reveal a scholar whose devotion to scholarship and objectivity clearly transcended the prevailing views on race that existed during his era.

Unfortunately, the raciocultural hegemony which governs how American sociological thought is viewed and around which it is written has served as a major hindrance to understanding the relevance of asking serious questions about Afro-American sociological thought. This is particularly the case when it comes to suggesting a theoretical approach that explores how the intellectual products of Afro-American social scientists become mainstreamed, marginalized, or excluded from the arena of scholastic discourse. This introductory essay to *Bitter Canaan* approaches the work through the framework of the sociology of knowledge and in so doing explains why Johnson considered this particular manuscript his best writing. Finally, some propositions are advanced to account for why the work was not previously published. In the epilogue, there is a brief attempt to revise common knowledge about Charles S. Johnson's career.

I wish to thank Dr. Maurice and Mrs. Patricia Clifford (daughter of Charles S. Johnson), for granting me permission to publish *Bitter Canaan* and special thanks to Mrs. Clifford for giving me access to correspondence between her father and mother that she had in her possession.

I am most grateful to the following individuals for their comments on the introductory essay: David Apter, John W. Blassingame, Rutledge Dennis, Edmund W. Gordon, Harriett G. McCombs, Charles C. Moskos, Jr., Earl Smith, and David Tyack. Delores Grillo, Kimberly Phillips and especially Francesca Polletta, who proofread most of the *Bitter Canaan* manuscript, while Carole D. Tiernan and Gayle D. White typed the manuscript. The research for the essay was financed by the Ford Foundation, Yale University Social Science Research Grant Program, the National Academy of Education, and the National Science Foundation. I am deeply grateful for their generous financial support.

Librarians in the following libraries assisted me in this research and gave me permission to quote from materials in their archives: Chicago Historical Society, Fisk University, National Archives, Schomburg Center for Research in Black Culture. Many thanks to Irving Horowitz, president of Transaction Books; Special Series Editor Wilbur H. Watson; and the diligent editorial staff of Transaction Books who made the publication of *Bitter Canaan* possible.

JOHN H. STANFIELD II

Introductory Essay:
Bitter Canaan's Historical Backdrop

Charles Spurgeon Johnson considered *Bitter Canaan* his best writing.[1] It is a historical sociological assessment of the Amero-Liberian elite's development of a caste-ridden society. The major emphasis is on the use of statistical and ethnographic data to analyze how various political, economic, cultural and societal organizations created a flourishing domestic and international system of slavery which was condemned by the United States and the League of Nations. *Bitter Canaan*, written as a literary essay, is a fusion of Johnson's skills in literature and social science. For twenty years it was Johnson's labor of love, written and rewritten during breaks from an incredibly busy schedule. Not getting it published was one of Johnson's greatest disappointments. But it could not have been published during his lifetime because it broke with too many traditions underlying the racial etiquette of the politics of scholarship.

Johnson wrote the first draft of *Bitter Canaan* in 1930 after he returned from service with the League of Nations International Commission of Inquiry into the Existence of Slavery and Forced Labor in the Republic of Liberia. Why the U.S. government took an interest in Liberian affairs and chose Charles S. Johnson as the American representative on the International Commission is a fascinating and little-known episode in U.S. history that deserves elaboration.

During the first quarter of the nineteenth century, Liberia was founded by freemen and ex-slaves sponsored by the American Colonization Society. Although the United States government gave minimal support to the country and in fact took many years before officially recognizing it, over the decades Liberia became known in world opinion as a ward of the U.S. federal government. The reluctance of the U.S. government to get involved in Liberian affairs unless unavoidable was part and parcel of the isolationism of American foreign policy up through World War I. The occasional American interventions into Liberian affairs usually came when Liberia, which was always in financial straits, could not get loans from other countries or when its European colonial neighbors threatened its boundaries. Also, the federal government occasionally helped Amero-Liberians to squelch native uprisings.[2]

It is important not to equate the lack of formal U.S. foreign policy in Liberia and in other parts of Africa with a lack of ideological position vis-à-vis the continent. The United States government did not criticize European penetration into Africa and indeed allowed American capitalists to profit from the activities of such colonialists. When European colonial powers, for instance, decided to cease using African societies as markets for liquor sales, the U.S. liquor market moved in.[3] Just prior to the Great War, State Department officials began to point out the virtues of Liberia, hoping that American investors would take advantage of such opportunities. However, the Great War distracted State Department officials from this public relations concern. The federal government became involved in Liberia after World War I, helping Amero-Liberians squelch a serious native rebellion in 1918 and by giving the Liberians a major loan. The loan was given on the condition that the Liberian government initiate a series of social and political reforms. It is interesting to note that the U.S. government became concerned about Liberian political corruptibility and problems of native mistreatment only when pressed by world opinion to answer the desperate pleas for help from Amero-Liberians.[4]

Otherwise, State Department officials turned their backs on the political atrocities of Amero-Liberians and their mistreatment of native populations. For instance, in the 1910s, the probability that neighboring Spanish African colonies were using forced Liberian labor came to the State Department's attention. The reports were merely filed away or used for other purposes. On 17 January, a State Department official noted that "Exploitation of the natives in Liberia has been occurring for many years. At least since 1914, when Liberian government officials contracted with the Spanish government to supply laborers to Fernando Poo planters, the political mold was set."[5]

In the early 1920s, the advent of American foundation and corporation interest in Liberia was to drastically change U.S. posture toward the country. The prevalent assumption in foreign policy literature has been that the U.S. State Department did not formulate foreign policies toward African national states until the decolonization period—the post-1960s.[6] This belief is more a product of the politics of the rediscovery of Africa during that time and the subsequent demand for informed contemporary literature on the matter than based on actual fact. Prior to World War II, U.S. African foreign policies were mainly shaped by missionaries, explorers, foundations and corporations informally representing the federal government. Only since the end of World War II has the State Department become the major formulator of U.S. policies toward Africa. Interestingly, the U.S. government's approach to Africa has paralleled its treatment of domestic Afro-American affairs.

State Department archives are replete with correspondence indicating that the ambiguous U.S. policies toward Africa prior to World War II had informal premises which were shaped by the reports and interests of American explorers, missionaries, foundations, and corporations. The activities of the U.S. liquor industry in the 1910s has already been pointed out. In the 1920s, missionary and foundation roles in developing and carrying out African policies with informal state department approval crystallized due to a dramatic set of circumstances. In a profound way, their central roles both converged and clashed with emergent American corporation interests in Liberia.

It was the American-based International Missionary Association that persuaded the state department to ratify the League of Nations' 1926 Antislavery Convention. This was an unprecedented feat. Since the U.S. Senate had refused to sign the Treaty of Versailles, the State Department was reluctant to involve itself officially in League of Nations affairs. But understandably, though always giving a noncommittal response to League of Nations mail, State Department officials kept close tabs on the leading figures of the League and the organization's activities. Once in a while, when the need arose, a private citizen on other business who just happened to be in Geneva served informally as the U.S. representative.[7]

There was a powerful international missionary effort to reform various aspects of European colonial rule in the Third World during the 1920s. One of the major efforts missionary groups rallied behind was the eradication of slavery throughout the world. The vehi e used to support this cause was the League of Nations' International Labor Bureau. Throughout the early 1920s, the International Labor Bureau worked toward worldwide agreement among members and nonmembers to outlaw slavery and labor systems analogous to slavery. By the mid-1920s, most major world powers had ratified the Antislavery Convention. The United States had not.[8]

State Department officials were kept abreast of the League of Nations' antislavery movement but aside from responding to a survey, kept themselves aloof with noncommittal responses to correspondence about it. The survey they responded to, which was sent to every national capital, asked if the U.S. or any of its territories had slavery or analogous forced labor systems within its boundaries. State Department officials posed this question to spokesmen in departments of Labor, Interior Army, and Navy. Since all of them claimed that slavery and its analogous forms did not exist in their jurisdictions, State Department officials informed the International Labor Bureau that the U.S. was free of the problem. This was an ironic gesture given the extensive southern peonage system, the Hawaiian plantation system, and forced labor conditions confining populations of Mexican descent in the southwestern U.S.[9]

Missionary association leaders began meeting with State Department officials after numerous major nations had ratified the Antislavery Convention. Their arguments were both moral and political. Missionaries pointed out the immorality of slavery and argued that the U.S. should conform to growing world opinion about the need to endorse its eradication.[10] Soon, missionary leaders won State Department officials over to their perspective through their reports on international slavery as well as, political and economic reasons to be discussed shortly.[11] These missionaries wrote the policy papers for the State Department to argue their case before the U.S. Senate which had to approve ratification of the convention and newspaper releases.[12]

But there were other reasons why State Department officials changed their minds so quickly and decided to lobby for ratification of a convention sponsored by an international organization which had a controversial image in the media and which the U.S. did not recognize. State Department officials feared that mounting international political pressure would give domestic labor unions an opportunity to raise the delicate issue of the relationship between imported cheap goods and the forced labor system which produced the goods.[13]

To head off this exposure, which certainly would be an embarrassing incident, State Department officials decided to push for ratification of the antislavery convention on their own terms in collaboration with an elite segment of the American religious establishment. Whatever they decided to do would certainly be more wholesome to ruling class interests than would be changes forced from the bottom due to adverse publicity. The ratification of the antislavery convention maintained domestically and abroad the image of the U.S. as a humane state sharing the international indignation about the existence of slavery. It also enabled business to go on as usual between U.S. industrialists and the forced labor markets abroad which produced commodities for American consumption so cheaply.

While American missionaries helped to raise State Department consciousness about the acute political consequences of maintaining an officially neutral stance, the Phelps-Stokes Fund, the Carnegie Corporation, and the Rockefeller International Education Board were becoming involved in European colonial educational affairs in Africa. The administrators of these foundations, especially Thomas Jesse Jones of the Phelps-Stokes Fund, were interested in applying the Tuskegee model of southern Black education to various European colonies and settlement societies in Africa. Their attempts were based on the assumption that, like the rural U.S. south, peripheral industrial education made African natives "adaptive" to their environments. By making them the passive subjects of colonial rule, such foundation-sponsored native education strategies became quite popular in British West and South Africa.[14]

In the 1920s, the Phelps-Stokes Fund and the International Education Board founded the Booker T. Washington Industrial School in Liberia. The school was controlled by the foundations, which had given the bulk of financial assistance and whose administrators sat on the governing board including Thomas Jesse Jones of the Phelps-Stokes Fund and Jackson Davis of the Rockefeller General Education Board and the International Education Board. The Booker T. Washington Industrial School enabied these men to be informal ambassadors of sociocultural solutions to Liberian underdevelopment and gave them the power base for being authoritative spokesmen on Liberian internal affairs. Jones' inroads into the powerful inner circles of British colonial administration in all parts of Africa gave him a special berth in the informal culture of the State Department. More broadly, the Phelps-Stokes Fund was an instrumental institutional surrogate for State Department African policy development during the interwar period. Indeed, for many years after Jones published major works on African native education policy on behalf of the Phelps-Stokes Fund, the foundation continued to be the most well-respected authority on native education in Africa.[15]

Missionary associations and foundations worked hand-in-hand in developing adaptive corporate forms of native African education. In Liberia this collaborative effort converged with interests Harvey Firestone had in developing rubber plantations in the country in the 1920s. Expanding American consumer demands for rubber goods, particularly those related to the automobile, as well as an expensive British monopoly on rubber production, inspired Firestone to search for territory to establish rubber plantations.[16]

Since the presence of the Firestone Company in Liberia would help to unburden the State Department officials of their wearisome ward, Harvey Firestone experienced little difficulty in persuading them to give him leeway in negotiating with the Liberian government. The Liberian government's dependency on the U.S., induced by deep financial difficulties and aggressive European colonial neighbors, added obvious leverage to Firestone's efforts to develop a massive plantation economy in the country. Also, the lack of a competitive economic base in Liberia made the offer quite inviting. Foundation and missionary administrators endorsed and later defended Firestone's efforts, since the presence of comprehensive American capital would aid the country's sociocultural development.

Thus, Firestone experienced little resistance in first renegotiating a U.S. loan made to Liberia in 1926 and then bargaining for a 99-year lease of one million acres of land. The lease terms ensured that Firestone would have an unquestionable right to influence property ownership and use for decades to come.[17] It would enable the State Department to keep a closer informal eye on internal affairs in Liberia.

The financial arrangements and the land-leasing agreement assured Firestone decision-making in internal Liberian affairs. This had to be in order to protect American corporate interests in an African region outside direct European control.[18] But, of course, neither the State Department, nor the Firestone Company ever admitted the "need" to keep Liberian affairs under the indirect control of White Americans. In fact, they went to great lengths to appear to be more concerned with developing the Liberian economy than indulging in neocolonialism.

The paranoia of State Department and Firestone Company interests regarding the slightest criticism of neocolonial linkages with Liberia surfaced behind closed doors in the late 1920s. A series of events that had the potential of tainting the American image abroad eventually led to the immediate circumstances behind Johnson's writing of *Bitter Canaan.* These events demonstrate that in the world of politics, image-maintenance often takes precedence over reality and, indeed, proceeds to become reality.

After the U.S. Senate ratified the 1926 Antislavery Convention, State Department officials continued their business-as-usual attitude toward Liberia with one significant difference. Between the late nineteenth century and World War I, the Liberian government was in frequent boundary disputes with its British and particularly its French colonial neighbors. Amero-Liberians often asked the United States to exert its diplomatic power and to provide financial assistance to enable them to ward off their European colonial neighbors. After World War I, the French resumed attempts to annex Liberian areas adjoining Sierra Leone. This controversy was resolved by the United States, which advised the Liberian government to make peace with France. The State Department was able to have such authority in Liberian affairs not only because it was requested by Amero-Liberians but also because, since the end of World War I, a federal loan to the Liberian government had been administered by American banking industry representatives.[19]

The boundary disputes with powerful neighbors who had imperialistic designs encouraged the Amero-Liberian leadership to strengthen its ties to American capital. Certainly, significant American economic activity would discourage further British and French efforts to liquidate Liberian sovereignty.[20] This assumption accompanied the search for expendable sources of rubber plantation development by U.S. industrialists. World War I stimulated demand for rubber products and consumer demands for automobiles.

Herbert Hoover as secretary of commerce was a major advocate of t. extension of U.S. rubber industries as a means to break up the monopoly in the production of rubber.[21] For example, Harvey Firestone was encouraged by Herbert Hoover and other government figures to seek out properties conducive to large-scale rubber plantation development.

Firestone believed labor was practically inexhaustible for such an intensified economic activity. Most of all, he realized the ease with which U.S. capitalists could control the Liberian political and economic climate. This process would assure a seemingly eternal flow of rubber dividends to the U.S. government and provide capital profits for Harvey Firestone. In the climate of the 1920s and indeed, of today, U.S. capitalists were hesitant to implant industrial activity in non-European nations without at least neocolonial control of their internal affairs. This mode of what has been called the development of underdevelopment was thought to be particularly necessary by U.S. capitalists to protect their interests in a country such as Liberia which was economically unstable and politically vulnerable in the face of aggressive European colonial neighbors and hostile native populations.

With the blessings of the State Department, Firestone succeeded in negotiating a lucrative agreement with the Liberian government. This agreement included a 99-year lease for up to 1 million acres which Firestone could develop (building highways, railroads, etc.), with minor profits going to the Liberian government. The Firestone Company had the exclusive right to construct highways, railways, and waterways for the efficient development of the property. However, Mr. Firestone declined to agree to the government proposal that these roads should be open to the public, a position which seems ungenerous in comparison with obligations of concession-holders in the Belgian Congo.[22] The government agreed to supply Firestone with some 300,000 laborers, a number it predicted would be sufficient to develop his rubber plantations. Liberian government officials balked at the provision that "the Liberian government should not make a new loan of any kind, whether for refunding or any other purpose, for a period of thirty years." After long debate, the period was set at fifteen years.[23]

But the proposition that "threw the city of Monrovia into furor" was the Clause K Firestone inserted in the agreement after the Liberian legislature had approved it.[24] Clause K, "relating to the million-acre concession, which declared that the operation of the agreement should be dependent upon the acceptance of a loan by the Liberian government on the same terms as the loan which the American Senate had rejected in 1921." If this loan had been approved by the U.S. Senate, it would have been a five million dollar senatorial agreement on the condition that the federal government had the authority to "appoint twenty-two officials to administer Liberia's financial, military, and native affairs."[25] Amero-Liberians feared that since there was no chance that the U.S. government would extend such a loan, Firestone would be the loan giver. Since Harvey Firestone would offer the loan, he would be able to appoint administrators who would constitute a powerful voice in Liberian affairs. There was a fear among Amero-Liberians that Firestone was trying to usurp their power through methods similar to those used by American corporations in Haiti.

Firestone and the Liberian government eventually agreed to seek the development loan from an independent financial source, the Finance Corporation of America. The Finance Corporation of America was not really independent at all since it was established by Firestone for the allocation and the administration of the loan.[26] Firestone set it up through the National City Bank of New York.[27]

There was the impending possibility that the Liberian government would try to refinance the loan to avoid longterm high interest rates. Government officials intended to approach the British or the French. To prevent this, and to protect his capital, Firestone insisted that the Liberian government not refinance the loan for thirty years. The Liberian president opposed any such plans for over fifteen years. Through American diplomatic pressure, he compromised on twenty years.[28] The terms of the loan required the appointment of a finance adviser to be approved by the U.S. president and appointed by the Liberian government. Other foreign officers were to be appointed to help administer the loan. [29] This loan agreement went into effect in 1927.

All of these points were taken from a massive study by Raymond E. Buell, *The Native Problem in Africa,* published in 1928.[30] It is no wonder that when State Department officials heard about Buell's book while it was going through final production stages, they were upset enough to attempt to neutralize its impact before it reached the public. This had to be done since Buell, formerly of the Harvard Bureau of International Research and a member of a foreign relations association, was a prominent international relations scholar.

Buell was in agreement with the Eurocentric justification for foreign aid for developing "backward societies" like Liberia.[31] Moreover, he did not think the State Department was purposely in conspiracy with Firestone interests. But his critical perspective and the extensive documentation of his argument posed a grave threat to the State Department and the U.S. image abroad—particularly the points he made about the inevitability of forced labor use by an otherwise "enlightened" corporation. Firestone would be embarrassed in light of the widely publicized international antislavery movement. Buell criticized Firestone's and the State Department's naiveté about the demographic and social organizational aspects of Liberia that would lead inevitably to Firestone having to use forced native labor to reach his economic goals. He pointed out how and why the British and French abandoned plantation agriculture based on native labor, and argued that Liberia did not have the abundant population for free labor use. To preserve his company's labor supply, Firestone would have to develop a forced labor system analogous to slavery.[32]

If Buell's well-documented allegations were not discredited, the U.S. image as Liberia's guardian would be tarnished domestically and abroad. Equally important, American neocolonial control over Liberian internal affairs would be exposed. State Department officials attempted to discredit Buell by preparing an immediate rebuttal through the Associated Press when the book reached the public.[33] Associated Press representatives were asked to stand by for denial claims by State Department officials. State Department officials wrote a denial speech for Liberian President King. Most of their efforts to deny the accuracy of Buell's perspective were published in the *New York Times*.[34]

State Department press releases denied that the Firestone interests enslaved natives and that Americans exercised great control in Liberian affairs. When Buell went to Williamstown, Massachusetts to continue his criticisms, State Department officials braced themselves for a prompt rebuttal. Their strategy was to counter Buell's claims so quickly that there was no time for negative public opinion to crystallize. The attempt by the State Department to manipulate public opinion in the *New York Times* and in other prominent mass media was a clear illustration of how governmental elites are aware of the fact that the politics of image control is at times more important than debating verifiable facts.[35]

Anson-Stokes, and especially Thomas Jesse Jones of the Phelps-Stokes Fund, aided State Department efforts through published lectures and through reviews of Buell's books. The convergence of the Phelps-Stokes Fund and State Department efforts to discredit Buell was evident when a review of Buell's book written by Jones was forwarded to the State Department to assist in their counter attack.[36]

In countering Buell, State Department officials and their allies distorted the researcher's argument in the extreme. Their claims that Buell's statements about the interests of American rubber were premised on circumstantial evidence were inaccurate given his efforts to document his points. In their criticisms of Buell's analysis of inevitable slavery in Liberia, State Department officals distorted the true thrust of his arguments, namely, the historical and demographic conditions which made slavery and other forced labor usage inevitable in West African plantation economies. Also, he did not oppose imperialism and in fact, was in favor of it as long as it was carefully applied in "backward" societies.[37]

The Buell controversy triggered recollections of the allegation of slavery by the American Legation in Monrovia. Apparently, State Department officials were not too confident in their stand. Indeed, if government files on Liberia are accurate indicators, one gets the impression that State Department officials were quite naive about Liberian internal affairs, particularly about the labor activities of the Firestone Company. Although for years State Department officials received routine reports about native forced labor sent abroad, there was no concerted effort to gauge the depth of the problem. World opinion did not demand answers until 1928. Several months after the Buell controversy ended, the U.S. minister to Monrovia reported to his superiors that he was receiving definite evidence of forced labor practices from a variety of sources.[38]

As the evidence poured in documenting a flourishing domestic and international forced labor market condoned by high officials in the Liberian government, State Department officials became increasingly concerned. Considering the smoldering controversy over Buell's book, U.S. government officials feared that adverse public opinion would actually indict the State Department of covering up if not contributing to the structures of oppression underlying the seemingly countless cases of slavery coming to their attention. What made State Department officials decide to act was a lengthy document submitted by the American minister in Liberia that offered extensive illustrations of pawning (a native quasi-slave system engaged in by Amero-Liberians as well.)

Henry Carter, a State Department official, wrote a memo reviewing the historical ties between the U.S. and Liberia. He pointed out how the country originated, its political and economic problems and the U.S. role as loan allocator. Carter stressed the moral pressure on the U.S. by the European international community to be the protector of Liberian sovereignty and the overseer of its conduct in world affairs. He warned that unless the U.S. took the initiative to reprimand the Amero-Liberian leadership and institute reforms to eradicate the practice of slavery, negative opinion about the U.S. would arise. Although there was a chance that Amero-Liberians would take revenge against Americans in their country, Carter discounted this as a real possibility since they could ill afford to anger the U.S. Interestingly enough, Carter failed to mention that natives who would be asked to give testimony about the existence of slavery would probably be persecuted if not killed.[39]

Based upon Carter's report, State Department officials decided to send the Liberian government a note. On 8 June 1929, the State Department informed the Liberian government about evidence of the existence of forms of domestic slavery and international slave trade to a Spanish African colony, called Fernando Poo.[40] This practice, that was said to involve high governmental officials, was in violation of the League of Nations 1926 Antislavery Convention, which Liberia had ratified. State Department officers, calling upon the moral obligation of the U.S. as Liberia's "best friend," ordered that the slave systems be eradicated and that high officials involved be removed from office. Also, they demanded that the Liberian government ratify the League of Nations' 1926 Antislavery Convention and subject itself to an inquiry by an impartial international commission which would investigate the extent to which slavery did exist. The commission would recommend reforms that would assure the eradication of slavery.

The Commission: The Politics of Selection and Organization

Needless to say, the selection of members and organization of the commission was quite political. Throughout the formative period, June to December 1929, the Liberian government and the U.S. government squabbled over key issues such as: should public, as well as private uses of forced labor be investigated? This question became particularly heated when the commission issue reached the League of Nations level in August. Although European colonial powers had signed the 1926 Antislavery Convention, in practice they did not adhere to its terms. Several colonial regimes in Africa violated the convention's rules on using temporary forced labor for public works. Liberian Secretary of State Barclay relayed to a U.S. State Department official the heated debates over this issue which ensued in the League of Nations' Geneva headquarters:

> League of Nations representatives of Belgium, Portugal, Spain, and France do not want an investigation of the conditions in Liberia of compulsory labor for public purposes. . . . He (Secretary Barclay) said it is no doubt true that Belgium, Portugal, Spain and France fear that if the League recommends a man to serve as a member of an intenational commission to investigate the conditions of compulsory labor for public purposes in Liberia, this will establish a dangerous precedent and later investigations may follow in other parts of West Africa of conditions with reference to this class of labor. These countries, therefore, are reluctant to have the League use its offices in such an investigation in Liberia. The Secretary said that the French are very severe and hard with compulsory labor for public purposes in French colonies and also others. He added that, of course, the United States' position is entirely different on this question.[41]

This concern among colonial powers was soon resolved since the organization and policies of the League were supportive of European colonial rule. In fact, the chief of the League's International Labor Bureau was a major endorser of colonial administration. Moreover, the committee organized in his bureau to draft the Antislavery Convention was dominated by colonial powers. This helps to explain the fact that, while the Antislavery Convention recommended the complete outlawing of private uses of slavery, it only partially prohibited the public use of slavery. In many of their subject territories, colonial powers needed such labor for public works.[42]

Another controversial point was the Liberian government's efforts to make the case for an investigation into the role of America's European allies, European corporations, and individual European citizens in encouraging traffic in international forced labor. U.S. State Department officials resisted these suggestions for the commission's work, refusing to believe that external powers were fundamental reasons for prominent Liberians engaging in practices of forced labor. Even in the face of verifiable evidence of the forced labor activities by Europeans, officials chose to ignore the documentation or accept alternative more status quo interpretations of its meaning. When officials of the Liberian government pointed out the role of a British company and British nationals in Monrovia, U.S. diplomats discounted the claims. Clifton Wharton, a chief U.S. diplomat stationed in Monrovia, at one point wrote to the secretary of state:

> In the present matter, I believe that the Department can get some idea of the present intention of the Liberian government to involve, if possible, British interests in slavery practices. While there is nothing illegal per se in the shipment of native laborers from Liberia, the Liberians knowing that an investigation will disclose incriminating facts, are anxious to involve as many foreigners as possible. In view of the known fact that W. D. Woodin and Company has been in some way connected in the shipment of laborers from Liberia, it is highly probable that the present claim is the first step in this direction. I have been informed that W. D. Woodin and Company claim to have nothing to do with the recruitment of laborers, and I believe that this is true.
>
> Along the same line of thought, I wish to inform the Department that the Liberian secretary of state informed me that in 1927 he learned that British nationals came to Liberia to recruit laborers said to be for work in British West African possessions. He further informed me that he later learned that Liberian laborers were shipped to British possessions, were there furnished with false British passports, and then reshipped to private individuals to Fernando and possibly elsewhere. He added that in 1927 he brought these reports to the attention of M. F. Gorden Sule, H.B.M. Charge d'Affaires in Monrovia, and he was informed by Mr. Sule that the reports [may not have been accurate]. The secretary added that any shipments of this nature were made over his protests. I feel that the Liberian government will not hesitate to bring these facts to the attention of the commission and are now attempting to link up W. D. Woodin and Company.[43]

As in the case of the Firestone Rubber Company, State Department officials and diplomats may not have been in a conspiracy with European interest groups which may have indulged in slavery practices or its analogous forms. However, their naive conservatism may have biased discussion away from serious consideration of this matter.

There was a third and most crucial reason that State Department officials pressured the Liberian government to respond quickly and positively. They feared that other persons who came to their attention would air the forced labor issue publicly before they had a chance to control the controversy. While preparing the telegram to the Liberian president, Assistant Secretary of State William C. Castle informed the secretary of state why it was important to move quickly:

> The reason it is becoming more or less urgent is that Dr. Patton has submitted to the Presiding Bishop of the Church a report on Liberia which goes into great detail about the situation. If it should get into the papers and the country believed that we had known all about it and had done nothing, we should be terribly criticized. The telegram, if you decide to send it, would not be published in Liberia because the government would not want to publish anything of the sort but when and if the story gets out in this country and there is a row in the press, we should be able to say that we have acted and what we have done.[44]

In the midst of preliminary discussions with the Liberian president about the implications of the American note to them, State Department officials were informed that the American minister in Monrovia had died suddenly. His untimely death would have ordinarily suspended discussions between State Department and Liberian government officials, but news about the forced labor issue began to leak out in the Black press in the U.S. On 23 July, Secretary of State Stimson wrote to American diplomats in Monrovia, recommending that the Liberian government announce plans for a commission of inquiry as soon as possible:

> It does not seem advisable to permit the matter to wait longer as Thomas Faulkner has just published in the *Baltimore Afro-American* of July 20, a vigorous and detailed attack upon forced labor and slavery in Liberia and it is likely that this article will be followed by other public discussion in this country and elsewhere.[45]

Stimson recommended the following political maneuvering:

> It is thought that unfavorable criticism which would inevitably arise in the course of such public discussion might to a considerable extent be forestalled and minimized by prompt action on the part of the Liberian government in the form of the announcement of the commission. It is therefore desired that you present a note as outlined in Department's July 12, 7 p.m. with the following changes.

In the penultimate paragraph of that note, change the phrase "has appointed a commission" to read "is appointing our international commission".

While in theory it might be preferable to determine upon the personnel of the commission before making announcement of its appointment it is possible that the publicity which seems likely to arise may render it advisable for the Liberian government to consider making the announcement that it is appointing an international commission before the actual personnel of the commission has been settled.[46]

Thus, in late July 1929, the political battle for the formation of the commission was set in world opinion.[47] The Liberian president published an appeal for an international commission to investigate the claim that some of his most prominent countrymen condoned domestic and international forced labor systems.[48]

The Formation of the Commission's Political Chemistry

After State Department officials charged Liberian President King with the responsibility of announcing "his" plan to organize an international commission, they moved quickly to control the political chemistry of the body and spent the entire summer and fall perfecting it in Washington, Monrovia, and Geneva. They decided three persons were enough and developed selection criteria that assured the dominance of their vested interests. They suggested to the Liberian president that a Liberian, a League of Nations representative, and an American be chosen.

Realizing the probable pro-Liberian bias of the person selected by the Liberian government, State Department officials were careful in applying the informal pressure needed to assure that the League representative friendly to the U.S. would be appointed. A sympathetic American was, of course, mandatory. With this strategy, State Department officials were confident that the League and American representatives would not align themselves with the Liberian representatives.

This strategy explains why State Department officials were so adamantly against having a Spaniard on the commission. This was because the forced labor issue evolved so much around labor problems in the Spanish African colony, Fernando Poo. Although State Department officials did not attempt to implicate Spain directly in the forced labor matter, their diplomats in that country submitted reports that indicated that Fernando Poo colonial administrators did engage in suspicious labor relations with Liberian workers. On 5 July 1929, an American diplomat stationed in Spain reported that a reputable informant told him that "Spanish authorities (on Fernando Po) had found it necessary to hold back a certain proportion of the (Liberian) laborers' pay, and only give it to them as they were actually embarking for the mainland, as otherwise the Negroes spent it all in wild sprees in Fernando Po and had no funds to return home with."[49]

Fearing that a Spanish member of the commission might have an interest in blocking a full inquiry and would perhaps side with the Liberian representative, State Department officials were understandably resistant to the idea of a Spaniard on the body. Thus, when the Spanish ambassador to the U.S. broached the issued to a State Department official during the month of August, the officer reported to one of his colleagues that,

> Spain wanted a representative on the commission. I told him that this was not possible as the commission would presumably be made up of one Liberian and one American and one person appointed by the League of Nations. It is perfectly obvious that if the discussion should be largely on the question of labor forcibly recruited and sent to Fernando Po [sic], the Liberian representative and the Spanish representative would be likely to vote together against the American representative. This, however, I did not tell the ambassador, who seemed personally eager to do away with any thought of slavery.[50]

During this period, Liberian government officials also proposed a Spanish representative in the League of Nations. The U.S., needless to say, put up an effective resistance.

Liberian government officials selected the elderly Arthur Barclay, a former president of Liberia and viewed as the most educated man in Liberia to be their commission representative. He was a prosperous lawyer in Monrovia who counted the Firestone Company among his clients. His patrimonial ties with Liberian government officials was characteristic of national and local administrative levels in the country. Wharton described him as

> The confidential advisor of the present administration and in times of stress, the government invariably calls upon him. He is father-in-law of President King, uncle of Secretary of State Barclay, and uncle of Attorney General Grimes. He is brother-in-law to Liberian Consul General Gabriel Johnson who is assigned to Fernando Po and through marriage is related to four different prominent Liberian families, having been married four times. Upon inquiry I have failed to learn that he is related to Mr. S.A. Ross or Mr. Allen Yancy.
>
> At present he is practicing law in Monrovia, Dean of Liberian War, best known lawyer in Republic, is attorney for the Firestone Plantations Company—great experience on commissions.[51]

If the Liberian government's selection of Arthur Barclay was an attempt to get a sympathetic hearing on the commission, it almost worked. Only after the commission was well underway did Barclay cease questioning procedures and terms of references and begin to criticize the slavery activities of his countrymen.[52]

The League of Nations General Secretary claimed that the organization lacked the funds for a representative and suggested that the Liberian government pay the bill. After an arrangement was worked out, and opposing colonial powers were assured that the ramifications of the commission's report would stop at the boundary lines of Liberia, the League decided to select a representative from a country with extensive colonial experience (the selection of the League representative will be discussed later).[53]

Prior to his death, the American minister in Monrovia nominated Emmett Scott for the American commissioner position. Scott, while serving as Booker T. Washington's secretary, was appointed by President William Taft to the 1910 American Commission to Liberia. During World War I, he was one of many Black leaders sent to France to advise Black soldiers not to expect changes when they arrived back home. After leaving Tuskegee, subsequent to Washington's death in 1915, he became treasurer at Howard University, remaining in that post for a number of years.

At last when State Department officers began to consider Scott, he was considered to be the "type of colored man" they wanted. Indeed, while the Liberian controversy brewed during the summer and fall months, State Department officials spent most of their time trying to persuade Scott to take the position. Even President Hoover intervened personally.[54] But Scott would not budge. He kept dodging the invitation.

In September, he turned the State Department down for some unclear reason. Then in October and November, with President Hoover's prodding, Scott turned down the offer for a more specific reason: he had to do budgetary work at Howard University by the end of the year. When State Department officials pointed out that he would not have to leave until after 1 January 1930, he said he would give the invitation serious consideration. But on 15 November, he turned down the call to Liberia for the final time, giving these reasons:

> After most serious consideration of the matter and with consultation with members of the Board of Trustees, with my family and my physician, it is with profound regret that I find it impossible to accept this unusual opportunity to serve in the high place to which the President and you have been good enough to call me.
>
> As I have expressed to [Assistant Secretary of State] Mr. Castle over and over again, it has been one of my hopes that I should be able to render this particular help, and thus round out for a third time a service in behalf of my country and my people. The members of the Board of Trustees did not meet until this afternoon, thus necessitating my delay in sending this word to you.[55]

We can only speculate why Scott was so determined not to serve as American commissioner. First, Scott may have been reluctant to involve himself due to a possible scandal surrounding the 1921 American loan to Liberia which may have included one of his close friends, an attorney, Charles Lewis, and perhaps the Howard administrator himself. On 10 September, Wharton raised this serious issue with the secretary of state in relation to a conversation with Liberian President King:

> Has the Department any information that Emmett Scott was implicated in [the] alleged scandal [of the] United States loan to Liberia in 1921? Last night for the first time, President King while not raising objection to Scott, asked in view of probability [of] Scott's implication in scandal, 'what effect would this have on Scott's impartiality if he is recommended by the United States to serve on commission?' I informed King [that it was] hardly possible [that] Scott [was] implicated, and assured [him that] Liberia, did not have to be apprehensive [about the matter]. King, when asked direct[ly], said he had no objection to Scott [and that] this question [was] premature [since he had] no definite information.[He] has no intention of raising objection if Scott [is] recommended.[56]

On 16 September, apparently after making brief investigation, Wharton wrote the secretary of state.

> I informed the President that I knew nothing about any scandal in connection with the 1921 loan and asked him what was the nature of the scandal. He replied that when it seemed that the 1921 loan would be granted to Liberia, certain colored American citizens attempted to obtain thousands of dollars from the Liberian government, claiming this money was due them for services rendered in getting the loan through Congress, for using their influence, lobbying, etc. He said that his government received a telegram from one colored [person], in plain English, claiming this money. He stated that it was rumored that Dr. Scott was one of the men who claimed a share. He said that such a charge was of utmost delicacy, that he was very hesitant to bring up the rumor, and indeed, did not know whether or not Dr. Scott was one of those involved.[57]

Inside the State Department officials searched through their files for further information on Scott. On 31 October, one State Department officer was able to report to another that,

> The only thing in the file concerning Dr. Scott's connection with negotiations for the 1921 loan was a letter complaining of the lack of attention received by Mr. King and his party while in the United States. It is well known however, that Charles Lewis, the Boston lawyer, presented a claim for $50 a day for work in connection with loan negotiations. Lewis is a great friend of Scott and they both worked together on the loan negotiations but I have never heard that Scott presented any claim for services.[58]

The President claimed he was not opposed to Scott but wanted the matter investigated. After Wharton defended Scott, claiming that a man "of his type" would not be involved in such dishonesty, the president reversed his stand. He then began to praise Scott's character and comment on his work on the 1910 American Commission. Wharton was bewildered by the president's vacillation. He asked the secretary of state to investigate the charges further.[59]

Although I could not find concrete evidence, there is a possibility that the real source of the President's worries was that Scott was at one time a Garveyite. In the 1920s, Marcus Garvey attempted to advance plans to settle followers in Liberia. Given the race consciousness and nationalistic fervor of Garveyites, the Amero-Liberian ruling caste considered them to be a dangerous internal political threat. Externally, Liberia's European colonial neighbors were quite disturbed by Garvey's plans and put informal pressures on the Liberian government to oppose his efforts.[60] This fact helps in understanding why the Liberian government did not want a Garveyite, even a former one, on the international commission. Scott's past alliance with the Garvey movement may have been enough to cause Liberian government officials to be wary of his possible appointment.

Certainly Wharton's request for further investigation into Scott's activities greatly sensitized this issue. What complicated matters more was that during this period, while negotiating with a reluctant Scott, Herbert Hoover invited Charles Lewis to the White House. While Castle attempted to persuade Scott to accept the position, the following quotation from an unsigned State Department memo about a meeting between Hoover and Lewis on 1 November 1929, suggests that Scott was not fully informed nor necessarily committed to serving on the commission:

> One thing Doctor Scott told me was a little disturbing. He said that the President had sent for Mr. Lewis, the colored lawyer in Boston, to come down to see him, that Lewis told Doctor Scott he had no idea why he had been sent for. Doctor Scott said he, of course, did not know either and before Lewis left he told him that the President wanted to discuss Liberia with him, wanted apparently to find out whether Lewis would possibly take a position on the slavery commission, with the understanding that after that work was over, he would remain as minister. The disturbing thing is that Lewis said the President told him he felt very strongly that whoever was the American commissioner should, after that work was over, remain as American minister. This is, of course, out of the question because if the commissioner does his work honestly, he will obviously be at outs with most of the people in the Liberian government and can hardly do this country any good by remaining as minister. I could not tell Doctor Scott, but said that I felt sure Mr. Lewis had entirely misunderstood.[61]

It would have been a sensitive issue if Scott or Lewis had involved themselves in such a scheme. For this reason Hoover's proposal was disturbing to the unidentified State Department official to whom Scott revealed this information in the 1 November meeting.

While Scott kept turning the State Department down, officials filed numerous self-nominations for the position and noted three recommendations made by Scott. They also discussed a Henry West, who was a "journalist of long experience, a former commissioner of the District of Columbia from 1902 to 1910. Since 1921, he has been president of the American Colonization Society, the organization to whose efforts and activities in the early part of the nineteenth century Liberia owes her origin. The Society has continued its active interest in Liberian affairs particularly in the field of education. In this area it has made large contributions and it is felt that Mr. West's nomination would be, in these circumstances . . . highly appropriate."[62]

In a 19 September letter, Scott recommended Charles H. Wesley, Charles S. Johnson and Colonel Hamilton as suitable alternatives to his own nomination. Scott had worked with Johnson in the past and, by the tone of his recommendations, seemed to favor him over Wesley and Hamilton.

The Selection of Charles S. Johnson as American Commissioner

Scott's final negative decision left State Department officials in a bind. There were signs that the Liberian government officials were becoming impatient. Also, throughout November and December, Liberian government officials began to squelch native leadership from the Liberian legislature, such as the expulsion of the prominent native leader Twe. They also began to hint that they would carry out their own investigation.[63] The indecisiveness of the leadership of the League of Nations about the selection of its candidate for the commission added pressure to an already highly volatile international affair.

State Department officials knew they had to act fast in selecting an American commissioner. But, given the race politics of the Republican Party and the power of the Black press which was in the main sympathetic to at least the symbolism of Liberia as a free African nation-state, State Department officials still wanted to find the "right colored man." An assistant secretary of state, probably William Castle, wrote late in November to his colleague Henry Carter to discuss West and Lewis, the remaining candidates:

> I am not perfectly sure about the West angle of this business. He is a pleasant little man, but I am, nevertheless, convinced that if a good colored man exists

we ought to send him, I wonder how Lewis in Boston would be? He is a conceited person, but able. The President saw him some time ago and I think discussed Liberia with him, but whether he suggested that Lewis go on this slavery commission I do not know. It might be well to telephone Scott and get his ideas. He has never been so helpful so far.[64]

Scott told State Department officers that Lewis was not interested.[65] On the same day, 18 November, another State Department officer wrote to Castle highlighting the urgent need to select a commissioner, even if it meant appointing the controversial W. E. B. DuBois.

I quite agree that it would be preferable under the circumstances to send a colored man as investigator to Liberia assuming that one who is suitably qualified can be found without delay. However, I feel that matters have reached a point where a *prompt* appointment is becoming more important than the appointment of a colored man as such and it was for that reason that I have suggested West's name.

[Scott] previously suggested the name of Mr. Charles S. Johnson of Chicago, who might be a possible choice, but I do not think much of the other two suggestions that he made in his letter to you. Lewis has made himself very unpopular with certain missionary and colored elements and was involved to a certain extent in the attempt made in 1922 by certain individuals including the Liberian Consul General in Baltimore to secure a commission for their services in obtaining the 1922 loan. President King has already inquired whether Emmett Scott was not involved in this and would, I think be certain to do so in the case of Lewis.

Another suggestion which has been in the back of my mind for some time, has been the possible appointment of W. E. Burghart DuBois. In spite of the radicalism and bitterness which marked him in previous years, I think he has calmed down very considerably and there can be little question as to his ability and distinction. He might prove somewhat difficult to handle, but I think that in the present circumstances it would be well to consider him seriously.[66]

Two days later, Secretary of State Stimson forwarded two names for President Herbert Hoover to choose between for American commissioner—Charles S. Johnson and Charles H. Wesley.

Appreciating the desirability of securing a colored man for this position on the commission, if one suitably qualified to serve could be found, I have made further informal inquiries and have secured the names of Professor Charles H. Wesley of Howard University and Dr. Charles H. Johnson of Fisk University, Nashville, Tennessee. Biographical sketches of these two men are enclosed for your further information and I am informed that they are equally well qualified for the position and that the appointment of either would insure to the commission the services of a competent and suitable investigator.[67]

Stimson then forwarded Scott's biographical sketches of the men to Hoover.

> Dr. Charles S. Johnson, a graduate of Virginia Union University and of the University of Chicago, is the outstanding investigator of his race. From 1917 to 1919 he was Director of Research and Investigation of the Chicago Urban League. He was also associated with me in developing the facts in connection with my Study of Negro Migrant Conditions, during the war, for the Carnegie Endowment for International Peace. He bore the main burden in connection with the inquiries and investigations which were carried forward by the Chicago Commission on Race Relations, beginning December 7, 1919.
>
> Mr. Johnson is a member of the Advisory Committee on Interracial Policy of the Social Science Committee, a member of the Editorial Council of the World Tomorrow and he also served on the Industrial Division of the National Conference of Social Work. He is now Head of the Department of Sociology at Fisk University, Nashville, Tennessee. His most recent piece of constructive work was the compilation of essential facts for the Report of the Research Committee to the National Interracial Conference, which held its meeting in Washington last December. Seventy-five cities were selected for special inquiry, and all of this work of investigation was carried forward under Mr. Johnson's directions. At this time he is also carrying forward a study for the Rockefeller Foundation having to do with Race Relations in the United States. He is about 36 years of age.
>
> Dr. Charles H. Wesley, Professor of History, Howard University. He graduated from Fisk University in 1911, with Degree A.B.; Yale University, 1913, Degree M.A.; Harvard University, 1925, Degree Ph.D. Attended Guilde Internationale, Paris, Summer Session 1914. He is author of "Negro Labor in the United States, 1850-1925—A Study in American Economic History." Other works are: "Comparison of Jean Froissart and Phillippe de Commines, Historians," "Problems of Sources and Methods in History Teaching," reprinted from the School Review May 1916, "Student Manual of European History, Part 1," designed for use of students in European History. He is about 38 years of age.[68]

Hoover selected Johnson as the prime candidate. Stimson proceeded to seek informal character references on the Black scholar. He first sent a telegram to Trevor Arnett, president of the Rockefeller General Education Board. On the strength of the word of Jackson Davis, his foundation's southern affairs program officer (officially assistant director of education), Arnett recommended Johnson highly (25 November):

> Your telegram of this date forwarded to me at Chicago. Mr. Jackson Davis, Assistant Director of Education of our board who is well acquainted with Charles S. Johnson of Fisk University, feels that he is well fitted by temperament, training and experience to serve on commission to Liberia for purpose stated. I am not personally acquainted with him.[69]

Castle thanked Arnett for his recommendation and in the process revealed still another reason why it was politically imperative to appoint the "right colored man" to the commission (26 November):

> We felt that, from many points of view, it would be better if we could get the right kind of colored man to have as our delegate. The whole slavery situation is apparently pretty bad and we must have someone who will not be taken in by the blandishments of the officials of the Liberian government. On the other hand, if the investigation proves that slavery, or something like it, exists with the convenience of the government, it would make for a much better impression among Negroes of this country if the report were signed by a man of their own race.[70]

Based upon Davis' initial recommendation, Castle decided to recommend that Johnson be appointed to the commission (26 November):

> On the strength of Mr. Davis' opinion, I have written Mr. Johnson asking him whether he would be willing to represent the United States on this commission to investigate slavery ... I wonder whether you would be good enough to ask Mr. Davis whether he would write me rather fully about Mr. Johnson's work, what he has done in the way of investigation for the Rockefeller Foundation or any other organization, and what he personally thinks of the man's capabilities.[71]

About a week later, Davis sent Castle a more lengthy appraisal of Charles S. Johnson:

> Mr. Arnett has requested me to reply to your letter of November 26. I enclose a statement of the record of Dr. Charles S. Johnson. I have known of his work for some time through the magazine *Opportunity* which he edited as the organ of the Negro Urban League. During the past year, Dr. Johnson was engaged to assist in a study of the Negro population of Richmond with particular reference to a program of social and recreational welfare. I became personally acquainted with Dr. Johnson in this study. The high opinion I had formed of his ability was confirmed by my personal impression and more intimate acquaintance. He had not only had thorough academic training, but he has had practical experience in all sorts of social problems and surveys. He has the objective attitude of the scientist and presents facts in such a way that they point to a logical conclusion. We found him very tactful and efficient and I believe he is discreet and entirely trustworthy.
>
> Certainly he is highly respected among the colored people of the South as a scholar and as a trained investigator of social and economic problems.[72]

Endorsements by such influential foundation officers as Trevor Arnett and Jackson Davis combined with earlier recommendations by Emmett Scott, Thomas Jesse Jones (Phelps-Stokes Fund) and James Dillard (Jeanes

Fund and General Education Board) were sufficient to assure Johnson's selection.

On 26 November, Castle extended an invitation to Johnson to become American commissioner. Of course Castle gave Johnson the impression that the commission was a fact-finding body, not, as it would be, an instrument to confirm a preconceived political stance. After Castle told Johnson about the commission's charge, his pay and the proposed starting date in early February 1930, he said:

> I cannot urge you too strongly to consider this suggestion favorably because I really believe that an honest investigation of this matter would be of great value to the world. If the stories are true, it is a tragic thing that Liberia, which after all was settled originally by freed American slaves, should itself have fallen into the crime of slavery. I think a commission making a thorough investigation of this matter and cleaning up a bad situation, if it is found to exist, would have an influence on the whole of Africa and by showing the evils of forced labor would have a most valuable effect on all other parts of the world where such conditions exist.[73]

Honored, Johnson responded to Castle by telegram on 2 December:

> I have just returned from a trip to Texas and Georgia to find your important communication, stop. Am favorably disposed to undertaking duties as this government's representative on the commission on Liberia, and regard consideration of my name a real honor, stop. However, it will be desirable to confer with University officials in New York regarding temporary release from certain urgent commitments, stop. Am leaving for New York and will wire final word not later than December sixth this delay is genuinely regretted.[74]

On 6 December, Johnson reconfirmed his commitment.[75] Liberian government officials did not raise objections to Johnson's appointment to the commission.[76] Relieved, State Department officials turned to other matters, including assisting the League of Nations leadership choose their commissioner; planning Johnson's itinerary; and refining their strategy for using the commission for their own vested interests.

State Department officials wanted to orchestrate publicity about the selection of commission members. Thus, their choice of Johnson as American commissioner was kept from the public until the League of Nations leaders finally confirmed their selection a little over two weeks after Johnson accepted Castle's invitation. The chosen League of Nations commissioner was Judge Meek. A Norwegian, Meek was a member of the Belgian Congo Judicial Court from 1906 to 1915 and was, at the time of his commission appointment, holding a judicial position in Norway. He had travelled to China, Japan and to the U.S., and was amiably disposed toward the U.S.[77] On 19 December, the State Department issued a press release announcing the selection of Charles S. Johnson as the American representative and Judge Meek as the League of Nations representative on the International Commission.[78] But that announcement occurred just weeks before a flurry of scheduling problems that would ultimately result in costly delays in the commission's work.

Ideally, the State Department wanted the commission to begin its proceedings in Liberia by the second week of February and finish up before 1 June when the rainy season would begin.[79] Between the end of December and the middle of January, Johnson would have time to consult with State Department officials and with contacts in Europe before moving on to Monrovia where Meek would meet him.[80] Meek would be ready to begin his duties in the last week in January.[81]

But Johnson had duties at Fisk that delayed his sojourn in Washington by several days.[82] He was not able to arrive in Washington to be briefed and to look over documents until mid-January. Given his need to travel to London, Berne, and other European cities, the earliest ship he could take to Monrovia left from Hamburg, Germany on 18 February.[83] Since that meant that Johnson would not arrive in Monrovia until the first week in March, the commission's work would more than likely run through the rainy season. This change in the commission's temporal structure was supposedly the reason Judge Meek decided to resign. Meek resigned on 27 January, just before Johnson once again changed his sailing plans from 28 January to 18 February. At least one State Department officer questioned the official reason Meek gave for resigning. The justification, of course, implicated Johnson for delaying the commission's work.

> Influentially, Dr. Meek places the blame for his resignation on the "delayed arrival of the American member of the Commission." While it is true that the appointment of the American member was unfortunately delayed, Drummond, and presumably Dr. Meek were informed on December 31 and again on January 11, that Dr. Johnson would not sail until January 28. In this connection it is interesting to note that Dr. Meek's letter of resignation is dated January 27,[84]

Since Johnson and Barclay were of African descent, there is a possibility that Meek may have feared the strain of being outnumbered. Some diplomats expressed their fear of Johnson siding with the commission's Liberian representative. For instance, a League of Nations officer,

> inquired whether Johnson might not be expected to side with the Liberian investigator and indicated that Meek might probably feel impelled to write a

minority report. I [Henry Carter] reassured him as to Johnson, but said that we would welcome a minority report from Meek if he should feel obliged to write one.[85]

Whatever the actual reason for Meek's resignation, the League of Nations leadership had to find a replacement quickly. The League's high command appointed Cuthbert Christy, a British explorer of Africa and health researcher. He arrived in Monrovia approximately two weeks after Johnson stepped on shore. These schedule mix-ups, the stalling of tactics of the Liberian government, and other problems, resulted in the commission working through the summer months and finally coming to a close in mid-September.

Besides organizing Johnson's itinerary and coping with Meek's untimely resignation, State Department officers fine-tuned their future plans for the commission's report. They knew evidence would be found that as a matter of course Amero-Liberian prominents at least condoned slavery and other forms of forced labor practices at home and abroad. As late as 22 December, an informant told State Department officials:

> Forced labor in the republic seems to have been and is an understood thing. There appeared to have been a custom to bring into the Liberian households, particularly the upper ones, the illegitimate native children, offspring of the heads of those homes and native women living in the interior, either on the farms owned by these Liberians or in the native villages. As these native children grew up, they were worked in the homes without pay, and we were informed, without receiving any educational training, as a rule. In some instances, however, I learned that a *boy* was sent to school. These additions to the families were sometimes spoken of to outsiders as 'adopted' children.[86]

In one remarkable memorandum written in late December, a State Department official outlines the history of Liberia, the need to reform the economy through foreign investments, and the questionable ability of Blacks to rule themselves. Almost to the letter, the points made in the memorandum materialized publicly as the means by which the State Department would use the commission report to condemn Liberia a year later.[87]

As Henry Carter observed, the real goal of the future commission report was to raise international moral indignation to whatever level necessary for the State Department to act. It was not to be a well-grounded empirical study. Moreover, given the circumstances, that may have been impossible to produce.

> In my opinion, it would be over-optimistic to expect the commission to produce a clear-cut case against the Liberian government as important wit-

nesses and documents would be no doubt missing, and most of the testimony would probably be either perjured or worthless from a legal point of view. I said that I hoped, however, the commission would be able to make a series of stringent recommendations designed to prevent any possible recurrence of such conditions and that we felt in any case the fact of the investigation and the commissioner's report and recommendations would serve to put an end—and had in fact, already done so—to the activities of the slave traders in Liberia. I further pointed out that the Liberian government could ill afford to lose the good will of the United States.[88]

Since the commission was to find certain conditions and report on them in a politically useful way, Johnson and the other commissioners had to be encouraged to conduct their investigation in a particular format. What was suggested in the following 16 December memorandum in regard to the commission extending its investigation into the hinterland was probably recommended to Johnson as a procedure for the reasons given. It is essentially what happened.

A trip back to the interior to see the recruitment and treatment of the laborers for Fernando Po as well as a journey to Fernando Po, will probably recommend themselves to the commission.

A superficial audit of the books of the recruiting agents, their bank accounts, and the books at Fernando Po if made, may disclose how the LIO, which it is understood is obtained for the recruitment of each man, is divided. This line of inquiry will disclose which officials are involved and to what extent they are benefitting. Even if such proof is not of a definite nature, it would seem that if the commission learns that by general repute, the "graft" is divided among various officials, that fact should be mentioned in their report and given the prominence it deserves even if there is only a moral certainty.[89]

Johnson was never told the true intentions of State Department officials. He assumed that the commission was, as publicized, a fact-finding body suggested by the Liberian president. As he packed his bags and began to research his task, be believed he was being commissioned as an impartial social scientist.

After being briefed, Johnson's most important task in his new capacity was to select a secretary. The State Department required him to hire a secretary to take minutes of the commission's proceedings and to assist in translations. On 30 December, Johnson gave James P. Moffat, the American consul, names of two friends he thought would make good secretaries, John F. Matheus and Arthur A. Schomburg:

Mr. John Matheus: about 40, graduate of Western Reserve and an A.M. from Columbia, who has studied at the Sorbonne; at present a teacher at West Virginia Collegiate Institute. Competent as a secretarial assistant; conversant in French and Spanish; has travelled in Cuba, Haiti, Italy and Southern France; health good; intelligent, loyal and a person with whom I have had some association in other connections. In a general way, he is very satisfactory to me and has indicated an eagerness to accompany me.

Mr. A. A. Schomburg: but for the fact that he is an older person (a bit over 50) he would prove very satisfactory. His knowledge of Spanish is equal to his knowledge of English, and he has a familiar knowledge of French; is a high Mason (which I understand is a help in gaining entree), is personally acquainted with a number of Liberians, and thoroughly trustworthy as a secretarial assistant on such a mission; has been connected with the Bankers Trust Company in New York; knows well the literature and history of Liberia, and has been of assistance to me before as an investigator. He probably is known apart from these qualifications as a collector of a race library of Afro-America.[90]

Johnson chose Matheus. Probably his choice was based upon Matheus' younger age, his linguistic abilities (he spoke at least four languages at the time and would add a few more in his long life), and his experience traveling in Europe. Also, Johnson was a man who liked being in control, and while Schomburg was more of an equal, Matheus was not. Johnson's role in the life of Matheus was more as mentor than friend. Johnson had sponsored Matheus' literary work while serving as *Opportunity* editor and assisted him in other ways.[91]

Matheus was, furthermore, an easygoing passive man who would not cross Johnson in a significant way. The same could not be said about Schomburg, who was more outspoken. Johnson would not be all that satisfied with Matheus, as his letters home and his diary revealed.[92] But at least he was in control of the commission's official interpretations. More important, his views would not be seriously challenged by Matheus if there were differences of opinion between them when they returned home. He was correct. If there were any serious differences of opinion between the men about what went on during the work of the commission, Matheus did not raise them, at least not in highly visible settings. After the men returned to America, they rarely communicated; when they did, it was once again on an unequal basis.[93]

Johnson's Briefing in the State Department and in Europe

While in the State Department offices in January 1930, Johnson was briefed by government officers and others knowledgeable about Liberia.[94] He was also given access to government documents and materials received from Liberia. He sailed for Europe in late January. While in Europe, he consulted with diplomats in various cities, and conferred with scholars who could help him understand the cultures of native Liberians. He believed that the problem of native labor in Liberia was "inseparably locked with the structure of native life [for example], social customs, religion, laws."[95]

His first stop was at London's International Institute of African Languages and Cultures where he wanted to become acquainted with the work of Diedrich Westermann, editor of the Institute's journal *Africa* and University of Berlin Professor of African Languages. Westermann "studied the Kpelle in Liberia, assisted Sibley in the writing of the book *Liberia Old and New.*" Also, during the briefing in the U.S. State Department, Harvey Firestone Jr., had mentioned that Westermann "was preparing a grammar of the Kpelle or Pesse language, which is expected to be useful to them in dealing with native labor through some dialect which is common over the wide area."[96]

Although Westermann was not in London, Johnson was able to speak with the assistant editor of *Africa*, Dorothy Brackett. Johnson wrote in his diary about the meeting with her that subsequently led to an appointment to confer with anthropologist Bronislaw Malinowski.

> I am interested in their [the Institute's] researchers, their literature, personalities, what not, with any bearing upon Liberia or even kindred situations. Of Liberia, she knows not a great deal, nor may the Institute concern itself with the political phases of the problems met in courses of their studies. Sibley, of course, is known, and the linguistic work of Westermann in the country. There is a problem of concern in the text books to be used in the native schools, embodying in their character and structure the new principles of native development. Some had been experimentally tried by Sibley in Liberia, but were objected to by the administrations of the government. I mention that it would be useful to me to talk with Malinowski of the London School of Economics. Maurice Delafosse of the University of Paris has done much directly in line with what I interpret my basic problem to be. I wish to know more of what anthropology has revealed regarding the native customs which are characteristically associated with the labor of natives either communally or for non-native enterprises. What control is exercised by chiefs over the labor of their subjects, at what point does labor required by the chief and accepted as a part of native culture, cease to be communal and take on the features of compulsion. What of the practice of adoption? Pawning? The mild forms of domestic slavery? Here she can help and reach Malinowski by telephone. He is agreeable to an interview.[97]

Originally, Johnson was to meet Malinowski in his residence but met him instead in the apartment of Captain Pitt-Rivers. Brackett, who accompanied Johnson to make the introduction and informed him of the change of plans, warned her visitor: "Professor Malinowski says not to be upset by anything that Captain Pitt-Rivers might remark since he is a pleasant

person with ideas sometimes considered odd." Pitt-Rivers was an anthropologist whose expertise was African cultures. While they waited for
Malinowski to arrive, Pitt-Rivers and Johnson embarked on an awkward
line of conversation (after Johnson greeted Pitt-Rivers mistakenly as Professor Malinowski and was corrected politely). After exchanging greetings,
Johnson said that Pitt-Rivers seemed "to ponder what next to do" as he
racked his brain for an opening conversation "which would last a few
minutes." Finally, Pitt-Rivers asked:

> "Did Malinowski say something about your going to Africa?" That is good. I
> can at least explain my mission. He observes that there is usually much
> misunderstanding about native life and a great deal of sentimental tosh. It
> happens to be a question of some concern because of British colonial posses-
> sions. I ask after a lull, [about his] writings. He seems for a moment to think,
> begin to speak and hesitate, with the same nervousness, then hesitates and
> says, almost apologetically, it seems to me, that his grandfather had written several volumes. . . . His grandfather had died in 1893 (I believe).
> Since that time the only Pitt-Rivers who had connected himself with any
> volumes on anthropology was probably himself. I mentioned that I had se-
> lected his volume on the *Contact of Cultures* as one of the few to take along
> with me to Africa.[98]

After discussing the Pitt-Rivers book briefly, Malinowski arrived, and the
three men discussed Johnson's mission. They agreed on the need to stress a
pro-native posture on the forced labor issue. "We are agreed, all three of us,
that in any approach to the questions in hand our sympathies are first with
the natives, in getting their confidence and trying as nearly as any European can to see things from that point of view. I can speak with no more
firsthand knowledge than he about the country, and offer a cursory summary of such anthropological studies dealing with indigenous Liberian
tribes, and such general observations as have been made regarding the
relations of Amero-Liberians with them."[99]

Undoubtedly, Johnson's conference with Malinowski and Pitt-Rivers influenced the formation of his pro-native stance in Liberia and his ethnographic approach to the native labor question. Malinowski's influence
on Johnson's methodology was particularly apparent in a more lengthy
meeting Johnson had with the anthropologist on the morning before he
left. In his diary, Johnson recorded:

> He asks my intended methodology. I suggest, first, getting documents, then
> selections of intimate visits inland, combining of sociological inquiry with
> the terms of reference, later hearings on the basis of such evidence as is
> disclosed. This he thinks sound. To it he adds comments that it would be
> important to take specimen censuses. Find out in what huts men are away,
> inquire into their economic system, i.e., land tenure, amount of labor neces-

sary, work of women, the problem of creating new values and demands. What does the native want when he goes out for shillings. Find a few cases of men who have been to Fernando Po, get their opinions of the place. What do they buy with their shillings. What did they do on the plantations. Why did they go. What means of pressure, if any, were used.

While at sea heading toward Monrovia, Johnson recorded his impressions about the ship's passengers and its crew in his diary. He also noted what he was reading. At one point he wrote, "I have completed the reading of Schuritzer's *On the Edge of the Primeval Forest*, a substantial part of Lugard's *Dual Mandates*, Sibley and Westermann's *Liberia*, Durant's *Liberia*, Lady Mills' *Travels*, and 2 copies of *Africa*. Buell has my attention at the moment."[100] He also recorded his initial impressions of the West African coastline and how he was received when the ship arrived in Monrovia's port on 8 March. Little did Johnson know that like British anthropologists before him whose work on "the native question" helped colonial administrators develop indirect rule policies, he would give State Department officials the sociological and anthropological data needed to refine neocolonialism in Liberia.

The Shaping of Johnson's Pro-Native Stance

No sooner had Johnson stepped off the ship at Monrovia in early March, 1930, than he became the observer and subject of a number of incidents that exemplified the paranoia of Amero-Liberians in regard to the true motivations of the commission, especially the American representative. The events also shaped his pro-native stance. He related to his wife:

> Until my very arrival the belief persisted that the commission would not come. Judge Meek's resignation, I am told, was greeted with considerable rejoicing in important quarters, and the rumor that I had postponed sailing for two months, reached such strength that a confirmation cable was sent from here to points in Europe to learn if I was enroute. One hour after arrival the rumors began to fly fast and thick—in one quarter speculations that the American member was the forerunner of American imperialistic policy.[101]

Two days after Johnson's arrival, he further learned about the deep-seated suspicions of the Liberian government toward his mission. He was informed that several persons wanted to see him, though he had not yet been formally presented to the president. He sent responses to these persons stating it would be improper of him to see anyone without first being introduced to the president. But rumors still circulated that he was seeing people and attempting to stir up trouble.

Throughout March, commission proceedings were delayed by Christy's late arrival after Johnson and then by Liberian government stalling tactics. After Johnson was eventually introduced to President King upon Christy's arrival, his excellency was afflicted immediately with a week-long illness that required confinement in his house. Writing home, Johnson intimated that:

> During the President's illness, it was suspected that important conferences were being held in his home . . . it was fully a week before the actual machinery of the government got going. Government officials during that period were either down country attending certain details in the hinterland work, or up with the President, or behind well-closed doors discussing the next move.[102]

More delays pushed the starting date of commission inquiries into early April. Johnson complained to his wife, "Everything conceivable is intervening to postpone the formal consultation of the body and beginning of its inquiry. As soon as the President was up the Secretary of State returned to his bed. It is now the first of April and I have been here three weeks, Christy for ten days and the issue has been postponed. . . . The Chief Justice of the Supreme Court came over and dropped hints." Finally on 2 April, Christy and Johnson sent a note to the president demanding to know when he was going to constitute the commission and received 7 April as a response.[103]

While these delays occurred, Johnson did two things. First, he had an opportunity to develop initial impressions of Christy. Christy had forty years of experience in exploring Africa and although he was in his late 60s, he looked 40. Johnson found him to be "a very congenial person, a naturalist, big game hunter for museums, as well as a sleeping sickness and malaria expert. Our long walks and chats, living as we do constantly together, are quite valuable education in new fields for me." He also noted, "I have, I believe, a decided edge on matters related to the presented inquiry and . . . he has been a good student."[104] Johnson's glowing evaluation of Christy would vaporize quickly once the commission began its proceedings.

Second, Johnson along with Matheus and perhaps Christy, explored Monrovia and its immediate rural surroundings. He wrote his wife about how much effort the government put into exposing them to pro-Amero-Liberian propaganda. Even when they visited churches they were preached to about the impressive ability of Liberians to survive despite tremendous obstacles. He was indignant at a hanging he observed.

> They hanged two poor culprits the other day, before a large audience. They were natives who had killed their wives (instead of returning them and getting back the dowry) for taking lovers.[105]

The paternalistic overtures that shaped interaction between European colonials and Amero-Liberians with natives as described, held his attention. Disgusted, he wrote to his wife,

> The little European colony is in the midst of it knows not what from the bland faces of the natives. They may be devising dire companions. They may be sneering behind the blank black cloaks of their faces. Always they respond, "BOY?" "SUH!" and the European colony knows it is in control of the situation. One of these says the fretful master expanding himself before friends calls "BOY" and there is no SIR. First, surprise, then anger, then alarm, etc., etc., etc.[106]

Although Johnson's initial impressions of Amero-Liberians were negative, he still could find a sympathetic posture toward their predicament.

> I hope personally that they will be able to save their faces. More, that they have nothing to hide. I do not see how it can be entirely successful. In which event, it is easier to understand the delays . . . the unexpected turns in affairs. I can understand why my chauffeur is a spy and letters that are sent through the open mail do not show up. So many of them are likeable people. They have so little to build a firm government on. So many natural difficulties, so much stealing of this land.[107]

Yet, given the extent of Johnson's culture shock—it was his first time in Africa—what he experienced in Liberia initially had a lasting influence in shaping his pro-native perspective, best illustrated in a diary he kept for his wife during commission operations, and in the writings of *Bitter Canaan*.[108] His letters to his wife during his first weeks in Monrovia, especially a lengthy 1 April log, were preoccupied with pointing out negative aspects of his experiences. His sad letters sent home also expressed homesickness.

Throughout the six-month period in Liberia, Johnson felt the brunt of loneliness, cultural isolation, and growing disdain for other commission members, particularly Christy. He did not enjoy his mission, which is probably why it was his first and last major effort in Africa.

The Commission's Work

The commission spent 14 to 29 April taking testimonies in Monrovia; 30 April to 9 May in Kakata (60 miles from the Monrovian coast), and 10 May to early July in the hinterland. It returned to Monrovia on 7 July and sat for another month, ending proceedings on 8 August. In total, 264 persons, comprised of government officers, natives, native chiefs, and Firestone Plantation Company officers were interviewed. Interviews were held in the morning and late afternoon. Arthur Barclay, due to age, did not accompany the commission into the hinterland.[109] On 1 May, Christy became seriously ill and could not go with Johnson and his staff to major areas in the hinterland.

As the commission went forth in its work, Johnson became increasingly incensed over the conduct of Christy. The African explorer's condescending and sometimes naive attitude toward Liberian natives was a thorn in his side. Christy and Johnson even argued extensively about the "questionable" capabilities of Black Americans. Christy's seventy-year old secretary, Major Jackson, also posed a problem until he resigned. Also, Christy was anti-Firestone and anti-American. During the proceedings, to Johnson's dismay, Christy manifested negative attitudes about American interests. In particular, he posed questions for the express purpose of uncovering Firestone involvement in encouraging the use of slave labor.[110]

Although Christy was made chairman of the commission out of respect for the League of Nations, Johnson was the man of ideas and knew how to express them on paper. He complained bitterly in his 13 July diary entry:

> Christy and I have our first important session on the report. For the past two or three weeks he has been trying to get down the first draft of a report. My card system for grouping all the data for study he has tried every way to criticize as less satisfactory than his own, which was writing the subject by the side of the testimony, and condensing the various testimonies. This did not offer much contraction, and was just as unwieldy and scattered as ever, with several or all of the points of the terms in one statement. Now he wants to use my cards; or, better still—"Suppose you make me notes on what information we have, so I can work it over and write it up." Naive. He began "his" draft of the report with the letter of transmittal which assumed that Barclay was to bring in a minority report even before we have had a single session; then the preface, which he tried to phrase before we had even read all the testimony, not to speak of making findings. His ["findings" included] . . . hysterical, extreme statements in summary fashion [that] [condemned] the whole government and [called] everything slavery, slave dealing, slave traffic, etc.
>
> My objections are: (1) We cannot make findings before knowing what we have—it would be better to state our observations and results of the testimony before beginning to plan a finding—psychologically this should come last, anyhow. (2) He is muddled on what is slavery. Capture and flogging need not be slave raiding, etc. We have seen no common slavery, but domestic slavery and pawning etc. Fernando Po cannot be regarded as slavery. I take exception to the League's definition as inadequate. Our findings, to create confidence, must be deliberate and analytical, etc.
>
> I showed him my summary of the Webbo (Fernando Po) material. He thinks it is too detailed, but wants to take it and condense it, instead of studying his material, for a section on which he can make a useful first draft also. The same thing applies to my draft of the Sinoe incident. Then he proposes that I not write up any more but give him narrative notes, embodying all the testimony, documented and let him write it. I am willing to do anything to get the business over, but I dislike the attempt to cover up ineptness both in

arranging his materials, memory for detail and sequence, and no writing, but taking my drafts and calling them his own. If he were even generous enough to be mutual on these matters I think I should even feel hesitant about turning over anything. He wishes to sign all papers, write all letters, except disagreeable ones, have only his name appear on state papers, acknowledge all courtesies personally, and do the social negotiating with Hines, etc., even though they are Americans; intensely jealous of any contact, he queries blindly about visits, keeping his own conversations with Ford, the British charge, to himself. Ford has given him papers from his office. Luckily I have them all. James of the Bank of British West Africa, it seems, keeps Ford informed.[111]

Johnson wrote the entire "Christy Commission" report, which as a result delayed his departure from Liberia until September.

The commissioners submitted a 207-page report to the U.S. State Department, the Liberian government, and the League of Nations.[112] Most of the report outlined the commission's mission ("terms of reference"); offered native and other testimonies of the existence of slavery and its analogous forms in Liberia; and presented evidence about the role of prominent Amero-Liberians in forced labor trade. The report also documented how the Firestone Company was unknowingly given forced labor through the corrupt actions of Liberian government officials.[113]

Many of the case studies Johnson presented in the report were incorporated into the *Bitter Canaan* manuscript. He also elaborated upon the report's recommendations and suggestions in *Bitter Canaan*'s final chapter.

When Johnson returned to the U.S. by way of Europe in late September, he submitted a supplementary report to the main commission report to State Department officials. Johnson's supplementary report was a minority position paper that offered much valuable historical background information about the work of the American commissioner and about "certain observations and incidents not included in the formal text, but which may serve a useful purpose in interpreting, in part at least, the significance of what is reported." He went on to give justification to his supplementary report:

> The character of much of the evidence, the procedure adopted in servicing and evaluating it, together with the somewhat unusual composition and task of the commission seem to make it desirable that the Department be informed in greater detail of the procedure of the inquiry, and the extent of its representation, in the formal findings through the American member.[114]

Johnson's supplementary report offered candid information about the other commissioners; particularly a negative assessment of Christy. He also presented biographies of major Amero-Liberian and native Liberian leaders. The structure of his analysis, with the exception of his remarks about Christy, was the germ of *Bitter Canaan*.

State Department officials took Johnson's comments seriously. Throughout his mission, State Department officials held his word in high esteem and spoke of him positively in their inner circles. Indeed, Henry Carter, who was sent to Monrovia to keep an eye on things during the commission's proceedings, once went as far as to risk criticism from his Washington superiors for openly siding with Johnson against the uncooperative Christy.[115] The only patronizing remarks I found were those of an American diplomat Johnson met in Switzerland on his way back to the U.S. who forwarded his impressions of the American commissioner to the U.S. State Department.[116]

State Department officials used Johnson's reports as the basis of their now well-known controversial attacks against the Liberian government. Throughout the 1930s, political elites in the U.S., the League of Nations, and Liberia played tug of war in debating over whether or not Europeans or Americans or just Amero-Liberians should take responsibilities for reform.

Johnson's role in the heated debate was quite marginal, with most of his efforts taking place in the early 1930s. In late 1930 and early 1931, he wrote to prominent figures who had misinterpreted commission findings, such as William E. B. DuBois, editor of *Crises* magazine.[117] He also passed on letters he received from Twe, the native Liberian leader, to State Department officials. The letters documented the reign of terror waged by Liberian government officials against natives who cooperated with the commission.[118]

From the 1930s until his death, Johnson displayed a deep interest in West Africa, particularly Liberia. Twe and he even corresponded about writing a book together.[119] He published a few articles and book reviews on his findings in the country and whenever he could, gave scholarship support to Liberian students. In the early 1940s, he served on the Phelps-Stokes Fund's Committee on Africa which was interested in the impact of World War II on African affairs. In a 26 July 1947 radio broadcast in London celebrating the Liberian centennial, Johnson said this, caught up in a radically changing international order:

> It was seventeen years ago that I paused briefly here in London, on the way to Geneva and then to Liberia as the American member of an international commission of the League of Nations. I am . . . convinced [of] a new relationship of this free nation in an Africa of colonies to the world outside its troubled borders. No young and isolated and underdeveloped country in Africa, whether dependent or free, could in this century escape the insistent currents of world economics and politics, or lag for long too far behind in its standards and practices if it was to survive and keep its independence. . . .

Liberia has survived the terror of the superior strength of acquisitive nations, the superior vitality of its aboriginal population, the hovering shadow of tropic death, and the ironic fate of starvation in a land of potential plenty. With growing strength it moves into its hundredth year as a sovereign state. In this decade of the century, Liberia is coming of age, and in the discovery of itself and in the development of its physical and human resources, it is commanding the respect and admiration of the world.[120]

Following is a detailed discussion of how *Bitter Canaan* fit into the flow of Johnson's intellectual career.

Bitter Canaan in Charles S. Johnson's Intellectual Development

Charles S. Johnson's Chicago School background and his independent ideas have never been explored systematically. In this section I analyze the importance of *Bitter Canaan* in Johnson's intellectual development as an effort toward a comprehensive understanding of Johnson's role in the history of sociological thought.

Charles Spurgeon Johnson was the first Black student of Chicago sociologist Robert Ezra Park. Park, who arrived in Chicago in 1913 from Booker T. Washington's tutelage at Tuskegee Institute, quickly established himself as the major race relations sociologist in mainstream professional sociology.[121] His ideas about the race cycle (racial contact, competition, conflict, accommodation, and assimilation), urbanization, collective behavior, and regional sociology would influence generations of sociologists. His unprecedented advocacy of Black graduate students in sociology would also have a lasting professional effect.

Park's profound influence over Johnson's professional and intellectual development cannot be denied. While reminiscing about the tremendous role Park played in his life and in establishing the Chicago Urban League, Johnson once remarked "in the spirit of profoundest respect and gratitude, I like to feel that it was he who blew the breath of life into me and into the Chicago Urban League at the same time."[122] Whether focusing on how Blacks were marginalized in northern industries, institutionalized on plantations and in Liberia, or exploring racial prejudice, Johnson used Parkian ideas to make his points.

The presence of Parkian sociology in *Bitter Canaan* is quite apparent. For years before going to Liberia, Johnson fully accepted Park's ideas about the assimilation of Blacks into the host White society. In his early Black migration studies, which have an interesting demographic perspective (Malthusian), Johnson assumed that Black migration north functioned to assist inevitable absorption into the city—or what Park presumed was civilization. Migration into the city changed the values, norms, social orientations, and other sociocultural characteristics of Blacks in a positive direction. Institutions such as the Urban League attempted to help to systematize Afro-American acculturation.[123] At the 25th anniversary of the Chicago Urban League, Johnson observed:

> The Urban League, in the strictest sense, is not so much a social work agency as a cultural agency. This observation may be questioned by some social workers and perhaps rightly so. But if questioned, the most valid rebuttal would be that social work agencies are themselves cultural rather than social work agencies. The responsibilities assumed by the League has been one primarily of reorientation rather than rehabilitation. It has been less interested in poverty and personal disorganization than in cultural status and cultural orientation. It has found itself involved in at least three of the most urgent and fundamental processes in our American society: migration and the shifting of the cultural levels of a large element in the American population; industrialization and the growth of the American city; and the democratic process in America which affects all of the people.
>
> Those of us who have been close to the Negro migration have tended to be preoccupied with the clumsy and somewhat gaudy exterior aspects of dishevelled newness, in personal habits, dress, public behavior, and industrial ineptness. What is most often overlooked is the fact that migration on such a scale is really a cultural crisis, a social phenomenon associated with the growth and internal adjustment of the nation itself. It is not a racial phenomenon as such, but a population problem emerging out of the pull and tug of the very forces that are shaping our destiny as a nation. If the Urban League did not exist as a functioning intermediary, it would be not only desirable but necessary for the nation itself to create such an intermediary agency.[124]

Predictably, the Parkian race cycle, which is the impetus behind acculturation processes in a society, materializes in Johnson's *Bitter Canaan*. The chronological historical framework Johnson uses to organize *Bitter Canaan* reflects a Parkian conception of the evolution of patterns of racial contact, competition, conflict, accommodation and assimilation. Rather than the cycle involving Europeans and Third World people, its participants are Amero-Liberians and native African tribes in a West African coastal society. In this analysis, Johnson offers a demonstration of how "race making" was used by Amero-Liberians to justify their domination over natives. Race was a sociopolitical construct which could be used as tool for status differentiation by a dominant population phenotypically similar to those it subordinated.

Johnson's ironic remarks about likenesses between Amero-Liberians and White American attitudes and behavior patterns was an interesting way of describing how the assimilation of Afro-Americans malfunctioned in Africa. He also believed, like Park, that since assimilation of dissimilar cultural and/or racial groups was the key to societal stability, the refusal of

Amero-Liberians to develop a qualified assimilation-oriented native policy was a major reason why Liberia was such an unstable society.

Johnson believed that the major problems of Amero-Liberians were economic. This is why he spent so much time reconstructing the economic history of the republic. He pointed to the Amero-Liberians' overly burdensome dependence on government for employment as a cause of pervasive political graft. The lack of a significant economic infrastructure resulted in the Liberian government engaging in *economic cannibalism*—contracting and selling labor abroad as a chief means of revenue.

Finally, Johnson's adoption of the Parkian notion of acculturation is seen in his views about Afro-American culture. Like most social scientists of his day, particularly Park, E. Franklin Frazier, and University of North Carolina at Chapel Hill sociologists, Johnson avidly opposed cultural pluralistic assumptions about Afro-American life. Blacks, Johnson believed, were Americans and did not have a culture outside the contours of American culture. At most, Blacks occupied different planes of American culture generated by different habits of life produced through social, political and economic isolation from Whites.[125] Although Johnson held this view about Afro-American culture, he did have an interest in a population his contemporaries considered to be an exception to this lack of unique Afro-American culture: the geographically isolated Gullah Sea Islanders of South Carolina.[126] As revealed in *Bitter Canaan* and in *African Diary*, Johnson also had an appreciation for indigenous African tribal cultures.

Throughout Johnson's career, particularly during the 1920s, he published arguments against biological notions about Black inferiority and low caste positioning. Park believed that racial prejudice was a psychological phenomenon. Johnson used the Parkian notion of prejudice as part of his macro arguments about the social basis of White prejudice.[127]

Johnson continually defined racism as a state of mind; a cluster of attitudes embraced and used by Whites to justify the oppression of Blacks and other non-European people. He was especially perceptive about how racial attitudes were power-linked phenomena. This is why he often commented on the negative consequences of the race prejudice of Whites in authority positions. Johnson found the cause of Black marginalization or exclusion in northern industry to lie in the attitudes and behavior of employers. In a 1923 article, "When the Negro Migrates North," he upheld an argument that he maintained for the rest of his life:

> Back of the attitude of northern employers unnaturally limiting Negroes in their industrial expansion, has been a prevailing skepticism concerning their adaptability for skilled work. The old myths about their improvidence, shiftlessness and general incapacity for sustained physical exertion or for performing technical tasks above routine processes have exercised an enormous

influence in keeping these workers from experiments to determine their fitness. These causal generalizations have an extraordinary potency and are more frequently remembered than the more recent experiences of employers who have seriously offered an opportunity to Negro labor on an equal basis with white labor.[128]

He went on to argue that, in many cases it was the racial prejudice of employers, not Black incompetence, that was the primary cause of the exclusion of Blacks from being employed by major industries.

Another example of Johnson's power-oriented assumptions about race prejudice was his 1939 review of Horace Mann Bond's *Negro Education in Alabama: A Study in Cotton and Steel*. Praising Bond's work, he said:

> Education for Negroes has too long been seen chiefly in terms of the lengthened shadows of selected Negro and white personalities without due reference to their social, economic and political attitudes, and interests. Dr. Bond's chief contribution rests upon his attempt to show the interrelationship between the attitudes and interests of personalities connected with cotton and steel and the public education in Alabama during the years when current patterns were being formed not only in Alabama, but throughout the South.[129]

In *Bitter Canaan*, Johnson details the prejudicial attitudes of Amero-Liberians and how such attitudes shaped their "native policy." He points out in his typical ironic manner how much the prejudices of Amero-Liberians against natives were analogous to ways in which Whites felt and acted against Blacks in America.

Johnson's Deviation from the Chicago School

As much as Charles S. Johnson was a protegé of Robert E. Park and the general Chicago School, he did deviate from his mentors in significant ways. The form and content of *Bitter Canaan* is the apex of Johnson's independent thought, particularly the manuscript's moralistic tone (i.e., muckraking sociology). There are five major concerns which began to germinate in *Bitter Canaan* and that became cornerstones of Johnson's innovative published thought: contextual analyses of Black migration; racial conflict; the folk Negro; racial caste; and dependency theory. These concepts plus Johnson's methodological perspective have been ignored or distorted in the effort to fit Johnson into the Chicago School.

The Black Migration

While Park and other urban sociologists tended to divorce human activity from social structure in explaining Black migration, Johnson's analyses were contextual. He examined how the migration of Blacks transformed the industrial institutions they were absorbed into, particularly in the human relations area. He used Malthusian and other demographic theories to explain why Blacks migrated in such large numbers from rural areas to cities both in the north and the south during the first quarter of the twentieth century.[130]

Similar to his early Black migration studies, in *Bitter Canaan* Johnson uses demographic analyses to explain how Liberian government labor policies and forced labor marketeers had an impact on the country's hinterland. He was especially perceptive in describing the negative consequences of depopulation as a process on the quality of life in native villages.

Racial Conflict

Like Park, Johnson was interested in how Blacks could best acculturate to mainstream society. In addition, he placed much stress on the processes and patterns of racial conflict. Indeed, more than any other Chicago product of his generation, Johnson was interested in race riots, racial conflict in industries, and strategies of conflict resolution in race relations.[131] This was not only because Johnson believed that White-Black conflict had to diminish dramatically before racial accommodation could be realized, but also because he believed that racial conflict was symptomatic of inequalities in power and privilege, particularly in the economic sphere.

By the 1940s, Johnson's concern about racial conflict and conflict resolution had become central.[132] This was apparent in his founding of the social action–oriented Department of Race Relations and the Institute on Race Relations, both established at Fisk University in the 1940s. His institute's journal, *Monthly Trends*, and his attempts to organize community-based human relations commissions reflected his acute concern about new macro patterns of racial conflict occurring during and after World War II.

In *Bitter Canaan*, Johnson casts the history of Liberia largely in terms of conflict, particularly in his description of Amero-Liberian clashes with European colonial neighbors and with native tribes. The recurrence of conflict was indicative of the political instability of Liberia.

Racial Caste in Industrial America

Most pre-World War II sociologists believed that racial caste relations were gradually being transformed into class relations. The advancement of urban industrialization and the progressive assimilation of racial minorities were the major stimuli behind the racial caste-class transformation. Johnson deviated from this dominant belief. He believed that although class was becoming increasingly important in explaining differential life chances and other issues between Whites and Blacks, he argued strongly that racial caste persisted as an explanatory variable. He argued as much in his 1936 article, "The Conflict of Caste and Class in an American Industry" (*American Journal of Sociology* 42 [July]:55-65). E. Franklin Frazier, however, criticized Johnson's perspective on caste, and advocated a class argument. In his rejoinder, Johnson responded:

> The article does not purport to be an analysis of the class struggle, as Dr. Frazier too hastily concludes. It is, as its title indicates, a discussion of the conflict of caste and class tradition.
>
> A very good summary is given by the reviewer of some of the materials presented in the article. He concludes that the arguments and conclusions seem logical, but adds that in view of what is known in the industry "the author has omitted to mention the most important factors, which are the economic conditions controlling working relations." In supplying these omissions, however, he repeats the controlling conditions already mentioned in the article, to wit: increased mechanization, the increase in white and female labor, lagging wages and labor policy, and employer control.
>
> The reviewer appears to recognize the absence of working-class consciousness, but attributes this to poor labor union leadership. This could almost be called naive in view of the obvious evidence that the persistence of the caste tradition prevents effective labor leadership as well as labor organization. One is led to believe that he expects abstract economic philosophies to operate automatically. What is influencing working relations most persistently is not the ideology of the labor movement, or the ritual of the conventional class struggle, but the cold imperatives of technological changes which tend, in the interest of the employers, to disturb the old caste alignments. The workers, in turn, defeat their own ends by struggling against each other rather than together for a common cause.[133]

Johnson's attraction to "racial caste" as a valuable way of organizing thinking about race relations explains why he thought highly of the anthropological studies done on southern communities in the late 1930s and early 1940s.[134] Concerning Dollard's 1937 psychoanalytic study, *Caste and Class in a Southern Town*, Johnson said:

> This is, in many respects, the most significant study of institutionalized race relations in the United States, so far made. The method of the study permits a vigorous and new interpretation of familiar behavior. The disproportionate rewards of upper-caste status, for example, are described under the concept of economic, sexual, and prestige "gains." The caste pattern is defined in education, politics and religion. The present-day emotional education of the Negro fits him for his caste role as his earlier education fitted him for slavery. Formal schooling, which is inadequate, nevertheless is an advantage to the Negro because, by introducing him to a wider culture, it tends to break down an unprotesting adjustment to caste status. Despite the dictates of caste, white southern people, as members of the major American culture, share the domi-

nant views which approve mass education. Politics are completely controlled by the upper caste, and religion, as he observed it, was largely an emotional outlet.[135]

In *Bitter Canaan*, Johnson used racial caste as a central analytical concept for explaining the institutionalization of Amero-Liberian oppression of the native populations. Through their paternalistic attitudes, social mannerisms, labor policies, and institution-building, Amero-Liberians created a caste-ridden society that drastically oppressed native populations. Johnson pointed out frequently the irony of Amero-Liberian patterns of language usage that structured paternalistic relationships with natives. For example, Amero-Liberian oppressors, like their White American counterparts, used the term "boy" to simultaneously signify the degradation of natives and reinforce their disenfranchised status in the social order.

Johnson used biographical and interview data to describe the patrimonial foundations of Amero-Liberian rulership. The fact that Liberia was ruled nationally and locally by a few extended Amero-Liberian families exacerbated the effects of caste on native life and facilitated the pervasive graft that engulfed that government. The ineffectiveness and the ethno-racism of Amero-Liberian rulers was so great that native tribes rebelled periodically and in some cases even wished to have rulers of European descent. Their rebellious spirits were met with Amero-Liberian hostility, sometimes backed by U.S. assistance.

The "Folk Negro"

Interwar literary and social science circles interested in Afro-American experiences focused on urban Afro-American life. This focus was understandable given the tenor of the times, such as the great Black migration north, the urban race riots, and growing middle class concern over the urbanizing southern migrant. This focus was also due to the assimilationist bias which guided so much thinking about urbanization and that considered Blacks a problem of absorption in the metropolis. This was most apparent in the assimilationist orientation of the National Urban League, most Harlem Renaissance writers, and the majority of journalists and social scientists writing on the race question.[136]

This stress on the assimilation of Blacks in urbanization processes ignored completely the "Blacks folks back home;" those non-assimilated kin still living in the shadow of plantations in the deep and borderland south. They were, in a sense, a source of shame, of the negation of Black progress for the urban middle class intellectuals and leaders who envisioned the absorption of Blacks into American civilization, particularly into the city. The only two Black scholars of national rank who described vividly the ways of the "folks back home" in a positive way were anthropologist and novelist Zora Neale Hurston and sociologist Charles S. Johnson.

Much work is being done on Zora Neale Hurston's study of the folk Black as part of the overdue contemporaneous effort to rediscover her as a seminal scholar of the Afro-American experience.[137] We have yet to do the same for Johnson, though his folk Negro concept runs throughout his *Bitter Canaan* and on through his extensive rural sociological studies during the 1930s and 1940s. In at least one unpublished document, Johnson expressed concern over the lack of social scientific interest in folk Negroes.[138] Whether writing about the culturally pluralistic attributes of Liberian native life, or the somewhat assimilated lives of Blacks in rural southern communities, Johnson insisted that the lives of ordinary people be studied in their own right.

Bitter Canaan, and especially his *African Diary* from which so much data for *Bitter Canaan* was drawn, is replete with sympathetic references to how natives lived and how externally imposed forces shaped their lives. In his effort to see the world through their eyes, he interviewed natives extensively and keenly observed their ceremonies. He recorded numerous protest songs as part of their resistance to the Amero-Liberian rulers. A major contention in Johnson's positive view of native life was that apart from oppressive external rule which was creating social disorganization (such as the depopulation of villages for forced-labor markets), native communities had their own internal logic which, when left alone, maintained a normal flow of life.

Four years after returning from Liberia to the United States, Johnson presented, in *Shadow of the Plantation*, a similar line of argument about Blacks in rural Alabama. He goes through great pains to describe the external oppressive forces and internal indigenous forces that shaped the lives of folk Negroes. Through studies of power and privilege he offered explanations of ways in which the Macon County, Alabama community he studied was oppressed in the plantation economy. He explained how folk Negro characteristics, such as quasi-family structures, were the result of a mixture of indigenous customs and the political economy of the plantation. This steered him away from pathological assessments of lower class Black families promoted by other Chicago sociologists.

Johnson's fascination with ordinary Black people who were not yet touched by the "ravages of civilization" continued when he began extensive studies of rural Black youth and how racial caste affected their personalities, interpersonal relations, and aspirations. His in-depth survey instruments and the life history data that empirically grounded his published work on Black youth, as well as his study of Liberian natives should be seen as attempts to interpret the realities of folk Negroes through their eyes.

A Prelude to Dependency Theory

More than Ernest W. Burgess and E. Franklin Frazier, Charles S. Johnson used contextual analyses to explain the evolution of poverty-stricken Black families. Frazier used the Burgess concentric zone framework to explore the relative moral strength and assimilation of Black families in urban settings. He concentrated on how the maladjustment of southern migrants to the urban northern United States created an underclass with pathological characteristics—high crime rates, pervasive illegitimate birth rates, etc.[139]

Johnson, on the other hand, focused on how structural, political, and economic attributes of local and regional environments shaped Black family organization and functions in rural southern United States and Liberia. For instance, in *Shadow of the Plantation*, Johnson explained the predominance of late marriage patterns, high illegitimate birth rates and variations in Black family life in terms of the impact of a plantation economy. Elsewhere, he expressed his criticism for pathological approaches to the Black family and stressed the need to consider the role of external environmental factors in shaping Black family organization.[140]

In Liberia, Johnson took his contextual perspective on development to the societal and international levels. Unlike most of his contemporaries in the field of African development, Johnson linked the crucial problems of Liberia to the political, economic, and sociocultural interests of European colonial regimes. The Liberian elites' inability to stabilize their nation-state economically and politically could be traced to their struggles with imperialistic European colonial neighbors as well as to their internal sociocultural and political problems. Paradoxically, due to their financial status, Amero-Liberians were periodically dependent upon European colonial powers for loans. Such financial assistance had strings attached, such as European control over Liberian financial affairs. Also, there was a large European community in Liberia, especially from Germany, that monopolized small business markets. Then there was the dependency on the U.S. for periodic military and financial assistance. Johnson documented how the U.S. used aid, especially military assistance, to quell native rebellions and as leverage for recommending internal reforms.

Johnson pointed out the dilemmas of the Firestone plantation developments that occurred in the United States. Rather than questioning the motives of Harvey Firestone, Sr., or the U.S. government, Johnson concentrated on the impact of Firestone interests on Liberian labor policies and on the republic's political economy.

In sum, Johnson claimed that the paternalistic attitudes and policies of European and Amerian elites that had shaped relationships with Liberia were central causes of the country's underdevelopment. Though not fully explained theoretically, Johnson's development of underdevelopment interpretation is similiar to what scholars of today call dependency theory.

Johnson's Methodological Perspective

Johnson's methodological approach to Afro-American experiences departed somewhat from his Chicago teachers and colleagues. Park urged his students to use life history methods for investigating sociological phenomena such as Afro-American social life. Burgess, being more quantitatively-minded than Park, trained his students to use census data to develop explanations about social issues such as family patterns, urban ecology, and delinquency. Both Park and Burgess advocated field study and participant oberservation as a means of rounding out data collected through other methodological techniques.

Methodologically, Frazier's approaches to Afro-American experiences usually came through life history analyses and census reports. In his Black family research, life histories generated needed experiential data.[141] Data from census reports gave a quantitative grounding for the moral, cultural, and ecological perspectives found in his scholarship.

Johnson was sensitive to the need to interpret the realities of his subjects through their eyes. Since he was a social situationalist, he insisted on using methods addressing the sociologically relative experiences of his subjects. More than other Chicago sociologists, he was an investigator of the social conditioning of Afro-American experiences. Johnson's philosophy of social research led him to use a combination of survey instruments, life histories, and participant oberservation techniques. Unlike Frazier, he shied away from being totally dependent upon census reports; he was more interested in firsthand data collection, in data that reflected more precisely the social situations of his subjects. When he did quantify data, whether from life histories, surveys, or census reports, it was to present statistical portrayals of Afro-American oppression or demographic characteristics. He seldom constituted statistical tables exemplifying Black pathology.[142]

From the 1920s on, Charles S. Johnson combined uniquely his literary and social scientific talents. During the 1920s, his social scientific interests were demonstrated in empirical race relations studies conducted for the Chicago Race Relations Commission, the National Urban League, and the National Interracial Conference. His literary interests were exemplified in his sponsorship of Harlem Renaissance writers through *Opportunity* literary contests and through informal mentorship.

Johnson never considered the humanities to be completely divorced from the social sciences. Social scientists had an obligation to grapple with moral and ethical issues as well as impartial empirical analyses.[143] Behind the numbers indicating patterns of human conduct were human beings: the field studies that Johnson became famous for—*Shadow of the Plantation* and *Growing Up in the Black Belt*—highlighted his concerns for the human story upon which data analysis was based.

Johnson's *Ebony and Topaz*,[144] an anthology of Harlem Renaissance writers and social scientists, was an indicator of Johnson's respect for both humanistic and social scientific depictions of Afro-American social life. Johnson's most dramatic attempt to bring the two intellectual spheres into synthesis was *Bitter Canaan*.

Methodologically, Johnson's *Bitter Canaan* is a striking literary essay grounded in a synthesis of data from biographies, life histories, archival sources, official histories, and ethnographic materials. Johnson's discussions with Malinowski and Pitt-Rivers in London as well as his Chicago training shaped his methodological tactics. His data presentations, particularly the ethnographic portrayals of the Liberian hinterland, offer a vivid narrative of native life and the negative effects of Amero-Liberian oppression and forced labor practices. Johnson's obvious pro-native sentiment comes through as he spends considerable time and space describing the customs and lives of natives disrupted by the paternalism and corrupt political motivations of the Amero-Liberian dominated government. As in the following diary excerpt, Johnson only faintly disguises his disgust for the unjustifiable pretentiousness of Amero-Liberians in contrast with the impressive qualities of other well-assimilated and non-assimilated natives. Johnson contrasted Amero-Liberian Victor Cooper with a native named Hodges:

> Victor Cooper, who styles himself a surveyor and disliked America because he couldn't stand the segregation, Jim Crow there. His people are from Barbados, and they are related to the other Coopers by marriage. We ate together. He has the table manners of a poodle dog, grim, surly, and growling; he put his head into his plate as he grasped his silver with a grotesquely permanent grip and began to feed himself, with hisses and hard breathing. The only indication he gave of company was an occasional shifting of his eye, without turning his head. He spent his time writing an article which he first made great disturbance getting typed (by Hodges) and later in reading and re-reading it, chuckling over it and handing it to various persons to read—sitting on the side, guiding appreciation by chuckling, raising his voice in laughter as he followed the eyes of his newest victim.

> I cannot understand this difference between Cooper, for example, and Hodges, a native Grebo. The first is uncouth, mannerless and of a bumptious puerility, and Amero-Liberian; the latter suave, gracious, well-read, keenly intelligent and native, sticking at times in the evening to his native dress—the lappa. Hodges does not dare appear in the first cabin where we pay the same fares, and Cooper feels warranted in a bumptious and patronizing air toward all the natives, including Hodges.[145]

As *Bitter Canaan*'s subtitle, *The Story of the Negro Republic* suggests, Johnson offered a critcal narrative voiced through the historical and recorded experiences of those who created the republic and most importantly, by those indigenous populations oppressed in the processes and structures of settlement.

As a contribution to what Gary Marx has called muckraking sociology, Johnson's *Bitter Canaan* dramatized the scholar's astute ability to synthesize techniques of humanistic and sociological discourse. Humanistic elements are found in Johnson's discourse, through which the book unfolds. His pro-native sentiments led him to attempt to construct the meaning of native life, not just measure or predict it. Johnson's recommendations, quite uncharacteristic for "official Johnson," indicate his understanding of the possible use of social science to expose corruption in powerful circles and to offer reformist or revolutionary solutions to eradicate such wrongdoing. In *Bitter Canaan*, Johnson highlights what he subdues in his published works: a persistent advocacy for the underdog.

Why Bitter Canaan Was Never Published

The question remains: why was *Bitter Canaan* not published? Before hiking to the archives and proceeding with the digging, I thought *Bitter Canaan* was too politically sensitive for the State Department and White publishers. But the more digging I did and the more I read about the politics of American-Liberian relations between the world wars, the more I began to revise my thinking. For one thing, as suggested earlier, State Department officials would have probably been quite receptive to the analysis of Liberian affairs Johnson offered in *Bitter Canaan*. Indeed, not a few comments Johnson made in his well-received supplement and final commission reports were incorporated in *Bitter Canaan*. If anything, State Department officials and certainly the White press would have been delighted to see a *Bitter Canaan* published by an eminent Black scholar. This was particularly the case since it was rather uncritical, though revealing, of American involvement in Liberian affairs.

Two more plausible reasons why *Bitter Canaan* was never published began to emerge as my archival research advanced, taking me to the National Archives, Fisk University, the University of Chicago, and the Chicago Historical Society. First, it became apparent that Johnson's wellmanaged but still overextended career was a major contributing factor to *Bitter Canaan* collecting dust in his files. In any rigorous schedule, some critical matters are overlooked or involuntarily given secondary attention. Thus, as much as Johnson considered *Bitter Canaan* his major work, it fell between the cracks of an incredibly busy schedule between 1939 and 1947, a period in which demands on Johnson were at their highest point. It was during that period that Johnson began his most serious effort to find a publisher for *Bitter Canaan*.

Due to unknown circumstances, University of Chicago editors became interested in publishing *Bitter Canaan* in the early 1940s. In the surviving correspondence that extends from 1941 to 1947, Johnson communicated with the editors about the progress of the manuscript.[146] Editors sent Johnson periodic notices about missing chapter deadlines and being over-due in submitting the entire manuscript. Since Johnson's activities accelerated during the World War II years, it is a wonder he was able to do the extensive revisions which gave *Bitter Canaan* its present form.

When he finally submitted the manuscript in 1945, University of Chicago editors sent it out for review. They sent it to Jackson Davis, of the Rockefeller General Education Board and soon-to-be-president of the Phelps-Stokes Fund. It had been Davis's recommendation of Johnson for the international commission post that was so highly esteemed by State Department officers in 1929. Davis liked the book, calling it an admirably detached study with a vivid, ironic style. He recommended that the book be published with some revisions.[147]

Davis's positive recommendations did not satisfy Johnson. He sent the manuscript to Eric Williams, Charles Thompson, and Claude Barnett for review. It was their comments that made Johnson hesitate about publishing *Bitter Canaan*. While University of Chicago Press editors became increasingly impatient about a manuscript they felt was beginning to decline in market value, Williamson, Thompson, and Barnett all discouraged the editors from publishing *Bitter Canaan*. The views of Williams, Thompson, and Barnett were illustrative of the dominant Black bourgeoisie's perspectives on Liberia.

Sundiata's *Black Scandal: America and the Liberian Labor Crisis 1929–1936*, details the various Black bourgeoisie's responses to the State Department's and League of Nation's efforts to pressure the Amero-Liberian elite into reforms in the aftermath of the international commission report.[148] Some bourgeoisie leaders, like the Amero-Liberian ruling caste, opposed Marcus Garvey's efforts in America and Liberia since it was a threat to Amero-Liberian authority. In the United States, Garveyism threatened the paternalistic White establishment that the Black bourgeoisie was dependent upon. Amero-Liberian leaders feared that Garvey's nationalistic plans in their country would upset their European colonial neighbors.

Other members of the Black bourgeoisie were entangled in American interests that attempted to exploit Liberian labor or to develop natives through foundation and missionary-sponsored education. The latter group was pro-Amero-Liberian in its attempts to legitimate its activities through developing working relationships with those Liberians in power and was anti-native in assuming that natives were a plentiful source of cheap labor, or were backward people in need of civilization. No effort was made to understand natives as people with unique cultures deserving preservation on a par with Amero-Liberian culture.

A third segment of the Black bourgeoisie was interested in developing economic schemes in Liberia which, of course, relied upon the cooperation of Liberian government officials.[149] A fourth segment of the Black bourgeoisie leadership class were post–World War II Pan Africanists. Yet, they were more of the elistist mold, since they emphasized nationalism from the top of African stratification systems. Since grassroot nationalism was really a form of militant tribalism that threatened sovereign statehood, it was not encouraged.

Although views about Liberia varied among the numerous factions of the Black bourgeoisie leadership, there was a common empathy toward the Amero-Liberian elite. For the sake of demonstrating the Blacks could rule themselves, the existence of Liberia was necessary. Native rights were irrelevant. At most, bourgeoisie leaders advocated the unqualified assimilation of natives as backward people through the promotion of Westernized education. At best, they were ignored or considered a hindrance to Liberian development.[150]

Charles S. Johnson's *Bitter Canaan* contained a paradigm that countered the popular ideological stances of the Black bourgeoisie on Liberia. It was anti-Amero-Liberian elite in its premises, data analyses, and conclusions. *Bitter Canaan* was pro-native in its sympathetic portrayals of native life and its destruction by Amero-Liberian labor practices and societal organization. Johnson, in his recommendations, urged that the structure of Amero-Liberian rulership be reformed and that natives be allowed more participation in the settler society, thus culturally pluralistic population.

Speaking from a pan-Africanist and Marxist perspective, Howard University historian Eric Williams raised doubts about *Bitter Canaan* before the editors of the University of Chicago Press. The year was 1947, when decolonization sentiment began to crystalize in the European world system. He argued that Johnson's *Bitter Canaan* would offer a negative criticism of emerging nationalist movements in Africa; also, the work was in need of serious revision that would require Johnson to return to Liberia for a short visit.[151]

Barnett and Thompson also discouraged Johnson from publishing *Bitter Canaan*.[152] Claude Barnett's ambiguous remarks about *Bitter Canaan* probably weighed most heavily in Johnson's mind. Barnett was a Tuskegee graduate and a devout disciple of Booker T. Washington and his successor, Robert Moton.[153] He was a great admirer of the Firestone Company's and the Phelps-Stokes Fund's activities in Liberia and in other parts of Africa. He was also the founder and director of the Associated Negro Press, which disseminated news to major Black newspapers and periodicals. Since the White press was seldom interested in Black news, the Black press and hence the Negro Associated Press were crucial institutions in Black America. Prominent Blacks and their major institutions such as churches, businesses, and colleges were dependent upon Barnett's news service to disseminate correct and positive information about them to Black newspapers and periodicals.

In 1925, while Firestone Company executives were planning negotiations with the Liberian government, Barnett offered to aid the development of a Black consensus in favor of the corporation's plans through his news service. Robert Moton wrote to Thomas Jesse Jones of the Phelps-Stokes Fund,

> I have just had a very interesting and satisfactory interview with Mr. Claude A. Barnett, manager of the Associated Negro Press, in which Mr. Barnett related to me certain ideas which he has for developing behind the Firestone Liberian project a sound Negro public opinion. Mr. Barnett's plans meet my approval and I have asked him to see you when such a conference can be conveniently arranged. I am sure you can be of great help to him in the furtherance of his plans, and whatever you can do in this matter will be very much appreciated by me.[154]

In the course of cultivating an accommodative relationship with Firestone executives and minimizing criticism about them through his Associated Negro Press, Barnett did not hesitate to reap personal benefits, or at least to attempt to do so. For example, he wrote the following 6 February 1937 letter to Harvey Firestone, Jr. about his wife, a talented singer:

> I feel confident that the (Firestone) company's radio program is built with an idea of developing good will. Therefore, I feel free to make the following suggestion.
>
> The finest—I am willing to modify and say one of the finest—voices on radio today is that of Miss Etta Moton. Returned from a triumphant South American tour, she is now giving concerts throughout the country. The attached press book gives you a description of her work.
>
> So popular is Miss Moton among radio listeners both white and colored, that I feel confident her inclusion as a guest artist at some time would be received with gratitude by the many.
>
> Incidentally, she sings in Akron on February 25 in concert at the Goodyear Theater. I feel certain you would enjoy hearing her.
>
> I am sometimes a bit diffident about extending her all the praise to which she is entitled, because when she is not Miss Moton professionally, she is Mrs.

Barnett. However, knowing she can deliver superlatively, I hope you will forgive my personal interest.[155]

At least from the 1920s on, Barnett held the racial philosophies of Phelps-Stokes Fund administrators in high esteem and disseminated their perspective through the Associated Negro Press. In 1925, Thomas Jesse Jones wrote Barnett a note of thanks for his willingness to promote "friendly relations between the races through his news service."[156] As their relationship grew, Jones did not hesitate to give Barnett confidential information or opinions which the director of the Associated Negro Press occasionally disseminated as objective news. In 1935, for instance, Jones wrote to Barnett about his views on Moton's successor at Tuskegee for the Associated Negro Press.[157]

The Phelps-Stokes Fund refused to broadcast criticisms about Liberia, and Barnett usually followed suit. One Phelps-Stokes officer, L.A. Roy, in the process of explaining why that was a set policy, revealed the inevitable dependency of education foundations and, indeed, missionary administrators on the goodwill of the Amero-Liberian elite:

> As our efforts are to cooperate with the Liberian government and work in harmony with them, we never release any news of an unfavorable character, nor do we often release anything about conditions in the country and even then only when they are sent to us from reliable sources for release. In almost all cases we know in advance that the president has seen the release before it is sent to us.[158]

Also, during the international debate over whether Europeans or Americans should be used to administrate reformed Liberian policies and institutions, Roy gave Barnett rationales for why Black public opinion should be pro-American. This view was in keeping with the beliefs of Barnett and other Black bourgeoisie opinion leaders who felt that some form of external intervention was needed to reform Liberia.[159] It is therefore clear why the ideology of the Phelps-Stokes Fund and Barnett's Associated Negro Press harmonized so successfully.[160]

When Anson Stokes retired from the Phelps-Stokes Fund Board of Trustees in 1946, Barnett was selected to take his place and graciously accepted the position.[161] He also sent Thomas Jesse Jones a touching letter upon his retirement in 1946,

> It certainly is with regret that I face up to your leaving the work in which you have engaged so successfully for so many years. I am confident that your spirit and most effective thinking will never be very far removed from it.

> While I know there are very many important activities which you will now be free to pursue, I trust that the causes of Negro and African education will still claim most of your efforts.[162]

Shortly after Barnett became a Phelps-Stokes Fund trustee, the foundation financed a tour of West Africa for him and his wife. In his lengthy "A West African Journey," Barnett praised the work of education foundations, colonial administrators, and the Firestone Company. He expressed the hope that Afro-Americans would be able to make contributions to "the upward progress" of Africans.[163]

Barnett, then, was a powerful opinion leader in Black America. He was instrumental in shaping positive public images about Liberian development via Amero-Liberian rulership and through American intervention. Barnett's conservative stance certainly explains his ambiguous response to Charles S. Johnson's *Bitter Canaan*:

> I really must applaud *Bitter Canaan*. It seems simply amazing that you could have found so much real and factual material and woven it together with the sort of philosophy and comment which brings it up to current thinking. The story is told in such fashion that there are no dull moments. One absorbs history while pursuing pleasant, interesting pictures.
>
> I found myself when I first read "Incident," wishing that the book would not begin on that note. I felt that, as sensitive as the Liberians are, they and perhaps many people would not get much farther than such a foreword because they would feel that here was another of those exposés which have been so popular about Liberia. Later I changed somewhat because the chronicle of lives of the early settlers showed them frequently as being sturdy pioneers. One had even a feeling of heroism on their part in some of their struggles. This rather leavens the first feeling. On the other hand, admittedly, you cannot gild the lily and declare that all was peace and light among a group of highjacking male slavers.
>
> Your report should be less objectionable by far than some of the books which have been written about Liberians, objectionable to them I mean. There is no way to escape the deadly facts which you assemble to buttress up the early chronicle, your notes and their damning evidence.
>
> You give me a new picture of the American Colonization Society. Why do you take so long to introduce it definitely? You keep saying "The Colonization Society."
>
> Just received "Into the Main Stream." I give up. Wish you would show me how to do one.[164]

Johnson, needless to say, was quite concerned over his critics' comments. Williams's remarks worried him; he did not want to be a stumbling block to the emerging nationalistic movements in Africa. He tried for several months to get Williams to confer with him about major revisions, but the historian was too busy.[165] Although no extensive correspondence between Johnson and Barnett was found, Johnson more than likely took the news service director's ambiguous comments to heart. Johnson was a man who shunned controversy; he would prefer to keep *Bitter Canaan* in his files rather than to enter a storm of controversy. Also, Johnson's encounter with Barnett and his other critics occurred in 1947, the year he became president of Fisk University. Fisk as well as Johnson could not risk being the subject of criticism by the Black and native African presses. He also did not want to stand in the way of emerging nationalistic movements in Africa.

Meanwhile, as Johnson pondered the comments of his critics while preparing to become president of Fisk, University of Chicago Press editors became quite impatient over the delays. Due to the rapidly changing international political climate, *Bitter Canaan* was becoming obsolete. Thus it was in need of serious revisions that would require Johnson to return to Liberia.

> We are very grateful for your letter of October 1, giving us the present status of your manuscript, *Bitter Canaan.*
>
> We are quite concerned about the delays that have occurred and perhaps may further occur with this work. Our recollection is not sufficiently strong to allow us the judgment whether any portion of the manuscript has in any way become obsolescent due to the lapse of time since it was first written, and we hope that this is not case. However, the possibility remains that at any time events may occur which might put the book out of date. For these reasons, we should be very grateful if you would do everything in your power to speed the work along and send us the final version as quickly as possible.
>
> It will not be feasible to publish the work in the spring of 1948. We should like to plan for publication in the fall of next year and, to make that possible, we would have to have the manuscript within a couple of months.[166]

When Johnson did not respond to this 9 October 1947 letter, his editor sent him the following 7 November rejection letter:

> The repeated delays which have, so far, prevented publication of your *Bitter Canaan* have made it necessary for us to study once more the question of whether publication of the work in its present version is at all advisable.
>
> Considerably more than a decade has elapsed since your book was first drafted, and there is no doubt that the intervening war has caused considerable changes in Liberia, changes which are probably still in progress. Under these circumstances, we are forced to the conclusion that it would be unwise to proceed with publication.
>
> If you were to find occasion for another visit to Liberia, and if that visit were to result in revision bringing *Bitter Canaan* up to date, we should, of course, want to have a chance to publish that revised version.

We trust that you understand, and agree with, our reasons for this decision. Please let us hear from you.[167]

A very busy Johnson scratched "ok" on the letter. When he did not respond to it, because he was preoccupied with his installation as president of Fisk and other activities, his editor wrote on 11 December:

We had hoped very much to hear from you in answer to our letter of November 7.

Although we can only repeat that, in our opinion, publication of *Bitter Canaan* in its present form would be exceedingly unwise, we want to make it quite clear that we believe this work could be developed into a highly important and excellent book. To do this, it would have to be brought up to date.

It occurred to us that, if your present duties would not allow you a stay in Liberia, you still might find an able collaborator who could spend a year or so in Africa and gather the information your manuscript now lacks. In this manner, *Bitter Canaan* might be made publishable. We are thinking, of course, of a collaborator skilled and intelligent enough to distinguish reality behind the latest facade of any statutes and post-war prosperity.

I hope that you will give this suggestion serious thought. If you feel it would be impossible to follow it, or to go to Liberia yourself, we are sorry to say that we see no other way but to drop the matter definitely. Unless we hear from you, we shall then assume that you wish us to cancel our agreement with you.[168]

Finally, belatedly and obviously disappointed, Johnson replied on 18 December 1947:

I must apologize to you for not giving earlier attention to your letter of November 7th. This was the date of my formal installation as president of the institution. From this somewhat active and distracting setting it was necessary for me to go immediately to the UNESCO Conference in Mexico City. I have just returned from this mission.

Regarding *Bitter Canaan*, it is quite agreeable to me to have the agreement on publishing cancelled. It will not be possible for me to spend any sustained period in Liberia at this time or support a collaborator there for a year or so.

As your files will indicate, I did not originally submit the manuscript to the University of Chicago Press. It was sent only after several urgent requests from the Press, and the agreement was drawn up after it had been examined and with full knowledge that I had no intention of going back to Liberia with the view to bringing it up to date. It has been revised since the first reading to correct such as might be adjusted by additional information from informants and publications. But, this is quite another matter.[169]

Bitter Canaan remained in Charles S. Johnson's file due to its obsolescence in the face of changing political climates in the international community. Also, the book would have raised controversy in Black bourgeois circles supportive of post World War II Liberia as a historic model of independent African statehood. Always a cautious man, Johnson preferred to give up trying to find a publisher. On 26 June 1948, he wrote the following letter to someone who had sent him materials for *Bitter Canaan.*

> I want to acknowledge with thanks the Legislative Acts of the Republic of Liberia which you were good enough to send. When I asked for them originally, I had in mind completing the manuscript which I had begun some time ago. In fact, shortly after my return from Liberia around 1930. I concluded, however, that events had moved so rapidly in the Republic, my material, except the strictly historical part of it, would be out of date, and so I decided not to publish the book. I have a tinge of regret about this decision because it represents, probably, the best writing I can do.[170]

Johnson's inability to get *Bitter Canaan* published was the result of problems which afflict any prolific, overly committed scholar. While pursuing so many high-powered projects, some activities, no matter how cherished, never get completed or are completed in a haphazard way. What primarily concern us here are the cultural taboos which contributed to Johnson's decision not to publish *Bitter Canaan.* As Carter G. Woodson learned in publishing *The Miseducation of the Negro* and E. Franklin Frazier in translating *Black Bourgeoisie* from its French text, there are matters that Black as well as White establishments do not wish to be aired.

For Johnson to publish a critique of Liberia, no matter when, would have been an unforgivable transgression in the eyes of the Black establishment. Then and now, the Black establishment has been hypersensitive to intellectually honest discussions about the negative as well as the positive attributes of Black African nation-states. We hear so much needed criticism about the dynamics of oppression in the Republic of South Africa, but such is not the case when it comes to countries tied to American interests such as Liberia (the only countries to get recent bad press are those outside the American orbit, including Uganda and Ethiopia).

This tendency for Black establishments to give uncritical support to Liberia is tied to a collective need to believe that somewhere Blacks are fulfilling the "American dream." *Bitter Canaan* with all of its realism would have demystified the Black establishment's heaven.[171]

Notes

1. Charles S. Johnson to V. Horatio Henry, 26 June 1948, CSJ.

2. *Bitter Canaan.*
3. League of Nations Papers (LAP), National Archives.
4. Indeed, even some American diplomats stationed in Monrovia, such as Clifton Wharton, did not try to stop forced labor and even condoned its use. The wife of the late Minister Frances related to State Department officials their discovery of the use of forced labor for public work in Liberia shortly after arriving in Monrovia: "The fact that this (public) labor was forced on the part of the Liberian government, the natives not being paid for the same, was first brought to our attention by Mr. Clifton R. Wharton, then the Legation Secretary, on the piazza at his home across from the park, where we were having our meals preparatory to getting the Segation Kitchen equipped for service, in November, 1927. Observing one day a host of natives at work in the park, levelling the grounds, demolishing the old frame bandstand preparatory to erecting a new one for the coming inauguration ceremonies, I inquired of Mr. Wharton what pay they received for this service and was informed that the natives were paid absolutely nothing (22 December 1929, Nellie Frances to William Castle, Liberia Record Group [LRG], National Archives, Washington, D.C.).
5. J.P. Moffat to Mr. Shaw and Mr. Cotton, 17 January 1930, LRG, National Archives.
6. I.K. Sundiata, *Black Scandal: America and the Liberian Labor Crisis, 1929-1936* (Philadelphia: Institute for the Study of Human Issues, 1980), pp. 1-10.
7. League of Nations Papers (LAP), National Archives, Washington, D.C.
8. 1926 Anti-Slavery Convention. LAP, National Archives.
9. Ibid.
10. Ibid.
11. Ibid.
12. Ibid.
13. Ibid.
14. Kenneth L. King, *Pan-Africanism and Education* (New York: Oxford University Press, 1971).
15. Thomas Jesse Jones, *Education in Africa: A Study of West, South, and Equatorial Africa by the African Education Commission* (under the auspices of the Phelps-Stokes Fund and Foreign Mission Societies of North America and Europe) (New York: Phelps-Stokes Fund, 1922).
16. Raymond L. Buell, *The Native Problem in Africa*, (New York: The MacMillan Company, 1928), vol. 2, pp. 704-888.
17. Ibid.
18. Ibid.
19. Ibid.
20. Ibid.
21. Ibid.
22. Ibid.
23. Ibid.
24. Ibid.
25. Ibid.
26. Ibid.
27. Ibid.
28. Ibid.

29. Ibid.
30. Ibid.
31. Ibid and Raymond Buell, *Liberia: A Century of Survival, 1847-1947* (Philadelphia: University of Pennsylvania Press, 1947).
32. Raymond Buell, *The Native Problem*, vol. 2, pp. 818-36.
33. State Department correspondence, 1928. LRG, National Archives.
34. Ibid.
35. Ibid.
36. Ibid.
37. Raymond Buell, *The Native Problem*, vol. 2, p. 853.
38. I.K. Sundiata, *Black Scandal: America and the Liberian Labor Crisis, 1929-1936* (Philadelphia: Institute for the Study of Human Issues, 1980), pp. 11-32.
39. Henry L. Carter, "The Special Relationship Between the United States and the Republic of Liberia," 13 May 1929. LRG, National Archives.
40. Secretary of State to the Liberian president, 8 June 1929.
41. Clifton Wharton to Secretary of State, 31 September 1929.
42. 1926 Anti-Slavery Convention document. LAP, National Archives.
43. Clifton Wharton to Secretary of State, 10 September 1929. LRG, National Archives.
44. William C. Castle to Secretary of State, 29 May 1929. LRG, National Archives.
45. Henry Stimson to American Legation, 23 July 1929. LRG, National Archives.
46. Ibid.
47. State Department memos about the international commission. LRG, National Archives.
48. Ibid.
49. Oggen H. Hammond to Secretary of State, 5 July 1929, LRG, National Archives.
50. William Castle to an unidentified State Department official (no date, probably written in August, 1929), LRG, National Archives.
51. Clifton Wharton to Secretary of State, 13 August 1929. LRG, National Archives.
52. *Bitter Canaan.*
53. State Department-League of Nations correspondence about the commission. LRG, National Archives.
54. W.T. Frances to Secretary of State, 14 June 1929; Henry Stimson to Emmett Scott, November 2, 1919. LRG, National Archives.
55. Emmett Scott to Henry Stimson, 15 November 1929. LRG, National Archives.
56. Clifton Wharton to Secretary of State, 10 September 1929. LRG, National Archives.
57. Clifton Wharton to Secretary of State, 16 September 1929, LRG, National Archives.
58. Unidentified State Department official to another unidentified State Department official, 31 October 1929. LRG, National Archives.
59. Clifton Wharton to Secretary of State, 16 September 1929, LRG, National Archives.
60. Sundiata, *Black Scandal*, pp. 112-15.
61. Assistant secretary of state memorandum of conversation with D. Emmett Scott, 1 November 1929. LRG, National Archives.

62. Henry Stimson to Herbert Hoover, 24 October 1929. LRG, National Archives.
63. J.P. Moffat to Secretary of State, 13 December 1929. LRG, National Archives.
64. Assistant secretary of state to Henry Carter, 18 November, 1929. LRG, National Archives.
65. Ibid.
66. J.P. Moffat to William Castle, 18 December 1929.
67. Henry Stimson to Herbert Hoover, 20 November 1919. LRG, National Archives.
68. Emmett Scott to William Castle, 19 September 1929.
69. Trevor Arnett to William Castle, 25 September 1929.
70. William Castle to Trevor Arnett, 26 November 1929. LRG, National Archives.
71. William Castle to Trevor Arnett, 26 November 1929. LRG, National Archives.
72. Jackson Davis to William Castle, 4 December 1929. LRG, National Archives.
73. William Castle to Charles S. Johnson, 26 November 1929. LRG, National Archives.
74. Charles S. Johnson to William Castle, December 1929. LRG, National Archives. Hoover's selection of Johnson marked the Urban League scholar's rise to international prominence. It also coincided with Johnson's growing restlessness with the Urban League. Johnson's position as research director required him to be on the road frequently, which created much unhappiness since he was so close to his wife and young children. His letters home were replete with complaints characteristic of a lonely man always gone on business. (Charles Johnson to Marie B. Johnson letters, in possession of Mrs. Patricia Clifford.) Toward the end of the 1920s, *Opportunity* began to experience financial difficulties, which certainly aggravated his restlessness. He had to get out and between 1928 and 1930, a series of events enabled him to do so.
    First in the late 1920s, Thomas Elsa Jones, the Quaker president of Fisk, received a large grant from the Laura Spelman Rockefeller Memorial which enabled him to organize a research-oriented social science program. Since Johnson had a national reputation as a moderate scholar, Jones approached him in 1928 or 1929 to become the department's director. Julius Rosenwald and Edwin Embree helped to interest Johnson by promising to support his research efforts through the newly reorganized Julius Rosenwald Fund. Since Johnson was completing his first book-length work, *The Negro in American Civilization*, and needed a change from the Urban League, he accepted the offer. When the Hoover offer came, he was just getting settled into Fisk.
75. Charles S. Johnson to William Castle, 9 December, 1929. LRG, National Archives.
76. Clifton Wharton to Secretary of State, 12 December 10, 1929. LRG, National Archives.
77. Swenson to Secretary of State, 19 December 1929; J.P. Moffat to Secretary of State, 4 December 1929. LRG, National Archives.
78. State Department, December 1929 memos. LRG, National Archives.
79. Clifton Wharton to Secretary of State, 30 December 1929. LRG, National Archives.
80. State Department officials to Charles S. Johnson, 11 January 1930. LRG, National Archives.

81. Swenson to Secretary of State, 19 December, 1929, LRG, National Archives.
82. Henry Stimson to American Legation, Berne, Switzerland, 31 December 1929. LRG, National Archives.
83. Henry Stimson to Clifton Wharton, 31 December 1929. LRG, National Archives.
84. J.P. Moffat to Mr. Gilbert, 5 March 1930.
85. Henry Carter to Secretary of State, 17 December 1929. LRG, National Archives.
86. Nellie Frances to William Castle, 22 December 1929. LRG, National Archives.
87. Memo of 16 December 1929. In this lengthy memo entitled "Liberia: Work of the International Commission to Investigate Alleged Forced Labor Conditions," the author noted under a subsection entitled "Recommendations of Commission":

> The report of the Commission should include recommendations for changes to be made not only to bring an end to the exploitation of native labor by use of forced labor for private and public purposes, but should also if need be make recommendations for future legislation. For instance, it is a very unhealthy condition to permit officials of the Government to engage in recruiting labor and laws should be passed prohibiting it . . . I think it needs no prophet to foretell that the Liberian member will fail to agree with any report in disparagement of Liberia and the present government. Life for him would not be worth living were he to do so. It is possible that the League of Nations member may only report generally that conditions might be improved. The American member will, I am sure, find what all our disinterested witnesses seem to agree on, that is, . . . condition[s] of native labor . . . , especially in connection with Fernando Po. I think it important, therefore, to emphasize the importance of the American member making, if necessary, a minority report and not to hesitate to describe fully conditions as he finds them. For obvious reasons, it is preferable that a unanimous report be agreed upon if at all possible. The findings in such [a] report should include unhesitantly the culpability of President King, if such is the case, either in his failure to safeguard the rights of the natives, or what is worse, in his profiting directly by the recruitment of forced labor. Even if the Commission has merely a moral certainty of this or any other facts, I think the whole world deserves to have the benefit of the opinion of the Commission. . . .
>
> It would seem to be that the report should, and such would be in line with their investigation, make certain recommendations concerning the use to be made of what is in reality a good labor supply considering the size of the country. The economic development should include greater cultivation of coffee. Liberian coffee, as is well known, is a very superior variety. Encouragements might be extended to American capital for coffee cultivation. Concessions might be offered for coffee growing and for the development of many of the economic resources, for the most part agricultural, which would enable Liberia to employ its native population at home and in a manner sanctioned by tribal customs. Certain changes, or course, would have to be made in the organic law, permitting foreigners to own land or it should be so arranged that exploitation might be carried out by civilized peoples, white or colored.

At present, Liberia is attempting to prove that a country can be run by colored people and [they] are making a mess of it to the dissatisfaction of every man, white or colored, who has an interest in the interest of the colored people. We are building on sand for Liberia . . . it is quite possible that Liberia can run its own affairs but possibly they were trusted too early with complete political liberty.

88. Henry Carter memo (around 13 December 1929). LRG, National Archives.
89. J.P. Moffat to William Castle, 16 December 1929. LRG, National Archives.
90. Charles S. Johnson to J.P. Moffat, 12 December 1929. LRG, National Archives.
91. For instance, see John F. Matheus, "Fog," *Opportunity* (1926).
92. Charles S. Johnson to Marie B. Johnson, April 1930. LRG, National Archives; Charles S. Johnson, *African Diary*, entries, CSJ.
93. Fellowship folders in CSJ.
94. State Department officials to Charles S. Johnson, 11 January 1930. LRG, National Archives.
95. Charles S. Johnson, *African Diary*, p. 3.
96. Ibid., p. 3.
97. Ibid., pp. 3-4.
98. Ibid., p. 5.
99. Ibid., p. 15.
100. Charles S. Johnson to Marie B. Johnson, April 1930. This 1 April letter was a short diary of March events which Johnson kept for his wife. In the possession of Mrs. Patricia Clifford.
101. Ibid.
102. Ibid.
103. Ibid.
104. Ibid.
105. Ibid.
106. Ibid.
107. Charles S. Johnson, *African Diary*.
108. Report of the International Commission of Inquiry into the Existence of Slavery and Forced Labor in the Republic of Liberia, p. 89.
109. Ibid.
110. Ibid., pp. 205-07.
111. Ibid.
112. Ibid., pp. 120-32.
113. Ibid.
114. Charles S. Johnson, "Supplementary Report," 1 October 1930. LRG, National Archives.
115. Henry Carter to Secretary of State, 15 March 1930; Henry Carter to Secretary of State, 5 May 1930; and Henry L. Stimson and J.P. Moffat, 8 May 1930. LRG, National Archives.
116. American diplomat (?) to Moffat, 30 September 1930.
117. Johnson to DuBois, 10 March 1930. LRG, National Archives.
118. Twe to Johnson, 13 November 1930, 22 November 1930, 12 December 1930; Johnson to Ellis Briggs, 19 December 1930.
119. On 12 January 1932, Twe wrote to Johnson: "Have you forgotten about the work we were to do jointly in anthropology and sociology?" Johnson responded, 27 February 1932, referring to his writing of what would be *Bitter*

Canaan: "Unfortunately I have been out of direct touch with affairs in Liberia for a number of months due to the necessary absorption in certain other studies. I cannot, however, divorce myself from the country, its fortunes, and its extraordinary personalities, and I have well along a text which attempts to interpret the situations which I experienced there in the light of broader sociological observations and the historical background of the country. I still entertain a hope that the country will right itself and eventually find a firm economic and social footing, and I shall be pleased accordingly to get from time to time your own observations and developments."

120. Liberian Centennial, script of four-minute broadcast, CBS-London, 1947.
121. Robert E. Park, *Race and Culture* (Glencoe: Free Press, 1950).
122. Charles S. Johnson, "The Cultural Mission of the Urban League," CSJ.
123. Most of Johnson's Black migration articles were published in *Opportunity*, popular periodicals, and professional journals.
124. Charles S. Johnson, "The Cultural Mission of the Urban League."
125. Charles S. Johnson, *Shadow of the Plantation.*
128. Charles S. Johnson, "When the Negro Migrates," *World Tomorrow* 6 (May 1923):140. Other major articles on the Black migration were: Charles S. Johnson, "The Negro Migration: An Economic Interpretation," *Modern Quarterly* 2 (4, 1925):314-26; Charles S. Johnson, "Substitution of Negro Labor for European Immigrant Labor," *National Council of Social Work,* 53rd annual session (Chicago: University of Chicago Press, 1926), pp. 317-27; Charles S. Johnson, "How the Negro Fits into Northern Industries," *Industrial Psychology* 1 (June 1926):399-412; Charles S. Johnson "The American Immigrant," *Proceedings of the National Conference of Social Work,* 54th annual session (Chicago: University of Chicago Press, 1927), pp. 554-58.
129. Charles S. Johnson, "*Negro Education in Alabama: A Study in Cotton and Stell* by Horace Mann Bond," *American Sociological Review* (December 1929), 907.
130. Charles S. Johnson, "When the Negro Migrates," *World Tomorrow* 6 (May 1923):140; "The Negro Migration: An Economic Interpretation," *Modern Quarterly* 2 (4, 1925): 314-26. "Substitution of Negro Labor for European Immigrant Labor," *National Council of Social Workers,* 53rd annual session (Chicago: University of Chicago Press, 1926), pp. 317-27; "How the Negro Fits into Northern Industries," *Industrial Psychology* 1 (June 1926):399-412; "The American Immigrant,: *Proceedings of the National Conference of Social Work,* 54th annual session (Chicago: University of Chicago Press, 1927), pp. 554-58.
131. Charles S. Johnson, "Race Riots," New Haven paper presentation, 2 April 1921; Charles S. Johnson, "Race Conflicts and Education," Joseph S. Rouchek et al., *Sociological Foundations of Race Relations* (New York: Thomas U. Crowell, 1942) pp. 419-37.
132. See n. 131.
133. Charles S. Johnson, "Caste and Class," Reply to Dr. Frazier's criticisms, 1936, CSJ.
134. He gave Hortense Powdermaker advice on how to go about doing her functional analysis of caste relations in a Southern community—*After Freedom.* See Hortense Powdermaker, *Stranger and Friend.*
135. Charles S. Johnson, "*Caste and Class in a Southern Town,* by John Dollard," *American Journal of Sociology* 43 (May 1938): 838-40.

136. Nancy Weiss, *The National Urban League, 1910-1940*; Nathan Higgins, *The Harlem Renaissance*; and Robert Hemingway, *Zora Neale Hurston*.
137. Robert Hemingway, *Zora Neale Hurston*; Zora Neale Hurston, *I Love Myself*. ed. Alice Walker.
138. Charles S. Johnson, "The Concept of Folk Negro," lecture written in early 1940s.
139. John H. Stanfield, "Black Americans and Race Relations: Research between the World Wars," *Journal of Ethnic Studies* (Fall 1983).
140. Ibid.
141. E. Franklin Frazier, *The Negro Family in Chicago, The Negro Family in the United States*.
142. This was even the case in his more abstract empirical works such as *The Negro in American Civilization* and *The Negro College Graduate* (Chapel Hill: University of North Carolina Press), 1938.
143. Charles S. Johnson, "Charles S. Johnson," in *American Spiritual Autobiographies: Fifteen Self-Portraits*, ed. Louis Finkelstein (New York: Harper, 1948).
144. Charles S. Johnson, *Ebony and Topaz* (New York: National Urban League, 1927). Also see, Charles S. Johnson, "The Negro Enters Literature," *Carolina Magazine* 57 (May 1927):3-9, 44-48.
145. Charles S. Johnson, *African Diary*, p. 198.
146. The correspondence between Johnson and the University of Chicago Press editors ranged from January 1941 through December 1947. About the origins of the correspondence see John T. McNeill to Charles S. Johnson, 7 December 1942, CSJ.
147. Johnson informed a University of Chicago Press editor: "Mr. Jackson Davis, who was one of the readers of the manuscript, was good enough to send me a copy of his report to the Press. The recency of his visit to Liberia made it possible for him to bring me up to date on a number of facts. He also sent me the page proofs of a volume which they are preparing. As a result of the studies made in Africa, I would like to have a chance to make the corrections indicated as desirable by Mr. Davis and to take advantage of his chapter on Liberia. Other changes involving correction of the tenses between pages 200 and 300 will have to be made. Would you like me to make these or can these be made by the editorial reader at the Press? I can send the page proofs from Mr. Davis' book on to you if you think it would speed matters any on the general editorial corrections" [Johnson to John Scoon, 7 February 1946, CSJ].
148. I.K. Sundiata, *Black Scandal: Americans and the Liberian Labor Crisis, 1929-1936* (Philadelphia: Institute for the Study of Human Issues, 1980).
149. Ibid.
150. Ibid.
151. Eric Williams' review of the "Bitter Canaan" manuscript sent to the University of Chicago Press editors and to Charles S. Johnson; Eric Williams to Fred Wieck, 23 June 1947; and Eric Williams to Charles S. Johnson, 30 June 1947, CSJ. Since Williams was a close colleague of Johnson's, his review of "Bitter Canaan" put him in an awkward position. He wrote to Fred Wieck, a University of Chicago Press associate editor: "Your request that I should read Dr. Johnson's manuscript on Liberia placed me in a somewhat difficult situation, which, however, I have done my best to deal with, within the limits that I thought proper. I am personally acquainted with Dr. Johnson, and, in fact, look upon him as a colleague. I would be glad, therefore, if I had your permis-

sion to send him a copy of these remarks, so as to be able to continue the discussion with him further, if he thinks that it is worthwhile. I am anxious to do this as quickly as possible, and I would prefer to do it with Dr. Johnson himself rather than through a third party" [Williams to Wieck, 23 June 1947].

152. Charles S. Johnson to Fred Wieck, 1 October 1947, CSJ. Charles H. Thompson, Dean of the Howard University Graduate School wrote to Johnson on 20 October: "I finished reading your manuscript last week, and I must confess that I have come to the same conclusion as Williams; namely, that it might not be desirable to print the manuscript in its present form. I think that it would be misunderstood, but not for the reasons that Williams gave. I shall be glad to talk with you about it when I come down to the inauguration at Fisk, as I plan to be there November 6th, 7th, and 8th" [Charles H. Thompson to Charles S. Johnson, 20 October 1947].

153. Claude A. Barnett to Robert R. Moton, 31 July 1933, Claude A. Barnett (CAB) Papers, Chicago Historical Society.

154. Robert R. Moton to Thomas Jesse Jones, 18 November 1925, CAB.

155. Claude A. Barnett to Harvey Firestone, Jr., 6 November 1937, CAB.

156. Thomas Jesse Jones to Claude A. Barnett, 19 December 1925, CAB.

157. Thomas Jesse Jones to Claude A. Barnett, 16 March 1935, CAB.

158. L.A. Roy to Claude A. Barnett, 22 September 1937, CAB.

159. L.A. Roy to Claude A. Barnett, 3 August 1933, CAB.

160. Claude A. Barnett to L.A. Roy, 5 August 1933, CAB.

161. Claude A. Barnett to Anson Phelps Stokes, 14 November 1946, CAB.

162. Claude A. Barnett to Thomas Jesse Jones, 10 May, 1946, CAB.

163. Claude A. Barnett to Exten Moton; Barnett, "A West African Journey," CAB.

164. Claude A. Barnett to Charles S. Johnson, 18 March 1947, CAB.

165. Charles S. Johnson to Eric Williams, 24 July 1947; Charles S. Johnson to Fred Wieck, 1 October 1947, CSJ.

166. Fred Wieck to Charles S. Johnson, 9 October 1947, CSJ.

167. Fred Wieck to Charles S. Johnson, 7 November 1947, CSJ.

168. Fred Wieck to Charles S. Johnson, 11 December 1947, CSJ.

169. Charles S. Johnson to Fred Wieck, 18 December 1947, CSJ.

170. Charles S. Johnson to V. Horatio Henry, 26 June 1948, CSJ.

171. As a lasting memorial to the Liberian natives he met and admired, Johnson and his wife named their second son, born in 1931, after an African chief who at one point save his life: Jeh.

PART I
INTRODUCTION

1

Passage to Africa

Tenerife juts suddenly out of a vast plain of ocean like a black con-
vulsion. Once an outpost of civilization, Spanish and isolated, it lives
behind a moving world of ships. By day swarthy south Europeans move
languidly about in a mellow glow of heat fanned from the tropics. Days
fade quickly, and at night the lights, viewed from shipboard, are like glitter-
ing fireflies impaled on a dark mound. It is here that spring suddenly
becomes summer and summer an intensity of humid heat.

Far out over the green surface of quivering water, where the sky touches,
there is a film of fog—all day, without change. The sailors, quiet and intent,
move about eternally scrubbing and painting or, grimy and black, twist at
heavy machinery. Canvas tops are threaded and tied into knots that will
resist a tornado. Now it is an African sea, smooth with little bubbling white
tufts, and the gentle but treacherous blandishment of the sun. Two days
later we are slipping through an oily sea. The tiny waves have ceased to
cavort. Instead, there are only long swells of heaving water, streaks of
turbulence. The color has changed fro green to foggy gray. The sun,
blanketed in its threatening mist, has roobed the waves of their color. The
atmosphere is heavy and depressing. The deck, washed as usual at
daybreak, is not dry at noon. Then, night again in the dreary monotony of
water.

Freetown

The pounding of the engines ceases. Across the way there are lights. It
is curiously quiet without the audible, throbbing heart of the vessel and the
splash of the waves. A Black official appears, clothed in the blue coat and
brass buttons of authority. He moves about the first mate's quarters, studying charts. Another in khaki asks with matter-of-fact crispness for pass-
ports. Here, one ventures, is Britain's new colonial technique. There are no
Whites in evidence except as visitors and passengers. The boat crew is
waiting for something. Then a soft, deep swishing of the water back in the
darkness, and someone remarks, "The Krus are coming."

3

Since Europeans first came down the coast these Krus have been their aids, as vital to transportation as the lighthouse and the surf boats. Even when slaves were being snatched from Africa the Kru boatmen negotiated the last brief but treacherous passage from shore to ship. They are still the eternal liaison with Africa. A huge tugboat with padded prow, its cabin high in the air, crawls through the water with slow dignity. It is piloted by an extravagantly dressed Black native in white, and tows a tandem of flat-top lighters. Standing stiff and erect on the prow of the first of these, like some fantastic masthead, is another Black, a band about his head, loose and flowing smock, wide trousers reaching to the calf of his leg, and a coil of rope on his arm. Behind him is a group, some sitting, some standing, all alert and straining their eyes upward, like one of the mass scenes from the modern theatre. Behind this lighter another and behind that still another, with its crew posturing near the prow, drawn along in slow procession by the tug, dipping and swaying across the waves.

From the ship two sharp beams of light streak down, throwing queer shadows of the moving mass of men against the bottom of the lighter. Across the way other streaks of faint light from the cabins of an anchored ship pattern the water with dancing yellow stripes. The boat crew clambers up the side of the boat, a jolly and noisy lot, and once aboard fall into casual postures, as if merely coming aboard were the object and end of all the excitement.

There is an endless diversity of dress within the limits of a few garments, and in these one sees the first half-absorbed stock in Europe. There is one in blue smock and another in khaki shorts and a felt hat, another with kerchief bound turban fashion under his hat. Some are in blue denims, some in linens, undershirts, sun helmets, sleeve holders. They talk in Kru dialect, which seems to have been made for deep voices and leisured conversation. The headboys and foreman rush about with preposterously wide gestures of concern and give their orders to the truly casual laborers in the familiar pidgin English of the coast. It is curious for its unexpected omission of violent invectives: "Come, come with me," one would shout with profane decorum, "Open these hatches!" "No! Go!" A ship without the Kru boys is a ship foundered in sight of land.

The unimaginative English have given, characteristically, blunt substance to colony building, even though at the expense of beauty and comfort as measured either by European or African standards. The imposing cement structure of the Government House with its high arches and ostentatious screening, is the heavy and immovable hand of the Empire itself. The streets are level, with deep gorges on either side to carry off the water. There are stretches of dwellings constructed of heavy metal, rows of "cabin tenements," painted red, with high doors opening up the entire front, veritable boxes, utterly devoid of grace or comfort. They are effective shelter; the materials are durable and transportable, but they fit neither into native lifestyles nor into the needs and moods of the people. The government hospital, the mission, and the cemetery are conclusive enough symbols of the blessings of civilization. Native vendors sit patiently behind their stands exposing cheap trinkets, tobacco, rice, and spices for their shillings—shaded by Sunlight Soap advertisements or cinema signs offering the incongruous art of Constance Talmadge. Native women with rigid spines and grossly animated hips weave in and out, bedecked in excessively brilliant kerchiefs and blouses, the gift of European cotton mills. Westmoreland Street runs with shabby dignity through a row of Kru huts. Syrian merchants sit back in shops with full open fronts, tempting foreign tastes with flaming gewgaws of incredible inutility. In the shadow of the hotel a gangrenous native woman, toothless and brazen, employs flip phrases of solicitation, borrowed whole, it would seem, from the port towns of Europe. On the curb sits a derelict White man, stupid with trade gin, receptive but incompetent.

The descendants of repatriated sons of Africa under the British are referred to as Creoles, and one may find a third generation of literates. As a coaling and military station, Freetown has offered jobs of a sort enough to turn attention away from agriculture. The Black "clarks" come near to representing the intellect and aristocracy of Casely Heygood, who died during the very month of this visit. The most dismal commentary of the future of Africa is the assumption of certain Britishers, from which they appear to take some satisfaction, that these Creoles and occasional natives have in all probability reached the highest point to which the African Black can aspire.

Monrovia

The view of Monrovia from the sea is perhaps its only advantageous aspect. The sun flashes brilliantly against red roofs set in green foliage. The houses, gleaming white and elevated, take on an arched dignity as they spread in hazy outline along the uneven but graceful contour of Cape Mesurado.

Incident

Tuwely Jeh, tall, bronzed, and magnificent, came from a proud family of tribal rulers famed for their unfailing courage and justice and their sustained eras of peaceful security, as well as for their imperial dignity which lent barbaric splendor to the long history of the tribe. Many generations before they had joined the trek westward, which continued until they found themselves triumphantly at the ocean's edge, where they settled. When civilization came to Africa, Jeh's people called themselves the Webbos.

Near the mouth of the Poo River, where Europeans in the early nineteenth century had set up their slave factories, was another tribe of the same Kru family, designated simply and separately as the Poo River people. They could "hear" the Webbo dialect, as they could "hear" the Grebo speech, but they disdained speaking either. When they found themselves in the line of the Webbos' natural outlet from the back country to the sea, they capitalized on this advantage and imposed heavy tolls on the Webboes for the privilege of using it.

In recent years these tribes had learned to settle their differences and keep the peace by arbitration and treaties. One bargain was that the Webbos, in return for palm nuts and oil, *piassava*, and wild rubber, should be permitted to pass unmolested through the Poo River country to Cape Palmas, a seaport and new center of trade. But truces are White men's brittle tools for keeping the peace—not African—and so it happened again and again that Webbo men going alone to market through the Poo River country were attacked and killed. But not only men were attacked; it even happened that two women traveling unprotected were killed. These outrages were nursed as bitter memories, and there was no Webbo youth who did not cherish the hope of some day avenging these deaths and even notching two for one on the handle of his cutlass.

Since the coming of the Black Americans, the Webbos' guns had been taken away, their age-old methods of settling their differences stiffly penalized, and their proud chiefs humbled and confused by strange courts of law. With each insult they had appealed to these new laws and, just as often, got impatient replies about being weaklings and eternal nuisances to civilized government.

A Poo River man one day landed from his canoe on the Webbo side of the river. Strolling casually on the beach, he came upon a dead fish that had been washed ashore. Excited by his find, he yelled across the river to announce it. This was either thoughtlessness or brazen insolence, and the Webbo fisherman who heard him relieved him of his find, arguing reasonably enough that, since they had set the traps and the fish had landed on their side, it rightfully belonged to them. Swiftly the old feud flared anew. The Poo River men, seeing one of their own in trouble, swam the river to his defense. A fierce struggle followed and continued into the night, resulting in the Poo River people recovering the fish but losing one of their men. At daybreak the contest was revived with blows, taunts, and arguments, and the Webbo people were accused of a cowardly murder. From such a base charge Jeh's people recoiled in soberness, suggesting that the man was probably lost and would turn up again eventually. The Poo River people taunted: "You are cowards. When we kill one of your men, at least we have the grace to dump him on your side for ceremonial burial. You should be men enough to *show* our man after you have killed him. We showed you *seven.*" The passions of the Webbo men broke loose with this last insult, and they fell upon the Poo River men and with their bare hands beat two of them to death.

This incident, trivial in itself in the life of the tribe and in the affairs of the smallest of states, developed into national proportions involving the full fabric of the government of Liberia and, because of the frequent inter-relation of world economics and diplomacy, eventually came to engage the ponderous attention of the League of Nations.

This is how it happened: The Liberian Commissioner of the Kru coast, when he learned of the incident, summoned King Jeh and sixty of his subchiefs. He ordered his soldiers to strip them and bind them with ropes. They were then flung across the road and lashed into the proper prelimin-ary respect for his authority.

He called the swollen and bleeding Jeh before him and imposed a per-sonal fine of 100 pounds and, on behalf of the government, he sent out his soldiers to apprehend the murderers. They picked up seven natives at random and brought them in. The commissioner then dismissed the chiefs and closed the incident.

Gaping and incredulous, the seven native youths were turned over to the county superintendent, who was also a recruiter of native labor and who shortly afterward became vice-president of the republic. This gentleman was about to send them the way of all stray natives when it was mentioned that a goodly sum of money had been paid to the commissioner. His brows puckered and the case took on more seriousness. The law had been of-fended, the chiefs had defied its dignity in an intricately pernicious fashion. Jeh was rearrested and impressed with the seriousness of his "rebellion" against the authority. He had to get lawyers immediately.

"But," protested Jeh, "I don't know a lawyer in Cape Palmas." The superintendent magnanimously named three, two of them senators and one the county attorney. He ordered Jeh to go home and bring 100 pounds for these gentlemen. Jeh called together his elders and the sum was finally collected in shilling pieces which his boys had saved from coast labor. He paid this over but was immediately sent back for 300 pounds more. This new sum Jeh borrowed from traders, thereby exhausting all further credit. He was released again. The incident reached the president of the republic, who, in his turn, reopened the case, called Jeh to Monrovia, imposed a new fine of 300 pounds on behalf of the government, and demanded that Jeh produce the murderers on penalty of having his towns destroyed. Jeh was then placed in prison until the new sums could be collected.

Tarplah and Karpeh, the two faithful attendants of the chief, were sent home from Monrovia to collect the 300 pounds. They were met at Cape Palmas by the superintendent who knew that Jeh's money was gone and his credit exhausted because he had been responsible for both. Playing upon the tribe's affection for its chief, he offered to borrow the funds, provided they agreed to turn over to him, without the necessity for chase and capture, 500 boys to be sent away to the Spanish island of Fernando Poo. The messengers demurred, because their men bitterly opposed going to this place from which so few ever returned. Besides, they were not empowered in native law to make agreements for the chief. Finally, the superintendent forced an agreement with the threat of further fines and punishment, and ordered the Spanish ship *Mont Serrat* to call at the Webbos' narrow outlet to the sea. Here the ship rested and awaited the delivery of the men. At midnight they had not arrived, and the beach town saved itself from destruction by marching its entire population aboard to be held hostage until the interior villages yielded enough men. At daybreak the broken subchiefs marched 316 of their young men down to the ship. The superintendent received fifty dollars for each man landed alive at Fernando Poo.

When Jeh returned from Monrovia, he found great consternation and grief in his towns. His women were weeping, his elders in melancholy council, and his strong men had been carried away. "What!" he exclaimed, "they break our country." They told him of the demand for 500 more. "They cannot go. It will destroy our country," he shouted desperately and as it turned out, fatally. The protest so vexed the superintendent that he sent his soldiers into the land of the Webbos to chastise this insolence and capture the men he needed. Under a dashing young captain, the Frontier Forces executed a clever and overwhelming maneuver. Quietly leaving the Cape, they marched peacefully through the Webbo towns from Cape Palmas to Julacan, the extreme border town of the section, and there they rested. When night came, they prepared as if to continue their decorous journey and, on a signal, fell suddenly upon the unguarded village, throwing it into a screaming panic. The younger men, swiftly comprehending the purpose behind this strategy, dashed madly through the lashing whips and swinging rifle butts and concealed themselves deep in the bush. The older men of the town, the traditionally respected elders, were caught, tied, flogged, and finally marched as hostages back toward the Cape.

The Frontier soldiers, who lived chiefly by plunder, being then more than nine years in arrears in pay, helped themselves to the town's cattle, fowl, and rice, while the commander imposed arbitrary fines as his share of the spoils. The raids were repeated in Obankin, Soloken, Jalateh, Kordor,

Webbo Beach, and the men taken back to the Cape, leaving women and children panic-stricken and weeping in their trail. "What be this matter!" the bewildered subchief Martin cried. "Be this more Fernando Poo palaver? The first men gone; 500. Why you not let me know you come for more?"

To impress the old men, the soldiers flogged them and required them to carry the captured goats on the long march until their arms were paralyzed with fatigue. These old men then were held hostage and required to work on the private farms of government officials until the younger men for exportation returned from the bush and surrendered. The ship sailed again with another cargo of "boys" consigned to the Sindicato Agrícola de los Territorios Españoles del Golfo de Guinea.

The "boy" traffic, so old to most Liberians that its stark angles have been blunted through familiarity, came eventually to the notice of the world. Despite a prevailing callousness to native interest in its own right, it became impossible for the nation to escape the blight of so vast and sustained an exploitation of its labor, an exploitation that stripped the country of its manpower while its monetary returns dulled the conscience of the state. The traffic revived the horrors of slavery itself and involved in intricate meshes the economic and colonial policies throughout Africa. That the Republic of Liberia became the focus of protest is a further incident, given the irony that this republic is itself a colony of ex-slaves. But to understand the charges and the presence of slavery, forced labor, and Black imperialism in the Republic of Liberia, it is first necessary to understand Liberia. And this is another long story.

Note

This chapter was omitted from the final draft, M.H. Johnson to Mrs. Allen, May 27, 1944, box 411, folder 12, Charles S. Johnson Special Collection, Fisk University.

2

Exodus

Get thee from out of this land,
And return to the land of thy kindred.

On February 4, 1820, the 2,000-ton frigate *Elizabeth* lay rigid and motionless all day in the icy North River, at the edge of Rector Street in the city of New York. Throughout the night, numb hands, hacking patiently but to no avail, fought the unyielding ice of one of the city's worst storms. Morning came, but the fury of the night had only gripped the ship more securely. No voyage outward from New York had ever been less auspicious in its beginning; none had been more blindly speculative nor more dismal in its first prospect. None had been compounded of stranger motives, for this was a voyage embarked upon by the first Black emigrants to Liberia. They were the Black freedmen, fugitives and manumitted slaves, and political remnants of a new American republic which had been fed and fostered by their tough hands; they were the objects of noble pity by those Fathers who so recently had struck a blow for their own freedom. These emigrants were going somewhere—home. What irony that in their bold launching they could not free themselves from the icy grip of America!

Crowds gathered during the second day to watch the little band of Blacks strain at the ice locks under the futile guidance of three White men, agents of the American Colonization Society and of the United States government. Into the crowd of onlookers strolled Cornelius Vanderbilt the First, rugged, bearded, and young, captain on a steam ferry running between New York and New Brunswick. He knew ships and he knew the New York harbor. He had ferried produce and passengers between New York and Staten Island, and had provisioned the vast fortification projects in the harbor. After watching the men's vain efforts for a while he turned away. As he threaded his way out of the crowd he commented: "They are not doing that right. I could get them out in no time." Someone told the agent who, in desperation, followed him. The captain's knowledge, however, was not without price: For $100 he made a sliding platform of plain boards on which he rested a heavy anchor. This was pushed forward toward the thin ice until it broke through. Eventually a path was cut and the ship was freed. Then silently it turned its prow eastward and headed out to the sea.

There was something bitterly valiant about this sailing. Here was compulsion sustained by blind hope; here was a slave's dull dream of freedom and of an empire about to take substance. Here was reluctant escape and adventure and the beckoning of other men's ideals, a challenge of the ability to rule of Blacks who had never yet been citizens. Here was a leave-taking impelled strangely and sternly by the first mutterings of a new spirit in the New World. Here was the first forewarning breath of a conflict that split a nation.

The year 1820 was weighted with ominous portents. The back of the slave traffic had been broken by an aroused world conscience. In 1806 England had checked its slave traffic to the West Indies and had turned its eyes toward the buried wealth of India and Africa. The passion for freedom which so recently had found fulfillment in the War for Independence tempered the thinking of the hundreds of thousands of slaves in America. This passion for freedom had developed a conscience on the rights of man. Thomas Paine's remark that "from a tiny spark kindled in America a flame has arisen not to be extinguished" came to have profound significance. It would have been a strange flame indeed that did not warm the desires of Blacks, both free and slave, as well as Whites.

The shrill cry of "freedom, equality, and fraternity" had shaken the Bastille only a few years before and had laid the foundation of the French Republic. Of more significance for Black slaves was the organization founded by Brissot, Les Amis des Noirs, which was directing fiery pamphlets at the world in general, and at Santo Domingo, close to America, in particular. At Santo Domingo thousands of Blacks chafed under French colonial masters. The revolutionary idealism of Lafayette, Robespierre, La Rochefoucauld, and the Abbé Gregoire, all members of this society, was the terrifying philosophy of the hour in Europe and in America, and helped apply the torch that inflamed Santo Dominican Blacks to one of the most astounding and bloody slave revolts the world has known. These people of "dull, deformed mentalities," which the consoling theorists of the "peculiar institution" had asserted were as inherently incapable of insurrection as their masters' mules, had rushed down from the hills, and with machetes and muskets massacred 2,000 Whites and destroyed $2 million worth of property within the first two months of their rage. This memory was as fresh in America as an open wound.

The same spirit that had forced the Somerset decision in England and had impelled Parliament to prohibit slave trade in the colonies had shown its catholicity by attacking White slavery in the factories of England and stimulating the passage of the Factory Act and the famous, though drastic, Poor Laws. The "genius of universal improvement" was stirring. Strange as it may sound, prayers were being offered for the success of the Society for Colonizing and Evangelizing the Jews—"the unhappy wanderers and outcasts of Zion through so many ages." During this period the foreign mission societies, now of universally conceded importance, were born and consecrated to Christian enlightenment throughout the "heathen" world.

The "immortal ordinance" prohibiting slavery forever in the Northwest Territory and the exclusion of the word slave from the Constitution indicated a desire in the recently established United States, to recognize the importance of a mental adjustment to the new independent status. The War of 1812 had brought the first real consciousness of nationalism, and just five years later, when New York abolished slavery, the final spiritual division of the Union into pro and antislavery states was foreshadowed.

Commentators of this period have remarked on the irony of the simultaneous appearance of the colonists' Declaration of Independence and the advertisement for a runaway slave in a Boston newspaper. The moral issue of slavery in America was slowly evolving from the pressure of conflicting self-interests. Thomas Jefferson was candid about it: Slavery may be profitable. Yet if it was degrading to the slave, it could also be degrading to the master. "The whole commerce between master and slave," he wrote in his *Notes on Virginia,* "is a perpetual exercise of the most boisterous passions, the most unremitting despotism on the one part, the most degrading submission on the other. I tremble for my country when I think that God is just, and that His justice cannot sleep forever. . . . The blacks may assert their freedom. The Almighty has no attribute which can take sides with us in such a contest."

There was ample justification for such fear and herein lay the root of much of the fervor for the distant colonization of Blacks. Between 1800 and 1830 the importation of slaves had been stopped by law, and smuggling was eventually made an act of piracy. There was actually a surplus of slaves in the population.

It was becoming increasingly expensive to retain large numbers of slaves for the amount of work to be done. Patrick Henry remarked publicly that they were being held more from a sense of habit than for any other reason, and George Washington was advising his friends to get rid of their slaves because they were no longer profitable. Masters were manumitting their slaves as much from economic as from humanitarian motives. The invention of the cotton gin had not yet produced its effect in revolutionizing the South into a new cotton era, although it had made its golden promise. Nor had Virginia yet become the "grand menagerie, where men are reared for the market, like oxen for the shamble."

At the end of the 1820s there were 1,500,000 slaves in a total population of 9,648,191, and nearly a half million free Blacks. These figures were a striking contrast to the 1790 count which had shown 757,178 Blacks, slave and free. The rapid growth of the Black population fostered sincere apprehension on the part of White Americans, who were advised by statisticians that they could anticipate 12,000,000 Blacks by 1880, and ultimately "a nation of slaves larger by 4,000,000 than the whole present white population of the United States." In a stretch of forty years Whites had increased only 8 percent while Blacks had increased 112 percent. There was the danger of plots and insurrections and the possibility that 'the tragedy of Santo Domingo and Haiti might repeat itself. The editor of the *Christian Spectator* wrote:

> For not withstanding all that may be done to keep the slaves in ignorance, they are learning and will continue to learn something of the tenure by which they are held in bondage. They are surrounded by the memorials of freedom. The air in which they breathe is free, and the soil on which they tread, and which they water with their tears is a land of plenty. Slaves are never slow in learning that they are fettered, and that freedom is the birthright of humanity. Our slaves will not always be ignorant—and when that righteous Providence, which never wants instruments to accomplish its designs, whether of mercy or of vengeance, shall raise up a Toussaint, or a Spartacus, or an African Tecumseh, his fellow slaves will flock around his standard, and we shall witness scenes which history describes, but from the thoughts of which the imagination revolts.[1]

Something had to be done; the Black "horror" was indeed impending. It had been foreshadowed in the Negro plot of New York and in the intercepted revolt of Gabriel in Richmond in 1800. Sullen slaves, with the aid of two Frenchmen, had devised a plot involving some 10,000 Blacks; they secretly forged swords, cast bullets, shaped implements into weapons, and emblazoned on their banners a defiant "Death or Liberty." They were foiled in this attempt because one of the slaves, who wished to save the life of his master from the general slaughter, informed. Down in Spotsylvania County, Virginia, a group of slaves had conspired to make insurrection and four of the conspirators were executed. Shortly after this, the governor of Virginia had been excited by an alarm in Smithfield over a plot that planned to draw in Carolina Blacks when the blow was struck. Still later, in Louisa County, another plot was barely suppressed in time. Nat Turner's revolt in Virginia was incipient, although it did not take place until 1831. The very year of "General" Gabriel's plot, an insurrection of slaves occurred in Charleston, South Carolina, an effort which was repeated in Camden, New Jersey, in 1816, and again in Charleston in 1822 when Denmark Vesey barely missed his aim—sudden, wholesale massacre and flight to free Haiti. Just four years later there were insurrectionary movements in Newbern, Tarborough, and in Hillborough, New York; and it was necessary, in the interest of public safety, to surround a swamp where the plotters were hidden and slaughter them all.

Thomas Jefferson, reflecting in the quiet aloofness of Monticello, made another entry in his *Notes on Virginia:*

> What an incomprehensible machine is man, who can endure toil, famine, stripes, imprisonment, and death itself, in vindication of his own liberty; and the next moment be deaf to all those motives whose power supported him through his trials, and inflict on his fellow-man a bondage, one hour of which is fraught with more misery than ages of that which he rose in rebellion to oppose.

He had accepted slavery and held slaves. He had also believed in freedom and liberated many of his own slaves, sending them to the free state of Ohio. He had believed in eventual emancipation and had proposed a scheme to accomplish it gradually. He had also believed in colonization and had solicited foreign suggestions for an asylum for free Blacks. In one breath he had flattered Black intelligence in the person of Benjamin Banneker, the Black astronomer, by sending his *Almanack* to the secretary of the French Academy of Science; in another he had declared, after reading the poems of Phillis Wheatley, that he did not believe a Black capable of uttering a thought beyond plain narration. There is no more brilliant example of the prevailing mood of indecision and doubt.

Slavery contradicted the primary principles of republican government. It was not, however, inconsistent with the primary principles of Greek and Roman democracy. It was in harmony with all the systems of government which, with the exception of Great Britain and Switzerland, prevailed in every province of the Old World, "from the frozen ocean to the Cape of Good Hope, and from the Bay of Biscay to the Pacific." But it stood in direct opposition to all the acknowledged maxims on which American political institutions were based.

There was one thought that spread terror over every aspect in which the subject could be viewed, and for which there was no remedy: The slaves and those who had been slaves were all marked and stigmatized with the brand which nature had stamped on them, their color. In Greece and Rome and in every other country where slaves had existed, "a slave might be made free, and then he was no longer a slave, but he was amalgamated with the rest of the community; and the road of wealth, or honor, or office was open before him and his interests were united with the interests of the republic." Here the thing was impossible and the idea repulsive. A slave could not be really emancipated: "You cannot raise him from the abyss of his degradation. You may call him free, you may enact a statute book of laws to make him free, *but you cannot bleach him into the enjoyment of freedom.*" Total or immediate emancipation was unthinkable. The numbers were increasing. The growing cupidity of the institution under the rich prospect of cotton drowned all the softer sentiments of abolition, of the abstract rights of man. Slaves were being smuggled into the country.

Metaphysicians might quibble about the subtle issues of abstract ethics, but there was no escaping immediate issues. Something must be done with these Blacks. There were too many. They were no longer profitable in Virginia, yet they prevented the rise of a hardy White yeomanry. It was as well put as possible in the despairing remark of one Virginian who wrote: "While he remains here, no white laborer will seek employment near him. Hence it is that in some of the richest counties east of the Blue Ridge the white population is stationary, and in many others it is retrograding. Virginia, once the first state in numbers, as she is still in territory, has become the third and will soon have to descend to the fourth rank." The waning importance of Virginia, the sparse population of White settlers, the deserted houses, and the fields without cultivation were attributed to the numerous slaves. "Even the wolf, after the lapse of a hundred years, returns to howl over the desolations of slavery," cried Custis of Virginia in the legislature.

The South was agricultural and comprised one-half of the nation's agriculture. The New England and middle states had two-thirds of the commerce and New England almost one-fourth of all the manufacturing. Whatever the moral issue, the lower South could be exploited only by slave labor. Thus the contest of the century began.

It would be futile to try to chart the temper of the period which drove the Fathers to desperation without giving due stress to their chief irritation, the free Blacks. They were a nuisance and all too sharp a challenge to the embryonic principles of liberty, equality, and fraternity. Thinking on the subject could be summed up in almost any comment picked from the literature of the time: "Causes beyond the control of the human will must prevent their ever rising to equality with the whites." Master and slave in ancient Greece and Rome were of the same color, and amalgamation was possible in a generation or two. In America there was "an insuperable barrier" against such a result. There had to be a solution and it was a compromise. The compromise was colonization, which was finally and triumphantly heralded as "the grand conservative principle of the American Union."

Colonization in Africa, the *natale solum,* was an evolution both of national expediency and a sudden overpowering solicitude for the souls of the "heathen." At an earlier period vacant territory in the United States had been considered—Texas, Louisiana, Mexico, but were altogether too close at hand; collusion with the Indians and boundary and international disputes were evils too imminent. The year after the Declaration of Independence, Jefferson's proposal to utilize vacant western lands had received but scant attention. The colonists were too exhausted after their late rebellion to undertake the costs involved. Twice in secret sessions of the House of Delegates of Virginia, following the insurrections, the subject had been discussed. When James Monroe was governor of the state, he had been instructed by resolution to institute negotiations with some of the European powers having colonies on the coast of Africa, with a view to locating an asylum to which emancipated Blacks might be sent. Jefferson, still later, applied without success to Portugal for a colony in their Brazilian possessions. The search for asylum, by private citizens and statesmen, included Madagascar, Sandwich Island, St. Helena, and Columbia. Finally, the Virginia Legislature in 1816 sent a resolution to the president of the United States insisting that an asylum be found. After all, there was excellent precedent in the British experiment of Sierra Leone on the coast of Africa.

A word is necessary about the Sierra Leone experiment. The revolt against slavery, in which England led the way, had begun in the seventeenth century, largely by the Quakers through the indomitable George Fox: "They lighted a candle which, though it flickered uncertainly for a hundred years, could not be put out." It spread to the Lutherans of Germany, Denmark, and Sweden. It flared as a movement in England in 1772 when James Somerset, the slave who accompanied his Virginia Master to England, declared himself free. Though most of the judges opposed, the lord chief justice, Mansfield, delivered the famous declaration which really fixed the law that once a slave touched British soil he was free.[2]

In the rebellion of the American colonies a number of Blacks had sided with their Loyalist masters. When Cornwallis surrendered, daring loyalty was rewarded with freedom and transportation to Canada and Nova Scotia. Slaves from the West Indies were likewise free men in England, after Lord Mansfield had spoken. The incongruity of Black and White free colonists and citizens in this new estate, and the sight of these impecunious Blacks living on the exhausted gratitude and sympathy of the nation, gave birth to the idea of colonization. Dr. Henry Smoathman, an English surgeon, had spent four years on the West African coast, and almost simultaneously the Swedish naturalist, Carl Berns Wadstrom, developed certain wild ideas about colonizing in the tropics. Jointly, they suggested the West Coast. The manner in which they settled upon Sierra Leone is of still further interest.

During the middle of the eighteenth century the vast slave trade between West Africa and the West Indies had developed a depot of European and mulatto slave traders and raiders at Sierra Leone, of which few speak without contempt. This strange, outlandish group had intermarried, founded considerable fortunes, and incidentally laid the foundation of a mulatto class of traders of remarkable cunning and brutality. Chief among these was a mulatto trader, Cincinnati. Starting as a cabin boy on a slaver, he was soon an assistant at a slave factory on the Sierra Leone River, and later became an expert slave trader. Combining his knowledge of native life with the civilized shrewdness of his White father, he soon amassed a sizable fortune.

If there were mulattoes in Sierra Leone—why not send the English-speaking Black colonists to them? And so a Sierra Leone Company was formed with the help of an almost hysterical philanthropy. The Blacks from America, the West Indies, Nova Scotia, and Canada were herded together for repatriation. With grim humorlessness, they added to the company sixty unreclaimable White prostitutes, fully confident that the new life and surroundings would change them into faithful and fertile spouses of the returned sons of Africa.

What was good for British Blacks was none too good for American ones. Besides, it would involve less exploration and inquiry, a consideration of some weight in the almost total absence of any benevolent knowledge of Africa in America. Thomas Jefferson in 1811 made advances, but suspecting political trickery, the Sierra Leonians declined his proposals.

One must go another step back for the seed in American conscience on slavery which found maturity in colonization. It probably started with Anthony Benezet and John Woolman, two stubbornly righteous Quakers with an interesting history of personal philanthropy and sacrifice in the service of abused human individuals, whether Indians, suffering soldiers of the American Revolution, or Black slaves. Benezet, a Huguenot, was erudite, indefatigable, and inspired. It was his *History of Guinea* that first inspired Clarkson of England to become one of slavery's most terrible antagonists. The polished, scholarly shafts of Benezet stung, with their unanswerable rebuke to public and official indifference to human suffering. So complete was his devotion that he went to his grave feeling ashamed to meet his Maker, having "done so little in His cause." He did not know that he had initiated a cause as potent as the religion he professed.

Dr. William Thornton of Washington caught the spirit which Benezet, Woolman, Lundy, and Lay had preached with such fervent conviction, and in 1787 proposed to conduct personally a company of free Black emigrants to Africa. But lack of money stood in the way. Eccentric old Captain Izard Bacon of Virginia took his fifty-two freedmen to Pennsylvania, hoping to find a means of transporting them somewhere overseas, and before the turn of the century a contrite Methodist minister, James Smith, set a further example by trudging from Virginia to Ohio with his slaves, trying vainly to colonize them. The stage was set for the young missionary Samuel Mills, who, save for his Liberian exploits, would have been forever obscure. He organized at Williams College in 1808 a society for missionary work which was transferred to Andover and later bloomed as the American Bible Society and Board of Foreign Missions. Frail, devout, and imaginative, he was interested in spreading the light of the gospel everywhere. It was a sort of birthmark with him. Even before he had been weaned, his pious mother announced: "I have consecrated this child to the service of God as a missionary." Blacks were a very special concern to him, and at one time he had dreamed of bettering their condition by founding a colony for them somewhere in America between Ohio and the Great Lakes. He went to Princeton to complete his theological studies and there continued to talk about his plan until he had irritated the Presbyterian clergy of the state to action. Dr. Robert Finley was one of those aroused, and it was he who called the first meeting on African colonization at Princeton. At this first meeting there were printed memorials to the Legislature urging the adoption of some deportation scheme. On the back of these he addressed a note to Paul Cuffee, a New England free Black who in 1815 had equipped a ship with his own funds and carried thirty-eight disgusted American Blacks to Sierra Leone. Awakened, and bent upon promoting the idea on a properly large scale, Finley went to Washington in 1816 with plans to found a Colonization Society.

Christian benevolence gave birth to the Society, but it was not long before it had become hopelessly entangled in politics. Slaveholders had presented objections to too much idealism on this matter of freedom. It was an attack upon property! And so began the rationalizations. On the fledgling ideals of the Society the powerful statesmen placed a neat and perfectly fitting gag. It was virtually pledged not to oppose the system of slavery; it aimed at the free Black population in America. Twelve of the seventeen vice-presidents were from slave states and all eighteen of the managers were slaveholders. General Harper, who gave the name "Liberia" to this far away asylum and called its capital Monrovia in honor of President James Monroe, and for whom the capital of Maryland in Liberia is named, let it be known what he thought of the free Blacks: "They are a greater nuisance than even slaves themselves." Vice-President Mercer of the Society characterized them as "a horde of miserable people, the objects of universal suspicion, subsisting by plunder." Henry Clay, one of the original members of the Society and a president, measured the distance between these strangely consorting aims when in one breath he declared: "Of all classes of our population the most vicious is that of the free colored;" and in another breath: "Every emigrant to Africa is a missionary carrying with him credentials in the holy cause of civilization, religion, and free institutions." Where was logic, where consistency, where sincerity? John

Randolph of Virginia, in the first meeting of the Society, asserted that it "must tend essentially to make slave property safe." The first president of the Society, Justice Bushrod Washington, defended himself against criticism for selling some of his personal slaves into Louisiana by asserting the right of every slaveholder to sell his property, and in this point of view he was comfortably sustained by Henry Clay, who very particularly pointed out that "from its origin and throughout the whole period of its existence the Society had consistently disclaimed all intention whatever of interfering in the smallest degree with the rights of property, or the object of emancipation, gradual or immediate."

The misalliance of aims prompted Von Holst, in his *Constitutional History of the United States*, to accuse the whole scheme of hypocrisy, falsehood, and swindle.

> The slave states knew exactly what they wished and laughed in their sleeve at seeing the philanthropists of the North fall so readily in the trap. A bait thrown out by the founders of the Society was the gaining of Africa to the Christian religion and Western civilization by means of the settlement of the Negroes there. But they seized every occasion to brand free colored persons as the refuse of the population, whose departure could not be too dearly bought at any price. . . . With every year not only did this show itself more plainly, but it was also roundly stated that the Society's aim was, in fact, the purification of the land from the rest of the free colored population in order to give security to slavery. . . . Such a piece of Don Quixoterie has never been indulged in more bitter earnest, and especially by such men. It would not have been possible if political thought had not already been perverted by the baleful influence of slavery.

The spirit of philanthropy in the South added to the problem of free Blacks through the process of individual manumissions. How else could the number of free Blacks have reached such a startling total of a half million, actually more than the number of slaveholders? The tragic concourse of conflicting principles again appeared in the misery to which these free Blacks were subjected. Nine-tenths of the free Blacks were consigned to the most menial of jobs; their associations were chiefly with slaves. "No merit, no service, no talents," it was admitted, could ever "elevate this great mass to a level with the White." They were hounded out of the Southern states and mobbed in the North. Louisiana's new ordinance fixed banishment for them sixty days after manumission. South Carolina forced them to put up bond of $500 or be resold into slavery. Mobs in Cincinnati outraged them, burned their homes, and forced hundreds out of the state to Canada. The fugitive slave laws permitted the capture of many of the free population to be resold into slavery. After the Missouri Compromise, the welcome to fugitives as well as to free Blacks chilled into intolerance.

They were unwanted in the trades, at the polls, in the schools. Mercer of Virginia, in a sort of delirium of reflection, saw them emerging furtively from their retreats beneath the obscurity of night, plundering the rich proprietors of the valleys, infesting the suburbs, towns, and cities, hiding stolen goods, and, schooled by necessity, cunningly eluding the vigilance of their defective police. The classic picture is Joel Chandler Harris' Free Joe, an exile to his own people and without status with the Whites, secretly envied and openly despised by the slaves, eternally suspected and hounded by his quondam masters. Abdy observed the more sophisticated ones boring pernicious holes in the Fugitive Slave Act by conspiring with dissolute White men in a traffic of forged manumission papers. The devout Mills, alarmed, exclaimed: "We must save the Negroes or they will ruin us."

The zealous missionaries had played the statesmen for their power; the statesmen in turn played the missionaries for their ideals. It was a bargain that squeezed the soul out of their first principles and could offer so sterile and tepid a compromise as this: "The difference in regard to slavery and the Negro population, between New England and Georgia, we owe not to ourselves or to our fathers but to the God who has placed our habitation where the climate forbade the introduction of Africans and where the hard soil could be cultivated only by the hands of freemen." The Blacks, now fully aware of their status, or lack of it, the responsibility for which had been palmed off on God, made objection. Three years before the *Elizabeth* sailed, 3,000 Blacks had assembled in Philadelphia to express their opinion as to whether they were willing to accept the views of the Society. They found themselves unanimously opposed, as they had known they would be. Fisher, of the House of Delegates of Virginia, exclaimed: "If we wait until the free Blacks give their consent, we shall wait until time is no more. They will never give their consent." Twelve years after the sailing of the first ship, these objections were more specifically phrased in the resolutions of a New Bedford meeting: "The Society, to effect its purpose, the removal of the free people of color (not slaves) through its agents, teaches the public to believe that it is patriotic and benevolent to withhold from us knowledge and the means of acquiring subsistence, and to look upon us as unnatural and illegal residents of this country; and thus, by force of prejudice, if not by law, endeavor to compel us to embark for Africa, and that too, apparently, by our own free will and consent." These objections and protests were often empty rhetoric, based on scarcely more than incensed feeling and flickering hope. These men had as yet little reason to feel in any way secure in this country, and had even less reason to cherish any hope. Ahead of them was the gloomy doom now sanctified in the chartered purposes of the society: "A dreadful collision at a future day of these two castes, which must inevitably be objects of mutual jealousy to each other."

True enough, there were the mulattoes, some with eminent White citizen fathers; they were within a bare shade or two of comfortable citizenship. This was just enough to stir the springs of bitterness. The Blacks had only their faith, but this sufficed to resist the dark speculation of Africa. The kindly and well meaning Augustus Washington of Hartford had sensed this when he declared: "I maintain that, clinging to long cherished prejudices and fostering hopes that can never be realized, the leaders of the colored people in this country have failed to discharge a great and important duty to their race. . . . Seeing this, I came forward alone, joining with friend and foe in moving the wheel of a great enterprise which, though unpopular with those it designs to benefit, must result eventually in the redemption and enfranchisement of the African race." The bolder Blacks could, in 1818, still speak defiantly about high principles, liberty or death, or eventual emancipation, and refuse to be interested in colonization, although the cords were tightening from that very date. The nation was moving on to a test of these very principles, even though Lincoln himself, who emerged a brilliant spirit from this tragic era and saw the Black as the "bone of contention," committed himself to a dark and dismal doubt: "If he is to be made free," he said, "God only knows what is to be the future of this race."

The free Blacks could shout until they grew purple with exhaustion that, if they were given the education White men received, they would be unfit for the debased position which they must here occupy and would gladly depart; that the country being denied them was at the very moment being opened up as a haven for the scum of Europe; that slaves and illiterate free men could not be expected to impart civilization and the arts and sciences to the heathen inhabitants of Africa; that the very cause which made colonization popular made it repulsive to self-respecting free Blacks; that the society had erected a platform so broad that the worst enemies of the race could stand upon it with the same grace and not be distinguished from the honest and true philanthropist. But shouting, reason, argument, were of little avail; stronger forces were now in motion.

In 1818 the Colonization Society sent Samuel J. Mills, the zealous young man of missionary spirit, and his companion, Ebenezer Burgess, to seek a location for the settlement. These gentlemen sought advice about Africa in England and decided upon Sherbro, just 100 miles from the British colony of Sierra Leone. Here they stumbled upon a most curious incident. They found a colony headed by a Black, John Kizell, of African parentage who had been born in the interior country of Sherbro. Kizell's brief personal history throws a ghastly illumination over the whole West Coast business. His father and his uncle were both chiefs, residing in different towns in Sherbro country. A favorite of both as a boy, Kizell was sent by his father to another village to visit his uncle. The night of his arrival a tribal war flared, the house was attacked, and his uncle and most of his people were slaugh-tered. A few escaped and some were taken prisoners; the boy was among the latter. Land and slaves were offered by his father to recover him, but his enemies refused. They carried the boy to an English slave ship lying off the Gallinhas, bound for Charleston, South Carolina. At the height of the revolution in America, he arrived at the port of Charleston, just a few days before Sir Henry Clinton captured the city. A proclamation to the slaves offered them the opportunity of joining the royal standard, and Kizell, finding one direction as easy as another, joined. At the close of the war he was sent with other slave loyalists to Nova Scotia, and in 1792 to Africa and home, as a colonist.

Kizell, now a trader and preacher and wise in the ways of both worlds, led the missionaries to Yonie, the royal residence of King Sherbro, who sat in state under a cola tree attended by Couber, his speaker, and the elders. Gifts were dangled and bids made for lands for the noble experiment of repatriating the lost descendants of Africans. They wished to return from a far and unfriendly country and settle peacefully in the dominions of King Sherbro. The crafty monarch turned to his minister, who hinted politely at difficulties preventing a prompt conclusion of matters. After a leisurely consideration extending over a week, the monarch made vague indications of agreement in a grand palaver, after which the gentlemen departed. Mills, with all his fine fervor, was already advanced with tuberculosis and died before he could return home. Buried at sea, Mills took with him more of the nobility of the project than we care to admit.

The drama of the Moors in Spain began an earnest reenactment in America. While Mills and Burgess were exploring the African coast, the Georgia legislature passed an act, under the license of Congress, directing that all Blacks brought into the state should be claimed by an agent desig-nated by the governor, taken to Milledgeville, its capital, and after sixty days notice in a public gazette, sold for the state. Slave running continued apace and finally a slaver with some thirty-eight Blacks was captured by a government chaser and brought into Georgia. With the events rushing to such a climax, the government had to act. On March 3, 1819, under the favorable auspices of Monroe, Congress authorized the president "to make such regulations and arrangements as he might deem expedient of the safe keeping, support and removal beyond the limits of the United States of all such Negroes, mulattoes, or persons of color, as might in this manner be brought within their jurisdiction; and to appoint a proper person or per-sons, residing upon the Coast of Africa, as agent or agents, for receiving the Negroes, mulattoes, or persons of color delivered from on board vessels seized in the prosecution of the slave trade, by commanders of the United States armed vessels." On May 3, 1819, the thirty-eight slaves brought into

Georgia were offered for sale at Milledgeville. Here was the chance for the Society; it availed itself of a clause in the act permitting it to purchase the victims and to assume all expenses incurred by the state.

The recaptured Africans thus provided the official sanction of colonization. Government, philanthropy, politics, and questionable economics joined hands in hastening the consummation of this mandate of eternal excommunication. The legislature of Tennessee, in 1818, and of Maryland in 1819, instructed their senators in Congress and their own representatives to give all aid to the government in colonizing the free people of color "in some distant country," and these were soon followed by Connecticut, New Jersey, Delaware, Kentucky, Pennsylvania, Indiana, Ohio, Louisiana, Massachusetts, New York, and a formidable list of ecclesiastical bodies. The exhilaration of a solution fostered numerous manumissions conditioned upon emigration to Liberia. The die was cast. The returned Burgess, picturing a refuge for these oppressed sons of Africa, in a land "whose hills and plains are covered with a verdure that never fades," began recruiting. He enlisted Elijah Johnson, an impetuous mulatto and son of a former Maryland slave, who had moved to New Jersey. The young Elijah moved later to New York, where he was trying to preach. Against the advice of his friends he subscribed himself, his wife, and three sons for passage on the *Elizabeth*. He was one of the brilliant survivors of this Mayflower party who helped shape such history as the republic has made. There was another, Mrs. Mathilda Newport, who succeeded before she died in inspiring a movement and a national holiday in her memory.

What a day in New York when these eighty-eight first sad pioneers assembled! A farewell party had been planned for the group that took passage on the *Elizabeth*. It was to have been a quiet gathering of friends to offer encouragement and "bon voyage" and perhaps a few useful tokens. In this expectation they went to the little Black church which had been engaged for the occasion. What was their surprise when they met there a mob of some 3,000 Blacks, for the most part indignant and protesting. Such foolhardy flight, they asserted, was nothing short of cowardly capitulation for such as professed to know what they were doing. The excited agents removed the emigrants as quickly as possible to the boat and the farewell ceremonies were never held. Before they could put off, the waters congealed into an ice block which held them cold and fast.

Edward Blyden, one of the few scholars of whom Liberia can justly boast, on looking backward at this first sailing, saw it in its own tragic light. These emigrants were leaving under circumstances peculiar in the history of the world. They were not a restless people who, finding wealth and honor too slow for ambitious and enterprising minds, resolved to accelerate the tempo of fortune under foreign skies. They were not fallen children of opulence and splendor, seeking new scenes to repair shattered fortunes. They were not balked political theorists, nor victims of religious persecution "fleeing the horrors of enthralled conscience." If they had been in any of these categories, they could have remained at home, content to reap small gains, rather than accept the eager gift of a remote home and, defenseless, face the dangers and privations of a land notorious for its unhealthy and dangerous climate. They were a peculiar people.

> They were those who themselves or whose ancestors had been, in the providence of God, suffered to be carried away from heathenism into slavery among a civilized and Christian people; and who, from the degradation necessarily attached in all countries to those in any way related to slaves, could not rise. The forces of circumstance over which they had no control kept them down, hopelessly down. They felt the depression; they saw its causes upon their minds and the minds of their children. And they found that it was useless to contend against these unfavorable influences. They saw clearly that to remain in that land and contend against what they could have no reasonable hope of overcoming would be no more than "beating the air."

Here was a mere handful of Black emigrants, whose deep, impenetrable past was before them, in whose minds there stirred no light of history or precedent to inspire them, whose only philosophy had been distilled from an unending chain of conflict with physical and moral adversity, whose prospects were as "dark and appalling as the memory of the past." Persuaded by the resolute will of the Fathers to be forever rid of them, they were going home! It was this feeble, flickering light that these Fathers had gravely commanded to blaze a way for the coming of Christ; to carry the love of art and literature, and a noble spirit of liberty to Africa. It was on such a foundation as this that men in America seriously professed to expect the rearing of a republic.

Notes

1. See Review of Reports of the American Colonization Society, reprint of article from the *Christian Spectator*, 1823.
2. The case was three times argued and the decision three times postponed. The chief justice was torn with doubts. Finally, on June 22, 1772, he delivered himself of the famed judgment which became the law of England: "There is no necessity to refer the question to the judges. Immemorial usage preserves positive law, after the occasion or accident which gave rise to it has been forgotten, and, tracing the subject to natural principles, the claim of slavery can never be supported. The power claimed never was in use here or acknowledged by the law. Upon the whole, we cannot say the cause returned is supported by the law: and therefore the man must be discharged." It set the point for a significant turning in civilized opinion on slavery.

3

The Land of Gold

Reckless Norman adventurers in the fourteenth century knew Cape Monte and Grand Bassa, the Petit Dieppe on the coast of Liberia; and Hanno the Carthaginian had sighted these shores with his Phoenicians five hundred years before Christ was born. The significant story of Liberia, however, begins with the Portuguese whose place names still linger like ghosts of dead masters to mark the conspicuous points of this little country. Prince Henry of Portugal, grandson of John of Gault of England, filled with missionary zeal, had entered Africa in the early fifteenth century. By 1441, a material incentive was added by the fabulous tales of spices and gold in Guinea. By 1448, the Portuguese had reached Senegal. Between 1448 and 1480 they had entered Bulombel, whose mountainous promontory jutted sharply upward like the walled end of the earth, and named it Serra Leoa, the lion-like mountain range where echoes roared. In 1461, just one year after the death of the zealous Henry, Piedro de Centra was sent out by King Alphonso to survey the coast of Guinea, the land of gold. He was the first of that memorable caravan of explorers to reach the coast of Liberia. By a great green forest that swept down to the sea, he dropped anchor. It was the present site of the sensitive and self-conscious municipality of Junk, whose name in English is an unfortunate corruption of the Portuguese word *junco*, reed. De Centra on this voyage named Cape St. Anne, the western promontory of Sherbro; Cabo de Monte, the high and pleasing Cape Mount of northern Liberia; Cape Mesurado, the present site of Monrovia; and all of Liberia's principal rivers. After conversations with the natives, he "detained a specimen" by order of his king who, with proper caution, had demanded that they "bring a man of the last country visited, by force or by love." This specimen, with his sleek black body and flashing teeth, his pierced ears and septum, was a rare spectacle in Portugal. He was loaded with presents and returned to what is now Liberia in 1462.

The voyage of de Centra continued southward past the Grain, Ivory, and Gold coasts as far as what is now Elmina. By 1471 he had passed the mouth of the Niger and the islands of St. Thomas and Fernando Poo, so tragically linked lately with Liberian history, and by 1481, following the Congo coast, he had crossed the Equator. Thus, from the Senegal River on the north to the southern limits of Angola, a coast line of 4,000 miles was laid open to slave commerce, and the Portuguese set out in dead earnest to monopolize it all. This monopoly lasted over one hundred years before it was broken, when these masters were beaten off by stronger and greedier ones. Albeit small atonement, the Portuguese left in Liberia the orange tree, the lime, the coconut palm, the pineapple, chili pepper, the tobacco plant, the hog, and the muscovy duck.

Piedro de Centra regarded himself as the first White man to visit Liberia, and indeed he may have been. However, one expectation of the Portuguese geographers at home in the detention of a "specimen" was that on arrival in Portugal he might meet some other person of his race who had learned Portuguese and, through him, give an account of his country. De Centra's Black actually met a Black woman slave in Lisbon who seemed to understand him. All that the learned geographers could extract from him, however, was that there were unicorns in Liberia.

From native folklore may be learned the story of the coming of the first White man. That vibrantly hardy tangent of the great Bantu race, the Krus, had, after unwritten centuries of migration, found themselves within marching distance of the sea and salt. Their towns were in the interior, but fighting villages were stationed on the coast and a comfortable balance of life had been struck by exchanging produce. The seaboard dwellers were fishermen and masters of their canoes, gracefully and symmetrically carved out of logs; often they ventured far and recklessly into the green endless waters.

Then came the Quees, or White men, and this is how it happened: A mammoth seagull, solitary and apparently motionless, appeared on the breast of the ocean. It grew larger, and the sun flashed against its white wings. Now it was no longer a seagull, but a vast egg, and as it neared the shore, it could be seen that there was motion and the forms of men within it. The startled Kru men rushed ashore and retreated with their families. Men from the strange ship came ashore with presents of bright beads, baskets, bracelets, tin pots, bells, coral ornaments, and boxes from which came curious sounds. These visitors stood on the shore making cordial gestures of friendship. Finding that these had no effect, they deposited their gifts temptingly on the sands and retired to the ship. The natives cautiously returned to inspect the presents and, intrigued by their flashy janglings, fell upon them eagerly.

The Quees came again and were ingratiating; they made music, brought more presents. They asked for a child, promising to carry him home as a precious guest and later to return him. With children plentiful, and boys particularly being of no pressing value, the visitors were easily accommodated. They carried a child away, taught him to speak Portuguese, tirelessly amused him, fancily bedecked him, and returned him eventually to incredulous parents. Other children were offered and accepted. The visitors kept some at home as curiosities and returned others, leaving gifts as tokens for those who failed to return. The introduction of the new articles created new desires; as a result, more children and a few older relatives were exchanged. The transition was easy. Before long, native kidnappers, now full of greed, waylaid the footpaths through the forest and made it unsafe for anyone to travel alone or from the interior to the coast with produce. And thus there developed both the provocation for and profit of more tribal wars. "Black ivory" acquired a value that made both White and Black men forget.

"No single, separate African race or tribe," says Sir Harry Johnston, "has felt anything like solidarity with the Black race in general; otherwise Europe and Asia would not continue to dominate Africa." Once the Portuguese and the Spanish slave traders had fired the desires of the natives along this coast with their gaudy trinkets, they became avaricious, plundering and pillaging their neighbors, kidnapping, pandering, and creating occasion for war. Perhaps this development was aided by that distinctively African type of village government and association, with its sharply discreet sociality reinforced through the centuries. It gave birth to that dismal, disintegrating psychology by which they gave both abatement and spoils to the traffic in their neighbors and in turn themselves, "which cost Africa in the dead and stolen nearly one hundred million souls."

The Dutch followed the Portuguese into the Grain Coast, coming just ahead of the English and the piratical John Hawkins' famed slaver, the good ship *Jesus*. At the beginning of the eighteenth century, John Snoek visited Liberia in the yacht *Johana Jaba*. He observed the Mandingoes, whose tall, erect carriage and sharp features suggested mixture with North African races. This tribe, through hundreds of years, had wound its way across the Sahara and trailed down from the Mandingo plateau into northern Liberia around Cape Mount. Snoek found the men wearing the large flowing blue gowns, a distinct touch of Islam, which they still use. The women were often naked on the present site of Monrovia, the natives (probably the basic and indigenous Kru and Kpessi stock) lived in large thatch huts of two and three apartments. These natives, longer used to the Europeans, were sophisticated, spoke a mixed jargon of Portuguese and English, had adopted European names, and indulged in a lively slave trade with the coast as a consequence of incessant intertribal wars.

The river Cestos, farther to the south, was the port of an agreeable and friendly country, and the principal village contained about sixty houses very neatly built, and so high that "some of them appear three miles out at sea." Cape Mesurado, the site of Monrovia, had become a strategic point in the long coast trade. It was necessary for ships to call at this port for wood and water, and there could always be found an abundance of rice, Indian corn, fowls, sheep, goats, and oxen.

When France entered again the slave trade, the Chevalier de Marchais was sent to visit the West Coast in 1725 and, because of the friendly intercourse between himself and the natives, the old king, Captain Peter, actually gave him the island and urged him to settle on it. De Marchais had plans for the establishment of a French colony on the very site of Monrovia. His memoirs, first published in 1744 and translated by Wadstrom in 1792, describe the natives as being of large size, strong, and well proportioned. "Their mien," he said, "bold and martial, and their neighbors have often experienced their intrepedity, as well as those Europeans who tried to injure them. They possess genius, think justly, speak correctly, perfectly know their own intents, and, like their ancient friends, the Normans, recommend themselves with address and even politeness. Their lands are carefully cultivated, they do everything with order and regularity, and they labor vigorously when they choose, which, unfortunately, is not so often as could be wished."

Although de Marchais' favorable account reflects the comfortable relationship with King Captain Peter, it is evident that the coastal natives between Cape Mount and the Cavalla River were by no means savage. As much cannot be said of the more interior tribes, or of certain branches of the Kru stock itself. Tradition, as handed down by the old men of the tribe, provides a clue to the selection and consequent division in the Kru stock along the Liberian coastline, so that it happens that, linguistically, a Kru man can "hear" a Grebo or a Bassa man without being able to speak his dialect. They live, essentially, as different races, and the intertribal warfare is an interminable reciprocity of bloody attacks over trivial insults.

In the days of the rampant slave trade, a great king of the Druin tribe, Kubahkaka, came to eminence and power through an unbroken record of ruthless victories. His truculent nature and savage raids spread terror throughout the country. Wherever he marched his forces, they conquered and destroyed everything. Whole districts were depopulated and laid waste for the sake of plunder and the "black ivory" which the Portuguese prized so highly and paid for so well. Kubahkaka had several large canoes, made at Druin, in which he traveled in great pomp and splendor. Smaller tribes near the coast, trembling at his rapidly increasing power and ruthlessness, sought plans to escape his attack as he neared the sea. They agreed among themselves to meet upon the large rock, Hedohpoleorh, on the coast of Berriby, near Tahon, "the rock of council," to discuss plans for safety. They arranged to assemble secretly one night, "hung head"—that is, deliberated—and went home. Their plans, as well as the objectives of the meeting, were to be withheld from the women and children, since it was barely possible that one of them might be related through marriage to Kubahkaka, who would eventually hear their plans and blast them.

It was useless to consider opposing him. Their major goal was to prepare, without directing suspicion upon themselves; to rise up quietly and suddenly on a dark night, take to their canoes, and desert the country forever. They could find a home elsewhere on the coast at a safe distance from the tyrant. The movements of the men excited the curiosity of the women, as their visits to the rock became more frequent. Although they explained that they were fishing, a reasonable enough occupation, nothing was ever produced for a meal. Late one afternoon, as the women were getting water, one of them, more crafty than the rest, saw her lover coming toward her and swore to probe the secret of the men, if it were anything short of the devil bush. She said to her friends: "The fish are as plentiful here as elsewhere in this season, and one need only strike his canoe against them to the windward of the school and get more than are required. How is it that the men never bring any home?" When her lover came nearer and addressed her with his usual familiarity, she affected an air of great injury and spoke coldly, passing on. The young man asked for explanations, and she replied ambiguously, "I am only waiting and watching the outcome of events." Puzzled, he pressed her for an explanation, and she answered with like vagueness: "Whatever one undertakes to do, he should always consider the end. Why should you see another's secret when you have taught yourself to conceal your own so well? Why should you conceal from me the dark treacheries of the men with whom you are conspiring against the women?" He swore that the accusation was false and promised to tell her alone the secret if she would swear to share it with no other woman. And he told her. Thereafter, the secret was too hot for her to hold and under similar pledges she committed it to a few of her friends who had heard her boast; soon it was common property. Alarmed, the old chieftains, who were but partially prepared for the migration, were compelled to embark at once and without regard for the condition of the sea. With their frightened families they plunged into the waters which were rolling threateningly. The most agile of them who were able to keep their canoes upright in the turbulent waters and reach a safe position far down the coast, were called Ggebos or Gdebos, meaning, so tradition says, the agility of monkeys. Those, however, whose deficient skill allowed their canoes to upset and who scrambled ashore close to the starting point, were called Wreboes. These Wrebos were left behind to feel the hard hand of Kubahkaka while the Gdebos, at a great distance, were able to encamp themselves upon high ground and build a strong stockade. This high ground, so tradition tells, was the point named

Cape de Palmo by the Portuguese. This is the story as the old men like to tell it, and the Gdebos to this day have a proverb linked with the tale: "Never tell a secret to a woman."

Kubahkaka's men, rushing headlong in search of plunder, making conquest, and taking slaves from the weaker tribes, eventually reached the Bassa Coast. Weakened in their march, they decided to "sit down" for a spell during the rains and fish. A storm of great violence and duration visited the sea and so cut them off from food that a great hunger seized the town. An old woman of the community was known to have a dog, lean, craven, and dirty, but emergency meat. One dark night this animal disappeared and the old woman, annoyingly suspicious, began prying about, casting hints. She demanded that a palaver be held. The medicine man was called but would give no verdict, saying that he had not had time to investigate the matter thoroughly. But suspicion attached itself to Kubahkaka's marauders and diligent search was made in the dump heaps for the carcass of the animal. This proving futile, it was reluctantly concluded that a leopard had carried the dog off. As the season for cassava planting approached, the women went to the manure heaps for fertilizer and to the amazement of all unearthed the lost animal's bones. Thus the accusation was confirmed, and Kubahkaka's men were given the name of Bittahs, meaning dog eaters, a name which still clings to them as a term of reproach.

Years later there arose another tribe which swept down to the coast pillaging as it went, and introducing a few new customs. For example, they built their houses of bamboo and thatched roofs in conical shape, curing these by smoke so that they would sustain themselves erectly for as long as forty years. They were agriculturalists and raised cassava, eddoes, corn, and rice, which they exchanged, when conditions were favorable, for fish from the Bittahs. "Hungry time" came in turn to the newcomers and in their desperation they fell upon the crabs moving obliquely through the sands along the shore. The Bittahs, who were skillful enough to brave the waters for fish, thereafter applied to these newcomers the scornful epithet of Carboes, meaning crab eaters. Many bloody battles have been the outcome of these designations. The Bittahs made contemptuous reference to their brave conquering neighbors who were too timid to get wet in the manly act of ocean fishing and thus had to depend upon the filthy crabs bedded in the sand. The Carboes would reply: "We are your equal in every respect save that of dog eating, which habit becomes no one so well as a Bittah."

The challenge of the seas was given and accepted by the Carboes, who eventually came to excel the masters, both in fishing and in the art of canoe making. The women of the Bittahs heckled and nagged their husbands for their sluggishness and eventually deserted them to throw themselves at the feet of the graceful and sturdy men of the new race. These men gave promise of being by far the best providers, and their gay strength commanded adoration. In retaliation and mortal pique, the Bittahs abducted women of the Carboes and a long succession of fierce hostilities followed.

The Bittahs, according to the lore, were the first proprietors of the coast from Buttah Point northward to Grand Bassa, called in their tongue, "Beeronn." The Carboes held a strip of territory extending from Sinoe, or Snoclee, to Sassytown on the south. Beyond this point and extending as far as Webbo was the area the Bittahs also claimed.

How interminable these tales are, and with what triviality of detail they are passed from generation to generation! It seems that the old men have a purpose in this occupation, and can fondle and nurse these petty grievances until the sheer weight of time and accretion give them potency. There is no better example of the power of these accumulated animosities than is afforded in the instance of the tribal quarrel over a dead fish related earlier, which, in the tangle of the new politics in Liberia, reached the League of Nations for settlement.

4

The Wilderness Years

A country that bloomed a garden and a grave.

For forty days and nights the *Elizabeth* sailed its way uncertainly toward the east. The bleak memory of America had been blasted suddenly by the hot breath of the tropics, without the leisurely routine of changing seasons. The tedium of the ocean and the endless plowing into the blue haze of a dead man's dream were eased by that first refuge of the slave and last hope of the free man—prayer. The first church of Liberia was organized on board ship by Brother Elijah Johnson.

Then suddenly across the straining prow, far, far away, a great chain of mountains loomed up with convulsive abruptness. Clouds hung low and heavy with rain. A musty, dark blanket of fog, like hot vapor, enveloped everything, bearing down on the travelers with a sickly languor and disgust. Here was Sierra Leone, and Africa—home! The thrill of seeing the fatherland was chilled instantly by the sight of the slave ships prowling around the harbor. The ships terrified the fledgling freedmen and brought nightmares of recapture and a second middle passage. They must find John Kizell. He was a Black like themselves. He had seen both America and Africa, and could tell them what to do, both for comfort and safety. His loud boast to Mills and Burgess had given them something to which they could cling. The agents, however, were not taking succor from Black men—yet; they would visit the White governor of Sierra Leone. In this far off wilderness of Blacks, White men could understand White men. And so the Messrs. Bacon, Bankson, and Crozier went ashore to call upon Governor Charles MaCarthy, to whom England had entrusted the destiny of its repatriated Blacks. The conference was a failure—MaCarthy promptly suspected political motives behind the enterprise, as indeed there were, although these agents were not politicians. He had no room in Sierra Leone for the Black colonists, but he suggested that they might find something down in Sherbro. It was, in fact, just the place for this party and as many more as they wanted to bring. Hauling anchor, the group headed south about 100 miles. It was now appropriate to think of Black Kizell and his influence with the native chiefs, for he would meet them and arrange everything.

A second landing was made at Sherbro. From the ship could be seen dull, squat huts stuck into a landscape tangled and wild with the exuberance of strange vegetation. Here they landed. But Kizell was nowhere to be found. The natives were sullen and uncooperative. The colonists could not turn back now; they must find Kizell. There came back to them in this dreary land of torrential rains, tangled swamps and hovering forests the erie tales the Sierra Leonians had whispered: that it was a country where nature itself was sullen and perfidious; where every object from the brittle and slippery sand of the beach to the bamboo chair upon which one sat possessed an evil intelligence and would "lay hands on" with a loathsome disease; where merely to brush oneself against one of the cottonwood trees spreading porous trunks at large was to invite the vile touch of elephantiasis; a country with a mysterious "holy city," upon whose soil no living man might walk shod and live to see the next day; a country so treacherous that even the hardboiled Briton contented himself with calling his conferences on the beach within sight of his ship. The appearance of the place gave a disconcerting substance to these tales. Campelar, Kizell's place, was no town at all. It was scarcely more than a mangrove swamp. And the rains . . .

Eventually Kizell was found, though he had been frankly avoiding the colonists. Evasive, equivocal, and full of specious alibis, he began to dally. Instead of taking them directly to King Sherbro, he went to Couber, an inconsequential subchief. Impatient with his chicanery and hastening to settle their charges and return on the *Elizabeth*, the agents made their first tactical mistake: They landed without the permission of the paramount chief. This was an unpardonable indignity to the chief of a country, and from this moment trouble began. The native chiefs were not anxious to have their lucrative slave business interfered with; many moons had passed since they had discussed the matter of land with Mills and Burgess, and they had been shrewdly careful to leave a loophole in the agreement big enough for even a fool to walk through. They had not even scratched their cross on a paper of agreement, and Mills, who had negotiated this hazy contract, was dead. When the agents eventually presented themselves to King Sherbro and announced that they had come to claim their land for the new home, the suave monarch lifted his skimpy eyebrows in surprise and with feigned naiveté inquired, "What lands?" He did not remember that any had ever been promised, or, really, that any negotiations had ever taken place. This was a surprise as overwhelming as the sudden disappearance of Africa itself would have been, and it left the agents speechless and without plan.

Days dragged on and, in the miasmic muck of Sherbro, the colonists began to fall ill and to lose all their illusions about adventure. Kizell, in spite of having boasted the virtues of the island, could not live down the resentment of the intruders or a malignant determination to make them pay for the adventure. When the provisions began to dwindle, and when the sick colonists required fresh nourishment, he set himself up as a huckster and charged them dearly. They were forced to pay him sixty dollars a month for the dreary, rain-soaked huts they occupied. The water to which he directed them with the smirking assurance that it contained "peculiar qualities conducive to health" was a spring of poison, which neither he nor his followers touched. The truth was that his personal influence with the King of Sherbro was negligible, for he himself was scarcely more than an intruder.

The languorous ailment which had sapped all enthusiasm from the party suddenly burst into a virulent fever. Bacon, in a dark hour of despondence, penned in his memoirs: "The consequence [of assigning the people to the labor of making a temporary home] was that their strength was exhausted with excessive bodily labor and imprudent exposure to the direct rays of a vertical sun through the day and the damp pestilential exhalations at night. Many of the Black people, at the same time, would scarcely take the trouble to prepare their food properly; by the indolence manifestly inviting disease and laying open the system to the worst effects of the malignant properties of water and climate." This regenerated marine was a powerful, if ungainly, figure, quick and violent in his passions, generous at times, then pensive, then storming with suspicion and rage. Without a break after his description of the exhaustion of the party from excessive bodily exertion, he complained with great irritability of the moral consequences of general idleness. He could not understand why these empire builders should complain about their lot or put responsibility for their hardships on the agents, since, as everybody in America had been told, it was their own voluntary party and they were going "of their own free will to tame this very wilderness." This idleness, he wrote, in a moment of impious wrath, "afforded to the seeds of dissatisfaction, which had never been entirely eradicated from their minds, a prolific growth. Scarcely a circumstance of their lot but administered some pretext of complaint." On April 6, Bacon continued gloomily:

> We have now twenty-one sick. We tried the country practice of bathing and find it successful in some cases. We have not tried it sufficiently to attest its efficiency. . . . I have heard the complaints of the people this day, because there is not good water to be had on the island, because they were brought to this place, because I did not take possession of the land by force, because the

> people are visited with sickness, because there is not fresh meat, sugar, mo-
> lasses, flour, and other luxuries to be distributed to them, because the "pal-
> aver" is not over, because the houses are not better, because they have only
> meat and bread to eat. They complain of everything they have; and are
> clamorous of everything they have not.

Harassed, almost apoplectic in his impatience, he began to sense mutiny in every whisper. He was disgusted with everything and spared no one of the charge of willful malingering: "We have suffered much from the de-predations of our own people! Even our high-toned professors of religion have been repeatedly detected in petty thefts, falsehood, and mischiefs of the most disgraceful nature. I am pained to the heart with these indications of gross hypocrisy. It is a dark picture, but its shades are truth."

Two days later the number of stricken colonists had reached twenty-five, and in a clearer moment he attributed this sickness to "a too free use of country fruits; the neglect of personal cleanliness; alternate exposure to the sun and the dampness of night; the want of flooring to the huts; constitu-tions not seasoned to the climate; and (for those working on the ship) excessive fatigue and anxiety of mind, remaining for hours in the water and in wet clothes, while landing the goods. . . . Wherever I move, I meet with little besides groans and tears." To strengthen his righteous contempt for this bilious indolence, he boasted that he had the spiritual concerns of the whole company to look after, went without stockings and sometimes shoes, scarcely wore a hat or coat, was up early and to bed at ten or eleven, ate little, labored more than anyone, "and yet, blessed be God, I continue in health." On April 19: "I last night contracted a slight cold." April 20: "Still sick." April 21: "The same." April 22: "Thy will be done."

On April 28, in this lingering agony, there came a ray of hope: A vessel from Freetown anchored and two representatives of the colonial governor, one of them a physician, landed. They were welcomed with unbounded joy. The visitors announced their object as some small and incredibly trivial matter of trade, made a leisurely and indifferent survey of the calamitous situation of the colonists, and with a shrug went back to their ship. The entreaties of the sick for medical attention, or even advice as to treatment, were refused. The official visitors did not leave, however, before they con-sented to remove the prostrate Bacon on their ship to Sierra Leone for medical treatment, and they set an hour for taking him aboard. Anxious, those Blacks who still were able to move about, placed Bacon in a small boat and approached the anchorage ground at an early hour. At the ap-proach of the boat, the vessel brazenly drew up its anchor and set sail for Sierra Leone. The dying Bacon screamed to his men at the oars to overtake it, and for hours they splashed and strained in futile pursuit, but the vessel gained in speed and hopelessly outdistanced them. One after the other the oarsmen collapsed with exhaustion and fell limply across his oars, and the race was over. On May 1 Bacon died on a little island where the group had taken refuge to ease the tortures of his last hours.

Dr. Crozier, the physician, lay aboard ship, stricken and helpless. Then, wearied by the futility of the negotiations with the natives and wounded by their duplicity, Bankson fell ill. He lingered briefly in a feverish delirium, then died. Five, then ten, of the colonists were buried in the mire of Sherbro. Dr. Crozier, feeling the approach of death, committed his charge to Daniel Coker, a Black preacher. The strange torturing malady was burning out the will to survive. In a fit of delirium, Midshipman Townsend broke from his berth and leaped into the ocean.

Coker was ecstatic over this heroic opportunity to lead the remainder of his own people into the promised land. In the midst of this swift, uncontrollable decimation against which he had neither defense nor plan, he sat down and penned a burning message home: "Tell my brethren to come—not to fear—this land is good—it only wants men to possess it." Before the next ship arrived, he had retreated to the security of Sierra Leone.

The *Nautilus* came early the following year, bringing twenty-eight more Black settlers and four new White agents: J. B. Winn and Ephraim Bacon, with his wife, as government agents; and Joseph R. Andrus and Christian Wiltberger for the Society. They secured permission to intern the entire company at Foura Bay, a cultivated plantation near Freetown, until the coast had been scoured farther down. On Monday morning, March 9, the Reverend Ephraim Bacon entered this note in his diary: "At six o' clock prayers in church. After breakfast it was concluded that it was expedient for Mrs. Bacon to remain in Mr. [Elijah] Johnson's family during my absence with Mr. Andrus exploring the coast. Although painful to the flesh, yet duty required it, and my wife readily submitted after uniting with good Mr. Johnson in commending us to God in solemn prayer." After doubling the cape, they headed out to sea, proceeding parallel with the coast some 250 miles southward to Cape Mount. Here reigned King Peter, one of the most powerful and bellicose chiefs on the west coast and more deeply engrossed in the slave trade than any of his neighbors. King Peter was also shrewd and aware of the agents' mission. At their first approach, he bristled with such determined menace that they passed on as if they had never intended to stop at all. As Bacon nicely puts it, "He dissuaded us from incurring any loss of time or expense in procuring an interview with him." Just fifty miles downward they came upon two small islands facing a rich and fertile stretch of elevated country. Here rose a detached mountain, steep and high toward the sea, but sloping gradually on the land side, its summit forming a level plain. To the east was an extensive bay, bordered by rich and uniform soil, and skirting it were hills of moderate elevation covered with trees. It was an ideal spot. The two islands facing it were pleasant and fertile. The kings of that section had used them for their own pleasure. The largest, which at one time had been offered to the French trader, de Marchais, as a mark of highest esteem, was now being used by John Mills, a mulatto slave trader of splendid English education. The smaller one was in possession of a native African named Baba, who likewise traded in slaves.

The chief of this region was a dependent of the terrible King Peter. Carefully, the Reverend Mr. Bacon selected a bundle of trinkets and dispatched them to the king, requesting at the same time the privilege of an interview. Within a short time he received his presents back with a curt refusal. There was nothing to do but move on. They went to Bassa and for a solid week jogged from one village to the other looking for His Majesty, King John. Finally they found him, lying in state in a palaver house, dressed in a fine robe, with a pair of new English boots on his feet—dead, as he had been for four months. After apologizing for having interrupted the funeral rites, they proceeded to a place called Jumbotown and there met King Jack Ben. At his feet they placed a gun, some powder, tobacco, pipes and beads, and began to unfold their mission. Bacon's brief diary carries this record of this interview:

> We stated our object to be to get land for the black people in America, to come and sit down [to occupy]. We told him that the people were very many and required much territory; that a few white men only would come along, to assist and take care of them; that we should make a town where ships would come and trade with cloth and guns and beads and knives and tobacco and pipes; and take in return their ivory and palm oil and rice and every other thing growing in the fields; that they would not then need to sell any more people, but might learn to cultivate the ground and make other things to sell for whatever they wanted.

During the deliberations, which were extended over a week, a squat, pugnacious Kru arose and in a fiery speech warned the king that these were hostile emissaries who meant no good. King and council withdrew and on their return demanded that the visitors "make book" that they would in no way give assistance to the armed ships sent to the coast to suppress the slave traffic. On this condition they were offered land. The agents finally agreed and departed. They had a home for their wandering children, but their consciences were not easy about the ironic stipulation that they would condone the slave traffic at its very source. It was, indeed, an empty success which conceded more in principle than the venture was worth. They returned to Sherbro.

Brother Andrus was now disgusted and gloomily considered foreswearing his impending martyrdom and returning to a White man's country.

More colonists had died. Kizell was haggling for payment for the six feet of mangrove swamp in which their corpses had been interred. The rains continued. There were no ships in the harbor in which to return, nor were any expected. While awaiting the arrival of a vessel, Andrus made a brief excursion to the Plantains, a tiny group of islands owned and cultivated by an African-born Black, George Caulker, who had been educated in England. Snugly ensconced in this remote and unsuspected quarter, he was found living the life of an English squire—whether comfortably or not—attired in well-fitting English clothes and deeply immersed in the preparation of an extensive manuscript. He had already translated the liturgy of the Church of England, and was in the midst of the translation of the Bible into the *Bollum* dialect. Although he made no mention of it, this was not his first contact with the leaders of the struggling colonists. The year before he had warmly received visitors Bacon and Lieutenant Stringham. Dressed in a flowing white robe and a turban of figured cambric, he had gracefully showed them into his own bedroom for the night, and had found comfortable accommodations for their boatmen. However, although suave and gentle, he was suspicious of their errand on the coast and expressed his disapproval. A considerable part of his wealth, they were certain, had been amassed through trading in slaves. On two sides of his enclosure he had built high strong walls, and about those were resting, most eloquently, five dismounted guns. Caulker gave the new visitors comfort in the selection of the Bassa country for settlement and, with a flourish, pointed to several specimens of fine cattle and hogs which he had brought to attest that it was good, that its soil was equal to any on the West Coast, its cattle preferable, and its people unwarlike and more hospitable than their neighbors.

Back at Foura Bay the gentle Mrs. Bacon, with true missionary zeal, had beheld with satisfaction the children of Ethiopia stretching out their hands unto God, but the evening before her husband's return she came down with fever. Although the scourge had taken twenty-two of the settlers, nothing could be done about moving to Bassa until after the rains. The questionable contract with the Bassa tribe haunted these pious minds like malignant ghosts and even with prayer they could not dispel this ugly memory. The Honorable K. Macauley of Sierra Leone had purchased a slave schooner which had been taken as a prize by the British, and was on the point of sending it to Barbados for sale. Andrus was in town with his baggage ready to go along as far as Barbados, having now convinced himself that so long as the Reverend Bacon and the rains remained, there was no pressing need of his services. But the pestilence still pursued and soon Bacon joined his wife in illness; Winn and his wife were stricken next. Mr. and Mrs. Bacon became so ill that Andrus finally felt compelled to suggest that he should remain in Bacon's stead, so that the couple might have the benefit of the sea voyage. Bacon demurred gently, reflected, consulted his physician, yielded to the will of the Lord, and wrote in his diary, "I feel much indebted to him." Six weeks after the ship had sailed without him, the disappointed Andrus died. Within a month both Winn and his wife had also succumbed. From the safer quarters of his study in America, Bacon phrased an eloquent tribute to his friend: "The sons of Africa shall tell to their latest descendants how these men of God left father and mother, and brother and sister, and all the sweet endearments of friendship and of home, to cross the wide ocean and dwell beneath the burning sky and the blasting heat of her inhospitable wilds, and counted not their own lives dear unto them, that they might preach the unsearchable riches of Christ."

The next episode of this dreary pageant of extinction opened with an almost incredible incident: An American vessel trading somewhere on the Liberian coast encountered a storm. After a number of vicissitudes it was forced to abandon contact with the coast and go home, eventually turning up at Baltimore with six Kru men aboard whom they had not been able to land in Africa because of the storm. Baltimore was the home of General Harper, an active member of the Colonization Society, and likewise of E. Tyson, who had on numerous occasions exercised himself in the interest of Blacks. This was distinctly and embarrassingly a difficult situation, since no one wanted any more Blacks in this part of the Union. To all intents and purposes, the passengers of the *Elizabeth* had been disposed of finally, though left quite helpless and in dire need of essentials and medicine.

President Monroe was profoundly touched by this affair and ordered a public vessel to be placed at the disposal of the Society for the removal of the stranded tribesmen to their home. In the necessary interval, the Africans had been taken in charge by Mr. Tyson and General Harper and were treated with the greatest kindness. On the ship that carried them back, the Society sent also a new agent, Dr. Ayers. When they had sighted the coast of Africa, they encountered another series of storms, and Captain Stockton, after missing his customary observations, termed the section *terra incognita* and was ready to let it go at that. The bustle at the sight of land, however, attracted the Kru men to the deck, and very soon, one of them rushed to the captain in great excitement and gratitude, exclaiming, according to their chroniclers, "Oh, good massa—too good to poor Kru man—dat Cape Mesurado—dat he home." As they bore closer to shore, they could actually distinguish people walking there. An aged native was among them; two of the Kru men, when they saw him, uttered a great shout of recognition and leaped into the waves to rejoin their old friend. This and the evidence of excellent attention which the Kru men had received at the hands of the ship's party laid the foundation for the first negotiations for land at Mesurado, King Peter's country.

Captain Stockton and Dr. Ayers, satisfied to accept this providential introduction, hauled their ship straight into the harbor and went ashore. It was not easy to find King Peter, but the road had been cleared, and after annoying delays they succeeded in getting an assemblage of the surly Dey chiefs. These chiefs were clever at sparring, and the palavers were dragged through several days. It was evident that there was discussion of their mission among the chiefs and that the repatriated Krus were apprehensive about the safety of the visitors. The discouragement of the agents grew when they discovered that their landing boat, the only means of direct communication with the ship, was gone. The still grateful Krus, on the chance of incurring Peter's wrath, recovered the boat, which had been brazenly hauled away by certain of the Dey chieftain's men. The following day the menace became a bit more formidable. From the beginning of the palaver, the captain had observed the peculiar movements of a Dey youth who had entered and seated himself arrogantly and prominently near the center of the circle. His eyes, hard and full of determined enmity, followed every gesture of the visitors and carefully appraised their means of resistance. Suddenly, in the midst of the sustained circumlocution of King Peter, the youth sprang to his feet, shouting "I know him, that man," he cried, pointing. "He no friend to Deys, no friend to traders. He be master of gunboat. He take ship with goods we sell. I be steward. He make masters wear iron. He break our trade." This, at any rate, was the thought and substance of his fiery remarks, to which he added a warning against any arrangement with Captain Stockton or his friends. The captain, in a hot passion over this new excuse for prolonging the drowsy bickerings, leaped to his feet whipping out his revolvers, defiantly admitting his occupation as annoyer of the slave trade, and made loud and dreadful threats in the name of powerful Christian nations. The gentle and uninitiated Dr. Ayers grew extremely uncomfortable and, casting his eyes about at the sea of Black menacing faces, cautioned the captain to command his temper and, if humanly possible, keep cool. Together they backed out of the palaver yard, the captain still brandishing his guns, the doctor nervously speculating upon the whims of the heathen, "infuriated by jealousy, intoxicated by drink, maddened by disappointment, incited by the slave traders."

Before they could reach their ship, however, they were overtaken by a small boy who made them understand his curious speech that the chiefs desired them to return to the palaver yard. After some hesitation, they went back and found that the mulatto trader, John Mills, had made effective intercession for them. A small bullock was tied up near the circle of men; a brief apology was made for the disturbance and the bullock was presented as a "dash." The palaver ended on Christmas Eve (1821) with an agreement to sell a strip of coastland 130 miles long and forty miles broad and the two islands to be used forever as a settlement for American freed slaves, for the following consideration: six muskets, one barrel of powder, six iron bars, ten iron pots, one barrel of nails, one box of tobacco pipes, three looking glasses, four umbrellas, three walking sticks, one box of soap, one barrel of rum, four hats, three pairs of shoes, six pieces of blue taft, and three pieces of white calico. This was all they had along with them. However, the agents promised to pay, when they could, six more iron bars, twelve guns, three barrels of powder, a dozen knives, forks, spoons, and plates, five barrels of salt beef and of salt pork, twelve barrels of ship's biscuits, a dozen glass decanters, a dozen wine glasses, and fifty pairs of shoes.

Practically none of this stuff was needed by the natives save, perhaps, as curios and for the purposes of intoxication. In fact, just two things were certain about this deal: The agents of the colonists believed that they had bought a strip of the Grain Coast and had the deed to it in the paper on which the chiefs had scratched a mark; the chiefs did not know that they were selling the country on which they had lived from the earliest memory of the tribe but, by the rules of Blackstone, they had bound themselves to the bargain by acceptance of part payment. And so they separated, each side satisfied that it had concluded a neat transaction.

5

Harsh Heaven: The Land of the Canaanites

On January 7, 1822, Dr. Ayers sailed into sight of the newly acquired Cape Mesurado with a small group of the sturdiest of his male colonists. The last stage of this trek into the promised land had its cloud of disappointment because he had been unable to persuade many colonists to leave Foura Bay. They felt they had gone far enough into the wilderness already. A stubborn group of settlers, including Daniel Coker, had already declared Black freedom a myth and had crawled under the aegis of Great Britain. As he gave his orders for landing, Ayers was filled with apprehension. There was a strange and foreboding activity among the natives. He soon learned the trouble. The neighboring Dey chiefs had been furious when they learned of King Peter's land deal and had gone so far as to threaten Peter with death unless he cancelled it.

Apart from the humiliation such a violent reprimand caused His Majesty, King Peter did not want to die and was dissatisfied with his transaction. The colonists met a bristling reception and were not allowed to land, even upon a larger island facing the Cape. It was necessary for them to take refuge on the site temporarily controlled by the mulatto John Mills. The tiny island was low-lying, rocky, without fresh water, only two furlongs long, and stuck in the Mesurado lagoon. Huddled there in discomfort, the pilgrims waited for the rains, now threatening again. King Peter was no longer polite. He returned the presents and ordered the intruders to get out. A few more colonists showed up from Sierra Leone and were forced to join the original group in their crowded quarters. The natives harried them constantly, sniping at them every time they ventured to the mainland for water. Ayer and Wiltberger went to Sierra Leone for more colonists, leaving the first arrivals to survive as best they could.

It was a sickly time, and the first showers of the dreaded rainy season had already fallen. An incident then occurred which complicated the situation even more. A British schooner which had been moving about menacingly off the coast within sight of the colonists had recaptured some slaves intended for a French slaver. In the rough waters the British vessel parted its cable, drifted ashore, and was wrecked. It is an old tradition of the coast that any wrecked vessel is legitimate booty for the natives. Accordingly, old King George, one of the chiefs of this section, sent out his men to take possession. Although the crew of the schooner put up resistance and beat the natives off, they were helpless to sustain this resistance and the captain made a forlorn appeal to the ragged little colony, packed against itself on the island. He expected a White agent to be in charge. As the natives were warming up for a secònd attack, a boat was manned and sent to his relief with the colonists' only brass piece. It was a real rescue, the natives were cowed after two had been killed and a number of others wounded. The crew and slaves were safely landed, but the vessel and its other cargo went to pieces on the rock.

Aroused to fury, the natives resumed the attack the following day and killed a British soldier and one of the colonists. When Ayers returned from Sierra Leone, he found the place in great excitement. The natives had connected the disastrous incident with the presence of the colonists and were calling palavers of all the chiefs over a wide area. The nights were thundering with the excited staccato of the drums carrying messages and the call to council from village to village. King Peter renewed his demand that the colonists get out. They in turn offered to pay the balance due on the sale, but the offer was refused. Ayers was reluctant to give up what had been gained so far and tried at a discreet distance to argue the matter with King Peter. He was invited to a palaver on the mainland, where he was held prisoner by the chief until he consented to take his trinkets back and leave the country. Peter's good nature, however, returned long enough to grant them permission to "sit" on the island until they could find somewhere else to go.

There was one old chief back in the Dey country, comfortable in his strength and holding a grievance against King Peter, who was reported to be friendly to the Americans; Ayers now turned to him for help. After listening to the story, old King Bristol decided that since Peter had been fool enough to sell his country and accept part payment for it, he must accept the consequences of his folly. The Americans should have their lands immediately, and anyone not satisfied with Bristol's decision was at liberty to protest it if he did not mind having his head taken from his shoulders. That his was not idle talk could be attested to by the fresh mourners on the coast for King George, who had been the last to dispute Bristol's judicial fairness. There followed a sullen truce, and the colonists continued to sit upon the island, nursing the shadowy right to possession of land on the mainland.

The rains burst, and their temporary quarters were scant protection. Another scourge of fever set in, and the provisions showed signs of early exhaustion. Both the agents were now drowsy with the first touch of fever.

Disheartened, Ayers proposed the abandonment of the project as a fool's errand, and announced that he would leave the settlers at Sierra Leone on his way back to America. One of the survivors of the *Elizabeth*, Elijah Johnson, emboldened by his endurance of this long succession of ill fortune and finally disgusted with trekking up and down the African coast, demurred in language which made him famous. He said: "For two years I have been looking for a home. Here I have found one, and here I remain." This firm resistance determined the fate of what is now Liberia.

Ayers wanted no more of Mesurado and departed for Sierra Leone, allowing his associate, Wiltberger, the unenviable opportunity of writing his name in the history of this illusory Black republic by leading the colonists from the island to the mainland. Thus weighted with responsibility, Wiltberger came down violently with fever and at the earliest possible moment joined Ayers in Sierra Leone. This left the bewildered colonists under the leadership of Elijah Johnson, the man who would not go any farther.

When Johnson could recover from the shock of new responsibility, he took a careful inventory and concluded that of his eighty colonists, male and female, adults and children, there were about twenty-five capable of bearing arms. Their stores were within a few days of exhaustion, their mud and thatch huts were dissolving under the first showers of the rains, there were no enclosures, or houses, or clearings for houses on the mainland, and the able-bodied were rapidly succumbing to the eternal plague of the tropics.

Taking the best of his men, Johnson went boldly across the lagoon and began clearing a space for a stockade. From the dark security of the surrounding forest the natives sniped at the laborers and offered various other distractions. These annoyances grew into attacks, and the attacks gained in intensity and determination as the clearing went on. Soon the settlers were devoting more time to beating off attacks than to felling trees. Suddenly, to their relief, a British gunboat appeared off the Cape. The commander offered to punish the natives if the colonists would cede just a small piece of their land to the British government and hoist the British flag upon it. Although not fully acquainted with the devious methods of imperial land grabbing, it seemed an odd proposition, and with admirable boldness Johnson replied that he did not want the flag staff, that it would probably be easier to whip the natives than to get it down again. The gunboat went its way and the colonists, maddened and desperate, made such resolute opposition to the attacks that they earned for themselves a brief respite.

Ayers and Wiltberger, meanwhile, had long been gone to America to acquaint the Society, they explained, with the difficulties of the mission. The Society, tossing upon a resistless and hysterical current of political support, reiterated its aims with reinforced eloquence and appointed Jehudi Ashmun to lead the next expedition. Fifty-three new colonists, including the recaptured Africans bought by the Society, and a supply of stores were put in readiness for shipment from Baltimore.

Ashmun was of rugged Puritan stock, handsome, sensitive, ascetic, and of tortuously disciplined emotions. He took his religion and his conscience seriously, and his God was one of terrors. It was characteristic of him that he could pray: "O heart-searching and rein-trying God! Who requireth a broken heart of all who worship Thee." He did not come to this mission through any original interest in Blacks or through any concern about settling them permanently in Africa as a solution to America's race problems. This was fortunate, for it permitted him to be just without being sentimental, and resolute without being heroic. As a matter of fact, Ashmun came to the mission through broken fortunes and an unfortunate love affair.

Following the wishes of his parents, he had begun preparing for the ministry at the age of twenty. At this stage he had been impetuous, self-confident, and ardently fond of "the graces of the female character." The priestly career proved difficult to sustain, and he took a position as professor in a ladies' seminary. In the same town he met a devout and rather attractive young woman of gentle breeding from North Carolina, also a teacher. In this first flush of youth he was attracted and later proposed marriage. She was noncommittal, whether through shyness or indifference he could never learn, for he met her only once or twice in the course of the next few years. As he grew older his ardor flagged, and in a moment of courtly impatience he requested her to say either "yes" or "no," but the lady continued noncommittal.

In the interval of her indecision there crossed his path another young woman "of radiant beauty," to quote from his biographer, the Reverend Mr. Gorley: "A vision of singular brightness rose upon his sight, and an image to him of unrivalled loveliness became enshrined in his heart. He felt the captivating effects of charms surpassing what he had imagined of beauty or excellence in Woman." In a moment of rashness he kissed her! This was something which he could not reconcile with his Puritanic notions of honor, and he fled from her presence, thereafter brooding over his unfaithfulness. Conscious-stricken over the deep stirrings of new emotions which he could neither quell nor forget, he sat down and pressed his earlier attachment for an answer. To his surprise, as well as dismay, she accepted him and they were married.

This episode was too much for the tight little New England town, and for a ladies' seminary. There were vague and injurious rumors. The gentle female students sought to be excused from Ashmun's classes. He found himself unable to press his claims to the ministry and a vocation as preacher. Finally, local gossip and his own state of mind forced him to resign his position and go as far away as his funds would carry him. They landed him in Baltimore. Here he learned that the Colonization Society was in need of a man to take charge of its undertaking at Cape Mesurado. He was ordained and offered himself as a missionary. Promptly he set sail with his wife, secretly nursing the hope that he would discover a means of rebuilding his fortunes through the development of trade with Africa.

At the brilliant threshold of a life of classic composure and that enviable security and stately ease of which all well-born New Englanders dreamed, Ashmun had stumbled. He could not escape, even in an overwhelming flush of shame, the stern Puritanic imperative implanted in his youth to preach something to somebody. And in his confusion this impulse had directed him toward a venture of missionary daring. But underneath there stirred his practical, self-seeking mind, piously calculating the chances of restoring his fortunes. He had failed so far at waiting, at teaching, and at preaching. Admittedly, personal sacrifice of some sort was demanded in expiation of the guilt which his sensitive conscience felt, if not as the inevitable price of success. And he was willing to face it. The African proposition, along with all the elements of a great humanitarian mission, offered him an opportunity to visit the African coast and give substance to the sudden wild dream of directing an extensive trade between Africa and America.

He mentioned none of his plans to the managers of the Colonization Society before leaving. But during the dreary eighty-one days of the voyage from Baltimore he brooded over them and amid perfunctory exclamations of piety he confided his reflections upon these mercantile possibilities to his private diary. Finally, in a letter to one of the managers of the Society, he introduced the argument that African trade could be most compatible to the aims of colonization. Properly conducted, he urged, the attention of the natives might discreetly be turned from the slave trade to an honorable commerce, and they would find it to their great advantage to remain on good terms with the colonists. American merchants might be in exclusive control of trade from a central station at Mesurado, the lush produce of the tropics could be laid temptingly before the eyes of the American people, there could be many ships, willing emigration, a waiving of half the expense of colonization to the Society. He offered to exert himself to the utmost to promote this project with the natives.

On August 9, 1822, the party landed at Cape Mesurado. The rains were in full flood. As far as the emigrants could see, landward was a wilderness of dense dripping forest, entangled with tough vines and brushwood. Nestling piteously against the edge of this wilderness was one tiny speck of cleared land, which had accommodated thirty huts, representing the continuous exertions of Elijah Johnson's desperate little band which had left its perch on the island for the mainland. A fire had destroyed nearly all the public property of the settlers along with their first rude shelter. There were no fortifications against the constant menace of the natives; there was not even temporary shelter for the new arrivals or their stores.

The whole population, including the new arrivals, totaled 130, of whom thirty-five were capable of bearing arms. It was a month before all the emigrants and stores were finally put ashore. In the face of these exertions and the dismal remoteness of all pleasing prospects, Ashmun laid aside his dream of commercial empire and set to work. For more immediate reasons than trade the chiefs of the country had to be bound to friendly relations. He sought out old King Peter, unctuously offering to instruct his sons in the English language. Peter listened to his proposals and asked bluntly if goods had been sent from America to complete the payment for the lands which had been ceded to the settlers. Ashmun was shocked at this impertinence and replied that the Society "believed that nearly the whole price had been paid to King Peter many moons ago, according to the contract, and so had sent out only a few goods for that purpose." Peter grunted, and Ashmun perceived that all was not well. Peter asked again, pointedly, if Dr. Ayers had arrived in America before he had left. Ashmun's indignation mounted as he replied negatively. He supposed that the next ship to leave America after Ayer's arrival would bring instructions and he commented upon the Society's being governed by the strictest justice. To Peter's disgust, all that he had was a letter addressed to King Peter and his headmen, which he would deliver whenever the king expressed his readiness to receive it. Peter took the letter, and seeing that for the moment nothing could be gained by heckling this novice so fresh from the gentle surroundings of a ladies' seminary, he put the letter away, muttering something about waiting for the next ship. He now made a suggestion which he thought anyone could understand: His age and rank entitled him, according to the country custom, to some consideration of respect in the form of a present. It need not be useful or valuable, just a "present." Ashmun, groping for dignity, expressed a reluctant willingness "in behalf of the Society" to signify this respect for King Peter's age by a small present which he would send to his town "as soon as convenient, after receiving the goods ashore."

Ashmun left the presence of King Peter feeling none too comfortable. He was dealing with unlettered savages, to be sure, but the manner in which they played with intelligent men's thoughts was, to say the least, uncanny. He went to King Bristol, who had shown friendliness in an earlier emergency, and proposed to open with him and his people a fair and mutually advantageous trade with America and Europe. Bristol, too, was a bit cagey. While reaffirming his friendliness to the colony, he warned Ashmun that the country was ruled by many kings and consequently many dispositions. That night Ashmun committed to his diary that "under smooth and friendly appearances, there lurks in the minds of many of the headmen a spirit of determined malignity which only waits for an opportunity to exert itself for the ruin of the colony."

Along with the plans for the separate colonization of his fifteen recaptured Africans purchased by the Society at Milledgeville, the induction of native labor to assist in clearing the ground for more development, and the planting of vegetables, Ashmun included some very definite plans for fortification and defense. Encouraged by the show of defense, and nervously impatient over the inevitable developments, he sent a message to the silent and invisible foe to the effect that "he was perfectly appraised of their hostile deliberations, notwithstanding their pains to conceal them; and that if they proceeded to bring war upon the Americans, without even asking to settle their differences in a friendly manner, they would clearly learn what it was to fight White men." But kings Bromley, Todo, Governor, Konko, Jimmy, Gray, Long Peter, George, Willy, and all King Peter's warriors had reached accord and knew in what anxieties this grandiose bluff had been born. They surveyed this handful of dusky "White men" with an embittered scorn and tossed the note aside without reply.

Ashmun had been led to believe that there was not sufficient unity of counsel among native tribes to result in effective joint action, and this confidence, though unwise, allowed the colonists to give more time to the normal routine of clearing themselves a home. When he finally took stock, he found that of his settlers, twenty-seven men, when not sick, could bear arms, but only a few of these had handled a gun or were in any sense instructed in the art of defense. They had about forty muskets, all of which needed repairing, five iron guns, and a brass piece. Of these, only the brass piece was usable. The guns required carriages and these were completely buried in the mud on the other side of the river. There was no abatis or fence work of any kind, nor any prepared ammunition, and it was only with great difficulty and delay that they loaded their only useful gun.

With unity of counsel among the natives actually materializing, the arrangements for defense reached a high point of excitement. The settlement, with its twenty-seven fighting men, was declared to be under military law. F. James was commissioned captain of the brass-mounted piece and given four assistants. Elijah Johnson was made commissionary of stores, and R. Sampson was made commissionary of ordnance. Lott Carey was made health officer and government inspector. A nightly watch was established which required twenty men and became more fatiguing than the daily labor of chopping away the forest. The organization sounded military at least. They took thirteen young Africans attached to the United States

Agency and tried to teach them, by daily drill, to handle the musket which the ordnance department had finally patched together. And then, on August 25, just about two weeks after landing, Ashmun came down with fever. Three days later Mrs. Ashmun followed him. By September 10 only two of the new arrivals remained on their feet.

The natives suddenly ceased communicating with the colony. It was a painful and foreboding silence. Ashmun tossed about in delirium, muttering over and over again orders to hasten the fortifications. There were mornings when he could be seen staggering from his cot, laboring through the mud of the compound, waving his arms wildly and shouting instructions to the settlers now growing listless in their exertions. It was trying enough to be ill, distraught, and useless in the presence of a dark fate; but there were stinging arrows of remorse as he saw his wife beside him on a couch dripping with water which the thatched roofs were unable to exclude. Helpless with fever and grotesquely disheveled from the writhings of pain, she died. There was misery for Ashmun, even in wanting to wish for her the ineffable peace of this escape, for it had been the love of Ashmun more than the love of Africa that had brought her there.

Deeper and deeper Ashmun sank in the African fever uncommonly prolonged. He no longer had energy left for the raving delirium which marked the earlier stages of his attack. Slowly, almost by imperceptible stages, the fortifications took random shape, the old gun carriage, unmired, was hauled across the river and mounted, and the military companies, composed of five and six men each, were given to understand that this new home which they had finally reached now had to be fought for.

6

Hunger and War

One morning a stranger, whose name has since become famous, came into the compound. (He informed the colonists that the fatal unity of counsel among the natives had matured and that, lashed to a fury of indignation and intolerance, they were forming for attack.) Sunday morning, November 10, after a 24-hour vigil, the colony sought refreshment and the mysterious consolation which comes from worship. While they were at prayers, word came, ominous and breathtaking, that the first hostile and concerted movement forward had been made to the bank of the Mesurado River. Now the colonists began to learn the black magic of jungle warfare. They were aware that the forests were thick with men, that for days vast numbers of natives, stripped and painted for battle and plunder, had been assembling almost within earshot, that a heavy menace more terrible than fever or strange beasts was bearing down upon them. Their patrols could see no signs throughout the day, yet all day the natives had been there, holding themselves fixed and still, indistinguishable from the snarled black confusion of the jungle.

At sunset they moved forward again to within half a mile of the settlement and dropped again to quiet invisibility. The pickets on watch, in stupid misinterpretation of orders, left their posts at daybreak instead of sunrise. They could as well have slept in their huts through the night for they had neither seen nor heard the enemy swarming under their very noses. The armed native force crept up as the pickets went off duty. Then came the awakening amid screams of fright and disorder, for there, just sixty yards away, packed solidly into a line ten yards wide, stretching endlessly, was the enemy—the resentful heirs of Africa, from whom the colonists must now wrest their lives as well as their homes. They rushed to their gun stands. Here, at this first brazen call of danger, without orders or warning, they had no precedent for action or ordered plan.

The native force delivered its fire and rushed forward to seize the post. In this volley three or four of the colonists were killed; the others in dismay left their guns without discharging a single shot and retreated so recklessly that the reserve guard, stationed in the center of the compound, was

53

thrown into confusion. It was a kind Providence that intervened, and one with a sense of humor. There was absolutely nothing to prevent the natives from pursuing their advantage. A single movement forward and the Republic of Liberia would have died in its struggle for birth. The first four houses of the settlement had fallen into the hands of the natives, but the first warriors stopped to plunder, and the movement of the main body was for a brief period impeded. At this point Lott Carey stepped into Liberian history. His towering black brawn began to move about among the disordered colonists; he drove them back to their guns. Two discharges of the brass field piece, double-shotted with ball and grape, brought the entire body of attackers to a stand. Ashmun later observed in his diary that "the gun was well served and appeared to do great execution." It could have done even more, but for the necessity of sparing a cluster of dwellings which were known to be sheltering twelve of the colonists' women and children. Elijah Johnson, with a handful of musketeers, at this point ranged around the flank of the disconcerted attackers and delivered another surprise by driving them into the mouth of the most effective brass piece.

The native custom of carrying off their own dead and wounded in the midst of battle, their inexpertness in loading and reloading their guns, and the peculiar alignment of their forces pressing into the compound added to the confusion. The rear lines, eager to enter the fray and share the plunder, pressed against the front lines which were the only ones fully exposed to danger. As they sought to escape the destructive violence of the settlers' field piece, they only plunged into the blind advance of their rear forces. The native warrior chiefs had at no time contemplated a complete reverse motion for so large a body, and like a mammoth scrimmage line they heaped themselves in direct range of all the guns. Eight hundred men were pressed shoulder to shoulder in so compact a form that a child could easily walk upon their heads from one end of the mass to the other. They presented in their rear a breadth of rank equal to twenty or thirty men, all exposed to a gun of great power raised on a platform at only thirty to sixty yards distance. "Every shot literally spent its force in a solid mass of living human flesh."

Beginning with discordant individual screams of horror, the forest shook with the violent screaming of a terrified host of native warriors crashing madly through the snapping underbrush. The shouting continued in full volume until it died away in the distance. Reaching the river, some swam across while others stayed to carry their sacred dead and their wounded to the opposite side of the Mesurado River. One canoe large enough to hold twelve men was observed to make a dozen trips across, bearing the bodies of the dead, and for two days friends crept though the woods gathering bodies for ceremonial burial. A party of friendly natives found twenty-seven more bodies which had been overlooked, and the putrid odors which clung to the forest for weeks testified to still more yet under cover.

Such had been the work of thirty-five settlers and six native youths under sixteen years of age, about half of whom had participated in the battle. The colonists were not without fatalities, but the survivors were incredibly hardy. Mrs. Ann Hawkins, who had been unlucky enough to select for shelter the first house taken by the attackers, received thirteen wounds, was thrown aside as dead, and recovered without the aid of medicines. Mrs. Minty Draper, fleeing the horde with her two infants, had been slashed in the head with a cutlass that beheaded her children, but the mother survived to bear more. Mary Tines, another young matron of the settlement, with an older companion who was the mother of five small children, had been in a besieged house. They had barricaded the door, seized axes, and for a while held their attackers at bay. Firing their muskets, they had attempted to escape to the safety of another house, but Mary Tines had been stabbed as she fled. The older woman had put down a suckling infant which crawled out of sight in its terror and was left behind as its mother escaped through a small window. Dazed by her loss, the woman had wandered between two heavy fires, unhurt.

The colonists, now sensible of the position, set to repairing their fortification even before taking up the melancholy duty of burying their dead. But spirits that had managed to sustain the onslaught now began to flag, and the men entered a mood of dismal, hopeless brooding. Was freedom worth this much? A check of the stores disclosed provisions for about fifteen days; there was no hope of food from the country in a state of war. The settlers' sources of secret information about the movements and plans of the natives had been abruptly cut off, but they were certain that reprisals were intended and that, although driven off, the natives were neither dispersed nor satisfied that the affair was concluded. Most disconcerting was the discovery that there was just enough ammunition for one hour's engagement.

In this extremity they sought to make a treaty with the chiefs. They sent assurances that the Americans were a friendly people and wanted peace, that they did not come to Africa to do harm. But the chiefs, still mourning the terrible slaughter of their sons, were silent, and the silence was another strategy. One afternoon about six o'clock a message was sent by the colonists offering peace and announcing somewhat desperately that the colony was prepared for even bloodier destruction in case of another attack. At daylight the following morning a reply came from the chiefs, observing in deliberate detail that, having bought the lowland of the Bushrod Island, the Americans had seized the Cape without right, that the natives visiting the settlement had been cheated and roughly used by the colonists, that the unctuous promises of the agents to instruct their children had not been fulfilled, and that not until they were given satisfaction on these points would they make peace. These messages continued daily while the chiefs recruited warriors from deep in the interior in deliberate preparation for a second attack.

The food of the colony was within about three days of exhaustion when a tramp steamer halted and consented to trade them enough food to sustain them a few days more. Then, when these supplies were gone, by that strange Providence which persistently nurtured this fledgling state, a British vessel under Captain H. Brassey touched the Cape and nearly exhausted its own stores relieving the distress of the sick, wounded, and hungry. The captain offered the benefit of his long acquaintance with the coast chiefs to overcome the hostility. He was unsuccessful, but his negotiations revealed that an attack had been planned for the very night and had been deferred only out of cautious respect for the ship's guns. The captain could not stay, but Ashmun addressed a forlorn letter to America and the armchair colonizers who were turning their neat, inspiring phrases about the redemption of Africa. Presumably it went on Captain Brassey's boat for it was dated the day after his arrival at the Cape. Ashmun wrote:

> All the tribes round us are combined in war against us. Their principal object is plunder. We are surrounded only with a slight barricade, and can only raise a force of thirty men. Have not time, limits, nor the means to erect an effectual and permanent fortification. Nor any means except what casually offers of sending to Sierra Leone for aid. We endeavor to make God our trust. I have no idea but to wait here for His deliverance—or to lay our bones on Cape Mesurado. Dear Sir, pray for us fervently, that if living, God Almighty would be with us.

At home it was remarked with pious satisfaction "by what pure Christian principles this good man, who in a very trying situation discovered so much ability and energy of character, was influenced."

The ship sailed on the day the letter was written, and at dawn the following morning the colony was aware that the second blow was falling. The natives assembled along the muddy margin of the river under the protection of the bank. Their scouts sat insolently and without gesture of concealment, observing every movement within the enclosure. Suddenly the forces rose, divided, and attacked the front and rear sides of the stockade simultaneously. The native forces commenced brisk musket fire as they rushed the enclosure. The iron guns of the colonists were touched off in reply. After three determined attempts, the natives were beaten off. Again the colonists maneuvered the native forces into position which exposed both their front and flank to the iron guns and the brass piece. In such a situation the native attackers were rendered unable to use their own arms effectively.

It was customary for the natives, in close action, to load their muskets, of enormous calibre, with copper and iron slugs to the measure of twelve inches or more. The havoc that a single discharge could inflict would have been enormous if there had been any important numbers of men in the enclosure to hit. Although all the chiefs had cannon, secured through trading on the coast, it required fully a half hour for them to load these weapons. The charging and firing of cannon at a rate of four to six times a minute was regarded as something close to sorcery. In the midst of the fourth assault a curious thing happened. The colonists were battling against exhaustion as well as angered warriors. Scarcely more than fourteen of them were able to continue in action. Huddled in the center of the compound with the women and children and wounded men was Mrs. Mathilda Newport, one of the oldest of the colonists, who had come over on the *Elizabeth*. Taut nerves demanded some vent. She asked permission to light her pipe. This granted, she took the coals and suddenly, in a burst of impatience, dashed them against the powder charge of the field piece. It exploded with a terrific force and the charge of the shot took off the head of one of the Gregre priests who had been brought along by the natives to render the cannon of the colonists harmless. There followed instantly the wildest panic. It was as if the entire force had become crazed with fear. They ceased firing, their mad yells were choked instantly and, on the signal for general retreat, every warrior vanished as if by magic. In the public square of Monrovia is a tall white obelisk erected and inscribed to the memory of Mathilda Newport, and no patriotic address is complete without its tribute to her homely courage and daring.

Although the colonists had again stood their ground successfully on two or three acres of the promised land, their numbers had been further reduced. Gardiner and Crook had received ugly and painful injuries and Tines had been killed. There had been no emigrants or stores from America since the *Strong* arrived in August; it was now December. There was neither medicine nor surgical dressing for the injured, and only three rounds of ammunition. For six weeks they strung themselves along on scant rations of meat and bread. Ashmun set up an ultimate, almost impatient prayer: "Almighty God, if you will not send us aid, at least prepare us, and the society at home, for the heaviest earthly calamity we could dread."

The waning stores, the dread of impending attack, and nerves stretched and torn by constant, wearing vigil, had their effect. One of the night guards at a crackling of the brush by an errant breeze became startled and fired his musket. To exhausted nerves the gnarled black forest had sprung again to menacing life. The thick foliage was the gaudy headdress of war, and in ranks more stiff and solid than those of the first attack the enemy was again upon them. They rushed to their guns and in the panic of their illusions, fired frantically into the still forest. Passing the coast far out at sea was the British colonial schooner *Prince Regent,* under command of Major Laing, the celebrated African traveler, with a prize crew commanded by Midshipman Gordon and eleven seamen of his British Majesty's sloop of war, *Driver.* To the old captain, the sound of cannon from the shore at midnight was an extraordinary occurrence and meant distress. He headed in to the Cape, landed with his seamen, and there beheld a situation which struck him dumb with pity and admiration. Here was a company of less than twenty men, gaunt with hunger, fatigue, and the wounds of two desperate engagements, fighting against the combined strength of nearly every tribe on this part of the coast—for scarcely more than the bitter privilege of dying later from hunger and exhaustion. The British crew responded with generosity and with a courage equal to that which they had admired in the colonists. Captain Laing, acting as a neutral, forced the chiefs to a truce and an agreement to refer all matters of difference with the colony to the governor of Sierra Leone. Midshipman Gordon and his eleven seamen volunteered to remain with the colonists to see that the agreement was kept. The captain of the *Prince Regent* remained four days, placed food in the empty warehouse, stocked the emigrants with ammunition, and then turned again to sea.

Through an inexplicable genius for survival with which only foundlings can be so perversely endowed, the little colony, ragged but reinforced, continued to live. Back in America the soft pink fingers of learned theologians continued to polish off phrases about "the love of Christian brotherhood, the heightening of every constitutional excellence through regeneration, the incorruptible treasures of truth"—and the erudite statesmen rationalized this voluntary crusade which entailed no obligation upon them either morally or financially. Within a month of the departure of the *Prince Regent,* Gordon and eight of the eleven seamen were dead. These sturdy sailors, as humane as they were fearless, were swept into a swift martyrdom almost before their ship reached England.

Seven months after the arrival of the *Strong,* Ashmun looked gloomily upon the graves of fifteen White men, all of whom had landed after him, and, along with the colonists, thanked God for an astonishing and incomprehensible preservation.

7

Promised Land

The return to the fatherland had been, so far, a dull succession of pestilence and warfare, two scourges which had exhausted the half-formed impulses to home building, discouraged the growth of habits of industry, and made the business of living for the colonists a desperate matter of keeping alive. When the fighting ceased and the surrounding tribes again showed friendliness, there was a respite from the constant warfare. The compact for survival dissolved into individual self-interest, and dissension flared over allotments of land and food, the pressure of administrative authority, and the stern requirement of labor. There was sudden awareness that there were free Blacks, ex-slaves, mulattoes, recaptured Africans, Christians, Methodists, Baptists, and unbelievers in the colony, each assuming special rights and privileges. The matrix of the inevitable schisms and caste separations was here exposed. The settlers became unruly, mistaking relief from the dread of native attacks for the long-withheld freedom to which they aspired, They expected this freedom to be as easy for them as they had sketchily observed it to be for their former masters at home. The harassed agent wrote in his diary:

> My predecessors stand accused in their absence of having rested and fattened on the Society's bounty; and consumed funds which were contributed for the comfort of the colonists . . . of permitting the people to furnish their own tables and wardrobes with an unseemly and disproportionate abundance . . . B.T., a man without principle and, as far as his wit lets him go, a mischievous calumniator, has accused agents of selling the charitable contributions to the stores of the Society for African produce and converting the proceeds to their own gain. The fear of the pillory only restrained the fellow's slander. Whoever shall connive at the repetition of it in my presence will discover a degree of malignity equal to his and a degree of cowardice which T. never did; for he, devil-like, dared to belch his scandal into my face.

Few of the settlers wanted to be farmers, for farming was serious, exhausting, and humble labor. Trading was both more profitable and more dignified, but trading on the coast came dangerously close to the notorious slave trading although, in the light of new estimates of the natives, this was a less repulsive idea than it had seemed before. The Grain Coast had again become infested with the slave traders whose market was chiefly in America. Two of these traders in particular, Theodore Canot and Don Petro Blanco, caused the colony immense irritation. They erected their barracoons or slave depots against the Liberian frontier. The conniving of the Spanish traders eventually created an intrigue within the colony against the agent who, acting on a humorless conscience, had begun a vigorous attack on the slave trade. News of this enmity in time reached the Colonization Society in America, some of whose members, already undecided about Ashmun's antislavery activities, thought he was going too far. As a reminder of their authority over his activities, they had held up his pay as well as the promise of future compensation.

On March 31, 1823, when the United States ship *Cyrus* came with emigrants and supplies, the colonists were again near starvation. The newly arrived captain repaired the Martello tower, their chief defense. However, after a sojourn of three weeks his crew was so devastated with disease that he decided to sail, leaving his chief clerk, Richard Seaton, to assist the agent. Seaton, following the ghastly pattern of his predecessors, died within three months.

In the midst of this disorganization, the *Oswego* arrived with sixty-one new colonists and with Dr. Ayers who, after thinking things over from the safe distance of America, had decided to return to the colony. Unsuccessfully he tried his hand at quelling the dissensions; he merely increased the bickering, and finally, disgusted, he went home to stay. The *Cyrus* followed in February 1824 and brought 103 new Virginia emigrants, for the most part listed as free-born.

Ashmun, wearied and ill, went to the Cape Verde Islands to rest. There he brooded over the abortive mission which had been entrusted to him and on the fickle nature of man in general. No longer wanted in the colony, he contemplated returning home in October, where his reception was even more doubtful. Of one thing he was certain, that the colonists were a lazy lot and habituated, as dependents, to charity. But his generosity of mind demanded hopeful speculation:

> At present I am pleasing myself with the supposition that the colonists are mostly on their own resources and are diligently and successfully cultivating the soil. If the older settlers are still receiving rations from the Society, they are ruined and the funds of the Society misapplied. Of the one or the other of these facts I am certain, and fully believe that nothing is accomplished toward the establishment of the colony till the settlers are brought to subsist themselves and very little, indeed, as long as a barrel of beef and flour continues to be imported of *necessity* from America.

Ashmun was entirely right. The colonists had no precedent for hardy self-support and, as might easily be expected in the circumstances, assumed that the Colonization Society and America generally were reaping sufficient rewards from their absence to be willing to support it. They had sent back to the Society so many strong remonstrances that the Board had decided on firm measures to prevent the collapse of the colony and the extinction of the hope of sending more settlers to it. This action the Blacks interpreted as effective protest on their own part. Ralph Randolph Gurley was sent out to make an investigation of affairs. He was as much concerned with studying the grumblings of the Blacks and Ashmun's personal relations with the Society as with the fact of the protest. On his way over he touched at the Cape Verde Islands and met Ashmun, whom he persuaded after a conference to return with him to the colony to introduce him to its affairs.

When Gurley asked the fractious settlers to make their charges, there was that silence so characteristic of rebellions of this nature. In their momentary freedom and self-determination the settlers had consumed all their stores, creating for themselves a serious dilemma. As a consequence, the investigator found them in the mood for receptive peace.

The business of putting the colony on a solid basis was begun: the name of the chief town was changed, with official sanction, from Christopolis to Monrovia; new laws were set up, which the colonists were apparently eager to accept; and new lands were acquired by purchase and treaty at New Cess, Cape Mount, and Junk River in the vicinity of Grand Bassa. Then with a feeling of having settled everything, Gurley returned to America.

Flushed with importance over the attention given their protests, the colonists decided to celebrate something and, accordingly, on July 4, 1825, they commemorated with quaint irony Independence Day in the United States. The Monrovia volunteers served a dinner consisting of the products of Africa as well as liquor in sufficient abundance to bring two of the diners before the justice the following morning. They drank grandiose toasts, compounded of gratitude and wistful speculation:

> To the present president of the United States: the champion of the people's rights, he deserves the people's honor.
>
> To the independence of the American colonies.
>
> To the Colony of Liberia: may the history of the nation which has founded it become its own.
>
> To Africa: may it outstrip its oppressors in the race for liberty, intelligence, and piety.
>
> To heroes and statesmen of American independence. They fought and legislated for the human race—even the people of England are freer and happier for their labors.

To Monrovian independent volunteers: armed for the defense of rights which it is the trade of war to destroy. May they never forget their character!

To General Lafayette in America. We honor him not because we are Americans, but because we are men.

To His Britannic Majesty, the Constitutional King of England.

To the health of the president of the United States, and prosperity to the Colony of Liberia.

The celebration of American independence, however, brought a chill of apprehension about the real significance of their own enterprise. At their very door and within sight of Monrovia, slave traders were openly and arrogantly plying their trade. The colonists knew by sight eight or ten vessels engaged in the traffic, and at the very moment they were aware that there were contracts for 800 slaves to be furnished within four months from an area scarcely eight miles from the Cape. Four hundred of those slaves were destined for America! From the promontory just a few days before, they had seen a French slaver with twenty-six slaves in irons upset and capsize—twenty of the miserable creatures were drowned. Just fourteen days after their celebration of American independence, the purchase price of 200 slaves, sent from America, was brought to their very door.

Despite the Society's problem of suppressing the trade, Ashmun decided to attack the slave factories by force. There were many traders hanging about the coast, but Canot and Blanco, in addition to being a constant nuisance, gave a touch of glamour to the whole business. While maintaining an outward aspect of courtliness and intelligence, they were yet the most efficient slave merchants on the coast.

The first of these, whose life story was told by Brantz Mayer in 1928 under the title *Adventures of an African Slaver*, was a flashing personality. Born in Florence in 1803, he early dedicated himself to a life of adventure. His father had been captain and paymaster in Napoleon's army and his mother a Piedmontese who was left a widow with six children. That his family was one of some prominence is borne out in the fact that through them he early met Lord Byron. At sixteen he was apprenticed to the *Galatin*, an American ship trading in the East Indies. He soon rose to the rank of mate on this ship and later was transferred to a British vessel. Some time afterward he was shipwrecked and captured by pirates one of whom, pretending a relationship, saved his life. Through this strange friend's advice, he engaged in a slave ship, the *Aerostatica*, bound for River Pongo on the West Coast of Africa. A mutiny broke out en route and Canot, after the captain had failed, quelled it by shooting five of the mutineers.

At River Pongo he struck up an acquaintance with the mulatto trader Mongo Ormond, son of a prosperous Liverpool merchant and a native.

Ormond inherited most of his father's wealth and became quite a figure in Senegambia; Canot got a job as his bookkeeper. Eventually the two quarreled and Canot set up as a slaver on his own account in partnership with an Englishman named Edward Joseph. The rigid hand of the English and the French eventually dislodged them. Ormond died and Joseph fled, but Canot was imprisoned by the French at Brest. He escaped and, still lured by the profits of the business, came again to Sierra Leone and later found his way to the Gallinhas country, where he entered into partnership with Don Petro Blanco. This glamorous gentleman was a master organizer, and Canot was given charge of the depot at New Cess near Grand Bassa on the Liberian coast.

Wealthy, polished, and with an excellent education, Blanco was a gentleman slaver if ever there was one. His barracoons were spacious and clean, and he surrounded himself with all the luxuries which could be brought from Europe. His credit was good at any bank in Europe or America and, although he was engaged in a dirty business, he enjoyed it. Eventually he retired to the quiet seclusion of an Italian villa, with a fortune estimated at $1 million, to devote himself to philosophy and ease. The two men had been an excellent team. They were the courtly traffickers in men, calling their depots "chapels of ease," entertaining lavishly, organizing games and dances for the recreation of their slave property and constructing, by paid labor, depots famed along the coast.

Canot, in his story, is firm in his assertions of a clean, gentlemanly life, although in the archives of the Liberian Department of State there are transcripts of the agents' protests. One of these refers to the captain's social habits:

> Some two years since, or more, when Canot was a frequent visitor, I might almost say a resident of this place, he formed an intimacy with a young woman here and finally took her away with him as a mistress; she has since kept up a secret intercourse with her family, and the persons alluded to, whom Herbert carried down to New Cestos, were two of her sisters, a brother and a waiting maid, who are to live with her, I have it, in the munificence of her paramour. But if they ever come within reach of my authority, they will get a practical proof that the way of the transgressor is hard.

In April 1826 the Columbian war vessel *Jacinto* arrived at Monrovia with orders to cooperate with the United States government agent Dr. Peace and Mr. Ashmun. With thirty-two volunteers they sailed for Trade Town where the Spanish traders were then in full force. They were joined by the *Indian Chief* and the *Vencedor* and the three united for attack. The surf was boisterous, breaking heavily over the notorious bar, and the passage to the shore was only eight yards wide. They took barges, and these soon filled with water within gunshot range of the Spanish traders. The flagboat carrying Ashmun was upset on the rocks, but despite injuries they sent the natives and the Spaniards to the forest and recaptured eighty slaves who were being held for shipment. The victory was inconclusive, however, and while leaving, they fired on the town as an afterthought. Flames spread to the ammunition stores and exploded 250 casks of gunpowder. The detonation shook the earth and seemed in its violence to hold the vast swell of the waves rigid and motionless. Trade Town was wiped out completely, but within three months it had been rebuilt and sufficiently fortified to resist any similar attack.

Illness, the recent injury, overwork, and worry bore down and Ashmun collapsed. He addressed a dismal farewell to the colonists, who now were beginning to feel a real affection for him, and returned, broken, to the United States, where he died about four months later. The colony was left in charge of the "Reverend Doctor" Lott Carey, a rough-handed and now seasoned pioneer. He was neither a trained minister nor a doctor, but nevertheless performed both roles with distinction.

Carey had been born a slave in Virginia and learned to read by one of the numerous devices employed by slaves. At twenty-four he was brought to Richmond and hired out as a laborer in the old Shockoe tobacco warehouse where his enormous strength and agility soon made him valuable. By saving the bonuses over pay from his master for his services, he eventually accumulated $850 with which he purchased himself and two sons.

Carey was from the first what Blacks like to call a "race man." With the news of colonization, he quit his job and prepared to go. "I am an African," he answered his brother ministers who questioned his folly in giving up a good job, "and in this country, however meritorious my conduct and respectable my character, I cannot receive the credit due to either. I wish to go to a country where I shall be estimated by my merits and not by my complexion, and I feel bound to labor for my suffering race."

When left in charge of the colony, he proved himself capable of dealing fairly with the natives and of promoting sanely the interests of the settlers. But he was constantly harassed by the slave traders, and before long he sensed the animosity of the natives rising again. First, he had to drive away three suspicious Spanish ships prowling around the harbor. Then, one of the colony's most desirable warehouses was robbed by natives. Carey's demands for satisfaction were answered with cold sneers. Later, a slave trader landed a cargo in one of the storehouses. A letter of remonstrance from Carey to the trader was intercepted by natives and destroyed. Christian patience was exhausted and Carey now called out the militia with the idea of making a show of force. On the evening of November 8, while he and a group of colonists were making cartridges by candlelight in the old agency house, a puff of wind upset the candle and the flame ignited some loose powder. The explosion which followed killed Carey and seven others, leaving the colony again without a leader.

When Richard Randall, the newly appointed agent, came in December 1828, he found that the colony had nearly wrecked itself in preparations against the new native disorders. He viewed this chaos and died, just four months after arriving. Dr. Mecklin succeeded him and his incumbency, although for the most part sustained in ill health, coincided with the final labor pains of the little republic.

Old King Bromley, a chief of the Deys, whose jurisdiction covered all the country on the right bank of the St. Paul River, had reaped generous profits from the slave trade by selling captives to dealers who were recruiting for American and British markets. Several of his slaves, as they were about to be sold to the Spaniards, escaped and took refuge in the colony of recaptured Africans. The chief's son, Kai Pa, just cutting his war teeth, came down to the colony and demanded them. Mecklin parried for a while and finally announced that he would protect them until old King Bromley himself came down to claim them. Back in Bromley's town, the old chief lay sick of a painful and loathsome disease, but he still sputtered defiance. He died before he could meet the colonists' challenge, and Kai Pa, young, impetuous, and strong, succeeded him. He carried on his father's hatred and determined upon a brilliant and final extermination of the interlopers in Africa. He planned an alliance with the Golas, a fierce, cannibalistic neighboring tribe. Their common hatred of the Americans accomplished a union which no other exigency in their history had been able to bring about.

King Willy's town, standing in the path to the deep Dey country, was selected as their stronghold; it was built into a fortress, walled about securely with thick logs. The Dey-Gola alliance became a dread union of ferocity, greed, and hatred. When the natives' plans were finally completed, they sent an arrogant challenge to the colonists that, if the Americans did not promptly meet them in the field, their towns of Caldwell and Millsburg would be attacked. To add to the provocation, they captured and imprisoned every colonist they could lay hands on. One of these, escaping, dragged himself to the palisade, slashed and torn by spears and knives, and gave the first real intelligence of the impending hostilities. Aroused again to the keen inhospitality of their neighbors, the colonists sent a messenger to King Willy's town with a note demanding the release of the captives. Kai Pa tore up the letter and flung the pieces in the messenger's face. With studied insolence he explained to the messenger that he was allowing him to return only because he wanted him to be the bearer of more bad news to the colony. On the following morning Kai Pa and his men appeared in an open field opposite Caldwell, fired their muskets, blew their war horns, and assumed arrogant postures, inviting the colonists to combat.

Mecklin was no soldier, Carey was dead, and there were still too few men to risk war recklessly again. A council of the older settlers was called. They had been insulted and the prestige of White men had been made ridiculous. But there was no hot-headed volunteering to avenge the insult, even though it seemed to involve the lives of the puny settlements of Caldwell and Millsburg. These colonists had been insulted before by experts, and Kai Pa could have the satisfaction of jangling his weapons and calling them names without disturbing their honor.

Their first stratagem was a compromise which provided a battle with the minimum of risk to themselves. They sent out a detachment of recaptured Africans, blandly instructing them to seize all the chiefs who had been guilty of plotting against them. The recaptured Africans, numbering 100 or more, headed in a straight line for King Willy's town and found to their dismay a large force awaiting them, taut for combat. Convulsed with fright, they retreated so promptly and so completely that only one man was lost.

Three days later the colonists concluded that it was necessary to fight their own battles and reluctantly began their expedition. It was a dreary and fatiguing march, hampered by the rains, fallen trees, and the thick growth of tropical vegetation which had to be cut through to permit the passage of their invaluable field piece. They advanced about ten miles in seven hours. As the colonists approached, Kai Pa, thinking better of the matter, led his men into the fortress. Elijah Johnson, captain of infantry, had been given command of the recaptured Africans, after they had been collected from the surrounding country. Backed by the settlers, Johnson led them in a more determined charge on the barricade.

It was a cleverly built, well-located fortress, but this was a new method of warfare for Kai Pa's men. At that first assault on their stronghold, they poked their muskets through the loopholes in the barricade and fired without aim completely over the heads of the attacking colonists. Such inexpertness emboldened the colonists and brought a thrill of military achievement. A charge of the field piece made an opening which Johnson's men enlarged. They stood aside and the attacking settlers, sensing an easy victory, rushed into the fortified town and suddenly found themselves crowded densely into a space of about twenty yards and looking squarely into the mouth of Kai Pa's three-pounder. But a stroke of sublime good fortune emerged for them, and so unplanned that no one knows who was responsible. At that very instant a musket charge took off a part of the shoulder of Kai Pa as he was in the act of applying a match to his cannon. He reeled backward with a scream of rage, and the colonists sheepishly but fervently thanked God for another deliverance. They examined the machine loaded almost to the muzzle with iron bolts and pot metal from which few of them would have escaped.

Worn down by the long march and the shock of their miraculous escape, they planned to stay in the captured town that night. As they listlessly threw off their equipment and began to relax, they discovered the town was on fire. They turned back to King Bromley's town only to find that the recaptured Africans, never right even by mistake, had set fire to the windward houses and the flames were rapidly spreading. And so they dragged themselves to their boats and returned to Caldwell to pass what was left of the night. Treaties later bound the chiefs to friendly relations once more.

The alliance of the Deys and the Golas dissolved under the defeat by the colonists, and, after the pattern of Africa, these two tribes resumed their immemorial sport of killing one another. The Golas, being stronger and more ferocious, so wore down the Deys in a two-year war that the pitiful remnant of this once proud people, who had been the first to oppose the colonists, sought refuge with the settlers. The bloody Gatumba one day came boldly into the colony and murdered four of his former enemies as they worked on the colonists' farms; twelve more he carried away into slavery. The governor of the colony sent a letter to Gatumba, asking for an explanation and a palaver. Gatumba sent an insulting reply and followed it · up with a savage attack on another settlement. All the colonists of this little settlement came together in the house of missionary Brown and withstood the attack until their ammunition was nearly exhausted. Suddenly Gotorah, a giant Gola known for his feats of cannibalism, with insolent confidence stalked out from the mass of native warriors into the open within a foot of the house. A musket packed to the muzzle with scrapiron and ball shot was fired full into his face, and he collapsed, a mangled mass of blood and torn flesh. The battle was over. A further attempt at reprisal was so completely frustrated by the colonists that Gatumba gave up his ambitions and came to terms.

8

The Nascent State

The first reaction of American free Blacks to colonization had been one of protest and defiance. But King Cotton had felt his strength by 1830 and thereafter was by no means gentle with their chimeric aspirations. Blocked off completely in the place of their birth, a few Blacks with education embraced the idea of colonization with something of the fatalistic resignation with which one leaps from a burning building. One of them was John B. Russworm, the first Black to receive a degree from an American college. After leaving Bowdoin, he had, in 1827, established *Freedom's Journal,* the first Black newspaper published in the United States. While editor of this paper, he had begun a second journal called *The Rights of All,* through which he gave expression to the wrongs of slavery and to the acute indignities to which sensitive Blacks were systematically subjected in America. He arrived in Liberia in 1830 and established its first press, the *Liberia Record.* Russworm, as ambitious as he was scholarly, saw his best chances in the colony of Maryland, set up independently by the Maryland Colonization Society under a White man, James Hall. Taking residence in Maryland, he became its second governor.

Meetings of Blacks, always debating the issues of colonization, fanned sentiment in the United States. Down in Charleston, South Carolina, there were fiery speeches which stirred hundreds of families to emigration. Julius Eden raised his voice in eloquent new praise of the fatherland: "The inhabitants," he cried, "invite us to come and possess it and to assist them to infuse into the natives notions of pure morality and to erect temples dedicated to the worship of Jehovah, where the injured Sons of Africa may enter and with united voices raise melodious songs of praise to Heaven's Eternal King." He had never been to Africa, of course, nor, apparently, been in close touch with the harassed colonists who were addressing Heaven's Eternal King in their own behalf. Charles Hendry, another speaker, a bit more cautious, said: "Africa, the land of our fathers, although surrounded with clouds of darkness, seems to me to be extending her arms toward us as her only hope of relief, and calling on us loudly for help, saying 'I struggle for light and liberty, and call upon you by the *name* of your ancestors to come to my *help* and your rightful possession. Tarry thou not, but come over and dispel the darkness from your benighted land. . . . Come and enforce the empire of reason, truth, and Christianity over our benighted minds!'" He also was very largely abandoning himself to oratory, for no list of emigrants reveals his name.

Pharaoh Moses, an ex-slave who retained memories of Africa, after hearing these grand expressions observed with some emotion, "If you, who are natives of this country, and have never seen Africa, speak so highly of her, what must I say who have trod the soil—the soil which gave me birth, and where yet live my relations and kindred, from whom by the hand of violence I was torn away and deprived of freedom, which thanks be to God I have again obtained." Here Moses was so much overcome by his emotions that he was obliged to take his seat. It would have been interesting to know what was passing in Moses' mind, for at that moment the little settlement which was the object of this eloquent sentiment was making a determined but puny stand against slave traders who were making fresh captures for the American market. Parliamentary documents reveal that within four years after 1840 these traders had brought 267,587 slaves from the African coast into America. The old Gaboon missionary J.L. Wilson was right in observing to Lord Palmerston that if they waited for colonization to stop the trade, "the world will have grown old enough for new geological strata to have formed over the surface of rocks of our day."

An emboldened philanthropy could now exclaim: "Let the regenerated African rise to empire; nay, let genius flourish and philosophy shed its mild beams to enlighten and instruct the posterity of Ham, returning 'redeemed and disenthralled' from their long captivity in the New World. But, Sir, be all these benefits enjoyed by the African race under the shame of their native palms. Let the Atlantic billow heave its high and everlasting barrier between their country and ours."

It came to be a philanthropic fad in America for branch organizations of the American Colonization Society to establish independent settlements in Liberia. Edina, a settlement on the north side of the St. Johns River, was named for Edinburgh, Scotland. Most of the funds for one shipment of settlers had come from philanthropic residents of that country. The Pennsylvania Young Men's Colonization Society, made up largely of Quakers, sent out a group of settlers under a charter which echoed the religious and ethical convictions of the Society of Friends. They foreswore wars and banned trading as a source of income. Their Black colonists were solemnly pledged to "temperance and sobriety," and to nonresistance as a principle of life. In 1835, just as soon as their pledges and abstinences were made known to their native neighbors, chiefs Tom Harris and Peter, the whole colony, consisting of some twenty or more men, women, and children, was massacred. Only the White agent, Hankinson, and his wife were saved by the help of some friendly Krus who smuggled them to Monrovia.

Thomas H. Buchanan, cousin of a president of the United States, was sent out by the New York and Pennsylvania societies at the head of a group which settled at Bassa Cove. The governor of this colony was I.F.C. Finley, a son of the Reverend Robert Finley who organized the American Colonization Society. In September 1838 he left Sinoe for Monrovia on a brief visit for his health and to attend to some business matters, carrying a considerable sum of money. At Bassa Cove, where he stopped to rest, he was murdered and robbed. Slave traders were clearly the instigators of this murder and rumor suggested that Canot himself was involved. In his reminiscenses, Canot refers to the incident but thought the victim was the governor of Sierra Leone, whose name was also Finley.

With the exception of the obstreperous colony of Maryland, all the settlements united for convenience of administration and for safety under Governor Buchanan. The slave traders, reinforced and supercilious, took up most of his time. They plied their trade brazenly and treated the protests of the colony as one treats the fantasies of children "playing house." This was certain to damage the colony's prestige with the natives. Humiliated, Buchanan decided to move in force against Trade Town. Elijah Johnson was again placed in charge of a land force while the agent and his men proceeded down the coast in two chartered steamers. Storms delayed them until Johnson had arrived at Trade Town by land. As Buchanan and his force approached through the surf, they were mistaken by Johnson for slave traders and a suicidal engagement with each other was narrowly avoided. Finally they concentrated on Trade Town. Many shots were fired, and though no serious damage was done, the traders concluded that they were in earnest and surrendered most of their slaves. There being nothing else to contend for momentarily, the colonists went home.

It was a reflection of the split conscience of the civilized nations of Europe that they prosecuted the slave trade as actively as they persecuted it. British and American slave traders alternated freely in the ports with naval officers and presented a prototype of our modern rumrunners. Buchanan wrote: "Whilst making various complaints against English traders, I cannot forbear placing in distinguished contrast the honorable and gentlemanly conduct of the naval officers of that nation. They invariably manifest a warm interest in the property of the colony and often lay me under their obligations by their kind offers of service." The newly designed Stars and Stripes of the free government of the United States floated over slave ships which openly maintained their trade on the coast, and neither England nor any other nation could search these American vessels. Not until 1842 would the United States take any formal action to stop the traffic. In that dark and bitter stretch between 1820 and 1842, only the casual help of the British cruisers curbed the wild growth of slave depots in the Bassa and Cape Mount sections of the little republic.

The zeal of Great Britain to suppress the trade, despite its fortunate humanitarian quality, was nevertheless highly colored with economic considerations. For sixty years palm oil had been recognized as valuable; the volume of imports to Liverpool had been increasing enormously and Britain was an almost exclusive consumer. The trade challenged the slave traffic in value and while interest declined in the old trade, it increased in the new, for Liberian palm oil was the most desirable on the coast. Traders from the adjoining colony of Sierra Leone lost their sentiment for struggling Black settlers and their new bonanza. They pushed over into this territory and attempted to bring the British flag with them. So openly contemptuous of the pretenses of the civilized Blacks did they become and so thoroughly did they harass them that the Blacks grew suspicious, not only of Britain but of the British Anti-Slavery Society itself. Buchanan was eventually forced to send an agent to England to make an appeal for more ethical conduct.

The all-important requirement of the settlers was an interest in agriculture, which they distinctly lacked. The land was rich, needing only to be tilled. The upland soil of two qualities permitted wet season crops, but the lowlands would yield practically any crop planted. Moreover, each variety of soil lent itself advantageously to special crops. Clearing had to come first, however, and this meant labor. Rice and corn, heavily demanded by traders and natives, grew easily. Cassava and yams could be cheaply produced and were an invaluable resource. Half an acre of cotton could provide clothing for an entire family. The utility of the coffee plant, of which the country provided a unique variety, was early discovered. Indigo was profitable and could be cropped at least eight times a year. Ginger, aloes, arrowroot, and paper were demanded for export. Bananas, oranges, limes, guava, sugarcane, pineapple, pumpkins, sweet potatoes, and almost any vegetable familiar to America could be cultivated.

The presence of the native population offered temptations to those indulgences which the colonists had both observed and experienced as a part of the only culture they knew. Some 30,000 or more natives with their cheap labor had come under the protection of the colony. The system of domestic service which quickly took root was the beginning of a caste system among the Blacks, following faithfully the American pattern. The native practice of pawning was adopted as an easy and inexpensive source of fixed labor, at first under the euphemistic term "apprenticeship."

Despite the prohibitions of slavery and trade in slaves in the various colonial constitutions, the colonists committed this offense and drew a hazy line between slavery and pawning. Roberts had complained to the

Society as early as 1831 that certain colonists were surreptitiously selling slaves to the Spaniards at the Gallinhas and at Cape Mount, and Mecklin was obliged to offer the curious explanation that they had not been stopped because of "want of power to inflict a punishment suited to the magnitude of the offense." Dr. Hodgkin wrote to Elliot Cresson in the 1840s about the pawning practice. "These pawns," he said, "are as much slaves as their sable prototypes in the parent states of America," and he added that almost all the labor was derived from a system of domestic slavery. By 1848 the caste lines were fairly well fixed and rationalizations satisfactory. The natives were looked down upon as inferiors. "If they are treated better," explained a Liberian gentleman, "they would be insolent and saucy and rise and cut our throats." Intermarriages between natives and colonists, through this prejudice, were taboo and only two or three a year occurred.

A preacher of the colony, the Reverend C.M. Waring, was the first to venture his own labor and funds in a new crop which, however, miscarried, completely through ignorance of the planting seasons. This provided an excuse for many who were trying to avoid this occupation. However, Waring tried again and got results. A colony of about sixty families of country farmers from North Carolina settling along the St. Paul made a successful venture and eventually became self-supporting. For the most part however, the colonists avoided agriculture with determined stubbornness, preferring trade. At the beginning of 1843, with a population of 912, there were only 104 acres owned and in cultivation in Monrovia; for the entire colony with a population of 2,390 there were only 3,432 acres in cultivation. The colonists owned eleven vessels with an aggregate tonnage of 198, and during the year 1843 they did a commission business amounting to $50,500. When Francis Devary, one of the earliest and most intelligent of the colonists, visited the United States in 1830, he told a committee of Congress that Waring had sold goods during the year in the amount of $70,000 and that he himself had many slaves amounting to some $25,000. Coffee growing was the chief interest of the farmers and they had planted some 21,000 trees, which grew in abundance in the high rocky ground. As for rice, so much in demand in France, there were only 52 acres under cultivation, and of sugarcane only 54. The combined value of all the farms was less than $12,000.

The first twenty years of colonization removed 4,456 Blacks to Africa. Nearly half of them (2,198) died before the first count, and sixty-two of these in the fearful muck of Sherbro and Sierra Leone. Somehow 108 got back to the United States, 197 went to Sierra Leone, 147 to Cape Palmas, the new Maryland colony, and 68 disappeared on foreign vessels without giving their destination. The cost of this great experiment so far was $589,012.31.

The Colonization Society, through some curious interpretation of its project, seemed to expect its wards to pay back the cost of transference. And naturally they would be watchful of the kind, quality and quantity of produce sent back to America in the returning emigrant vessels. Buchanan was sternly rebuked for the pitiful and slovenly character of his agricultural exhibits. In turn, he could only make biting remarks to the colonists about self-respect and self-support. Such observations always provoked grumbling among the colonists, and their smoldering indignation offered a most fitting setting for the intrigues of the Reverend John Seyes of the Methodist Episcopal Church, a new agent. Misguided and opinionated, he succeeded in dividing the colony completely over an issue of dutiable goods which was none of his concern. Worn down by the intrigues from within and the even more formidable annoyances from without, his spirits fell. Crossing the notorious bar at Marshall one day, he fell into the water. Fever followed, and he died in ten days. Seyes was the last of the White administrators in Liberia.

Joseph Jenkins Roberts, an octoroon and the vice-governor, succeeded Seyes. His sharp, chiseled features, brown hair, blonde mustache, and gray eyes marked him as Black largely by courtesy. He had a good mind and a hard fist and, although conscious of the sensitiveness of an overwhelming majority of Blacks from America, he commanded a position of considerable respect and confidence in the colony. A general of the Liberian force when the colonists had waged its war against Gatumba, his prowess in arms made him a logical successor to Buchanan. From the point of the ascension of a Black to full and permanent command in the colony, the Society's interest began to wane.

Roberts paid a visit to the United States to give a visible assurance of his ability to carry on the experiment and to try to obtain more emigrants. Following this trip, an American squadron visited the West Coast but helped him very little in the troubles now hanging perilously over his head. He soon ran afoul of the French over possession of his Cape Mount, Bassa, Butu, and Garraway sections. These together comprised a large part of Liberia. Under Louis Philippe the French had begun to dream of an empire in Africa. So far their holdings on the West Coast were limited to the course of the Senegal River. As a nation France had been interested in suppressing the slave trade as an echo of its earlier zeal for liberty, equality, and fraternity. But as with England, this was probably not all. The French were intensely jealous of the British, who were reaping a measure of success from the West Coast colonial ventures in palm oil, and it seemed as unnecessary as it was unseemly for Britain to be the sole beneficiary of the coast.

From the beginning of Roberts' administration, the French had begun to lay hands on all territory not pinned down with guns south of Gambia and above Sierra Leone. These new possessions became the first vital links in the vast chain which eventually gave France an area in Africa of nearly 1.5 million square miles (excluding the first mandated territories) and dominion over 12 million natives. It was easy to buy the country over again from the wily chiefs who had already sold it to the Liberians. At Garraway, between Monrovia and Cape Palmas, the French flag was actually raised by royal authority. The titles were so vague, however, that when Roberts protested, they permitted the matter to rest for fifty years before reviving it. By that time, of course, Roberts was dead, the chiefs and their marks long gone, and the scraps of paper only as valuable as superior guns could make them.

The colony needed money. With the French issue temporarily settled, the new governor together with the scholarly Russworm, now governor of Maryland, worked out a uniform 6 percent ad valorem duty schedule on all imports. He received his first economic shock, however, when the foreign vessels refused to pay the duty. If Blacks were ever going to run their own colonies, this was a poor beginning. Remembering his military prowess he decided upon measures of force. When the English trading boat *Little Ben* refused to pay, he seized it. Retaliation came swiftly in the seizure of the *John Seyes*, belonging to Benson, a Liberian trader; it was actually sold for £2,000. There was nothing else to be done now, for the colony could not fight Great Britain. Helplessly, Russworm appealed to the United States government. An extravagantly modest note was sent to Great Britain, which merely asked in substance what Roberts was talking about. An answer came which was neither modest nor gentle. Great Britain replied that it could not recognize the sovereign powers of Liberia, which it regarded as a mere commercial experiment of a philanthropic society. The Society was stunned and the government felt itself getting embarrassingly into hot water. Neither could do anything about the situation; it was a crisis which came violently and unexpectedly out of space. Already weakening, the Society resolved in 1846 that it was more expedient for the Liberian people to take the management of their affairs into their own hands. The Society then severed its relations with the colony.

The following year the Liberians called a constitutional convention, made a Declaration of Independence on July 26, designed a flag, and adopted the Constitution of the Liberian Republic, patterned closely after the only model they knew, the American government. There is one important variation from the classic phraseology of the American Declaration of Independence:

We, the people of the Republic of Liberia, were originally the inhabitants of the United States of North America.

In some parts of that country, we were debarred by law from all the rights and privileges of men—in other parts, public sentiments, more powerful than law, forced us down.

We were everywhere shut out from all civil office.

We were excluded from all participation in the government.

We were taxed without our consent.

We were compelled to contribute to the resources of a country which gave us no protection.

We were made a separate and distinct class, and against us every avenue to improvement was effectually closed. Strangers from all lands of a color different from ours were preferred before us.

We uttered complaints, but they were unattended to, or met only by alleging the peculiar institution of the country.

All hope of a favorable change in our country was thus wholly extinguished in our bosom, and we looked with anxiety abroad for some asylum from the deep degradation.

PART II

THE WATERS OF MARAH

And when they came to Marah, they could not drink of the waters of Marah, for they were bitter.

—*Exodus*

9

Nationalism

An anomaly of government, unique in the history of modern times, faced the founders of the new republic of Liberia. The logic of political egalitarianism, borrowed from America, demanded a government founded upon the principle of equal representation for all citizens. The constitution, patterned faithfully after that of the United States, provided for a president elected by popular vote and three departments of government: legislative, consisting of a Senate and a House of Representatives; executive; and judiciary, with the familiar secretaries of state, war, Navy, treasury, an attorney general, judges of courts, sheriffs, coroners, marshalls, justices of the peace, and a military organization. There was likewise a provision for a decennial census which, incidentally, has not yet been initiated. Not only the constitution, but the color and symbolism of the flag were almost directly copied from America, as America copied from England, and England in turn from the Dutch. The abstract rights of individuals were conceded with the theorem that "all men are created free and equal"; yet the aborigines were disregarded just as the Americans' slaves had been disregarded. Slavery was forever prohibited in the commonwealth, despite the virtual institutionalization of the system of domestic servitude and pawning.

There were, however, notable exceptions to the American pattern. The state was conceived as a haven for oppressed Blacks. Accordingly, only Blacks were permitted citizenship and only citizens could own property. There was a confusing vagueness about the citizenship of the aborigines from the beginning, a vagueness which has continued. Elections were held every two years, throwing the country into regularly timed political convulsions. Although intended to insure a fluid democracy, this provision contributed as much as any other force to the universal fixation of interest in politics. It tended, inevitably, to turn the office of president into an electioneering post and to discourage inauguration of sound measures of public value. There was no closed season on the assaults upon administrative policy by scores of hopeful aspirants, and this led to systematic and continuous counterparty vilifications. The power of the president to dismiss government employees indiscriminately and with pleasure helped create a "spoils" system with ruinous results.

The territories purchased from the natives and under the control of the colonists at the time of the adoption of the constitution extended about 600 miles in a forty-mile-wide coastal strip. Although the colonists assumed jurisdiction over larger areas farther in the interior, the constitution actually controlled only the coastal strip and, for that matter, only the towns within the strip. No relationship between the aboriginal kingdoms and the colonies was defined or even suggested in the rules of the government. It was evident that a dual control was imperative for the dual cultures, but the working out of this was left to fate, and fate did a bad job.

The constitution was a quickly drawn instrument, conceived more in the minds of American philanthropists than in the minds of the colonists who knew little of political science and less of the actual method of sovereign state functioning. As a matter of fact, the constitution was framed by Professor Greenleaf of Harvard, who had never been to Africa, and it was forwarded to Liberia by the American Colonization Society. The borrowed pronouncement that "governments derive their just powers from the consent of the governed" could no more have conviction for them than for the American state which was governing its million voteless and voiceless slaves. The logic of the new environment and responsibility demanded a sort of class rule, in fact, which belied all of the democratic principles by which the Liberians expected to govern themselves. The only patterns of government in Africa dealing with the aboriginal population were colonial governments, and these made no pretense of democratic principles.

There was thus at the outset the question of the feasibility of a republican form of government in Africa, unless it restricted the free and equal doctrine to the colony itself. No less important was the question of the full comprehension by the colonists of these principles of government which they had so readily adopted. It was inevitable that older political principles should begin to operate. Economic classes depend upon the character and distribution of property, and governments tend to shape themselves according to the classes formed. In America, there was among the White population a closer approximation to the democratic ideal than was possible in England. There was no recognized clergy or aristocracy or even pronounced peasantry. Americans could with some grace espouse the principle of equality in breaking away from the rule of King George III.

The only contact with this principle on the part of the founders of the Liberian state had been in its very exceptions, namely the practical and conceptual relationship of the republic to its slaves. The ex-slaves had learned all the prejudices and passions of their masters and acquired their aspirations and their power. This institutional pattern they carried over as faithfully as they had carried over, undigested, the American Constitution. They found themselves suddenly with all the responsibilities of men without having passed through the careful discipline of political childhood. Even the United States had a hundred and fifty years of colonial discipline; theirs had been but twenty-five years of tutelage. Independence had in no sense been self-imposed. They were cut loose. Thus, it was to be expected, as Blyden himself observed, that in their impatience with the curbs of arbitrary will, in their vacillating fancies and blindly selfish impulses, they should exhibit the traits of spoiled children.

The population divided itself promptly into four classes: the officials, including the trader class; the common people; the aborigines; and the recaptured Africans. Here was, again, a challenge to the fundamental principle of republican government. It was inevitable that the propertied classes should secure the greater share of representation and eventually relegate to a vague political oblivion the voiceless native majority. Moreover, there was an acute color division within the Amero-Liberians which expressed itself in countless conflicts. The mulattoes had been taught to believe that exposure to the climate had a more deleterious effect upon them than upon the Blacks; and that being in part White, they were thus much nearer the qualification for officialdom. They insisted that because of an inherent qualification the Blacks should devote themselvs to agriculture and permit mulattoes to run the government. The blue vein society of Charleston, South Carolina, appeared accentuated in this remote setting, and a bold effort was made to restrict marriages of mullattoes to mullattoes, as already the American Blacks were forbidding intermarriage with natives. It was out of this mulatto "upper class" that the first Republican Party was formed.

Shortly after the assumption of African statehood, the United States government sent, among the recaptured Africans, 1,639 Congos to Monrovia, providing by congressional enactment $150 for the annual support of each Congo. It was expected that these people would be educated by the colonists and turned into useful citizens of the republic. But the social as well as economic patterns had already been set. The recaptured Africans were divided among the Amero-Liberians as wards, and the money was used by them for their own ends. This wardship easily degenerated into domestic servitude, and the plans for the education of the Congos were completely ignored.

The beginnings of party division could be observed in the sharp class divisions. The Republicans, who began with the mulatto class, later rationalized their platform into a liberal policy toward foreigners, encouraging Black immigration with a view to citizenship and also admission of other foreigners to the full advantage of the country. The Whigs evolved a policy of race and color-conscious insularity and exclusion, with the ultimate view of development a truly Black state in Africa. This latter policy, which became dominant with the eventual elimination of the Republican Party, has appeared under such significant modifications as "Old Whigs," "Whigs," and "True Whigs." With the steady rise of the Blacks there finally remained in the field only one party, the True Whigs, until the emergence of the People's Party (under T.J.R. Faulkner), which violently introduced the rights of the aborigines. The colonists accepted for their legal system the common law of England and an arbitrary combination of British and American legal decisions.

From such a beginning it was difficult to evolve a self-conscious nationality. A first result could be observed in the curious individualization of the citizens, an unconscious divorce of ethics from politics and heedless programs of specious advantage which tended to ignore the state in the zeal to promote the interests of the individuals of a class. Nor was it entirely a class-conscious program; rather, there evolved defensively an official class, without mutual aims or sympathies, and unified almost wholly on the basis of necessary mutual protection.

The first struggle of the state was for recognition as a member of the family of nations. The British government that had precipitated the sudden independence was the first to give recognition. To insure this, Roberts, the first president, made a tour of Europe. Viscount Palmerston and the Right Honorable Henry Labouchere signed the treaty for the British government. Queen Victoria received Roberts and the British government gave him a vessel, *The Lark*, for coastal transportation, and a sloop of four guns, *The Quail*, to assist him in patrolling his coast. He proceeded to France and then to Belgium, where he was kindly received. Back in England he was dined by the Chevalier de Bunsen, ambassador of Prussia. At the dinner he complained to the Bishop of London, one of the guests, about the slavers at the Gallinhas. The Bishop and Lord Ashley raised money from British philanthropists, and Roberts concluded treaties with the natives of the country, purchased the slaving area, and eventually succeeded in suppressing the trade.

The greatest difficulty was recognition by the stepmother country, America. The controversy over slavery and the rights of Blacks was too bitter to permit discussion of the question. There was the gross anomaly of recognizing the national equality of a race which, by nature and policy, was considered as ineligible for status of political equality in America. Henry Clay favored, but Congress continually put up objections. At the opening of the 37th Congress in 1861, President Lincoln recommended it, although Garrison thought his representations "feeble and rambling."

One of the hidden stumbling blocks to recognition came out when, in commenting upon Charles Sumner's bill to appoint diplomatic representatives to both Haiti and Liberia, Davis of Kentucky declared, "If, after such a measure should take effect, the Republic of Haiti and the Republic of Liberia were to send their ministers plenipotentiary or their *charge d'affaires* to our government, they would have to be received by the President and all the functionaries of the government upon the same terms of equality with such representatives from the other powers. If a full-blooded Black were sent in that capacity from either of the two countries, by the laws of nations, he could demand that he be received precisely on the same terms of equality with the White representatives from the powers on the earth composed of White people."

Saulsbury of Maryland made the objection even more pointed. "How fine it will look," he exclaimed, "after emancipating the slaves in this district, to welcome here at the White House an African, full-blooded, all gilded and belaced, dressed in court style, with wig and sword and tights and shoebuckles and ribbons and spangles and many other adornments which African vanity will suggest . . . If this bill should pass the Houses of Congress and become a law, I predict that in twelve months some Black will walk upon the floor of the Senate and carry his family into that which is apart for foreign ministers. If that is agreeable to the taste and feelings of the people of this country, it is not to mine."

It was not until 1864, over fifteen years after Liberian independence, that recognition was given. Significantly, Haiti received at the same time the recognition it had patiently awaited for sixty years.

Recognition was the symbol of revived American interest in the Liberian experiment. The sudden emancipation of four million slaves stimulated philanthropy to new inquiries. When the young and alert Liberian, Benjamin Anderson, visited America, he was able to lay plans for a next essential step in national growth. The interior boundaries had remained largely theoretical for some twenty or more years after the assumption of jurisdiction. A group of Americans suggested the wisdom of effective and final demarcation for the future protection of Liberia. Anderson, fortunately, had some knowledge of surveying and with funds provided principally by Henry M. Schieffelin, undertook the hazardous exploration of the hinterland. He did a good job, in spite of the obstructions of the chiefs along the route, and the result of two such journeys was the extension of the Liberian hinterland territory to include the kingdoms of the southern Mandingos and the tracing of a jagged boundary from Sierre Leone to the Cape. It was a fortunate action and the treaties, incontestable in their validity, were turned over to the state.

A group of West Indians numbering about three hundred came as a colony in 1865; this group later became the distinguished Barclays.

Successive administrations revealed a gradual weaning away from American influence, and a consciousness, at least, of purely African problems. The earlier presidents, from Roberts to Gardner, whatever the slant of their administrative policy, were all men born in America and exposed to its culture. Hilary Johnson, a son of Elijah Johnson, the pioneer, was the first president of Liberia born on Liberian soil. The administrations from Johnson to Coleman reflected a situation of desperate detachment and an intensified consciousness of statehood. Beginning with Barclay, the attention turned to the hinterland, and out of this interest grew policies of internal development and administration which completed the shift from trusteeship to the significant concept of a distinctive African state.

10

The Native

There is something fantastic about the spectacle of a group of 12,000 to 15,000 American Liberians, concentrated in six small towns on the coast, presuming to control an area of 43,000 square miles and an unknown native population of about 1.5 million. British and French colonists have found themselves similarly disproportionate, but behind them always has been the inflexible arm of a determined and secure mother country. It was an almost criminal anthropological irony that the American Blacks going to Africa retained their cultural memories sufficiently to give them an understanding of their contemporary "ancestors." They were themselves creatures of transition, shut off from any native culture. Now they were the rulers of their fathers. Sitting perilously on the fringe of a mysterious continent, they asserted their pretensions after the fashion of imperialism the world over, forever aware of the pressure of the vast aboriginal mass against them, crowding them into the sea. Such a situation leads easily to wasteful and even wantonly cruel tactics of survival.

The tragic element was that the interests of civilization and of colonization in Africa, whether by Whites or Blacks from another world, were forever in conflict. The natives were essential to the colonists if the latter were to survive, and all the pretty talk about spreading civilization became irrelevant in the face of the simple issue of material survival. It was not only that the two groups were vastly different culturally, but that they differed infinitely within themselves. A feature of native social systems was the confusion and endless variety of its patterns. They could not be controlled until they were understood, and a full century after the first arrogation of jurisdiction by these amateurs, the best anthropological thought of England finds itself asserting that no one yet knows much about the principles of native life.

There is perhaps no area of similar size on the West Coast of Africa which holds such a wide variety of tribes. Three principal native stocks predominate in Liberia: the Krus, who are regarded as the original stock of West Africa and embrace the Bassas, Deys, and Grebos; the Mandingos and Vais, who migrated more recently from the Sudan and are related to the Kpessis, Buzis, Mendis, Gbandis, and Gbundis; and a third group, the Golas and Kissis (Westermann's classification). There are other tribes in the interior, intensely primitive, among which are the Pahns, Guios, and Manas. Sir Harry Johnston characterized the interior of Liberia as the least known part of Africa. The range of culture is as varied as the stocks, from the sophisticated Vais, the single example of an African tribe known to have invented its own syllabarium and writing system, to the barbaric and cannibalistic tribes of the interior, who, as recently as twenty-five years ago, according to Edwin Barclay, came down to Bassa and sold human flesh as beef in the open market.

The seeds of the most constant native difficulties can be found in their naive concept of land tenure, economics, jurisprudence, and even religion; against the harsh wall of these differences the administrative problems of the Liberians crashed. And where weak, inefficient, and blundering policies failed to accomplish acculturation, they nevertheless created opportunities for exploitation, of which, in the later schemes of government, many took advantage. Native land tenure and ownership, for example, is most complex. The basis of native ownership is communal; in contrast, that of the European culture is individualistic. The translation of native ideas into current terminology is difficult even for the specialist, for, like the rights and powers of chiefs, ownership takes on a curious variety of forms. Ownership, as Malinowski so well describes it, is a matter of uses, and these uses may be associated with native systems of kinship, sometimes a mixture of mother right and father right; sometimes the stress is utilitarian and sometimes it is associated with magic and mythological rights.

The internal history of Liberia is virtually one long harangue over land, either between natives alone, whose endless quarrels over farming areas, village sites, migrations, and population expansion have required the arbitration of a central government; or between colonists and natives over the alienation of native lands by the colonists within the coastal area. There has been constant encroachment upon native reserves. Native customary land ownership has been too obscure to avoid it in many cases, and too weak in others to defend itself against the arbitrary decisions of the civilized courts and vagrant officials. The land muddle, as well as the associated exploitation, is well illustrated in the complaint of old Chief Bodio of Fishtown:

> They told us to go and divide our land with Garraway people who spill the blood of our sacred men. We went. Then Garraway asked Superintendent, "How about the £80 we give you to give us that land and you bring Fishtown people to take it back?" We went off and hung head and when we came back Superintendent said give him £25. Then he say he have land surveyed and that cost £40, and after that we did not get the land and we go to President.

•

He said: "I have divided land, go give Garraway people £80 back." We come home and Superintendent say if we want land we must bring him £90 and he will take it from Nihwie people and give it to us. He take it and Nihwie people come and kill us mercilessly and in a bad state. We go to government again to decide. The Nihwie people kill us. The Garraway people spill our priest's blood. Superintendent take our money. We have no land. Something must be done to cool our hearts.

As it was with land, so it was with the role of the chief, the most respected of African political institutions. He may be the spirit of the tribe incarnate, father, guide, counselor, or friend—in each case with elaborate rights stretching back into a traditional pattern. His office may be bound up with religious beliefs of the tribe or in other ways inseparably related to some mystical symbol. The endless troubles with one section of the Grebo people, for example, over a Liberian civil commissioner's thoughtless taking of a belt, along with other loot, constituted a deep and abiding injury to the tribe and expressed itself in stubborn resentment against the government.

It is regarded as essential to all enlightened administrators to know what to discourage and what to retain as a safeguard against the complete disorganization of the native social order, before adequate substitutions can be made from the new culture. Bound up with the chieftaincy are the native councils, rules of succession, inheritance of property, and even the communal tenure of land. To disregard these is to court disaster because they are problems of great delicacy. Wherever the tribes were brought under the jurisdiction of the Liberian government, the policy of arbitrarily commissioning an individual into chief was followed. From the point of view of native society, the value of the institution disappeared. Under a loose administration and with the cheap native commissioners available, the practice degenerated into the selling of commissions.

The process was simple and rarely got attention unless some crisis drove it to the foreground. At Grand Cess, for example, there ruled Paramount Chief Gbe (the father, incidentally, of the young African Gbe Pleyneno Wolo who had a brilliant record at Harvard). Gbe died and the superintendent began investigating the matter of a successor. Jack Jaraca, a wily old codger with a long experience as a laborer on the West Coast boats, asked the superintendent for the job and was appointed. The elders objected to Jack, because "all clothes lie that Jack puts on," and they insisted further that a paramount chief should be the choice of the people. They finally appealed in a delegation to the coast commissioner, who asked how many were opposed; twenty answered. They were sent to Picnicess barracks and confined until they paid him £200 for their release. They said: "We still don't want Jack Jaraca." The superintendent came into the case again and promised to remove Jack for £300, which was given to the superintendent.

Jack stayed. The superintendent went to the inauguration of the president and on his return was visited by a representative of Jack's who brought him £40. He replied that Jack had been dismissed and that it would require £60 more to reinstate him. This was brought and Jack remained paramount chief of Grand Cess.

The same principles of tribal difference and customs hold for labor, detection and punishment of crime, sex divisions of labor, health measures, religion, and the whole confusing welter of social relationships. Liberia, for example, is the southernmost point of the spread of Islam, and Edward Wilmot Blyden brilliantly advances the view that Mohammedanism is a more congenial religion for the African than Christianity. It is more readily understood by them, adjusts to their best traditions, is of African origin, and is self-sustaining, imposing salutary disciplines. The religion of the non-Islamized tribes is a form of fetishism or ancestor worship, compounded with magic, highly resistant to the abstract conceptions and doctrines of Christianity, and unlikely, except at the expense of long education, to produce other than the useless and obnoxious "mission boy." Christian doctrines persist longest when implanted in minds detached from native conceptual patterns and given wholly new frameworks of Western ideas to support them.

The problem of cultures alone is full of difficulties for the Liberian administrators, but it has been further complicated by the effort to do by force what they have, as yet, been incapable of accomplishing by enlightened strategy. Out of touch with the world and having no sure guides to administrative behavior, they were forced to rely on clumsy tactics. The system of control, loose and inefficient, spread into a network of blind exploitation which, to both the native and the world in general, is indistinguishable from the policy of government itself. It evolved naturally and its familiarity gave it the dangerous stamp of normalcy.

In the institution of domestic slavery, the social institutions of the natives had an insidious element which the Liberians did not escape. Slave traffic was old to Africa, with the holding of domestic slaves an integral part of the social structure. The Krus have been among the few that did not subject their own tribes to bondage, nor have they been enslaved by other tribes. They have been, throughout history, the great transporters of slaves; and while maintaining freedom for themselves, they have held other tribe members. In a great portion of the Liberian interior the system has not been extremely oppressive on the slave, and it is difficult for the stranger to distinguish a slave from a free member of the native household. They can, however, be easily enough recognized by natives; though living and working with the masters, they lack minor privileges. The Krus have had the peculiar custom of sending the sons out with their slaves to cut palm nuts.

It was imperative that the son scale the trees, even though dangerously high, to cut down the nuts; the slaves gathered them and brought them back with the tools. Back of this tradition is the idea of qualifying the son to meet any situation.

The Mandingos and Vais were most harsh in their treatment of slaves. Averse to agriculture, they had greater need of slaves and of a rigid decorum to govern the relationship of master and slave. The Pwessis were the traditional slaves of Liberia; the value of able-bodied ones was $30. Young female slaves brought slightly more; the minimum for a boy was $15 and for a girl $20.

This practice is contrary to the laws of Liberia, which have been on the statute books since the Constitution was first framed. A slave might get relief, if he made proper appeal for it in court, in a section under the statutory laws of the state. The interior has not been under the statutory laws, and the practice of slavery was almost indistinguishable from "pawning" and "adoption," which the Liberians themselves practiced in one degree or another since the founding of the state. The practice by Liberians of high position of selling Pwessi boys to the Vais and Krus and even to men of the south who visited the country was criticized severely by the Liberians themselves.

Pawning is likewise an old native custom. It is a system by which one person may exchange another person—a son, daughter, wife, or another pawn—for a sum of money, usually £10 to £15 to redeem him *at any time*. The indefinite aspect of redemption virtually gives it the status of slavery, for individuals may remain in pawn ten, twenty, fifty years, or even a lifetime. The government officially recognized pawning in a set of regulations which made the shadowy fact of the passing of a token the distinction between legalized pawning and unconstitutional slavery.

Curiously enough, the natives have divided on the abolition of the practice. The pawns are never articulate, but the pawner and the owner have agreed that in the transitory state of native economics, pawning is the equivalent of a native banking institution. The disastrous consequences of the institution's acceptance were recognized in an official report to the government by an inspector in the Kakata section in 1923, who wrote:

The native African Commissioners appointed by the Government, Justices of the Peace, and the so-called "American friend" [American-Liberians without official rank] going into the Pwessi districts to settle palavers and administer to the peace and general welfare of those whom they are pleased to style their *retainers* carry on a system of "bluff" in their court sittings which works successfully in extracting money from the Pwessis and forcing them to do farm service for little or no pay. For example, if whoever a palaver "catches" has not the wherewithal to pay the cost of the court, he is expected to put himself in pawn to the Justice of the Peace or the Native African Commissioner, as the officer may be, or to some civilized spectator at the court sitting. If he becomes a pawn to the Judge, he must work on the pawnee's farm for the time agreed upon for which a ridiculous and privileged sort of rifacimento of Blackstone's forms of promissory note is executed with due formality. If the unfortunate person whom the palaver "catches" is pawned to some person other than the Judge, the latter causes a strongly worded note to be executed with the view of protecting the interest of the one who has made it easy for the court to collect its costs. The absent days of the pawn from work are carefully noted, together with his sick days, and any dereliction of duty: and such memorandum calls for an extension of the time laid down in the promissory note at the discretion of the pawnee. Thus the lawsuit business runs, and persons have often served as pawnees for three years in satisfaction of a five pound sterling court debt.

The coast Krus have been longest in contact with the White man and were among the first to resist the coming of the colonists. Throughout the first century of Liberian history they were in opposition. They regarded themselves as the true owners of the country and more than once tried to throw off the rule of their Black lords. In each case the colony was saved from possible extermination at the hands of natives by the intervention of the United States. In 1854 the *John Adams* was sent to help President Roberts put down a revolt of the natives; two years later the Grebos took up arms against the government over the land question. In 1875 the Gdebos effected a union of tribes in the Grand Cess area and tried to drive out the entire Liberian colony. The occasion was a dispute over land which the Liberians at Monrovia claimed the Grebos had ceded to the Colony of Maryland before the two sections were united. Again an American cruiser saved the colonists. The southern end of the country has been sporadically in revolt for the last sixty years and the interior generally has been in disorder.

Following the visit of the first American Commission to Liberia in 1890, the United States sent military officers to the republic to assist the government in organizing its Frontier Force. The most accomplished and highest-ranking Black officer in America, Colonel Charles Young, was dispatched on this mission. Associated with him were two other Black officers, Major Ballard and Captain Roundtree. They carried both sympathetic concern for the native population and a high regard for the experiment of blacks in self-government. They were in Liberia when, in 1915, the Kru rebellion flared along the Sinoe and Bassa coasts. The Liberian government encouraged Major Ballard and Captain Roundtree to assist them in putting down the Kru rebellion. The situation, developed many times, became more threatening. President Howard appealed to Colonel Young and the American diplomatic officers to request American aid in preserving his government against annihilation. Young saw the predicament of the Liberians and sensed their fate if the Krus persisted. The American officers and officials agreed to request American assistance if the Liberian government would bind itself to make immediate reforms in its policy of native administration. This agreed upon, on November 8, 1915, the U.S.S. *Chester* appeared off the coast of Monrovia bringing 500 rifles and 250,000 rounds of ammunition. Just ahead of the *Chester*, however, had come, unannounced, H.M.S. *Highflier*, offering assistance in restoring peace. This was uninvited and questionable relief, particularly since the Krus had expressed a desire to place themselves under British rule and had, on one occasion, flaunted a British flag. With World War I in progress, a point could be made of British violation of Liberian neutrality; the vessel withdrew. The *Chester* remained, patrolling the coast from Monrovia to the Cape, and on several occasions took the president on a tour of inspection along the coast.

The Krus, thoroughly awed by the presence of the American gunboat, laid down their arms and, on the assurance of Captain Roundtree that the matter would be adjusted, surrendered to the government. When their capitulation was reported to Monrovia, the chiefs of the Krus were ordered to Blubarrow Barracks to conclude the terms of peace. They presented themselves with their retinue. A list of the names was then made and sent to the president, who announced, "There is now peace on the Kru Coast. There will be no more war." Nothing was done about the reforms which were the condition on which American aid was given. Instead, three weeks later, without consultation with the American officers and against the advice of the attorney general of Liberia, the president declared martial law in Sinoe. A military commission of sixty-three men was appointed and sent down the coast, and a shocking orgy of recrimination followed. Seventy-two Kru chiefs were executed. The president in Monrovia, with a list of native names before him in the untrustworthy orthography of his agents, sent his orders:

> The enclosed are the names of those upon whom you will carry out the Death Sentence—see list—and the others you will retain in confinement until further orders.
>
> In Lewis McCauley's evidence he says that William Purser and Bleede carried two of the Deo people on the beach and shot them. If this Bleede is the same one as Blee Dee, No. 34 on your list, then add his name to the enclosed list.
>
> After executioning these, I would like for you to give me as much information as you can about the remaining ones as to what tribe they belong, etc., and any other important facts about them.
>
> These instructions do not refer to the man I just sent you. If it is proven that he was the one who went first to the boat which had Diggs in it, and then gave

information to the town people and caused Diggs and the others to be killed, then hang him, or if he is found guilty of treason like the rest, then execute him.

The Krus revolted again in 1932, instigated by American-Liberians who made them think that White men would take control of the country as a result of the investigation by the International Commission on Slavery which declared that they need pay no taxes. This rebellion was also put down with severe reprisals.

The memory of gratuitous violence remained fresh in the minds of the tribe for many years, and it was only recently that the chiefs of the Kru sent word to President Tubman that they now considered themselves at peace with the Liberian government.

The attempt to extend effective control over the various native elements would be expected to meet with difficulties. A first step was the universal disarming of the natives. Although they claimed that the step left them defenseless against marauding wild animals, it was a more comfortable situation for the Liberians. Again, official cognizance was given to the flagrant cases of ill-treatment, the circumstances of which came within the definition of slavery, when these natives found their way into the courts. The attorney general was called upon to make a decision in the case of a complaint of eight boys against Senator M.T. Vampelt of Bensonville. A part of his decision, which reflected the character of the case, stated:

> The record of the investigations shows that the aggrieved persons SIX-CENTS and JUNE corroborate each other in the statement that the defendant, for some petty offense, compelled them to eat cow dung; the evidence of the said SIX-CENTS to the effect that he was made to eat the "cold" out of his eye is supported by the testimony of JAMES and KLEENE, who testified substantially that they had suffered similar ill-treatment; while the only substantial variance in the testimony of BISMARK, JUNE, and JORQUELLE is to the number of days they were respectively confined in a water closet; and there are other statements on record of floggings, gross neglect during illness, etc., which it is not necessary specifically to mention now.

> Candidly, the subscribed found it difficult to give credence to such allegations made against a person of the social and other standing of Mr. Vampelt, and eagerly turned the pages of the record to find the character of the defense. Beyond a mere categorical denial of the charges, his own statement is not only irrelevant but also exceedingly far fetched.

> The opinion of the undersigned is that the charge is sustained by the record, and the prosecuting attorney for the county who made the information should take steps to vindicate the rights of the aggrieved. And since several times during the said investigation allegations of involuntary restraint savouring of peonage were made, it is hereby ordered that the eight (8) persons be sent to our colleague, the Honourable Secretary of the Interior, with a

copy of this opinion, for such further action in the premises as falls within the purview, when such allegations are made by our aboriginal brethren against their "masters."

President Arthur Barclay was perhaps the first to break the strict policy of division between American-Liberians and natives and suggest the ultimate necessity of incorporating these elements into the body politic. He invited the chiefs to his inauguration festivities in 1904, called the first Congress of Chiefs, attempted to organize the interior for administrative purposes,and applied the term *Liberians* to all inhabitants of Liberia, colonists and aborigines. But his interior policy was never understood by the people. The concept of the African state which had been slowly taking form from the first illuminating suggestion of Blyden was, under Barclay, recognizable as an attempt to mold the policy of government and life according to the unique demands of their African setting: "What we need is wider and deeper culture, more intimate intercourse with our interior brethren, more energetic advance to the healthy regions."

This policy, with some vacillation, gained strength under President King. There was still a difference of views on the objectives of this intercourse which, as late as 1930, was manifested in a division of the cabinet between King and Edwin Barclay, his secretary of state. King's idea was to have the natives retain all their customs and communities and to help them to do this, utilizing the full unit of tribal life and interfering only when necessary to develop a civilized section in the native area. Barclay conceived the first objective of Liberian colonization to have been the provision of a refuge for emancipated, recaptured, and oppressed Blacks in America. When this necessity diminished after the Civil War, the second most important objective of colonization would be the civilization of the native peoples. He would thus gradually introduce the native elements into the civilized areas, share the culture of these areas with them, and eventually incorporate them into the full responsibilities of citizenship and statehood. King's policy led to the introduction of foreign capital and a stupendous road program based on free native labor; Barclay's logically led to a closing of the door to further American Black immigration and a concentration on internal problems. Neither of these policies could be fully sustained against the pressure of factions to be conciliated and outside forces to be reckoned with.

The civilization of the aborigines, which under White rule has taken the anomalous aspect of detribalization, has attached to it, in Liberia, less conspicuous tensions. Once a native acquires the English language and puts on shoes, he is not very different from a Liberian. It appears that proportionately more natives than Americo-Liberians find their way to foreign institutions of learning, largely through the medium of the mission schools, and nine-tenths of the children in the mission and public schools are natives. The same general sequel to detribalization is manifested; once educated, the natives seldom go back to their people, even as missionaries or teachers, but seek instead to find positions in the civilized government. Their constituency may be native, as in the cases of Momolu Massaquoi, Didhwo Twe, and H. Too Wesley, who rose in King's second administration to the position of vice-president. The relationship between natives and Americo-Liberians is not without elements of prejudice similar to that existing between Whites and Blacks in America, and Wesley's position was an unprecedented elevation for a native. Full incorporation into the Americo-Liberian pattern involves acceptance of the Americo-Liberian attitude toward the native, and some of the educated natives have leaned backward in demonstrating their fitness for government. As a consequence, they have drastically alienated themselves from their own tribal connections. Those who have retained an intimate interest in the native which has run counter to special interests of Liberian officials, as in the case of Didhwo Twe, who proposed the bill in the legislature to stop the Fernando Poo exportations, have simply been politically and socially expelled. The intense tribal schisms further prevent concerted tribal support of a native of any one tribe, and conversely, it is difficult for an educated Vai or a Kru to regard with sympathy the native population beyond his own tribal connection.

The waning vitality of the Americo-Liberian stock and the gradual shrinking of the population have produced more favorable sentiment toward cautious intermarriage with the native population. The social taboo has relaxed at least to the point that Americo-Liberian men may on occasion marry educated native women. The principle is that when a man marries a native he takes the woman out of her culture and places her in his own, where incorporation into the accepted customs involves no loss. When an Americo-Liberian woman marries a native man, however, he takes her out of her setting into his own, thereby weakening an already uncertain cultural nucleus.

Under President Tubman the movement toward integration of natives and American-Liberians has gained greater impetus. His eventual long-range goal is one nation of citizens with equal social, political, and economic rights. Despite opposition from the "old guard," he has been able to introduce such reforms as a graduated income tax, a law giving aborigines representation in Liberia's legislature for the first time in the history of the country, and a decree forbidding forced labor during the planting season; and his program seems to be stoutly supported by the natives themselves. At the Salala councils he affirmed his belief that tribal lands unlawfully taken must be returned or paid for satisfactorily. The very enunciation of such a belief by the head of government indicates a reversal of policy and hope for the future of the nation. Indeed, the zeal of the natives for education, their tradition of labor and ready adaptability to new forms of work, their vitality and surprising mental acuteness, seem to mark them as the ultimate salvation of the country.

11

The Tragedy of Loans

The first twenty years of sovereignty were sufficient to mature a new generation of self-conscious republicans and cover with the glamour of caste the privilege of officeholding. As political office and proferment increased in importance, schisms developed on international and internal policy, on the Constitution and new laws, on principles of trade, and around the tragic irrelevancy of color, alluded to earlier. This last, however, took on a very real importance in the beginning of a fiscal travesty, the effects of which have steadily magnified over the one hundred years of the republic's existence. The preponderant Blacks of the republic had welcomed self-rule, but emotionally they had never accepted Roberts, the mulatto. They were, for one thing, suspicious of the basis for his easy relations with English, and even Virginian White people. They distrusted not only Roberts and his White friends, but themselves, and they made it rather pathetically obvious by supplanting Roberts, the mulatto, with Benson, the Black. It was aptly, even if inelegantly, put by one of the inchoate political philosophers when he said: "The folks say as how we ain't fitten to take care of ourselves—ain't capable. Roberts is a fine gentleman, but he is more White than Black. Benson's colored people all over. There's no use talking government and making laws and that kind of thing, if they ain't going to keep them up. I vote for Benson, Sir, because I wants to know if we's going to stay niggers or turn monkey."

Benson was elected and he was followed in office by the "Black" Warner, who went him one better and permitted his sons and daughters to adopt the life of the indigenous native population. This was going too far, and in 1868 James Sprague Payne, another mulatto, was put in by the Republicans.

Then was born the Whig Party to oppose the Republicans, and Edward James Roye, another "Black," was made president. It had been a test of political strength and sagacity; in the struggle the unmixed Blacks found themselves with a distinct numerical advantage. Mulattoes more readily became free men in the United States through the graciousness of owners, who frequently were influenced by blood ties, and their lot was a bit more

97

tolerable than that of the unmixed Black in America. They protested most vehemently against discrimination, but were less amenable to suggestion of migration and colonization.

Under Roye, the Whigs settled down with an air of finality and permanence to run the government. However, several problems stood in the way. First, the presidential term was too short. It admitted embarrassing caprices of popular sentiment. Second, the government needed money to extend its public works and to exploit the fringes of its rich hinterland through trade, the principal interest of the new citizens, apart from government itself. Roye set out to do something about both. The state had little or no credit, except on its customs, and these collections were indifferently organized. The natural resources of the country were there, but the government was in the vicious circle of first needing money to develop these resources before these could be used as security for loans of larger sums of money. Unable to exploit the hinterland unaided, it nevertheless opposed concessions to more experienced European and American concerns.

Efforts had been made in the United States under earlier administrations to secure a loan, and President Grant had promised to present the appeal to Congress. The matter apparently slipped his memory; whatever the Congress might have decided to do, the appeal was never presented.

Roye turned to England; the consul general for Britain in Liberia was a diplomatic adventurer by the name of David Chinery. He had friends in England engaged in international banking, whom he recommended to the Liberian president. This was scarcely distinguishable from an official British suggestion, and the Liberian government accepted the recommendation with unrestrained eagerness. The plan contemplated a loan of $500,000 of which $100,000 was to be used to pay off the existing public debt; $100,000 was to be deposited in the treasury as a basis for the issuance of paper currency, and the remainder was to be deposited in a safe banking institution as an emergency fund to be drawn against by an act of legislation.

There was objection to a loan of this size as unnecessary, and a general suspicion that such an amount of money would place temptation in the way. While the legislature was supposed to be the safeguard against irresponsible conduct, Roye had his own plans. Any members of his cabinet who expressed candid opposition to his tactics were ousted. H.W.R. Johnson, his secretary of state, who had accompanied him to London, came home. Roye, expecting his return, quietly appointed two senators, W.S. Anderson and W.H. Johnson, and Chinery as agents to go to London and conclude negotiations for the loan. Then came the news of the terms. Chinery's bankers offered to make the loan of $500,000, but found it necessary to discount it at 30 percent. The offer was accepted. Thus bonds to the amount of $500,000 were issued against a payment of $350,000. Moreover, the full amount was to carry interest at 7 percent, payable three years in advance. This meant further reduction to about $245,000. The entire loan, including interest, was to be repaid within fifteen years, which everyone knew was unfeasible. This would have meant that within fifteen years the government would have paid Chinery's bankers about $600,000 for the actual $245,000 delivered.

At the point where the bankers left off in their notorious bargain Roye began. The administration and its diplomatic corps and agents had needed money so long that the prospect of it threw them into a flurry of extravagant desires. Roye immediately issued a personal order to the amount of $70,000 against the remainder of the loan before it could even be paid into the treasury and before the legislature could either authorize or accept it. Every European luxury that he had been denied in Liberia Roye ordered Chinery to buy, and when he had exhausted his dreams, he drew a further order on the treasury to the amount of $50,000 which he turned over to an imaginary member of his family. To make it "legal" it was charged to the government. The veteran ex-president Roberts referred to this orgy of high-handed waste and malfeasance as "speculation and fraud unparalleled in any public loan transaction of modern times." For more than a quarter of a century this debt cast a blighting shadow of defalcation and criminal irresponsibility on the infant republic. Of the original $500,000 the government realized less than $125,000, but found itself under the terrifying stress of having to pay to the bankers $600,000, within fifteen years.

Angered by the yoke of debt which their president had hung upon them, the people rose up and prepared for drastic action. It was none too soon, for the brazen Roye, after the manner of the heads of certain South American republics, was busily preparing to perpetuate himself in office. His term nominally expired on January 1, 1872. In October 1871 he issued an executive order extending his own term of office for two more years. When a physical contest threatened, he armed his supporters and prepared to carry his wishes by force. Findley, a reputable and respected official who was known to be in embarrassing opposition to Roye's schemes, was murdered in a public street. The armed supporters of the president then attempted to seize a building in Monrovia which had been used as a bank. In the fighting that followed several were killed. Burly and bullheaded, Roye rushed into the street and flung crude hand grenades into the crowd. He was given pause when a well-aimed cannon ball ripped through the presidential mansion. Only then did the seriousness of his predicament dawn upon him. In a moment of frustration he took the seal of the Executive Department and ran down to the waterside. In so small a community he could only conceal his plans in overobviousness. But as he walked non-chalantly along the waterfront, an officer appeared and placed him under arrest; his entire cabinet soon joined him in imprisonment.

In the trial that soon followed, Roye was convicted of high crimes and official misconduct. During the proceedings, Senator Johnson, one of his agents, arrived by steamer from England. Having heard nothing of Roye's official collapse and, to insure a full surprise and the recovery of goods, he was allowed to assemble all his paraphernalia and land. It was known that he was carrying a considerable sum of money; later an officer was sent (behind him) to get it. The officer got the box in which the money was supposd to be, but when the committee from the legislature opened it, they found nothing but glass and brick dust. No one knows yet who got the money, and the officer who brought in the box was not exempt from the cold accusing stares of an outraged legislature. There was nothing left to do but take Johnson to join Roye. A provisional government was hastily formed and three Republicans were designated to constitute a permanent government. They were the Reverend Amos Henry, one of the signers of the Declaration of Independence, R.A.. Sherman, and Charles Burgess Dunbar.

On a second steamer, Anderson, the other Liberian agent sent to England by Roye, arrived. He, however, was more sensitive to the signs of trouble and continued on down the coast. The wily Roye lost no time in bribing his guards to permit him to escape. He went further and made careful plans to be met by a surf boat at a certain point on the beach and then to be taken to a passing ship bound for Europe. Using his natural complexion as a disguise, he stripped to a loin cloth in an attempt to be mistaken for a Kru man. With his bag of gold and the Executive Seal he repaired to the spot and waited the signal of the surf boat. His plans had been carefully made and the escape was a neat one. By morning he would be well on his way with enough money to live comfortably until the scandal was forgotten.

The signal came, and he plunged with his bag of gold into the surf. The money was heavy and, though a strong man, Roye had some difficulty in floating. Suddenly, to his great consternation, there was the sound of a second plunge from his hiding place. The strange new figure swam with rapid strokes and an unmistakable intent. In a panic of fright Roye made frantic efforts to reach the surf boat with his bag, but the figure overtook him, and without a word, knocked him senseless with a stone. He was dragged back to shore and the alarm was given. As the infuriated crowd attacked him and began to beat him, his wife, with a strong regard for modesty, rushed home and returned with a quilt to cover his near nakedness; the mob pommeled him back to jail, where he died shortly afterward.

The bag of gold was never seen again nor was the mysterious patriot, native or Liberian, ever identified. All that is certain is that the state got none of the money from the bag.

Roberts, the mulatto, was returned to office and permitted to use any advantage he might have for extricating the government from its new predicament. At first the government attempted to repudiate the transaction, but this was impossible since they had been credited with spending over $100,000 of the money. For twenty-five years they haggled over this obligation, to the further injury of their national credit. All the while, their internal affairs grew steadily worse. Finally, in 1898, under the guidance of Arthur Barclay, then secretary of the treasury of Liberia, they made an honorable settlement with the bondholders, committing the government to approximately $375,000.

The tragic consequences of this first financial episode blasted faith in the republic's ability to manage its affairs and appear today as a deep shadow, slanting across the entire history of the experiment in self-government. A sensible fiscal policy would have provided from the loan a basis for bolstering the rapidly depreciating currency. The sad and prompt end of the venture left the Liberians infinitely worse off than they had been before.

To remedy the situation they began soundly enough with regulatory legislation, but soon found themselves plunged again in new measures of desperation with further complications. A law was passed to the effect that one-half of the paper currency paid into the treasury should not be reissued, and one-tenth of all gold paid in should be held to meet foreign claims. Officials were paid one-half in gold and one-half in paper currency. Gradually the Liberians were putting their paper currency out of circulation, but an unfortunate tribal rebellion interfered and distracted them.

As the paper currency decreased further in value against the pressure of new debts and the insistent demands for current expenditures, they resorted to what has been described as the "order" system. The European merchants in Monrovia agreed to accept government orders for supplies and to use these in payment of customs revenues and anything else over which the government had control. This system was extended to the point of paying officials half their salaries in script and half in cash. The merchants profited handsomely by this arrangement while the government became increasingly entangled. Three sets of prices were established: one for cash, a higher one for purchases made in kind, and still another, the highest price, for a "half-and-half" order. In the end the purchasers received about half the value of the goods they bought, while the merchants were able to present the script in payment at par. Governmental expenses increased and revenues were cut because their customs receipts had been compromised to meet this further contingency. They were compelled to go again to the merchants for advances in cash, for which they had to pay 25 to 30 percent interest. They were now at the mercy of their local traders as well as of foreign creditors abroad. In 1904 the national debt was over $800,000, and of this amount $480,000 was a hangover from the profitless 1871 loan.

Something had to be done; another loan was imperative, although officials were aware of their lack of credit. However, in 1903 the legislature voted hopefully to try to get money from some source. In their darkest hour there came to the rescue another internationally famous Englishman, an old African traveler and student, Sir Harry Johnston. As early as 1882, when Sir Harry was traveling on the West Coast with Lord Mayo, he had been interested in the country, and in his reminiscences he speaks of the unforgettable impression made on him by the magnificent forests of the country which reared themselves so close to the waves. He had also, when serving as consul in the Niger Delta, encountered the Kru men and had determined to visit their homeland to study their habits. Still later he came to develop a commercial interest in the Krus' part of the coast. French and Dutch enterprise through an experiment with a chartered company had stopped, he thought, just short of reaping high rewards and the chartered company had been allowed to die. Britain was favorable to the extension of its commercial enterprise in Liberia to block the steady French advance on the area. Sir Eric Drummond, since a secretary general of the League of Nations, was just then launching his diplomatic career and was British counsul general in Liberia. He sensed something of the potentialities of the wild rubber forests and the rich mineral deposits, and spoke encouragingly of the prospects of extensive commercial exploitation in the country. To his judgment was added that of Colonel Powney, explorer and officer in one of the guards, who had served in the Sudan. In a casual exploration in Liberia he had found both gold and diamonds. Sir Harry Johnston was finally convinced, and in 1904 went to Liberia.

Since Whites were barred from owning land, any commercial exploitation required government participation in some form, and for the success of the venture it was best that its participation be not too aggressive. Sir Harry began making friends with the administration and traveling through the country. It was a thorough and painstaking examination of its resources, which not only accomplished its first purpose but contributed to Sir Harry's reputation as a scholar. The monumental two-volume *Liberia* which resulted became a reference work, not only on the history and ethnology of Liberian peoples, but on the flora, fauna, and mineral wealth of the country. The study became a prospectus extraordinary for a new loan—and for a new financial disaster for the republic.

The chartered company was revived by Colonel Powney with Sir Harry as director-manager. President Arthur Barclay, with the endorsement of his cabinet, offered suggestions as to what might be done to develop the wild rubber on which their interest settled. Some capital should be put forward by the company, he thought, in return for the concession, and with their influence and diplomatic connections they should be able to get the consent of the British government to aid them in settling the troublesome British and French boundary disputes. This was promised. It was agreed further that German claims in the old company should be bought, annulled, or otherwise transferred to British hands. Austin Chamberlain, chancellor of the Exchequer, was a friend to the venture; he helped the British Foreign Office arrange for a loan and the British government consented to recognize the appointment of an Englishman as comptroller of Liberian customs as a guarantee of security to the bondholders of the existing Liberian state debt.

The banking house of Emil Erlanger represented British interests in the new loan of $500,000. The terms of the loan provided that $25,000 should be used for imperative Liberian obligations, $125,000 for the payment of domestic debts, $35,000 to be loaned to the Liberian Development Company sponsored by Sir Harry Johnston, and the remaining sum of over $300,000 to be turned over to the company for the purpose of banking and promoting road schemes in the republic. As security for the loan two British officials were appointed as inspectors of the Liberian customs, the chief inspector serving as financial adviser. Thirty thousand dollars annually were to be paid until the whole loan was paid, and 10 percent of any excess over $250,000 in the annual customs revenue was to go to the Liberian Development Company. The company had responsibility for returning the loan to Emil Erlanger.

For the rather considerable sums entrusted to them, the company showed at the end of two years fifteen miles of dirt road, a small launch, and two automobiles, and quietly announced that all the funds were exhausted. The government, finding itself helplessly and inextricably under a new debt, made bold to ask how the money had been spent, but the company indignantly declined to make an accounting. Actually, all the salaries of their prospectors, workers, and directors, the rents, and traveling expenses had been paid out of the funds borrowed on behalf of the republic. President Barclay rushed off to London to confer with Sir Harry Johnston and his associates. He believed that, as reasonable men friendly to the republic, they would recognize the ridiculous features of the arrangement. Instead, the gentlemen offered him the privilege of buying out the company for $500,000. To put an end to the impossible situation, the Liberian government secured an agreement by which the unused balance of $150,000 should be returned to Liberia, took full responsibility for paying the Erlanger claims directly, and severed relations with the development company.

Stern reprisals followed promptly. The British government bluntly demanded the appointment of three more British customs officers, the establishment and maintenance of a Frontier Force under European officials, and reform of the treasury and courts within six months under penalty. Some of these reforms were begun hastily. The Liberians employed the three additional British customs men, organized a Frontier Force, and put British officers in charge.

Once entwined in the dangerous network of debts and obligations, everything the Liberians touched failed. Even the reform measures held for them the bitter results of intrigue and further diplomatic bungling, almost costing them their autonomy. The British officer of the Frontier Force, under the guidance of the British consul general, whether with or without official sanction, engineered a coup which barely missed adding Liberia to the territory of Sierra Leone.

In desperation President Barclay, although a former British subject in the West Indies, was compelled to turn to the United States for aid. A delegation appealed to President Taft, who, to its surprise, gave it a sympathetic hearing. The president sent over a commission consisting of Roland P. Falkner, George Sale, and Emmett J. Scott. Among its recommendations was included the suggestion that a loan be floated in the United States to pay off Liberian obligations, and that the Liberian customs be placed under American officials.

At the end of the second loan episode, the national debt stood at $1,289,570. Complications followed thick and fast. The requirement for funds increased as resources and credit declined. France had loomed as a menace to Liberia's territorial integrity, and Germany was for some reason now showing a suspicious eagerness to make the republic a new loan. Germany had been the least aggressive of the strong neighbors and had sent many traders to Monrovia who were on friendly terms with the government. This lent a certain reasonableness to the German offer.

Promptly after the termination of the arrangement with the Liberian Development Company, M. Dinklage, a German, was appointed by the legislature to negotiate a loan. Following the lead of Sir Harry Johnston, Gustav Lange, another German, published a report on Liberia and later presented the "Lange Proposition" to advance Liberia 2,000,000 marks for the purpose of taking up the foreign and domestic obligations of the country. It was further proposed to make an immediate ad interim loan of 200,000 marks. The Liberian customs were again to secure the loan and, if necessary, other Liberian public revenues would be pledged. A commission with important powers would administer the customs while a bank would be established to administer the finances of the country. It was the same old story.

The U.S. Department of State was approached by Mr. Warburg, of Kuhn, Loeb, and Company, on behalf of its German branch to secure American support for the Lange proposition. Encouraged by the new German and American interest, the Liberian government arbitrarily reduced the salaries of the British inspectors of the Liberian customs. It was a stupid gesture, for the salaries had been established by the British loan contract of 1907. For reasons best known to the Department of State, the United States declined to support the German proposition, although it seemed to envisage a loan in which British, French, German, and American bankers would participate jointly.

The situation would perhaps have quieted if there had not developed during the negotiations a rumor about the discovery of gold in the hinterland. Promptly the old, moribund interest in the country flared again. First came a gracious note from Britain to the effect that it would not interfere in Liberia so long as that government kept faith on its obligations. The arbitrary reduction of the salaries of the British customs inspectors under the earlier receivership developed into a blunder, for it had given some excuse for intervention. Then came a note from France informing Liberia politely but firmly of the existence of certain ancient treaty rights which had been overlooked for many years and which had just been discovered. The Germans pressed the Lange proposition, and the British quietly pressed for additional mineral concessions.

The policy adopted by the United States finally led to the establishment in 1912 of the joint international loan of $1,700,000 at 5 percent, to mature in 1952, participated in by bankers of the four countries allegedly interested. A customs receivership was set up under an American receiver general assisted by one receiver of each of the other interested nationalities—the British, German, and French. The American bankers who entered this agreement were: J.P. Morgan, Kuhn Loeb, the National City Bank, and the First National Bank of New York. As might have been foreseen in such an international receivership arrangement, trouble developed immediately. For example, British and French assistant receivers denied the right of the American receiver general to make appointments where he wished.

The Liberian government, cautiously quiet during the negotiations, now awoke and, either in blatant disregard of the terms of the agreement or in ignorance of the legal terminology in which the terms were couched, passed laws in direct conflict with the agreement. It made rules and regulations of the receivership subject to the approval of the Liberian secretary of the treasury and required all bills and payrolls of the receivership to have his approval. It created cashiers to handle the funds of the receivership and tried to prevent this fiscal body from making appointments without the sanction of the Liberian president.

It was a characteristic action. The little coterie of a governing class, racially self-conscious, zealously guarding its autonomy and independence, and traditionally disregarding the necessity for a laborious economic development to ensure its security, had placed its faith again in the magic of legislation. With the blurred vision of hungry men, they had misread the implications of a loan to a nation that lacked the customary security. They had sold themselves again but refused to believe it. The situation produced innumerable points of friction between the receivership, secure in its legal agreement, and the government, bolstered by belief in its sovereignty.

The financial difficulties were not limited to the receivership. The short-term loans which the Liberian government had been obliged to make of the Bank of British West Africa, pending the conclusion of the loan negotiations, brought heavy demands at the outset; native uprisings introduced unanticipated but necessary expenditures; and the opposition to the receivership from foreign traders who had profited by the heavy discounts on government script made affairs tense for the new financial government. Then came World War I and with it the retirement of the German member. All the other assistant receivers for one reason or another withdrew and the American receiver general was eventually left holding an empty bag. When trade was suspended as a consequence of the war, the revenues of the receivership were precipitously cut down. It was necessary finally to enter into a contract with the Bank of British West Africa for advances of $9,000 monthly to meet bare governmental expenses.

This new predicament made negotiations for another loan imperative. This time it had to be much larger, because the debt was greater. It would prove more exacting, the Liberians knew, because their credit and resources were poorer; more hopelessly permanent in its burden, because the country could not develop its resources until it could pay off its debts, and the country could never pay off its debts until it developed its resources.

In January 1918, while World War I was still on, Liberia requested the United States to advance it not less than $5,000,000 to refund the 1912 loan, centralize control of the receivership in American hands, liquidate internal indebtedness, stimulate industry, and to inaugurate such public works as would operate to rehabilitate the country financially and economically. In a spirit of recurrent humility the assistance of American agents was requested to aid the government in the effective administration and control of its various departments. Liberia offered, in consideration of such a loan, to throw off all European control and accept United States control.

The finances, boundary demarcation, frontier force, interior administration, sanitation, education, and agriculture would be controlled by American experts. They would reform their judicial system under American supervision and turn over the German wireless and cable station at Monrovia to the United States. This was offering everything they had. To make it a good case, they offered even what they did not have. In the preliminary talks they intimated that they were in position to furnish 200,000 men to the Allies!

Since Liberia had entered the war on the side of the Allies, at the suggestion of the United States, a loan of this character was possible as a war emergency, and the U.S. Treasury Department actually held that it might properly be made to the Republic of Liberia under the authority conferred upon the president by the Second Liberty Loan Act. This act permitted him to make loans for the purpose of "more effectually providing for the national security and defense and prosecuting the war." President Wilson agreed and the Liberian government was informed that a credit of $5,000,000 had been placed in its favor.

This action was incredibly prompt and at first the Liberians could not believe it because there was so little basis for expecting the credit. The old government script again took on exaggerated value with the prospect; merchants eagerly advanced goods and even funds; contracts were made for building materials which were to be paid for when salaries were finally paid; indeed, salaries could be increased when the loan funds were delivered. But the matter was not so simple as it had at first appeared. Both Britain and France registered objections, or modifications of the American proposal, the latter nation demanding a tripartite agreement in which there would be equal participation by the British, French, and American governments. Further international discussion of the loan carried the French recommendation that the final arrangement be made at the Peace Conference in Paris.

The loan prospect began to wobble disconcertingly as it shuttled through endless formal actions. First, an advance of $12,000 was recommended by America to get the Liberian delegation to the Peace Conference. Then the Treasury Department ruled that no money could actually be spent until a receivership had been set up. Congress, favorable to the loan, was about to adjourn before international fiscal agents could be named to receive the money. At this point John Lewis Morris, secretary of the treasury of Liberia, appeared in the United States. The point of view on the loan which he presented was at wide variance with the original petitions. The people of Liberia, he said, were suspicious of American financial aid, fearing control and ultimate supervision of their Constitution. They wanted Black instead of White officials, except for certain specified officers, and generally speaking believed that the proposed American treaty amounted to a protectorate.

The Liberian delegation, however, proceeded to the Peace Conference, led by Charles Dunbar Burgess King, then secretary of state. The transfer of negotiations to Paris, a part of the French plan, offered the opportunity for those European powers interested in Liberia to demand concessions at the expense of the country as a condition of adherence to the American treaty plan. The hand of France was promptly exposed. In return for its approval France demanded a concession of rights for a railroad through the Liberian country from the extreme hinterland post of Tinson to Monrovia on the coast, a share in the credit and administration of the Liberian hinterland, and assignment of the former German-Monrovia-Pernambuco cable to a French company—all of which were granted. The British, less flagrant, demanded equality of commercial treatment for all nationalities, impartiality in administration of special customs privileges, American support of claims on behalf of British subjects in Liberia, and acknowledgement by the American government of British claims against the Liberian government amounting to about $1,500. The demands as a whole were excessive and threatened to make the republic merely a pawn in the imperialist plans of colonizing nations. The Americans could sense this, and a new diplomatic struggle followed.

Secretary King accepted the agreement for Liberia and wrote to President Howard: "We shall have to give America a free hand in our affairs and be prepared to make some sacrifice of what we have called our sovereign rights. We shall have to put up with some of the bitter drugs which may be found necessary to put us on our feet in a sound and healthful condition." When he returned to Liberia, he furiously repudiated the agreement, giving as excuse the fact that he had been deceived about its terms. When he became president shortly afterward, he adopted a hostile attitude toward America, surrounded himself with men who would not challenge his judgment, and prompted the Liberian legislature to enact more laws breaking the control of the receivership. He then withdrew the internal revenues of the government as security for the loan of 1912.

The new loan discussions were not ended. Popular opposition demanded modifications of the terms and a delegation was selected to visit America. For the sake of continuity, the American government requested that President King head the new delegation. He deliberately prolonged the negotiations in the face of a changing administration in America, hoping that some other power would come forward with a new proposition. None came. The Liberian government needed money, and despite King's futile optimism about a fresh prospect, the country faced what seemed to be its ultimate financial disaster. The American government attempted to revise the financial plan and bring it nearer to the Liberian government's wishes. King continued to postpone the beginning of his journey. When he finally sailed, he dallied through England and France, arriving in the United States a few days after the Wilson administration had retired and the new Harding regime had been inaugurated.

With a new administration and Congress, new negotiations were required. The War Emergency Act could no longer be invoked and the loan had to go anew to be debated in Congress. On May 11, 1922, the House of Representatives passed a joint resolution authorizing the credit, but in the Senate the loan conditions met the determined opposition of Senator Borah. Said he:

> I had rather go down into the Treasury of the United States and take out $5,000,000 and hand it to the President of Liberia than to turn it over in this way. Then, if the Liberian people could not administer it, it would be their fault; but I am not in favor of taking over Liberia and bringing her under our protection and control, establishing our authority upon the West Coast of Africa, becoming a part of this imperial scheme of finance, which is now one of the curses which are leading the world into another war. I would rather give them the money outright then get messed up in African affairs which will cost us many millions to get away from.

When Senator Curtis referred to the valuable resources of the country that could possibly be developed to repay the loan and at the same time provide operating expenses of the government, Borah replied: "The best evidence of the fact that there is nothing there to satisfy the keen financial appetite of Morgan and Company and Great Britain is that they are trying to get out and they want us to pay so they can get out."

The Liberian bill was carried forward as unfinished business; in the 76th Congress it came up again. On November 27, after bitter discussion, the bill was recommitted to the Committee on Finance and was never again reported to the Senate.

All fears of American control were dispelled with the failure of the loan. But with the failure went likewise all hope of financial aid. Anticipations of promissory notes, artificially accelerated business, plans of further credit purchases predicated on this loan so nearly within grasp and now gone—all collapsed. The first reaction was bitter disappointment, with the accusation that antagonistic American interests had blocked the loan to imperil Liberia further. Greatly weakened, Liberia sought to interest American capital in a concession as a means of repairing its sad finances and binding the interest of America, thereby raising the threat of implied American protection against the new aggressiveness of other countries.

This serious national crisis coincided with the interest of the Firestone Company in developing rubber plantations, as a means of breaking the

British and Dutch monopoly which had forced crude rubber to the almost fantastic limit of $1.21 a pound. The result was a vast concession, bound by three famous agreements, to the company. In one of the agreements between the company and the government the eternal nemesis quietly appeared again in a clause to the effect that the Firestone Company would "use its influence to secure a loan either from the United States, or, with the approval of the Secretary of State of the United States, from some other person or persons, not exceeding $5,000,000, for public development, the terms to be subject to the approval of the Liberian legislature." In the impoverished state of the country, these public improvements were necessary and it was to be expected that they would be insisted upon. The Liberians had welcomed the company joyously as a possible source of income to the natives and, in the inevitable logic of their economic arrangement, to themselves in turn. The prospect of the loan, however, brought the usual popular apprehensions. The country had not been free from the burden of indebtedness since Roye's foolhardy venture fifty-four years before. The weight became greater and more hopeless with each new remedial venture. More important, however, in the popular opposition was the fact that a loan could mean but little to the people in general since it would do scarcely more than refund old debts.

It is impossible that the Firestone Company could have correctly interpreted the temper of the people on this matter, or they would not have so lightly anticipated their acceptance of the now famous Clause K in one of the proposed agreements, which made ratification of the terms of the loan virtually a condition of the acceptance of their plantation agreements. The Liberians objected, first to the loan itself, then to the fact that Firestone himself was planning to make it. To meet the latter objection, there was created the Finance Corporation of America, which made the loan using the National City Bank of New York as fiscal agent.

In substance, under the terms of this new loan the Finance Corporation agreed to buy to the amount of $2,500,000 forty-year 7-percent bonds. The second $2,500,000 the government could sell, but the corporation was under no obligation to buy. It required that they redeem all outstanding 5-percent 1912 bonds amounting to $1,185,200, although these were not due until 1952. The remainder was to be used to pay the costs of preparation of the agreement, executing the bonds, etc., and $35,610 to be paid to the United States with interest, as the sum advanced for expenses of the Liberian delegation to the Peace Conference. After this, the government might pay off its interest and floating debts.

The criticisms of the loan were that it required retirement of a 5-percent loan, due in 1952, with a 7-percent loan due in 1967, adding $100,000 to $175,000 expense annually to the government. The cost of administering the loan added a new salary item of $42,000 which, with $8,000 for stipulated military officials and $35,000 a year for the sinking fund, raised the annual expense of the loan to more than $250,000. It set up a financial adviser with some then subordinate but high-salaried officials. Finally, it gave a veto on any new Liberian loan for twenty years.

The channels of responsibility of the fiscal agents were not clearly defined, nor was their relationship with the government sufficiently clear to avoid friction. The fiscal officers were designated by the U.S. State Department but were responsible to the National City Bank. Their role made them borrowed Liberian officials and thus, as Raymond Leslie Buell pointed out, they were technically responsible to the government although they were expected to control the financial affairs of the government.

As soon as the first loan money had been delivered, official salaries were raised, that of the president being increased to $15,000, and the old psychology of an outraged and indignant sovereignty returned. The terms of the loan were kept in constant ferment and there were breaches of the agreement on the presumption that the failings of a weak nation would be excused. The government, for example, failed to observe the provision which authorized the financial adviser to apply assigned revenue and denied his authority to prepare administration regulations specifically provided for. It failed to account for consular fees or effectively prosecute officials shown to be guilty of malfeasance in office. In return, the Finance Corporation, within its legal limits, simply withheld the next delivery of $100,000 originally planned for public works.

The temptation to profiteer on the loan at the expense of the natives could not be resisted. Apportionments had been made from the loan for the payment of arrears of about nine years in salaries of the Liberian Frontier Force. It was difficult because of the lack of complete records and their bad condition generally to determine the exact amount due these native soldiers, but an arbitrary sum was set aside for the purpose. Under the system of disbursement drawn up by the Treasury Department, each individual soldier had been issued a certificate containing the amount due, and these were made payable at either the Treasury Department or the bank. The endorsement of the soldier on this certificate could make it transferable under the system at face value. When the certificates were issued to the soldiers, they were ignorant of their possible value, and as the loan negotiations proceeded, they were induced to assign the certificates to various government officials for a mere fraction of their face value. There was another confusing factor relating to the certificates from which the officials and other shrewd Liberians profited. Upon presentation of a certificate at the Treasury Department for payment, soldiers were told that a countersignature of the Secretary of War or of the Secretary of the Treasury was needed; the soldiers were offered sums representing a fraction of the certificate's value; if they refused, they were told they would probably have to wait many months for the countersignature to make the certificate negotiable; they were then offered again the fractional sum and as a rule they accepted.

The value of this loan was the retirement of the 1912 loan, just as the 1912 loan's chief value was the retirement of the 1906 loan—which, in turn, retired the loan of 1871 that had initiated the tragic fiscal cycle. Over 90 percent of the $2,500,000 advanced was used for existing obligations, among which were debts due the United States. Liberia thus became the only other nation besides Cuba to pay its war debt to the United States in full.

Following the report of the Slavery Commission in 1930, the League of Nations, at the request of the Liberian government, appointed a committee of eight to suggest means of implementing the recommendations of the commission. The plan of assistance proposed by this committee included modifications in the 1926 loan agreement. Taking a cue from this plan, the Liberian legislature in December 1932 declared a moratorium on the loan until government revenues reached $650,000 for two succeeding years. With considerable forebearance the Finance Corporation worked a revision of the 1926 loan, contingent upon Liberia's canceling the moratorium and accepting a revised League plan of assistance. Using familiar tactics, Liberia accepted the first plan and, despite British and American pressure, then rejected the revised plan, charging violation of national sovereignty. The result was to draw upon itself a threat of expulsion from the League of Nations. As a gesture toward reformation, President Barclay devised a three-year plan by which eight "emergency" specialists were engaged to help direct Liberian development. These specialists had no authority and were in continual conflict with government officials. At the end of the three years their contracts were not renewed. But the main purpose of staving off foreign intervention was accomplished. By direct negotiation between Liberia and the Firestone interests the 1926 loan agreement and plantation agreement were revised in 1935, and the 1932 moratorium and other acts violating the first agreement were repealed. The United States then recognized President Barclay and England followed suit. Liberia found that once more it had escaped foreign political control.

After supplementary agreements in 1937 and 1939, the loan agreement of 1926 was permanently amended in 1944. The interest rate was lowered from 7 to 4 percent until 1950, when it would continue at 5 percent until the loan was paid off. If government receipts fell below $565,000, interest might be paid in bonds instead of cash. The loan still constitutes a first lien on customs, head money, land rent, and rubber revenues. The contract stipulates that Liberia's budget shall be divided into two parts, the basic budget of $710,000, providing $565,000 for operating expenses and $145,000 for amortization of the loan and excess revenues. Ninety percent of government revenues amounting to a million dollars or more a year may be appropriated for the basic budget. The remainder is allotted very specifically to other debts and public improvements. When revenue is as high as it now is, there is a substantial amount for internal development.

Liberia's budget has been balanced since 1935, during a period of world depression and financial chaos. All the arrears on the 1926 loan have been paid off, and it is expected that the internal debt will be wiped out in two years and the foreign debt before 1966, the date originally set. The American financial advisor has praised Liberia's national credit as "worthy of the highest admiration." Acknowledgement would also be made to Firestone, the National City Bank, and the U.S. Department of State.

12

Foreign Aggression

Our enemies have been legion. Foreign influences have formed weapons against us. We have suffered. They have tried to take our country; maligned us. These weapons, praise God, have not yet availed. Now in this moment of a new national crisis we must appeal again from our weakness to the strength of Almighty God. We have committed sins; we have not always been right. O forgiving God, forgive the weakness and sin of those who have faltered. O saving God, save our country. O patient God, give strength to our leaders and guide them. Forgive those who trust alone to diplomacy, forgetting Thee. Remember, God, if You can, the prayers of Elijah Johnson a hundred years ago when You led him to this place. This is our home. We have no other place to go. America is not our home. You were with me there, God, in 1928 when I found that out. England is not our home. France is not our home. All that we have is this little strip on the West Coast of Africa. God spare it.

The miracle of the survival of the republic in the path of the aggressive empire building of Europe in Africa can be partly attributed to the implications of the American Monroe Doctrine and partly to the intense rivalry of those nations competing for territorial advantage in Africa. Liberia is potentially a rich little country, strategically located—flanked on the north by Britain's Sierra Leone and to the east and south by vast French possessions. Although Liberia is territorially essential to both these rival powers, neither has been willing to concede the area to the other. When Germany came to the African field years after France and England, it found Liberia still unclaimed by a European power.

The policy of these land-hungry nations has alternated, curiously and persistently, between commendable benevolence and shameless encroachment. Paradoxically, the very desirability of Liberia has been its greatest protection. Its situation has afforded the undignified spectacle of powerful nations eating into the boundary of a tiny, physically helpless state. The very territories which British philanthropy aided, the republic in securing to itself British imperialism took away without a shadow of excuse. Successive Liberian administrations have looked first to one, then to the other of the nations, accepting in turn a temporary and qualified succor. Each appeal afforded an opportunity for one or the other of these nations to point with righteous scorn at a giant's oppression of the helpless until, in turn, the countercharges became so familiar and so mutually applicable to be meaningless. The connection of the United States with the origin of the republic gave it the traditional position of "next best friend," and its good offices have been sought and given, in certain international emergencies, with remarkable consistency for more than a hundred years. But it did little else for its African step-child.

With Lord Ashley's money, President Roberts concluded treaties with natives and purchased before 1860, with full titles, all the area to the north of Monrovia extending from the Mano River to the Sewa and Sherbro Island on the west. This included the Mano, Sulima, and Gallinhas territories, all of which were recognized as being under the jurisdiction of Liberian law. Taking possession of the country had entailed negotiations extending over seven years; also, there had been considerable difficulty in expelling slave traders' activities, a difficulty which reinforced the purchase with as strong moral right as any of the nations could claim. An English trader, John Myers Harris, came into this Liberian territory in 1860 and began operation of his factories in flagrant disregard of all the commercial regulations of the republic. After several protests had gone unheeded, President Benson, who succeeded Roberts, attempted to do what the British at home had told Roberts to do about his trade. He sent the revenue cutter, *Quail,* the gift of the British government, to seize the two Harris schooners, the *Phoebe* and the *Emily,* and bring them to Liberia for adjudication. These schooners were taken between Cape Mount and Mano Point, indisputably Liberian territory.

Although legal and warranted, this act of the Blacks irritated the governor of Sierra Leone, and he boarded a British gunboat, came to Monrovia, and recovered the schooners. The gunboat's commander imposed a penalty on the Liberians of £15 a day for nineteen days' detention of the ships. This was making Benson's attempt to exercise his clear rights a ridiculous gesture. He put his *Quail* aside and, gathering up his treaties, took ship to England to lay the matter before the Foreign Office. Lord Russell examined his claims and the British acknowledged the rights of Liberia to the territories in question. While he was gone, however, Sierra Leone formally annexed a part of the area. Harris refused to move but continued to harass his government about protection. A mixed commission of British and Liberian members was named to investigate the matter further. The British members acknowledged some of the claims and refused others on the highly questionable basis of recent letters alleged to have come from chiefs of the sections. Since the Liberians could show clear titles, the British members, unable to invalidate these, withdrew, leaving the issue unsettled. Despite the failure of the commission to reach an agreement, the British government felt justified in recognizing Liberia's right to only part of the disputed territories. So went another slice from the northern area.

The smuggling continued. Other traders, together with Harris, eventually aroused the natives; bolstered by support at home, the natives became more daring. Harris irritated the Vais to the point that they threatened reprisals without waiting for Liberian aid. In reply Harris organized the surrounding Gallinhas tribes to fight the Vais, to whom the Liberian government then sent aid on the ground that they were theoretical subjects. The Gallinhas tribes consequently were defeated. Losing patience with Harris, the Gallinhas tribes then turned on him and in a remarkably mild expression of their resentment destroyed one of his factories. This was made the ground for damage charges against the Liberian government. The period thereafter was one of harrassing confusion. The native tribes eventually became uncertain of the prevailing authority and destroyed Liberian settlements. Troops sent to put them down destroyed the property of squatting British owners and more damage claims were forthcoming.

A new commission was appointed and an American, Commodore Shufeldt, was named as arbitrator. Harris was now demanding $30,000 in damages. The British members of the commission were open in their contempt for their Liberian associates, and kept them waiting for three weeks after their arrival in Sierra Leone before even acknowledging their presence. They looked at the title deeds held by the Liberians and sent out for oral testimony to dispute them. When the Liberians showed their claims to the areas of Sugaree, Mano, Rock River, and Sulima, they dismissed the claims by simply declaring that no such territories existed. When Schufeldt reduced Harris' claims to $15,000, the commission broke up again without settlement. The British then offered the questionable judgment that Sierra Leone should have the protectorate over the whole disputed area in the interest of tribal order, giving as the reason that the Liberians could not successfully fight the traders and that in any contest the traders could always get the named interference of the Sierra Leone government. Matters dragged along until 1880, when Sir Arthur Havelock came out as governor of Sierra Leone and, at the same time, as British consul general to Liberia.

An article in the *Liberian Observer* for June 10, 1880, well describes this state of affairs and helps also to explain the closed-door policy of the republic that has, in a commercial sense, destructively cramped its development.

> The accession to power in Great Britain of a liberal Ministry with so distinguished a statesman at its head as Mr. Gladstone leads us at this time to call attention to the unsettled Northwest Boundary Question. Particularly so because the present Premier has earned the proud distinction of being called the "friend of Oppressed Nationalities." That the Liberian Government has

been very unjustly treated in the whole business must be apparent to any impartial spectator. The original dispute, if we remember correctly, was in relation to the Gallinhas, Cassa, Muttru and Bumbo territories. The area of country to which the title of Liberia was disputed was gradually extended until it comprised Mano, Manna Rock, Sulima and Sugaree. When the English interfered, they professed to have no interest in the question themselves, but they were only solicitous to see that the tribes whose territories were claimed by us were fairly dealt by. The Liberians, unsuspecting any sinister motive, readily agreed to the surveillance of the English Government. The Commission which met at Sulima in 1879 revealed to Liberia the unpalatable fact that she had been outwitted. Some discussion was had about the Manna Country, but the Commission was never regularly constituted and was broken up by the refusal of the English Commissioners to conform to the terms of the protocol of Lord Granville which provided for the formation of a Mixed Commission for the settlement of the disputed question.

It would be unjust to charge the Foreign Office with having deliberately planned the miscarriage of the Commission, but it does seem that it saw it mismanaged and the Commission obstructed by their Agents with a certain degree of pleasure and complacency. All the Sierre Leone officials engaged in this wrong have been rewarded and advanced. The Marquis of Salisbury up to the time of his retirement was too much engaged to vindicate the honor of his government and do justice to Liberia. Indeed the Liberia Commissioners while at Sulima received a broad hint as to the feeling of the English about the question. Mr. Streeton, the present Chief Justice of Sierre Leone, remarked, "If we allow your claim to the territories in dispute, what will become of the Sherbro trade?" Mr. Streeton showed some ignorance in making this remark. The trade of Sherbro would not at all have been injured. If the natural outlet for the trade of Northern Liberia was the Sherbro, it would have continued to have gone to the Sherbro. Is not the trade of Liberia mostly done with Great Britain? Assuredly, and the tendency is not to dissever but to draw closer the commercial connection between the two countries.

All these things, however, have gone by and Liberia, if justice is speedily done to her, will be glad to forget that there was aught in the way the Boundary Question was managed that savored of injustice.

But it is obviously the duty of the Government to press for an expression from the English Government of their real intentions. Is another Commission to be appointed? Has Her Majesty's Government any intention of acquiring the territories of Gallinhas, Bumbo, Cassa and Muttru in the interest of the Sherbro traders, or does it intend to maintain the independence of the Chiefs of those territories? These are questions which Her Majesty's Government should be pressed to answer. We hope to hear that our Government intends dispatching a suitable person to Great Britain for the purpose of bringing the matter to a termination. We are aware that there are some who are inclined to allow this question to drag along until the Liberian Government is in position to do justice to itself and to take military possession of the disputed districts, but to this policy we are opposed unless indeed the Government could act at once. It will not do to allow a foreign power to be continually interfering with our internal concerns or to give foreigners a chance of exciting sedition among the aboriginal population. Settle the matter and shut the door.

Sir Arthur Havelock determined to force Liberia's consent to the restriction of its frontier. On March 20, 1882, he appeared suddenly at Monrovia with four gunboats and peremptorily demanded consent to the delimitation of Liberian territory from the Gallinhas down to the Cape Mount section and payment of claims amounting to $42,500. Gardner was then president of Liberia. Alarmed by the gunboats, he agreed to pay the indemnity and give rights to territory west of the Maya River. When Sir Arthur returned with his gunboats to get the treaty ratified, the Liberians contented themselves with putting two questions. The first was: If the territory in dispute was British, why should the British government demand indemnities of Liberia for the conduct of their own natives in that area against British traders? The second question was: If Liberia accepted responsibility, as it had already done, and agreed to pay the indemnity, on what grounds then did the British government propose to take the territories that were Liberian by acts of purchase admitted by the British government? The litigation had already cost Liberia close to $100,000 and much of the territory. The treaty generously provided that a sum of about $24,000 should be returned to Liberia as the amount originally paid for the purchases. The French and Belgians severely and self-righteously criticized the British government for taking such an unfair advantage.

The treaty of 1885, which forced the boundaries of Liberian territory down to the Mano River, was vague regarding the interior boundary. The Sierra Leone government suddenly began imposing customs duties and other charges on Liberians for the use of the boundary river. Another mixed commission was formed in 1901, with the three Liberians who were members going to London. The agreement reached amounted practically to a new British concession and proved the beginning of new troubles. The British government would deputize a British officer to demarcate the Anglo-Liberian boundary, lend a British officer to the Liberian government to demarcate the French boundary, and the Liberian government would pay for the cost of the survey. The governor of Sierra Leone would be relieved of his extra assignment as Consul General to Liberia and another officer would be sent to Liberia. Someone would also be sent to survey the Kru coast, and Liberia was to throw its native ports open to foreign trade. In consideration for these blessings to their state, the Liberians might use the river as long as they did not consider it an actual right. They must also allow the government of Sierra Leone to build bridges and ferries across the river to connect with trade routes to the Liberian interior. All this was done in the spirit of utmost friendliness to Liberia. Besides, the British government stood ready to advise the republic on all matters affecting its general welfare. The Liberian members left the conference with the dizzy conviction that there was something queer about this bargain. When they got home, the Liberian senate proceeded to tell them what was wrong; they talked loudly about honor and justice, but to themselves. They tempered their objections almost to a plaintive murmur in their amendments before ratification. They asked timidly that a Liberian officer be allowed to go along with the British surveyors in demarcating both the Anglo-Liberian and the Franco-Liberian boundaries, said that they were afraid as yet to throw open their coast to all foreigners, and limited the bridges and ferries to one each. This called for another joint commission in 1903, which eventually settled the new boundary.

The town of Kanre-Lahun, under the new agreement, fell on the Liberian side. There were British troops already in the area when the Liberian commissioner, Colonel Williams, put up the Liberian flag. The British forces simply remained, and there was nothing Liberia could do about it. The following year, the British complained that the Kissi people, as a result of a tribal fight, were coming into British territory, and asked permission to send British troops further into Liberian territory to quiet the disorder which, they insisted, threatened British interests. This was granted and British troops advanced to Mafisso, later reporting that order had been restored. Nothing was heard of the matter until two years later; a Liberian officer, Captain Lomax, assigned on the Franco-Liberian boundary, happened to go into Kanre-Labun and discovered a British garrison.

A chief of that section, Fabundah, complained that the native escort of Lomax had been plundering his territory. It was at this point that the Liberians turned to the United States on the joint problems of their boundary and a loan. In 1911 the British took the whole of the Kanre-Lahun district, a rich and populous area and, to ease their conscience on the matter, gave Liberia a practically worthless strip of thick forest lying between the Morro and Mano Rivers, and £4,000.

In meeting the demanded reforms, Captain Mackay Cadell, a British officer who had served in the South African War, was placed in charge of the Frontier Force and given the rank of major. His first demand was for two British assistants and ten sergeants from the Sierra Leone Frontier Force. Setting to work with great energy and good humor, he built barracks on the edge of Monrovia, enlisted 250 natives for service, ordered weapons, arms, and ammunition from Great Britain, and with his Scottish accent and bluff cajolery soon bolstered up a little confidence in the Liberians. One minor feature of the organization puzzled them: The military insignia were mostly all British. This had been passed over when it was observed that the ranks were being filled quietly with soldiers from Sierra Leone. The French were the first to notice and protest this, calling it sarcastically but in a spirit of warning, a "British army of occupation." They demanded that an equal number of French native subjects be added to the force. When the Liberians asked Cadell about the matter, he boldly denied that he had any British soldiers and, without investigating the complaint further, the Liberians entered an official denial to the French government.

Cadell was a shrewd fellow and knew what he was about. He continued to flatter the Black officials and made himself thoroughly useful to all departments of government without compensation. They were only too eager to let him do their work if he was willing, and it was not long before he got himself placed in command of the local police force, was made street commissioner, tax collector, and city treasurer. He ousted the Liberian Krus on the police force and substituted Sierra Leonian Mendis. So long as he was doing local officials' work without compensation, no amount of protest could shake his hold on the republic. (A later investigation showed that he was acting largely on the direction of the British consul general, Wallis, in Monrovia. It was quite possible that Wallis overplayed his hand in guiding this coup and that in the effort to establish a good reputation in the Foreign Office for Colonial Service, he employed those criminal artifices to create a result which he had already reported as occurring in the natural course of events.)

When Caldell felt that he had the important offices of government in his hands, he stopped cajoling the officials and began acting on his own authority. He was no longer carrying out the president's wishes and openly resented his interference. Monrovia awoke to the purpose of his good fellowship and eagerness for work, and forced the legislature to protest his summary behavior to the president. Cadell refused to resign any of his posts or turn over any of the city property except on payment of an impossible bill, carefully itemized, which he presented. Moreover, he resented the suggestion of supervision by the president, and refused to dismiss any of his British subjects.

The British consul at this point called a meeting of the Liberian cabinet and delivered a message purporting to come from the British government, in which that government threatened to unite with the French to disrupt the republic if certain things were not done. And as the cabinet puzzled over the meaning of the consul's mysterious message, Cadell sent another note to the president informing him that the native soldiers were in danger of mutiny because of salary arrears and that, if this and other grievances were not adjusted immediately, he could not be responsible for what happened.

The American commission sent over to investigate Liberia's sad muddle gave an account of this extraordinarily dangerous and suspicious sequence of incidents. Notice of the threatened mutiny had been cabled to London a week before the president of Liberia had even been informed of the danger. Sergeants in the force testified that Major Cadell had fomented the mutiny himself, going so far as to appoint certain ones to insult the president, arrest him, and take him to the barracks. On the scheduled day of the mutiny the British gunboat *Mutin* appeared in the harbor. A British officer was in command of the Liberian Frontier Force with a large number of British subjects in the ranks; one British officer was in charge of the Liberian customs, another in command of the Liberian gunboat *Lark,* and a British regiment was in the streets of Monrovia. The British government merely explained that its consul general had gone beyond his authority and transferred him to Dakar in Senegal, the finest consular post on the West Coast.

While the British were chipping off the northern boundary, the French, after their indignant protest against the unfair imperialism of the British, began chipping off the southern boundary. The Maryland settlement, at first an independent colony, secured its land through treaty and purchase from the Grebo chiefs, and the boundaries had been recognized even in the official maps of the French. This territory extended to the San Pedro River, some sixty miles east of the Cavalla River, which constituted fortunately both a geographic and ethnologic boundary. The section, well populated, held a most valuable and useful labor supply.

It was in 1885, the year of the famed Berlin Conference, that France's Liberian operations gained earnestness. Stanley had just founded Leopoldville in the Belgian Congo. The Berlin Conference had talked of humanitarianism and the welfare of the natives, while with mutual distrust the delegates had agreed that no new protectorates should be declared without first giving due notice to other powers to enable them to make equivalent annexations. France became excited and put in a bold claim upon Liberian territory which would have extended its Ivory Coast boundary into Liberia as far as Garraway. This piece of deliberate encroachment was invoked under the alleged provision of Article 34 of the Acts of the Berlin Conference. The territory in question extended about sixty miles along the coast and was a fairly wide strip.

The American government had been observing the menacing gestures of the French since the year before when, to prevent them from getting a foothold on Kent's Island (the probable boundary between Liberia and Sierra Leone), it registered a sharp protest. At that time something close to a policy toward the Liberians was formulated: In view of the intimate relationship between the United States and Liberia, any assertion of claim to any part of Liberia, as defined by accepted limits, and any enforcement of a settlement of alleged grievances which might take place without the United States being allowed to arrange the matter, would produce an unfavorable impression in the minds of the government and of the American people. With the new French threat, the American government protested again. This time the claims were reluctantly modified and were withdrawn to a moderate extent. . . . [Several pages from the original manuscript here were never found; the missing material apparently dealt with the French-Liberian boundary dispute.]

The beginning of the new deliberations was still more inauspicious, for they carried with them a fresh British ultimatum which made amicable settlement of the Anglo-Liberian boundary conditional upon their success in maintaining their integrity against the French.

A treaty was promptly laid before the new delegates which neatly marked off as French 2,000 square miles of the richest territory in the most flourishing section of the republic. Broken, outraged, and helpless, the commissioners stumbled out of the conference room and decided to seek the American ambassador. He could have helped them earlier, but at the point the negotiations had now reached, he could only advise them to sign the treaty before the French presented a second proposition which might take even more territory from them. The representatives signed.

No small nation with territory so valuable could expect to be secure even in such a bargain. The treaty stipulated an international boundary commission which, when formed, was known as the Richard-Nabors Commission. This group began work in 1908. They were forced, however, to suspend activities for three years while the French tried to subdue the tribes in their newly acquired territory. In doing this, they pushed four miles farther into what was left of the Liberian country and remained there. After a boundary had been established, the French began harassing the Liberians again, this time for rectification of certain lines. Zinta, a particularly fertile section, had been placed on the Liberian side by the International Commission. The French wanted it and to get it, after the decision of the commission, they raised a theoretical question about the precise location of the meridian of eleven degrees and fifty minutes. Anticipating the Liberians, they requested of the United States that an American engineer be sent to accompany their own surveyor, M. Villete, and to decide where the meridian of eleven degrees and fifty minutes fell. Before a formal decision could be made, the American engineer was sent over to resurvey the line and he gave the area of land back to the Liberians. World War I interrupted the dispute, and a plan for running a railroad from French territory at the rear of Liberia down through the country to Monrovia developed. This would provide a connection with the 2,500-mile chain of railroad communication which completely surrounded Liberia and provide them a ready access to the sea. The war was demonstrating the value of African troops and likewise the necessity for their facile transportation. The French argued that the railroad would be useful to Liberia, but insisted on cession of a right of way one mile wide on both sides of the road. This would virtually cede a two-mile strip to the French through the center and heart of Liberia. They almost got this at the Peace Conference in return for their consent to the American war loan of $5,000,000 to Liberia.

The boundary question was held quiet for a period and no amount of urging by the Liberians could induce the French to take it up seriously. This forboded a new danger, for the Liberians sensed what they believed to be a plan for some even more drastic action. They appealed again to America and also the State Department, and approached the Paris Foreign Office through the American ambassador and suggested renewal of the work of delimitation. French action was delayed and four years later French troops crossed the new Liberian border and occupied ten villages.,

In 1923 the commissioner general of the Liberian hinterland complained of disputes instigated by the French commandant at Macenta over Ballabala and its surrounding country. There was constant bickering and tribal disturbances. The commissioner general reporting the matter to the Liberian Department of the Interior said:

> It is not to be doubted that the French have both the ability and the disposition to give us continuous boundary worries. They have a thorough scientific knowledge of the topography of the region through which all rivers named in the delimitation treaty flow and where all demarcation lines are to lie. The very treaty is an instrument of their own creation, every vulnerable provision in the instrument is, of course, known to them. All things considered, therefore, it seems that the very best course of immediate action which can be followed is that of urging the French to appoint their engineer for boundary delimitation so that the work may be resumed and completed without further delay. It is obviously advisable for us to secure, just as quickly as we can, a well defined frontier with known rivers and streams, and with cairns fixed by a just survey, even though we lose a little more territory.

The aid of the United States was again needed, and this time it was decided to make it enduring by the concession of important commercial privileges to American capital. Edwin Barclay, secretary of state, was sent to Washington and propositions were made concerning a concession to Firestone and a new American loan. With this important American interest looming on the horizon, the French resumed their boundary demarcation and in a new survey placed Zinta on the French side. As evidence of their good grace in the matter, they turned over to Liberia another town on the border. Thus ended, for a time at least, the persistent peril.

The Germans were more sporadic in their imperialist programs so far as Liberia was concerned, and less acquisitive. For many years they had held some commercial prestige and on occasion had shown a surprising neutrality. It came, thus, as a painful surprise to the Liberians when, on January 26, 1898, the German man-of-war *Nixe* appeared in the Monrovian harbor bringing the governor of the Cameroons (who was, at the same time, the German diplomatic representative to Liberia) on a "serious mission of state." He marched to the department of state and made a demand for $13,000 as damages for injuries to two Germans residing in Cape Palmas. One of these Germans, a consul in Cape Palmas, claimed that an uncivilized native had destroyed some of his coffee trees and, when rebuked, had drawn a knife. The other charge was of a breach of contract between a German trader and two Liberian citizens. At the meeting, the German consul produced a paper which he claimed to be power of attorney from the Kaiser of Germany to make Liberia a German protectorate. The Liberians rejected such a crass and clumsy piece of diplomatic horseplay. When they refused the demands because the question had never been broached in Cape Palmas for settlement, the Germans sullenly withdrew, leaving the whole matter to be settled by the Liberians.

When Liberia joined the Allies in World War I, it found itself at odds with an old commercial relationship with the Germans. The government was under the embarrassment of having to appropriate a number of the most substantial buildings in Monrovia which had been erected by traders. As these served very comfortably as government buildings, the embarrassment faded as time went on. On the morning of April 10, 1912, a submarine stuck its head above the water within ripple distance of the *President Howard,* which constituted the Liberians' sole naval defense. Two sleeping watchmen aboard were aroused and in a spasm of fright dived into the sea. One was drowned, the other swam to shore and rushed in great excitement to the executive mansion to report what he had seen. Commander Gerche of the submarine waited until 9 a.m. and then sent a peremptory message to the president demanding the surrender of English and French residents, the hauling down of the French flag over the French wireless station, and the dismantling of the station. To make certain of the dismantling, he intimated that he expected the apparatus to be delivered to him on the submarine. He promised them, should they fail to comply, the excitement of seeing the wireless station destroyed by his guns.

A conference was hurriedly called of the cabinet and all allied representatives in Monrovia. The British representatives saw the folly of resistance and advised meeting the demands promptly. The matter seemed scarcely debatable but, after all, Liberia was a nation and an ally. Once before, on a threat from a British gunboat to bombard the city unless certain demands were met, a president had exclaimed, "Bombard and be damned!" and the commander had sailed away with a shrug muttering, "Your strength is in your weakness." The cabinet now decided to refuse the German demands! Promptly at 11 a.m. the fateful message was delivered to the commander by Wilmot Dennis, secreatary of war, and T.J.R. Faulkner, mayor of Monrovia. At 1 p.m. a shot from the submarine sank the *President Howard*. A breathless silence fell over the city, for the submarine remained. In a burst of fright, men, women, children, natives and Liberians, sought the surrounding woods. At 4 p.m. a shell, with uncanny precision, picked out the French wireless station and crumpled it to a mass of splintered wood. The captain then appears to have indulged himself in a bit of recreation—he exploded shells at intervals about the city. Although the shells caused little damage, messages were cabled for aid. The only reply was that no warships were available. About three weeks later an American gunboat arrived to inquire what had become of the nation.

The approach of World War II brought a strong revival of interest in Liberia because of its strategic geographic situation on the coast of Africa nearer to Natal by air than Dakar. In 1937 the effort of a Dutch mining concern, backed by Nazi capital, to develop a concession in the Bomi Hills iron area was discouraged, presumably by American pressure. In 1938 a United States warship visited Monrovia in anticipation of a similar visit by a German warship. When war broke out, Liberia declared its neutrality and maintained it until 1944.

German submarines sank a number of ships off the Liberian coast, however, and the United States found it expedient to consolidate its military position in the country. In 1941 Pan American Airways received the right to operate in Liberia and a ten-year lease on Roberts Field, where Firestone created one of the best land-plane fields in the world. A seaplane base was built at Fisherman Lake. Liberia permitted United States troops to enter and in 1942 signed the Defense Areas Agreement, giving the United States the right to build military and commercial airports and "to assist in the protection and defense of the republic" during the war, and getting in return help in road construction, "certain monetary aids for defense purposes," and assistance in training Liberian forces. Germany protested the entry of American troops as a violation of Liberia's neutrality, but the Nazis did not seem to consider it a violation of a neutral's rights when in 1942 they used their radio to urge Liberian natives to revolt. Their diplomatic officers were requested to leave the country. In 1943 Liberia and the United States signed a lend-lease agreement, and on January 27, 1944, Liberia declared war on Germany and Japan, becoming shortly thereafter the thirty-fourth country to sign the United Nations Declaration.

The Port Agreement, providing that the United States build in Liberia with lend-lease funds a port to be administered by an American company until the loan was amortized, was completed in 1943. The amount is believed to be $12,500,000 and is so large that, although apparently non-interest bearing, it is doubtful that Liberia can ever pay it off, even granting that lend-lease obligations are not supposed to be repaid in cash. The Port Agreement also permits the United States to maintain forces in Liberia for use in military installations.

There can be no doubt that with military installations in Liberia the United States is now firmly established there. Whether American policy will operate for the good of Liberia as a nation remains to be seen. Certainly, Liberia, well in the shadow of its "next best friend," need not fear for its boundaries.

13

Economic Foundations

The love of Liberty brought us here
—Motto of the republic

You free till you fool
—native comment

The compulsions to labor, under the institution of American slavery, were external. It seems to require, however, more than the habit of labor to make independent pioneers, capable of evolving from their own inner driving forces a secure economic structure for a sovereign state. Among the early immigrants to Liberia were men long familiar with toil, skilled carpenters and mechanics. It was, perhaps, too much to expect that mentalities dulled and impoverished by the institution of slavery should immediately respond to the subtler implications of freedom, out of which philosophies and ethics evolved. It was early evident that for the mass of emigrants to Liberia freedom meant, foremost, freedom from the cruel exactions of labor. No one generation of Blacks (or Whites, for that matter) could conquer Africa, or any important section of it. The situation might have adjusted itself in time with the development of new and more secure habits but for the presence and availability of a cheap and almost inexhaustible supply of native labor. From the time of Ashmun to the present the doom of the state has been read in the neglect of agriculture and industry, in the specious emphasis on trade and borrowed capital alone, and in general habits of indolence, rationalized into the natural prerogatives of civilization.

From the first founding of the colony the provision that each emigrant should receive a town site and twenty-five acres of agricultural land for development has existed. The town sites have been taken, but the agricultural sites neglected, although enough skill has emigrated to make a reasonable beginning. There were, in the first flutterings of the infant republic, men who rose to some eminence in trade. But trade was a "gentlemanly enterprise" which flourished on the surface and failed to take root. The children of the founders, in turn, reared in the inescapable atmosphere of native subordination, have eschewed labor as degrading, with a prejudice no less marked than the "poor Whites" of America exhibited in their attitude toward slave labor. They must be traders or government officials, or nothing. Frederick Starr quotes the lament of the Liberian S.D. Ferguson over the economic plight evident even before a second generation had passed:

> Compare, you say, the present with the past. Where are the schooners and cutters that used to be built right here in Liberia, when nearly every responsible man had his own? Where are the tons of sugar that used to be shipped to foreign ports by our fathers, and the barrels of molasses, and the tons of camwood? Where are the financial men of the country that looked upon the holding of public offices almost beneath them, who had to be begged to fill the offices? Where are those who, when they had made their farms, lived off the farms? Oh, where are the honest, upright and loyal government officials of 1847? You answer for yourselves. Where are the great Liberian merchants of Monrovia, Grand Bassa, Sinoe, and Cape Palmas? Gone!

It is not enough, however, to lay responsibility merely on psychological factors. Native labor can readily be made as competent as that of the American-Liberian, and the living standards of the two are widely different. The prevailing West Coast rate of pay for the native is about 18¢ a day, and until a native has acquired the taste and habits of civilization, he can live in comparative comfort within these limits. His diet is chiefly rice, cassava, palm oil, and dried fish. The Liberian requires more, not only for his necessities but for his pretensions. The simple pressure of competition would be sufficient to eliminate him unless he could develop superior skill and inventiveness, neither of which he appears to have attempted.

In South Africa, where there is a White artisan population below the level of competent administrators, adjustment to the native standard is made through the notorious "color bar" legislation. The Liberian adjustment has been made by letting the native have all the work. In South Africa, however, it has been more than a matter of taking in one another's wash—the same agencies which supplied the work were developing the resources of the country and creating wealth. This the Liberians have been unable to do. Theirs has been a failure written in the tradition of loans and in their present and well-nigh hopeless poverty in a land eagerly fertile.

There is not at present in the entire republic a single major development under Liberian control. Before World War II over 95 percent of all trade was in the hands of foreigners—German, British, French, and Syrian traders. Most of the civilized population derives its support, directly or indirectly, from the government. There is one qualified physician in

Monrovia, apart from those supplied by the missions, Firestone, Pan American Airways, and those connected with American military installations. Until 1931 there was not a single Black physician practicing medicine in the country. (A Black physician, graduated from Meharry Medical College, went to Liberia in March 1931).

With the possible exception of T.J.R. Faulkner, an American-born Black who lived in Liberia for about forty years, the Liberians have revealed complete lack of commercial enterprise and mechanical skills. Faulkner operated an ice factory and an ice cream plant, and at one time he installed and maintained a local telephone system. He became the most useful man in Liberia, the only person able to cut the sandbar so obstructive to harbor traffic and to erect and repair major machinery. He soon rose to importance and became a threat to the entrenched political party. Political opposition lost for him his telephone and other franchises and consumed his energies in what amounted to a world campaign for reforms within the state.

The dearth of mechanical skills has been pathetically marked in the prompt collapse of practically every impulse to modernity. In one gesture, for example, a government telephone line was built from Monrovia to Bassa, a distance of about sixty miles. It operated two weeks and broke down; it was left unrepaired. On the advice of one of the early American receivers, two second-hand boats were purchased at Las Palmas in the Canary Islands. They were partially paid for, and under marine law the government was required to employ and maintain a registered captain and engineer. This was done for five years, while the ships remained in the harbor at Las Palmas, 1,000 miles away. Finally the purchase was completed and the vessels were brought to Monrovia. They made several trips from Monrovia to Cape Palmas; then the engines went bad and they were allowed to rot in the harbor.

A government engineer attempted to erect a cement bridge on an appropriation of $6,500. He succeeded in getting up one huge and useless buttress before the money was gone. Firestone engineers were employed to rebuild the bridge at an expense of $2,500. The ferry across St. Paul's River, between Millsburg and White Plains, when built was a useful and substantial aid to communication. The cable snapped and for want of skill to repair it, the ferry lay idle for two years. The power system of Monrovia was suspended for several years because a part of the diesel engine was broken and the city remained without lights, although light taxes were collected from the Krus despite their bitter protest. Building is done without plan by natives under the direction of either a European trader or a Liberian. With all its wealth of lumber, Liberia has but one sawmill and most of the work is done by hand.

A coast Kru who operated the single barbershop in Monrovia reflected the native attitude toward the surrounding indolence:

I used to work on a ship. When the war stopped the ships and we can't go out, I barber. I'm a Kru. I have my house down in Americo-Liberians who want to sit down all the while and make us work; drag our men and boys out of their houses to work on the streets, for no pay, with no tools and no food. Do they go out to work? No! That's what they want the natives to do. That's why they are no further now. Lazy. Over a hundred years they have been here and look at the houses. Look at the streets. Full of the same rocks they found here. All the rich palms and coffee go to waste while they sit down. No farms, no businesses, no nothing. All of them want to be government. All of them want to be lawyers. Look at the other towns on the West Coast. This is the raggedest part of it. Look at Lagos, Secondi, Accra. See how the natives live. Good houses, good money, good streets. I used to go down there on the ship to work. Stayed there once fifteen months. Came back happy. Made money. We spent it buying our women clothes. We didn't need the money for food, for we have our own gardens. But these people, when they can't make money any other way make it selling our boys. My own cousin and nephew were caught and sent off to Fernando Poo. One came back after three years. I drawed his money myself from the Spanish Consul. One pound, six pence—for three years. He came back sick and soon after he died. Sammy Ross took hundred of them from Sinoe. Yancy is doing it right now in Cape Palmas. I went over to cut the Spanish Consul's hair. He said, "Why you people make so much fuss about the boys who go to Fernando Poo? There are 8,000 boys who go out to work on ships and only 3,000 of them go to Fernando Poo. Why don't you talk about the other 5,000?" I wait a long time before I answer him. I say, "Mr. _____, when I come up here to cut your hair, you get up and say it's all right and pay me two shillings. I go away and I come back when you send for me. Suppose I cut your hair, and instead of giving me fourpence, you give me nothing and give the money to somebody else, and when you call, he make me to come again and I get nothing for it. Am I his slave?" These people can't stand. . . . They can't rise and they hid book from we natives. Say they have schools for natives. Where they? When you go up to country, you try to find them. They don't like American Negroes to come here because they work. They want them to treat the boys like they treat them, so they be all the same. They say you have to treat them this way, and if you don't they don't like you.

The country will yield almost any variety of green vegetable grown in America, but there are no developed truck gardens. Practically all food used by the Liberians is imported. Rice can be grown in the country and is grown by the natives, although in insufficient quantities for their own demands; large quantities are imported despite the law forbidding its shipment into Liberia except in emergencies.

At one time in the history of the republic, there was the prospect of a valuable asset in coffee. It is, incidentally, an interesting coincidence that the coffee plant was first discovered and developed in Abysinia, the only other Black-controlled country in Africa. Liberian coffee has a characteristically pleasing flavor, and in its wild state has larger leaves, flowers, and fruit and a more robust and hardy constitution than any other known species. It flourishes in a variety of altitudes and soils, and blooms in any month of the year. Specimens of the coffee received awards at the World's Columbian Exhibition in Chicago in 1893. Thirty acres of land could sustain 16,000 trees with room to spare for other essential crops, and there was considerable demand for it in Europe. It required about five years to develop a coffee farm and, although the yield from thirty acres at early prices could bring $3,000 or $4,000 annually, deliberate cultivation of the plant never became popular. A market of some sort could always be found for the wild coffee and with a few exceptions trading was limited to this type. Liberian coffee scions, however, were carried in time to Ceylon, Madagascar, and Malay and given intensive cultivation. The crude methods of gathering coffee at home, and the persistent attempts to market it without clearing, grading, or selecting, undermined its popularity even before the enormous Brazilian coffee development swamped the market, lowering the price so tremendously that it was unprofitable to gather it. The old coffee farms reverted rapidly to tropical bush.

The palm tree is perhaps the most useful and profitable product of the tropics. The oils and kernels are used in making soaps, candles, and lubricating oils, and have been in great demand in Europe since their introduction in 1850 by a Liberian trader. Moreover, Liberia first introduced *piassava* to Europe. This is a sort of tough raffia made from the raffia palm, from which stiff brooms and brushes are made. The making of *piassava* has been confined entirely to native industry and, although the market demand has continued, it has not been consistently developed for large-scale exportation. As with coffee, the failure to grade and select the fibers eventually gave new West Coast competitors an advantage in the market.

Sugar making was formerly a paying industry, and the cane grew luxuriantly along the fertile banks of the St. Paul. Cheaper beet sugar entered the market, no attention was given to improving the plants or purchasing new machinery, and the industry was neglected in favor of wild coffee which at the time brought good prices.

Rubber grows wild in the country; it was with a view to systematic collection and marketing of this commodity that the Liberian Development Company inaugurated a commercial experiment that ended disastrously for the republic. Cocoa can be grown abundantly, but trees must be planted and cultivated. Natives on the British Gold Coast just a short distance away raised nearly two-thirds of the world's supply, and Spanish planters in the tragically unhealthful island of Fernando Poo developed a considerable market by using exported native Liberian labor.

Camwood was once an important article of trade, bringing as much as $250 a ton; butuline dyes destroyed this trade as they destroyed the indigo industry. Kola nuts are found in abundance and can be widely used in Europe and America as ingredients for tonics and beverages, but this trade has been neglected because of the difficulty of getting the produce from the interior.

The mineral wealth of Liberia is practically unknown. Until recently surveys by experts were discouraged as likely to reveal resources too tempting for the greed of stronger nations. Mining concessions have been at times granted to foreign concerns but have been withdrawn before they could be developed. These uneasy suspicions created an odd situation. Without exact knowledge of the resources, foreign capital was unwilling to take concessions unless they could be so broad as to include all contingencies of property. Sir Simon Stuart and J.H. Myring went out to Liberia in 1902 on behalf of the West African Gold Concession, Limited, and reported finding a number of gold reefs, besides coal, tin, and various other minerals. There were *micaceous schist* in the formation of a large portion of the country, and large outcrops of graphite, but the extent of these deposits has not yet been thoroughly investigated. Development requires capital and the large-scale investment of capital brings with it stringent demands. "Our real mineral wealth," said one Liberian writer, "is imperfectly known and if it were, we have not the means of developing it ourselves and would have to invite foreign concessionaries who would demand terms which would help us very little. Further, it might cost us our autonomy. South Africa did not draw the envious eyes of England until gold and diamonds were discovered."

With the advent of World War II this position was changed and Liberians are now looking for private American capital to exploit their natural resources. The United States Geological Mission which visited the country in 1943 reported high-grade iron ore in the Bomi Hill area that could be obtained by surface mining. An American concern, the "Christie Group," has been granted a concession to develop mining in this district.

The market fluctuations may affect export prices on certain commodities, but there seems little excuse for failure to supply domestic needs. More than a fourth of all imports has been food, most of which could have been grown easily in the country. The short crops of the natives have been deliberate, the intention being to raise only as much as they themselves expect to consume. The surplus, they claimed, was so regularly taken from them by the authorities in the form of monthly rations for the government or by the marauding soldiers, that they refused to grow more than they needed for immediate consumption.

The neglect of the very sources of national wealth and the ignorance of scientific agriculture resulted, until recently, in a dangerous unbalance of trade. Regularly, imports exceeded exports, an exceedingly bad state of affairs. The only resources to balance exports with imports was the money spent by foreign missionaries residing in Liberia, the expenditures for maintenance and development of the Firestone plantations, the money brought in by Kru boys working as stevedores and deck hands on steamers, exchange charges of the bank for transfer of funds to and from Liberia, and a string of inconsiderable, miscellaneous items.

One perpetual handicap to trade development has been the lack of roads and adequate trade routes to the interior. The absence of work animals and the condition of the roads restrict transportation of all produce to head loading, the most expensive transportation in the world. Thus, the possibility of large-scale trade becomes dependent on the development of a system of interior roads, which in turn is dependent on a supporting trade.

The logic of a sound economic program, envisaged by President King as the crowning of his administration, demanded a widespread system of trade routes through the interior. A road program was begun, an ambitious scheme which, if it had been possible to carry through, would have made a sound contribution to internal development. But there were no Liberian engineers, and the government was disinclined, for unbelievably trivial and in some instances grossly unsound reasons, to employ competent persons. The old colonial trick of bribing the government-appointed chief or inducing others, by means fair or foul, to supply road workers with or without their consent, was resorted to in carrying out this program. An average of 6,000 natives were kept daily building roads without pay. They were required to purchase and use their own tools and feed themselves. In addition they were subject to fines, both authorized and unauthorized, for infractions of regulations which they could never fully understand. It was a wasteful procedure and the roads dug out, for the most part, reverted promptly to bush. Between the two fires of exportation and forced road labor, the natives lost spirit, forgot their home industries and art, and refused even to grow enough food for their own consumption, saying that the American-Liberians always took it from them.

The road program is again in process of development. Following the conclusion of the Defense Areas Agreement, the United States sent Black troops to Liberia under Brigadier General P.L. Sadler who, in addition to helping train Liberian forces, aided in the construction of roads both for military and economic purposes, and there are plans to complete the road from Monrovia to French Guinea begun by the U.S. Army. A good network of roads is essential, not only for the economic development of Liberia, but also for the political unity of the country.

With skill, capital, and tools lacking, the only financial resources of the government for the year 1928–29 were $1,170,185.20, and of this $584,946.92 was from customs and head money, and $200,244.47 from hut taxes. However, the customs and internal items steadily declined and no other source of income was in sight. The estimated total revenues from all sources for 1931 was $772,500, and the financial adviser was obliged to repeat the warnings begun by Ashmun a century before:

> There are no signs that the bottom of the decline in customs collections has been reached, and unless active measures are taken to improve the agricultural conditions of Liberia, no substantial improvement can be expected. Liberia is not an industrial or a manufacturing nation. For its purchases abroad, it must sell products of the soil which are principally palm products, coffee and *piassava*. Exports of these vary little in quantity from year to year, but unit prices have declined abnormally. There is but one way open to increase the purchasing power of the people of Liberia, and that is to make it convenient for natives to bring their agricultural products to Liberian port towns, or to sell them near their homes to traders who will.

To this situation was added the uncontrollable factor of a decline in produce prices after 1928, the only item of Liberian export products remaining stable in price being *piassava*.

It is a curious fact of economics that the volume of overhead costs never scales down proportionately to the volume of trade. Charges were thus disproportionately high for such "invisibles" of the balance sheet as freight, marine insurance commissions, brokerage, interest on government loans invested in Liberia, insurance premiums, repayment of the foreign loans, expenditures of nationals in foreign travel and education, travel of Liberians between ports on foreign vessels, losses in exchange and contributions to meet Liberia's apportionment of expense to the League of Nations, and other international commissions and bodies.

"Our only truly exploitable commodity," said the secretary of state in 1930, "is labor." And herein lay the root of much of the difficulty of the republic. The Krus have been the seafarers and coast laborers of the West Coast since shipping became important. Deck hands were taken on at Monrovia to load and unload the ships on the trip down to the coast and back, where they were returned to their homes. A major government revenue was the "head money" imposed on each laborer taken on a ship for work. These fees, amounting to $1 per head for each trip, were levied in 1929 on 4,498 workers who brought into the country over $100,000 in wages. Native laborers shipped out of the country on contract yielded compound fees which included headmoney of $1, light tax of $1, a certificate of origin of $1, a recruiter's fee of $2.50, recruiting agent's fee of $2.50, hut tax of $1.00 and, on their return, customs duties. It was an easy step from this legitimized dependence on native earnings to the uncontrolled and nationally disruptive practice of exporting labor permanently out of the country.

The recruiting of labor was first capitalized in a concession to a German firm in 1897. A law was passed in 1903 setting the recruiters' license fee at $250, requiring a guarantee of $150 on the return of the laborer, and imposing a fee of $5 for each laborer recruited. This fee came out of the first earnings of the native. The gradual drawing away of laborers brought a protest from farmers in the Mesurado, Cape Mount, and Bassa sections, and in 1908 a law was passed prohibiting shipments from those points. In 1911, concession was granted to Messrs. Benarkis, Makrides, and Andronicos, general contractors of the Transvaal Mining Company of United South Africa, to take workers from Sinoe and Maryland to the Transvaal. This yielded the government a $4 head tax and bonus from the company for each laborer exported, $4 more from each native, and a special bonus of 50¢ a head from the company for the privilege. As coffee declined in value, the stress fell increasingly on this native labor as a source of income, and three years later a labor bureau was created in an attempt to regulate the handling of the labor and stabilize the revenues.

Without specific legislative enactment, native laborers for many years were recruited and sent to the Spanish island of Fernando Poo, to the Portuguese Island of Principe, and to various French possessions. Growing dissatisfaction over the great mortality rates from sleeping sickness, the excessive cruelty of the masters, and the permanent loss of Liberian labor as well as subjects, led to a legislative prohibition against these exportations. The Spaniards protested and complained that this action was ruining their agricultural program. On the expectation of getting a preferential tariff on coffee, a formal convention was drawn up in 1914 with the governments of Spain and Liberia to the effect that Liberia would provide laborers for the cocoa-growing island under certain nominal safeguards. The arrangement brought to the government about $5.50 for each "boy" shipped. As the practice grew, the Spanish government succeeded in having the restrictive legislation removed against Bassa Country.

Bitter protests from natives on their own behalf and from the Liberian farmers who depended on native laborers, together with the unsavory reports of ill-treatment and death in Fernando Poo, made it impossible for the government, with any conscience, to renew the convention. The pressure for laborers for Fernando Poo continued, however, and the want of money in Liberia was chronic. Two government officials, Sammy Ross, postmaster general, and Allen Yancy, vice-president of the republic, stepped in and, on special consideration of the president, secured the exclusive rights to recruit labor under a new contract with the Sindicato Agrícola de los Territorios Españoles del Golfo de Guinea, which raised the price to $50 a head for native "boys." Then followed an exploitation which has seldom been surpassed anywhere in its disgraceful disregard of native rights, humanity, and the welfare of the government of which the perpetrators were responsible officials. The system, as it grew, involved a network of public officials, acting with the implications of full government authority. The laws regulating the traffic and safeguarding such remaining rights as the natives had were violated. Eventually the government itself found it impossible to collect the headmoneys which, sadly enough, were being used by the receiver general to pay off the loans. To circumvent this tax the recruiters began shipping their laborers down the coast as passengers. No less than 10,000 "boys" were sold out of the country by these two contracts alone. A bill introduced by Twe to abolish the practice of recruiting and shipping native laborers of the republic outside the country was passed in the House but defeated in the Senate, and the practice went on until the coming of the International Commission in 1930.

Harvey Firestone, Senior, says his attention was first called to the country of Liberia in 1923. The British and Dutch monopoly in rubber had forced the price to $1.20 a pound, and the United States was using annually over 300,000 tons. Firestone sent a representative to Liberia to investigate the feasibility and possibility of a concession. This investigation would most likely have met the fate of earlier efforts to enter Liberia but for the extraordinary influence of several inescapable difficulties: the helplessness of the Liberians under the constant harassment and acquisitiveness of the French, the failure of the American loan, the collapse of the coffee market, and a stringent need of money, in the absence of commercial developments of any sort in the country.

The investigators were therefore cordially received; later they reported favorably on the prospects. Three agreements were drawn up: the first to cover the Mt. Barclay plantation of 2,000 acres, representing an earlier experiment of the Liberia Rubber Company, rights to which had been forfeited to the government; the second covered leasehold on 1 million acres of land over a period of ninety-nine years; the third covered plans for a harbor.

The terms of the loan constituted a weird entanglement of interests and defenses. The government conceded leasehold to the company for a period of ninety-nine years on 1 million acres of land—or on any lesser area, to be selected from time to time during the period—certain tax exemptions for the company as such, the rights to all timber cut (provided it was not sold), the right to engage in any operation other than agricultural on the land, provided that in the case of mining or like operation it be subject to the existing laws of the republic regulating mining concessions. It was also conceded that the company have the right to develop and use its own natural water and hydroelectric power, to construct and maintain power lines over any government lands by way of conveying power between selected tracts, and lines of communication for its own purposes, but not as common carriers; access to all ports and plots of land to ports upon favorable terms; and support and assistance in securing and maintaining an adequate labor supply.

The company promised the government to select and develop from year to year land suitable for rubber and other agricultural products in convenient and economically sound quantities (a minimum of 20,000 acres to be developed within five years) and to pay annual rental of 6¢ an acre in advance on land selected, and after six years a revenue tax equivalent to 1 percent of the value of all rubber and other commercial products shipped, calculated at the market rate on arrival in the United States. It gave the government the privilege of regulating and collecting taxes payable under the laws of the republic from employees of the company up to the limit of the average number employed during the year, and agreed not to import labor unless the local supply proved inadequate and then only to take workers acceptable to the Liberian government. Likewise, it agreed never to sell or transfer the rights of the agreement without the prior written consent of the government. Finally, the company offered to use its influence to obtain a loan either from the United States or from some other person or persons, not exceeding $5,000,000, for public developments, the terms to be subject to the approval of the Liberian legislature.

The mutual fears and distrust were not wholly groundless, for invested capital, despite original good intentions, has its sacred imperatives, while independent statehood has its inviolable prerogatives; and these, in the very nature of things, do not always coincide. It is inconceivable that the investors of $1 million in a foreign country, where land ownership was denied to all foreigners, would be content to trust entirely to the caprices of an unstable government. The loan, with its corollary of a receivership, and the stipulation regarding the submission of questions of differences to an arbitration committee, were intended as safeguards to capital. The Liberians, on the other hand, demanded that no more than 1,500 White employees should be used, and that failure to operate particular areas of land over three consecutive years would extinguish the rights to these lands. They also required the right to regulate the labor supply officially, and for the first period of operation they attempted to do this by reviving the defunct labor bureau established in 1918.

The terms of recruitment, under the provisions of the bureau, included fees for the government and for chiefs and headmen for each laborer hired. A natural result was that recruitment proceeded under very much the same conditions as before. The district commissioners recognized the company as a new source of income, and insisted on having their commissions. The natives could make no distinction between compulsory recruitment for

Firestone, of whom they knew nothing, and recruitment for any other kind of labor in or out of the country. There was the redeeming feature, however, that a laborer once hired under this arrangement was free to discontinue his services at will and even to limit the number of working days in the week. Deductions were made from the pay of the laborers for nonworking days, which they, in their ignorance of these methods, attributed to the familiar causes—"Government eating our money."

The Americans brought over by Firestone to conduct the plantations were unseasoned to Africa and unacquainted with native customs, and there were, therefore, many early mistakes in their relations with the natives, in the buildings constructed for themselves, and in medical precautions. Most of these mistakes were rectified as the work developed. The problem of pay, for example, made trouble whether given in full in cash wages of one shilling a day for the number of days worked, or partly in rice rations. Again, the season of plantation clearing, from November to April—the period of heaviest labor and largest number of workers—coincided with the natives' farming season. Among the tribes in the neighborhood of the Du Plantation, the men did the clearing while the women did the planting and hoeing after the rains set in. Under the communal system the chiefs required further labor from the men for their own farms. A result was an uncertain labor supply when most needed. One method of meeting the difficulty was that of domiciling entire tribes within the plantation area. There were objections to this, however, from the government, which feared losing control over both the natives and the hut taxes. Otherwise, there was the other questionable expedient of discouraging the cultivation of rice entirely and importing this grain from Ceylon. This the company does, and justifies itself by arguing that the wasteful crop rotation system of the natives contributes to a dangerous deforestation, and that it is cheaper anyhow to import rice from India.

In the southern plantation at Gyidetarbo in the Cape Palmas district, the Grebos who inhabit that area have a different division of labor between the sexes, as compared with the Pwessis, who prevail in the neighborhood of the Du Plantation. The men are warriors and hunters. The Grebos were the last tribe to lay down arms against the government. Their women have had so large a share of the essential hoe culture of self-maintenance as to give the stamp of "women's work" to the most essential labor of rubber cultivation. Money as an incentive failed to break this fixed custom. A first expedient, also unsuccessful, was a different pay arrangement, offering part cash and part rice. The company then turned to Liberian officials of the district who "knew the natives" of that section. They got laborers, cleared certain areas as they had built roads, but kept the natives' wages as well as their own commissions. This practice was abandoned when it was discovered, but not before these natives, returning to their villages, had reported that Firestone work was like government work—no pay. The company then insisted on doing its own recruiting in the interior and could not, even if so disposed, employ any other compulsion than the stimulation of desire for money. It is impossible to say what compulsions might have been felt if the venture had proved immediately profitable. Under no circumstance could the million acres be placed simultaneously under cultivation to require the number of men originally indicated by Mr. Firestone, for the conditions under which the growing is done would have prohibited it. But the price of rubber declined to 8.375¢ before the first trees matured, and operations were for some time largely confined to maintenance of the land in development.

During World War II Firestone's operations expanded under the stimulus of need, and Liberia became the primary source of rubber under Allied control, excepting Ceylon. In 1945 on 57,209 acres of rubber varying in age from four to twenty years the company produced 43,314,009 pounds of dry rubber and latex, employing 17,654 tappers on a schedule 50 to 100 percent above normal. It was planned to abandon the system at the end of 1946 and revert to usual production as the urgent need for rubber passed.

This activity brought economic prosperity to Liberia during the war years. Rubber made up 92 percent of the country's exports, and gold 4 percent. Both imports and exports steadily increased and for the last few years Liberia has enjoyed a favorable balance of trade. In 1944, $10,139,000 worth of goods was sent out of the country, chiefly to the United States, while imports, nearly all from America, reached $3,800,000. Native production of coffee, cocoa, and palm kernels made up less than 1 percent of exports.

Firestone is about the only large and definite source of money income for native labor within the country. Its importance to the country is obvious, but its implications are generally questionable. Fear of White control, although unlikely under the present arrangement, has been responsible for endless irritations. Various departments of the government may issue regulations which interfere with operations and which, unless checked by some stronger consideration, go to ridiculous extremes. Such a regulation was the so-called Wage Act passed several years ago at President Barclay's suggestion, increasing wages of all except government employees 50 to 200 percent, and obviously aimed at foreign employers. Although the courts are frequently called upon, many personal factors may interfere with just and amicable settlement of cases. Common standards of honesty are not always observed, and unnecessary embarrassments to various officials are sometimes deliberate as a means of stressing the fact of alien status of the company and its officials. These in turn call forth resentment, outraged discussion, and ridicule among the Americans—usually, however, within the privacy of their own circles. Inevitably, this strengthens the desire of the company officials to have a more secure hand in the making of an administrative policy as a measure of self-defense. The tact of the important officials has been responsible for keeping a balanced relation so far. The officials have been well-liked by the native workers, and have been on terms of mutual understanding with the government, with which most of the employment dealings were negotiated.

Liberian objections to the company include its connection with the loan, the fact that no Blacks hold any of the higher positions of management, its aloofness as a colony, and a suspected desire to interfere with methods of government. To the Liberians, the company represents money and, as such, it is exposed to many schemes, sometimes clever and illegal, to draw upon this source. Most dangerous to the Liberians, however, is the growing dependence on the company for public facilities, goods, and services, which they are expected to render without pay. And although the company has felt obliged to provide many of these against its will, the result is exactly what the Liberians oppose and continually preach against—control by the company.

Indications of this dependence appear not only in personal appeals of high officials for gifts and services (from sewer pipes and automobiles to free transportation through the country), but formally, in the president's address of 1929 to the legislature, in which he accused Firestone of precipitating a national depression by the reduction of the labor force.

Since the coming of Firestone, Liberians themselves, taking advantage of the offers of free seed, scions, and supervision, have a total of about 2,500 acres in rubber. Among these farms are those owned by ex-president Barclay, James F. Cooper, and Luke, a native who had already developed a small rubber plantation when Firestone came in 1926. Rubber was then bringing 70¢ a pound on the New York market; and he received about $600 monthly over a period of eight months. He had no equipment for handling the product; he simply rolled out the sheets with bottles.

Among other accusations leveled against the company has been that of fixing the price of independently produced rubber by virtue of its monopoly. The failure of the natives to help develop the wild rubber program during World War II, however, was found to be due, not to the price, which was set by the U.S. Rubber Development Corporation in agreement with Britain, but to the fact that the Liberia Export-Import Corporation, with which President Barclay had insisted the Rubber Development Corporation should deal, was paying the natives in valueless script and keeping the money paid by the Development Corporation. Only eight tons a year was being produced. In 1944 Firestone became the agent for the wild rubber program with the right to deal directly with the natives, resulting in increased production.

The presence of the company has meant for the Liberians a measure of contact with large-scale industrial processes and modern standards. The settlement at the Du has the aspect of any middle-class suburban development, with its ice plant, water system, cold storage, and lighting, and with close supervision of the water supply and sanitation. The Firestone Company has brought engineers for building their own roads and bridges which at least offer an example of skillful economy. Two hospitals have been erected of steel and concrete and are well equipped and staffed with five American physicians, in keeping with the agreement. A prenatal clinic with instruction in child care and a school for nurses which has graduated fifty Liberian nurses are maintained. The company hydroelectric plant of 1,500 KWH power trains Liberian employees. The company also supports a research program of experimental tropical agriculture, and has made contributions of a general cultural nature from an anthropological survey to the publication of a grammar in native Kpelle. It has established a public radio service and has given $65,000 for the improvement of government roads, exclusive of those on its own property. The building of the harbor, which was included in the terms of the original agreement, after the expenditure of a considerable sum of money by Firestone, was abandoned as unfeasible.

The exploitation of native labor as a chief commodity with the accompanying and almost traditional dependence on loans is an impossible economic foundation, and can never give security. During the century of the republic's existence, the character of the governing population has changed materially. With this change has come a distinct shifting of emphasis from internal development to the purely political aspects of government itself. This is nowhere more evident than in the overwhelming proportion of the American-Liberian population deriving its support from the government. Such a dependence gives abnormal importance to politics, to the neglect of practically everything else.

Primarily, agriculturists are needed, and there must be aid in securing a footing on the soil and in the slow process of developing a market. Trained agriculturists are necessary, not only to restore the dignity of this occupation, but to set new standards in seed selection and grading, and intelligent diversification of crops. Native confidence must be restored and the natives encouraged to cultivate independent farms. Skilled craftsmen are required also and new standards of precision and thoroughness must be established.

To help such a program, the U.S. government has lent an expert to Liberia, at that country's expense, to assist in improving agricultural methods. World War II brought Liberia what may well be the beginning of a carefully planned and productive economy when the U.S. Foreign Economic Administration sent a mission to Liberia with instructions which Earl Parker Hanson, the head of the group, interpreted as follows: "(1) Liberians were to be helped to produce plenty of good quality cocoa, palm kernels, *piassava* and kola nuts, for which the United States now offers a good market . . . ; (2) Liberians were to be encouraged to start, either on their own or with the participation of American private capital, whatever small industries they can manage; (3) large corporate concessions should go to American rather than European firms; (4) the country's independence should be protected." The plans and recommendations of the mission touched most of the institutions of the country. Mr. Hanson noted the "downright avidity with which the aborigines themselves took to new ideas, new methods, new items in their diets, and the small new sources of income that enabled them for the first tiime in years to meet the tax collector with ready money." The mission introduced a few donkeys to take the place of head transportation and the experiment was well received, forage crops for the animals being grown successfully.

The lack of harbor facilities is being remedied by the construction with lend-lease funds of a port at Monrovia under the supervision of the U.S. Navy in consultation with the Foreign Economic Administration and the Liberian government. It is expected that the work, authorized by the Port Agreement signed in December 1943, will be completed by 1947. Although the United States will have the right to use the port for strategic defensive purposes, the improved harbor will inevitably be of benefit to Liberian trade, as are the air and seaplane fields established at Roberts Field and Fisherman's Lake.

In 1938, Liberia and the United States signed a "friendly relations" treaty, and during World War II, by arrangement with the U.S. Treasury, Liberia replaced British currency with American money as the official exchange of the country. All these things, of course, mean that Liberia is being bound firmly within the economic orbit of the United States.

The economic weakness of the republic, for which the government has been in large measure responsible, raises the question of drastic reforms in every department of the government. Liberia requires capital; it also requires fresh immigration, new skills, new standards of industry, and, on the part of the Liberians, a fuller understanding of the movement of the civilized world around them.

The British and French are finding it necessary to revise their native policies to give increasing representation to their natives. Their present native courts are gradually becoming effective and there is increased native awareness of their own position. On the Gold Coast, at least, the British learned that with proper guidance and education, the economic returns of an enlightened policy could be as considerable as under more drastic systems of exploitation.

The logic of native development in Liberia is full incorporation into the life and government of the state and into the fabric of Liberian society. Such a consummation could be long delayed in the surrounding colonies. The situation contains a challenge for Liberia, for there is yet some question whether these surrounding colonies do not find it to their advantage, unfortunate as it might be, to have in Liberia the example of inadequate government. The implications for administration and for native psychology of a flourishing and well-administered Black republic could well be viewed as disconcerting. It would be infinitely better for Liberia to have inefficiency revealed and corrected than for the country to continue revolving blindly in a dismal circle of poverty, pretense, and dependence, meriting the taunt that it is the "lowest form of government in Africa."

14

Politics and the Public Weal

Let us take warning, fellow-citizens; we are fast hastening to the point when our government will be no longer a government of the people but a government of party. . . . It is not to party that I object; for I believe that the existence of two honest, earnest, zealous, active political parties in the community, is wholesome. But what is lamentable is the party spirit manifesting itself among us—discoloring or coloring every action to suit itself. There is not an act, however, virtuous and honorable, which may not be distorted to suit party purposes. . . . These things are sapping the foundations of society. Every man is becoming distrustful of his neighbors. . . . But there is a disposition the opposite of party spirit, which is, if possible, still more reprehensible. It is that careless, listless living for one's self; caring for nothing that does not come immediately in contact with one's personal interests [Edward Wilmot Blyden, a secretary of state of Liberia].

The original constitutional provision limiting the Liberian president's term of office to two years permitted no period of recovery from the stress of one election before another was on. The term was extended to four years during the administration of President Arthur Barclay, but it had continued long enough to give a "set" to both political and social habits. The dependence of so large a part of the population on government made the field of politics a natural and almost exclusive source of interest. In a country with no other outlet for ability and virtually no other source of income, there could be no such thing as retiring from public life, except to face starvation. It is scarcely to be wondered at that officeholding in the republic, from cabinet to clerkship, became a matter of life and death; that every device within the reach of cleverness and even chicanery should be employed to perpetuate tenure in office and to draw from this office all that it would yield. There is no civil service. Although the civilized population of Monrovia is less than 5,000, there are more than 100 lawyers. Law is a favorite profession because it leads to cabinet positions, and there are few barristers who do not aspire to fill some day the chief post of the nation.

In no other republic has there been such an unbroken fixation on politics. It is the national interest, sport, occupation, and emotional vent. That it has only once reached the point of physical violence, as in Latin Amer-

147

ican republics, is most extraordinary. The subject of politics is almost the entire concern of Liberian newspapers; the young men's clubs are political clubs. Whereas the church and the lodge absorb the potential political energies of American Blacks, politics in Liberia absorb energies that normally would go not only into church and lodge, but into trade, agriculture, recreation, education, creative writing, and art. No question of the common weal, however nonpartisan, has been able to escape it. Neither the loans, the native people, issues of national security, nor the concert of international condemnation of government practices escaped specific political interpretation or, more dangerous still, escaped being used to advance a special political interest within the state. The political scene is one uninterrupted campaign of vilification, from which no man in public life escapes. So paramount an interest seems to transcend even the welfare of the state. Foreigners have held their noses over the spectacle, and have been open in their sneers, but they could be no more energetic than the Liberians themselves, either in rival parties or in factional divisions of the Whig Party, in exposing their dirty linen to the world.

When the disgraceful conduct of Roye on the loan of 1870 restored political power to the Republicans, they were able to retain it only about six years. After a fiery contest, the Whigs, whose platform was both more racially and nationally self-conscious, succeeded in placing Gardner in the presidency in 1879. They remained securely in power and were never challenged until 1923 when the People's Party was born. Political activity during this long period was mainly between factions within the Whig Party.

To the looseness of the electoral system and the extravagance of the spoils system might be attributed some responsibility for the systematic abuse both of the electorate and the principle behind its establishment. Suffrage was limited to males, aged twenty-one and over, possessing real estate. A commissioner of elections for the five counties was appointed by the president, who in turn appointed township registrars. The men received pay for one month prior to the election, and, in addition, 2¢ for each person registered, a fact which helps to explain the wholesale fictitious registrations.

A voter did not need to register in person; he had only to send a deed or statement that he owned property. The practice was to send in long lists of names which were registered without challenge by the clerks appointed by the registrars, appointed in turn by the commissioner who himself was appointed by the president. If there was an opposition party, it might appoint a judge at the polls, but the system allowed an individual to bring along Liberians or natives to answer to the one or more names when called, and vote the entire list.

The question of the native franchise was handled by the provision that certain civilized natives, on becoming of age, should receive a land allotment with a deed. In practice, the opinion of the "degree of civilization" of the native was in the hands of the Liberian Bureau of Registration, and the hazy line between "civilized and uncivilized" made possible a wholly unmanageable electoral situation. In the interior there was no legal registration. Prior to 1919 the total number of registered landowners and voters was between 6,000 and 7,000. The limits to which these electoral excesses could be carried were well exposed in the case of the opposing People's Party which arose in 1923.

Charles Burgess Dunbar King had been a member of the Howard cabinet and after a prevailing custom, was chosen as Howard's successor in 1919; he was unopposed at the polls. Differences developed as King, undoubtedly one of the shrewdest of politicians, began to entrench himself firmly in his leadership, and Howard, to curb a dictatorship, organized the People's party in 1922. Four years later King was opposed by Harmon, who received 7,000 votes while King was credited with receiving 40,000. It was clearly a case of fraudulent voting, but the results went unchallenged. It was expected that, following the usual custom, the president would not attempt to succeed himself for a third term. During his first term King had been firm in his party discipline, but unassailable on matters of official misconduct. In 1925 he inaugurated his road programs, began to feel the thrill of power, and became less circumspect in his official acts. The House of Representatives and the Senate were his by virtue of his skillful manipulation. All the offices of the government were appointive and in consequence became his by right of appointive power. He declined to announce his intentions concerning the third term. In a cabinet meeting two members objected to the principle of a third term and soon found themselves in the street. Acting on this cue the remaining members of the cabinet met, in secret session, as six other Whig candidates made bids for the favor of the party, and nominated King for a third term, with Yancy as his vice-president. The nomination was promptly accepted. The election officers printed 250,000 ballots, over forty times the number of voters and more than enough for the entire hinterland population, and these were distributed on the streets in large bundles.

T.J.R. Faulkner opposed King in the 1927 election as a candidate of the People's Party. The returns showed 9,000 votes for Faulkner and 235,000 for King. In Bassa Country, for example, where there were not more than 3,000 legal voters, 32,000 names were registered and 72,000 voted. The case was protested in court, and brought immense embarrassment to the Whig judges appointed by the executive. They soon were made aware of their status when the judge was fined $150 and the sheriff who was sent to get a letter from the president was fined $50. It created a difficult situation, indeed, for the judiciary. When the legislature was compelled to get the ballot boxes from the State Department for a recount, they found stacks of ballots unfolded and even uncut. They ordered them burned at once. The president entered his third term, and the commissioner of elections was sent to prison for the illegal registering of voters. No satisfactory explanation was ever made of the figures.

There were other factors responsible for the defeat of the People's Party which reflected the state of politics significantly. It had but few men in it who were experienced in the higher branches of government. Those who had held high office before, or who were in office, whether in sympathy with Whig policies or not, were Whigs, because it was their livelihood. A very real courage was required to face the chances of disfavor of the perennially dominant party. The entrenchment had other conspicuous features about it. Cabinet officers were simply rotated within a small group which remained intact so long as it found itself in harmony with executive views. It was a fact that the recent cabinets had held along with others, perhaps the most skillful and competent men in the state. There was also a very real question about the wisdom of a sudden wholesale ousting of the administration, and the substitution of an entirely new regime of the permanent "outs!" There were too few men of experience in the republic to make such a procedure unqualifiedly sound. There is a strong likelihood that President King's superior political skill and his firmness, although at times dictatorial, might have contributed to sound progress, had power been properly directed.

The crystallization of a permanent official class tended to give both the aspect and reality of "family rule," which was no infallible guarantee of competence. One family in particular had been the source of much criticism for its practical usurpation of the reins of government. To this family belonged the president's wife, the secretary of the treasury and national chairman of the Whig Party, the chief immigration officer, commissioner general of the interior, the undersecretary of state, the consul general at Liverpool, and the chief nurse of the government hospital. Still another member of the family, who was secretary of war, died in office.

The platforms of the rival parties were as vague and undetermined as the familiar American party platforms. But they suggested the dominant direction of wishful thinking. The Whig Party favored equal commercial opportunity for all nations; a strong financial policy, with no repudiation of debts, whether owed to private individuals or nations; honest, efficient, and economical expenditure of public funds and close cooperation with the financial adviser; entry of foreign capital under constitutional limitations and development of natural resources by nonmonopolistic foreign concessions; a strong interior policy, cooperating closely with the aboriginal population and equal education privileges for it; noninterference so far as possible with native tribal government, collection of taxes to be made through chiefs, and equitable portion of revenues received to be expended on works of benefit to native taxpayers; a strong public school policy and appointment of teachers on a nonpartisan basis; encouragement of home industry and agriculture and cessation of the exportation of native laborers from the country; reorganization of militia and maintenance of a disciplined and effective Frontier Force; inauguration of road-building programs to open up the interior; and encouragement of selected colored immigration from the United States and elsewhere.

The People's Party platform was almost wholly an opposition program. It favored passage of constitutional amendments decreasing the president's power, especially his appointive power; removal of the seal of government from Monrovia to the interior, thereby developing the latter through forced influx of the civilized element; thorough reform in militia, finances, and judiciary, and establisment of a civil service; closer cooperation between government and business; entry of foreign capital into the country without special concessions; more stringent laws covering debt evasion and establishment of debtors' courts; increased appropriations for education; specialized scientific and technical efforts to aid agriculture, principally for coffee growing; unhindered selection of legislative candidates by the people; freedom of speech and press; restrictions placed on the importation of trade spirits; reform in the administration of the hinterland districts.

President King resigned in 1930 as a result of the investigations of the League of Nations Commission on forced labor. He was succeeded by Edwin Barclay. Barclay induced the legislature to pass a law criticizing the president or the government's native policy a penal offense. In 1943 he passed on his office to a chosen colleague, W.V.S. Tubman, formerly Supreme Court justice. The experience of the opposing Democratic Party, led by James F. Cooper, a former secretary of the interior, in the election of 1943 followed the traditional pattern. The Whigs refused to appoint a judge and clerk from the Democratic Party at each voting booth. The *Weekly Mirror,* a Democratic organ, cited the case of a small village of about twenty-four houses in the Territory of Marshall, which has a population of less than 1,000 men, women, and children "including all domestic animals," polling 5,100 for the Whigs and seven for the Democrats.

The group in control of the government today is almost the same as that involved with King in the slavery scandal. President Tubman was Yancy's legal adviser, and Vice-President C.L. Simpson also had a hand in the forced labor activities. The natives have had no right to elect a president.

Efforts have been made recently, however, to give them representation in the national legislature. Early in 1945 a constitutional amendment revising the system of representation and extending the rights of universal suffrage to citizens of the hinterlands was approved by the legislature. Each of the three hinterland provinces will send one representative to the national legislature. All citizens of these provinces aged twenty-three and over who own a hut and pay its tax will have the right to vote. This amendment will go into effect when the president directs.

Despite the gradual extermination of the civilized population by disease and the loud protests of practically every European nation with commercial or diplomatic representatives in Liberia, neither of the political platforms mentioned sanitation. The blight of yellow fever and malaria, small pox, and other scourges, correctable in some degree through sanitation, clings to the country like a curse. The attitude toward these complaints has been similar to the early attitude of American Blacks on the matter of their high tuberculosis and venereal disease rate. It has simply been put aside as part of the general slander of Blacks and nothing was done about it. The West Coast of Africa has long had a reputation for being unhealthful for Europeans. Even in the adjoining colony of Sierra Leone there was the familiar quip in the British Foreign Service that it always had two governors: one returning dead, the other on his way to the post. The mortal dread of the West Coast entertained by Europeans no doubt explains their intense and persistent concern about sanitation, and this became a definite irritation to the sensitive Liberians.

Lack of sanitation was the reason given by the Bank of British West Africa for withdrawing its Liberian branch, in 1930—the only bank in Liberia. In 1929, during one of the periodic epidemics of yellow fever, important natives of Britain, Germany, France, and the United States died. Among these were the U.S. minister, William J. Francis; the educational adviser for the republic, James L. Sibley, and a high officer of the Bank of British West Africa. In a joint address to the Liberian government the four nations urged the inauguration of a sanitation program. As a result of a memorandum agreement with the U.S. Public Health Service, Dr. H.F. Smith, an officer of the United States Public Health Service, was detailed as health adviser to the president.

The American medical officer undertook a thorough investigation, and as a preliminary measure, collected a stupendous heap of trash, tin cans, and bottles that had been cluttering the streets and lots for years. His actions were, incidentally, responsible for the first full count of Monrovia's inhabitants in about eighty years. This figure was given as 9,691, of which 3,839, or 45 percent, were native Krus, living in Krutown. In explaining his population figures, Dr. Smith paid his compliments to the official interest in sanitation:

> The actual population is slightly in excess of these figures, but owing to the absolute lack of any spirit of cooperation on the part of certain government officials, among whom may be mentioned the secretary of the treasury, the attorney general, the county attorney, the postmaster, the commanding officer of the Monrovia arsenal, the chief clerk of the municipal board, and a few other citizens of such refractory and antagonistic nature, such as are usually found in a cosmopolitan community, an absolutely accurate census could not be obtained. With the exception of the above omissions, however, which may really be considered as negligible, the figures as shown are as accurate as human endeavor could render them.

The city itself covered about three square miles, but only about 30 percent of this area was occupied. Within the houses available for the civilized population, there were about seven persons to each home. But in Krutown, near the waterfront, some 3,839 natives lived in their windowless bamboo-mat and thatch houses, within an area of about six city blocks. The average was nine persons to the house. The water of the city in the dry season was drawn from 317 shallow surface wells; in the rainy season it was caught in containers ranging in character from gasoline tins to cisterns. There was no modern sewerage disposal from the civilized population, and the Krus, following an ancient tribal custom, repaired to the beach at the edge of their village. The city's prowling animal scavengers, the goats and sheep, were relied upon to dispose of garbage and refuse.

The dread yellow fever carrier is the mosquito stegomyia calopus. It is found in or close to human habitats, breeding in almost any receptacle holding water. Sixty-five percent of the water barrels around the Monrovia houses were breeding *stegomyia* mosquitoes, and 81 percent of the city's wells were producing larvae as recently as 1930. The same mosquito-breeding prevalence was found for roof gutters, pools and depressions, weeds, and travelers' palms that held water.

The government's chief medical officer was the president's aide-de-camp, Colonel T. Elwood Davis, formerly a noncommissioned officer and medical orderly in the U.S. 10th Calvary. It was under his direction that the first garbage cleanup, stimulated by the foreign governments, was undertaken in 1929. The Health Department was practically a nonfunctioning organization, with the most casual record keeping, taking no notice whatever of communicable diseases. There were food control laws but no agency or personnel for enforcing them, and the maritime quarantine was in the hands of a person without medical training. The mortality records were in the form of "permits to open a grave," and these permits were not always required, so the death rate was impossible to ascertain. It was even impossible to know, because of faulty diagnosis and recording, the extent of deaths from yellow fever. Defensively, it was insisted in known yellow fever cases that the disease was simply "yellow jaundice."

The handicaps of a sanitary program for Monrovia were easily recognized by the visitor. The city was patched with rain-washed rocks which were difficult to control. Weeds and brush grew as fast as they were burned. Unless a health conscience was created, the only remedy was the development of complete immunity, and the colony at its 1930 rate could scarcely survive to achieve this happy state.

The U.S. Public Health Mission under Senior Surgeon John B. West, although sent to Liberia in 1944 primarily to aid in the control of communicable diseases in the vicinity of American military installations, is expected to improve, both directly and indirectly, health conditions in the country at large. It has recently extended its clinical activities into the hinterland and hopes, within the next two years, "to make a survey of all diseases thought to be endemic to Liberia; to recommend programs for the control of these diseases; to promote a system of vital statistical reporting and recording; to complete a modern health center at Monrovia; to aid the Liberian government in obtaining a water supply system and a sewage system for the city of Monrovia; and to aid the Liberian government in reorganizing its Bureau of Public Health and Sanitation into a modern public health unit capable of administering a public health program fitted to the needs of Liberia." If this program is successfully established and efficiently maintained, Liberia will have advanced a long step toward conquering its health problems.

Both party platforms desired to improve education and this, if accomplished to any degree, would be a judicious step in the direction of good government. In 1923 there were forty-six public elementary schools for Liberians and natives, with forty-six teachers and an enrollment of 2,704, and Liberia College had six teachers. For that year, $20,000 was appropriated and $4,950 actually spent. In 1929 there were sixty-three public schools. The expenditure for public instruction in 1929, including the secretary of education, Liberia College, and the sixty-three public schools, was $39,380. This amount was just $10,000 more than the salary and prerequisites of the office of the president. The pay of teachers ranged from $100 to $400 a year, and in addition, a contribution of $1,000 was made to the Booker T. Washington Institute for natives at Kakata. In 1944, from a total budget of $1,000,000, the appropriation for seventy-eight public schools enrolling 4,591 pupils with 160 teachers was $60,000, which included $12,000 for Liberia College. This is improvement, but until public instruction is able to take care of the need without dependence on private sources, the amount appropriated for education must be substantially increased, particularly since this is one of Liberia's most pressing problems. It is estimated that about 95 percent of the population is illiterate. Where the money is to come from is another problem.

The principal volume of funds for education has been contributed by missionaries of about ten Protestant and one Catholic organization. These, in 1928, maintained fifty-eight schools and were giving instruction to 5,752 children. In 1929 the sixty-three public schools and sixty-five mission schools represented a total enrollment of 10,250. In 1944, the total enrollment was 11,722, of which 7,131 pupils were in 109 mission and private schools employing 209 teachers. The mission schools are largely limited to natives, and a good grade of elementary instruction is provided. Fewer than 150 children, Liberians or natives, of the 10,250 enrolled in 1929 in all schools were of high-school grade and about twenty were of college grade.

Unquestionably, the schools are in a seriously impoverished condition. The "colleges" are, in fact, elementary and high schools and with few exceptions are poorly conducted. The native population, away from Monrovia, is almost neglected in such public provisions as are made. A good beginning may be found in the Booker T. Washington Institute at Kakata. The Suehn Mission, under Sarah Williamson, was a magnificent example of the possibilities of small funds intelligently handled. The Lutheran Mission at Muhlenberg is perhaps the best equipped of all the mission schools, but the enrollment is always small.

The National Baptist Convention, which supports the Suehn School, also maintains a hospital in Monrovia and stations at Bendu and Fortville. The Episcopal church has stations in the Cape Mount and Cape Palmas areas as well as in Monrovia; the Protestant Episcopal church, whose work has been under the careful direction of Bishop Campbell, stationed at Monrovia, penetated the interior, establishing native boys' schools at Pandemai and Masambolahun.

Liberia College is the highest institution in the public system. Its equipment is inadequate, but it is making good use of what it has. In 1944 there were twenty-eight students in the college, sixty-six in the high-school department and five in grades six to eight.

The entire system of education requires emphasis on practicality and utility. Greater stress on the industrial arts and agriculture, particularly, is needed. There could well be instruction in native administration. If the present generation of Liberians is to continue in control, it should be possible for selected ones to be educated in America, returning home to teach or engage in agriculture, the trades, or the professions. In line with this reasoning, the Liberian government has granted six scholarships to Liberian students for work at Howard University.

Under the stimulation of the Phelps-Stokes Fund, which has supplied both funds and intelligent direction to its philanthropy in Liberia, the various educational mission boards operating in Liberia were drawn together, for administrative unity and economy, in an advisory committee on Liberian education. James L. Sibley, until his death, was the executive officer for this committee and during 1931 he was succeeded by another American educator. This committee, among other things, has established teachers' institutes, devised texts for native children (with a content closer to their environment than the European readers), and has begun the long task of raising educational standards. Booker T. Washington Institute is an outgrowth of the interest of Dr. Sibley. Its purpose is to serve the hinterland as well as the coastal area as a center of trade and agricultural training. The war taught Liberians the value of such training, and the products of the institute and the subjects taught there were eagerly sought. Jackson Davis suggested that this school "holds the key to practical development of the Liberian people through the use of machinery, scientific knowledge, and technical skill." President King was instrumental in the establishment of Booker T. Washington Institute, and it is an indication of his potentialities.

It is astonishing that the Liberians have been able to develop to the extent that they have, in view of the character of their schools. Education for them has been a largely informal process developed through contact and familiarity with the instruments of culture. There are few, if any, American Blacks who combine such intellectual sureness of wide reading with the experience of Arthur Barclay; and few who can equal the erudition of Edwin Barclay. Louis Grimes, despite the absence of law schools in the republic, was an accomplished public advocate, whose decisions and legal diction would have received recognition in any country. There are others who have been educated in the United States, and who send their children to Sierra Leone or America for their education.

No one denies the educational limitations of the general population, and this fact in itself is a good sign. There could be, unquestionably, mutual benefit in the immigration of technically trained American Blacks, who find it difficult to express their special skills at home. Neither group, however, seemed in the proper mood, in the early 1930s, for the contact. Indeed, the immigration of American Blacks has not been seriously invited since the passage of the new alien acts and creation of the emigration bureau.

When the Garvey Back-to-Africa movement was at the height of its popularity, an attempt was made to effect an arrangement for colonization in Cape Palmas in southern Liberia. A few months' exposure to the relentless nature of Africa would, no doubt, have adjusted the potential migrants to reality and added fresh citizens of no less intelligence than the mass of Liberians, but a strange combination of forces kept them out. The political wishfulness of their leader, Marcus Garvey, had logic and precision. However, he could not, as he had promised, "put King George out of Africa," nor France, nor Belgium. His confident assurances irritated England at the same time that they tickled the illusions of his followers. For while the pretenses of the movement itself were harmless, even if serious, the spirit of unrest generated by them might have led to considerable difficulties for colonizing powers in their leisurely program of native development.

The Garvey program was theoretically a militant one, in a universe of combat to which few, if any, of his followers had ever been exposed. To any observer, the spectacle of a weak American Black peasantry arrayed against the entrenched colonial policies of major European nations, however righteous the cause, must have seemed a tragic farce. Liberia had often enough felt the hard hand of its stronger neighbors on less provocation than the Garvey situation promised. It is quite understandable how President King became wary as soon as England and America gave signs of disapproval. An executive order therefore prohibited members of the Universal Negro Improvement Association from immigrating; legislative enactment later sustained the order.

There was more apprehension in the exclusion, however, than the international relations factor. The vigor of the newcomers would most certainly have challenged the closed circle of government in the country. The new population very soon could have controlled Maryland County, thus challenging the central government at Monrovia. There is no certainty that they would have escaped all the errors of earlier colonists, but there would have been a new ferment in the state with as many potentialities for good as for mischief.

It has always been stressed in the faint-hearted invitations to American Blacks that only "high-type" immigrants of financial standing and education should seek a home in the country. This, however, is exactly the type of American Black who has been finding America reasonably tolerable since the Civil War. President Tubman, in his inaugural address on January 3, 1944, invited Afro-American immigration, but "carefully planned and selected." Since the coming of World War II American Blacks, under U.S. government auspices, have been helping with the development of the country in the fields of agriculture, engineering, and sanitation, and Liberia has welcomed persons with technical training. Also, a law making persons who have not lived in Liberia twenty-five years ineligible for the presidency of the country has been passed. This law was aimed, presumably, at American Black troops who might decide to stay in the country.

Liberia is an American colony. . . . It is unnecessary to argue that the duty of the United States toward the unfortunate victims of the slave trade was not completely performed in landing them upon the coast of Africa, and that our nation rests under the highest obligation to assist them, so far as they need assistance, toward the maintenance of free, orderly, and prosperous civil society. The welfare and progress of the millions of American citizens of the black race in the United States also furnishes strong reasons for helping to maintain this colony, whose success in self-government will give hope and courage, and whose failure would bring discouragement to the entire race [Elihu Root, secretary of state to President Roosevelt, 1909].

In 1929, following representations of certain citizens of Liberia to the League of Nations regarding internal slavery, this writer was appointed by the U.S. government to serve as the American member of a commission of three to investigate the charges that slavery and forced labor existed in Liberia, a member nation of the League.

The other members of the commission were Dr. Cuthbert Christy, an Englishman who had lived many years in Africa, and the Honorable Arthur J. Barclay, an ex-president of Liberia and its elder statesman.

The inquiry consumed the greater portion of a year, during which long periods were spent in the coastal towns and in the many villages of the interior. On one three-month journey into the interior, this author traveled by foot or by human carrier a distance of 300 miles. The remainder of this volume is based in part on the author's diary and in part on general records, observations, and conversations with hundreds of natives, with American-Liberian citizens and officials, and with Americans and Europeans stationed in the country.

15

Pillars of the Republic

The outstanding figure of the 1920s in Liberia was undoubtedly Charles Burgess Dunbar King, three times president of the republic, a master politician, who spun a web of statecraft of so fine a texture and so intricate a design that he collapsed in its tangles. I first met him on the occasion of a formal presentation to the government at the Executive Mansion. The ceremony was stiffly formal, as was essential to the establishment of any sort of status for a visitor, and attended with all the bustle of the military guard, loud commands, the slapping of rifles against hard hands, and the slapping of harder bare feet against the cement flooring of the mansion veranda. There was a period of waiting, under the affable chatter of the aide-de-camp, Colonel T. Elwood Davis. Then, suddenly, there came a heavy, muffled thud and a door to the side broke its warped and paint-stuck binding and was flung open, revealing the very erect and graceful figure of a man advanced in middle age, trimly and formally attired, the lines of his dark face set in the heavy composure of dogged self-confidence.

The aide-de-camp snapped to attention, and in an impressive whisper announced: "Gentlemen, the President of Liberia," as if he were sharing for the first time a tremendous secret. Across the room the president strode with a heavy, very firm step, followed by a pet collie that had resolutely refused to be left in the president's private office. As the first introductions were exchanged, the collie was alternately sniffing at the feet of the visitors and jumping at his master's hand, all the while eluding the efforts of the aide-de-camp to capture him. Finally, he settled down at the feet of his master, there to remain throughout the visit. It was a sufficient diversion to break the tenseness of the event, and relax both the face and conversation of the chief executive. He talked quietly and haltingly, as if selecting his words rather than his thoughts. Something about the friendly intimacy of his interests, the homely figures of his speech combined with his easy familiarity with a wide range of questions, marked him, on first contact, as an extraordinary personality.

Subsequent meetings confirmed this estimate but added others; the president had an uncanny aptitude for sensing and achieving expression in

homely language of the precise sentiment for the occasion, however difficult the situation. He had been heard to talk for an hour, through two
interpreters, to a group of Mohammedan Vais with the same ease, sim-
plicity, and happy selection of sentiments that he commanded in addressing the assembled nationals and diplomats of Europe, or the Firestone
officials in the presence of persons unfriendly to the company. To an American in Liberia, he could say that America was traditionally Liberia's best
friend. To the Firestone people, he could say, as he did in a speech at the
opening of a new development; "Liberia must have something. The Gold
Coast is the greatest cocoa-producing area in the world. Why cannot Liberia be the greatest rubber-producing country in the world? The work of the
company is an accomplishment of which to be proud by those most concerned." To the British, he could say, as he did on his visit to England: "The
one thing that has struck me about England is its extraordinary sense of
justice. I read the other day of an English judge who, when some ex-
criminal brought an action, commented that even a criminal should have
the right of the road. That struck me as essentially British." To the French:
"France strikes me as being the happiest country, excepting my own,
through which I have passed. My own country is exceedingly happy. There
is no rent to pay, and few social troubles." To his colonial neighbors who
feared a general awakening of Africa's Blacks: "I am working for the Liberian nation and not for the Black race. The Black race was there before
Liberia." And to the excited question about Reds and communism getting
a foothold in Liberia: "We have no Reds, only Whites and Blacks." To
Blacks: "God must have had plans for a people who could survive so long
in Africa, and when uprooted and transplanted to America keep alive and
flourish." Native chiefs upon whom he wished to impress the need of
cooperation with the government could at least understand his pleas for
cooperation when he used their own proverb: "One finger cannot pick a
louse."

He held his office with calm dignity. Only deepening grooves of care in
his face betrayed the weight of his responsibilities. Behind quiet eyes, alive
to every word, gesture, and intonation was, without doubt, the most astute
political intelligence in the republic, indeed one of the shrewdest minds in
Africa. Nothing escaped him, either of subtle flattery or subtler intrigue.

Born in Liberia in 1877 and educated in Monrovia and Sierra Leone,
King followed his father into politics and held important offices of the state
for twenty-five years. As secretary of state, he headed the Liberian delegation to the Peace Conference, and among his medals of honor is the Order
of Commander of the Legion of Honor with which he was decorated by the
French government.

Two great mistakes marked his administration. One of these was his unconquerable love of power, which had to be maintained by an increasingly precarious structure of gossip, espionage, and crude reprisals for disloyalty. The other tragic error was political entanglement with men more brazen in their unscrupulousness and less clever in their devices. Together, these led eventually to the collapse of King's administration.

In March 1931, he and Vice-President Allen Yancy resigned, following the publication of the findings of the International Commission of Inquiry, and the legislature's sudden courage in threatening impeachment. Under the disadvantage of an overwhelming world disapprobation, King, the master politician, in retiring gave a parting exhibition of his incomparable skill. He accepted the commission's report, designedly ignoring the legislature. He issued executive proclamations abolishing slavery and stopping exportations; his executive commitment to reforms drew indignant challenges from the legislature on the score that they usurped the complete authority of the state. His impeachment was threatened (not initially on the commission's charges, although he was implicated in the findings) on the score of official high-handedness. Thus it happened that, whatever his personal views about reforms or the charges, he retired from office on the side of reform and a clean government, leaving the legislature ostensibly opposed to reform, at the very moment that it was beginning to measure out punishment for official misconduct. King's influence unquestionably continued to be felt in the republic, although his attempt at a political comeback in 1935 was a failure.

The most hated and one of the most lonely men in the republic was Thomas J.R. Faulkner, leader of the People's Party, the Liberian citizen who first laid charges against his government at the door of the U.S. government and the League of Nations. Fearless, eternally active, of powerful physique despite his sixty years, he had been a relentless foe of the administration, a friend of the native, whose zeal for reform became almost an obsession. He was defeated by fraud in his campaign against King; he was the leader of a party that Liberians have not dared openly support, despite their sympathy with its aims; his business was destroyed by political prejudice, and through it all he opposed the dictatorship of King and the Whigs with ever-increasing fury. Indeed, it was difficult at times to distinguish between pure humanitarian sentiment and personal grievances. He could have justly been accused of intemperance in his charges against the administration, of stirring up native unrest against the government in his determination to air their grievances before the world, but although he held public office and was active in the country for over forty years, no one, not even his political enemies, ever accused him of dishonesty or of deliberate injustice. Because of his activities the government threatened to try him for treason; the most bitter pens of the administration attacked him, impugning his motives; even assassination was attempted, but Faulkner continued unabated, a painful, albeit salutary, thorn in the body politic.

At a time of tenseness and fear, when the Commission of Inquiry began its hearings, he broke the spell by opening the testimony, leading frightened natives down to Monrovia to report the brutalities of the interior officials. He shouted:

> I am the one Liberian who has confirmed the statements that have been made by writers and other reporters of conditions in Liberia. The natives have no representation—they are the oppressed people. They have no friends among those in authority. And since I have been the complainant, the native element is looking to me personally to get their grievances heard. The government is endeavoring to use the chiefs to depose on behalf of the government. If those who have been flogged, fined, and put to forced labor are ready to speak, let them be heard. Public sentiment is in this country! We have no press. Public speech is frowned upon, and we dare not discuss the actions of our officials. The people know that everything possible will be done to hamper inquiry. The people have been terrorized.

It was Faulkner who, when events moved too slowly, rushed into the Gola country, intercepted a group of laborers on their way down to work at Firestone's, and sent them home; who at Kakata addressed a group of gaping natives about their rights; who exclaimed before a Monrovia audience of Liberians: "I see mandate for Liberia written in the sky" waving before them documents of dire import which he believed foretold this fate, but which he did not know had been shamelessly forged. He traveled in America on his own funds awakening this country to the scandal of Africa, sought capital, men, and a sympathetic interest in a country which he had painted as wholly corrupt. He could work; he was a master artisan; he was certain that he could build up the country if he could escape the throttling prejudices of an almost permanent family of rulers of the country. The veto power of the president had balked every material advance of the republic. He said before a Monrovia audience: "I tried to install an electric plant for the streets of Monrovia, to give public light which would be an asset to the country. I appealed to the commonwealth for permission, and they sent me to the secretary of state. When I appealed to him, he sent me to His Excellency the President, who directed me to the legislature, which began the same circle again." There was but one way, he believed, to escape the thralldom of this prejudicial and disastrous veto, and that was to take over that power and use it for the advancement of the state.

Officialdom lapsed from dignity into blind rage when his name was mentioned. Luckless natives were thrown into prison, mercilessly manhandled for appealing to him. He moved openly, without guards, with his enormous jaw set, through the city of Monrovia on the strength of sheer fearlessness. The bitter significance to the world of his death by violence provided for him a shadowy protection even from the most cowardly of his enemies. He was the most useful man in the country. His word was his bond; he paid his laborers and his public debts. He loved the native and he loved Liberia. But the very intemperance of his zeal to destroy the enemies of good government, more than anything else, kept him out of the presidency. His death was a loss Liberia could ill afford, although the news was undoubtedly heard with relief in some quarters.

It is not without good reason that the report of the International Commission mentions conspicuously the name of Allen Yancy in connection with the scandalous regime of corruption in the state. His career was a rapid, notoriously brazen elevation to power through clumsy intrigues, extortion, chicanery, malfeasance in office, destructive cruelty to the native population, man-stealing, and an utter callousness to the ultimate welfare of the republic. For this, or in spite of this, he was rewarded with the office of vice-president of the republic, and was actually a candidate for the presidency to succeed King in 1931.

It was at Cape Palmas that I accidentally encountered him during a visit to Governor J.S. Smith of Maryland County. He turned out to be a small, ferretlike individual, whose head, sloping violently backward, was capped by a pompadour. He talked always with the air of a proprietor, gesturing at the town of Harper after the manner of one referring to his private farm. He had been irritated by a confidential report which the secretary of the interior had sent to the president regarding his recent activities. The president's secretary, who was managing Yancy's campaign for the presidency, had sent a copy to him. "It's a political move," he explained to Smith, "They are trying to hurt me with the voters." His restless energy, his Napoleonic complex, the cold cunning of his tiny bright eyes, gave some credibility to the reports.

Sometime later, and shortly after we had successfully completed a journey down the swollen and treacherous Cavalla River by canoe, Yancy was present at our meeting with Perry, the collector of customs. Perry had turned to him with a troubled look and reported that a mutual friend had just sent a frantic appeal for help, saying that the rampant Cavalla had undermined his house and threatened to destroy all their possessions. Yancy advised that he put his family in his little house and float on down to Harper, treating himself to a free boat ride.

We talked with him about Liberia, and he talked freely about what he would do if he were made president. "If people knew what I would do to develop the country," he ventured, "they would assassinate me. I would make them work." He referred modestly to his "little farm of 15,000 rubber trees," to his wife's farm, his coffee farm, and he told how he had struggled to build these up. "I say, give me eight years and if things aren't better, you can have the country."

Yancy was born in Cape Palmas in 1881, the son of the Reverend Allen Yancy, a minister of the A.M.E. Church, who, with his wife, migrated to Maryland County from Hancock County, Georgia, in 1873. His father had been first a farmer and then a blacksmith, and had taught these trades to his son. After Yancy Senior died, the son added wheelwrighting to the business for nearly all the trading firms at the time in Cape Palmas. Having learned to speak the Grebo language well, he was able in 1902 to woo and marry a native woman of the powerful Nabo (Bigtown) clan of the Grebos, Gertrude Seton. They had eight children, six boys and two girls.

Yancy's political career began in 1905 when he was appointed justice of the peace under President Arthur Barclay. During the war in 1910, Yancy, although a captain of the Liberian Guard, decided on a neutral status, and remained at home repairing guns of the Grebos at excellent profit. Later on, his friends persuaded him to take more interest in the serious crisis that confronted the republic, and he assumed his duties as an officer. Knowing the Grebos to be excellent fighters when called upon for an attack upon Waduke, he addressed his men on the uselessness of wars, insisting that it was the big men who had caused the war and expected the little ones to fight it. His company mutinied against the government and fled in the face of attack. His lukewarm patriotism played him ill, however, for when the Grebos learned that he had led an advance, they became incensed; between the two fires, he attempted to leave the country for Secondi. He was arrested and returned for disloyal and treasonable conduct, court martialled, sentenced, but saved through the intervention of friends.

He devoted himself largely to his business between 1911 and 1917, and persuaded Woodin and Company, a German firm, to open a trading store for him in Philadelphia. The friendship with Edwin J. Barclay bloomed during these years, and in 1918, through the assistance of Barclay, he was appointed county attorney of Maryland, though knowing practically nothing of law. With his entrance into public life, his expenses increased; circumstances forced him to give less attention to business. A serious shortage developed in the trading firm's funds, and as action was about to be taken, the Woodin store was mysteriously entered on the night of June 9, 1919, and all account books and other documents were removed. Woodin's firm has not yet recovered from that incident, for their important books and papers were carried off with all their personal accounts, and the firm has been unable to collect the large amounts owed.

While the audit injured his character, it did not interfere with Yancy's promotion in office. As county attorney he never appeared in court. Later, as governor of Maryland County, he was given charge of the new road-building program of Maryland. The excesses of this road program extended to brutality, extortion, and general exploitation of native labor. His bank account, automobiles, and concubines increased so rapidly there was always widespread comment, but never action. He developed his private farms and built houses from timber felled by free native labor, designating this as public work. He became known as "the millionaire of Maryland County."

His power grew enormous and unquestioned. He controlled the offices of his county, from governor to collector of internal revenue. J.B.S. Tubman, senator, and J.S. Brooks, superintendent of Bassa County, were then revenue collectors of Maryland County. Among these three gentlemen, the sum of $67,000,000 was lost. The government at Monrovia, hearing this, sent J.H. Dent, later Judge Dent, to investigate the affair. Dent, endeavoring to be honest, went carefully into the matter and found that the money had been squandered. Matters were going very badly against the collaborators, when President King, who had been out of the country, returned. When told that Yancy had been implicated in the shady affair, he was reported to have said: "What? My Yancy? Leave him alone." At any rate, the irritation ceased, and as he continued in office, Yancy became more open in his official misconduct. Aggrieved persons, both native and Liberian, reported him to the president as the only curbing authority, but nothing was said or done to check him. His political services were all too apparent. In the 1927 election, he took the ballot box to his house before the returns were counted. When the results were announced, King and Yancy led in Cape Palmas by a majority of 23,000 votes, more voters than there were in the republic.

While he was vice-president, personal charges were made and sustained against him: that he surreptitiously took Mr. Verdier's house from him and gave it as a "dash" to President King; that he called another Liberian, Victor Cooper, into his house and with a revolver forced his signature for the purchase of his house and lot; that he killed a man in his house at night and dragged his body to the street the next morning, later deciding to report that the man had visited him with the intention of stealing. He was accused of complicity in the murder of Joe Gibson, an active political opponent, and actually removed witnesses out of the way of the state. The story of his land policy is one of blind and cruel extortion.

The end of Yancy's political career came with the same violence that had characterized its beginning. He was forced to resign from office, and when faced with charges and the prospect of having to return money extorted from the natives, he flew into a rage, rendering himself a helpless paralytic.

Didhwo Twe was an educated native Kru of unusual intelligence. For a number of years he lived in the United States, serving for a while as a valet for Mark Twain, and later for a wealthy banker. Among his personal possessions incidentally, were several lengthy and intimate letters from Mark Twain reflecting the author's views on the American race question. Twe represented that very perplexing type of native who had been educated and fully adjusted to Western civilization without losing his tribal loyalty. He retained contacts with America, and, as a big-game hunter and prospector found a basis for friendly relations with many Europeans traveling along the African West Coast. Above all he was an intensely tribal-minded Kru. He represented the Krus in the legislature, and was expelled from that body by the most questionable methods for urging protective legislation for the native population. Both hated and feared by the administration, his life was more than once in danger. With his excellent command of English and his orderly mind, he proved an effective speaker, who relied on the weight of carefully marshalled facts.

Everyone in Monrovia knew that he had cause for grievance against the government, but as Liberia's new crisis developed, he confided to few, if to anyone, his plans. Methodically he went about the country, gathering evidence of indisputable validity, compiling documents, storing them away. When he was ready, he made his attack. With a cold, deadly, and implacable directness, nothing could stop him. He was offered reinstatement, golden promises; but he continued to unfold his case, as he called it, with devastating thoroughness. The expulsion from the legislature had burned into his pride, his hopes for the natives, his own people. He said: "When I saw that the exportation of men from Monrovia was in violation of the law, I drafted an Act to put a stop to the recruiting business. This act was drafted by me. This act was killed in the Senate; I repeated the act in 1929, and there was a tie vote. Senator Vampelt, the president pro tempore, cast a deciding vote and killed it." He spoke quietly, each word falling with the weight of unquestionable truth.

The same afternoon, as I was passing, Mr. Phelps, the president's secretary said, "Honorable Twe, I have just returned from the senate and I remained there until your bill was killed. We cannot allow you to pass a measure of that kind now. We all know that the shipment of boys to foreign countries is wrong, but we are not going to let *you* stop it, for we are not ready to stop it."

The following morning I met Mr. Parker, the Spanish vice-consul, who said that he had heard that I offered a bill that was killed. He said to me, "I advise you to leave it, because the power behind it is strong." I told him that I would continue.

On the 24th of October . . . twenty-four boys were forced by the police into a surf boat to be carried along side of a Spanish ship. . . . I ran to the secretary of state and reported it. . . . Two days afterwards, while the House was in session, I came downstairs, and there I met Mr. Eddie Barclay, the president's younger brother, and in the presence of Abayomi Thomas, A.J. Padmore, and W.C. Purser, he attacked me personally saying that I was the one who carried the report to the secretary of state, and that if his brother had been in the city he would not have stood for such a thing. I replied that if his brother had been in the city I would have carried the report to him. . . . When the president arrived in town, he asked me about it and I told him. He said no more.

On the 24th of November, twenty-four men were shipped from the government wharf in Monrovia. I have one of the men here who will tell you how they were flogged. Honorable Simpson, my colleague in the House, accompanied them on board and delivered them to the officer of the ship. . . . The speaker of the House called a meeting at his house. I went but they adjourned to another room leaving me. I heard them say, The president says that Twe must go. I asked the House committee to submit the matter to the entire House, but Honorable Sims told me that it would do no good to argue if I talked until the next morning. I asked them to produce witnesses, and that was denied. They would not even provide me with a record of the action, only a statement of my expulsion and a bill of costs.

Twe knew the chiefs up-country who had been beaten down by the hard and clumsy hand of the government; he gave them courage to make their grievances known. His was a bitter revenge, at the same time that it was a battle for the right of the natives to their own lives and labor. But beneath this concern about forced exportations was the deeper wound yet unhealed, inflicted on that tragic day when the government, under the shadow of an American gunboat, had shot down ninety of the chiefs of his tribe.

It fell to Arthur Barclay, an ex-president of Liberia, elderly and wide, to sustain the most difficult role in Liberia's 1930 crisis. As the sole ex–public official whose record invited international confidence, he was expected to examine impartially those charges against the republic which he well knew were in very large measure true; as "Father" Barclay, Nestor of the state, whose own hands had helped to shape its destiny, he was expected through some miracle of his wisdom to defend the integrity of the state before the world. The "old man," as he is affectionately called, belied his eighty years, with his brisk step, firm bearing, active erudition, and incredibly incisive wit. His head and face were covered with a grizzly mesh of white hair, and his mouth was made prominent by two enormous and solitary foreteeth.

One sensed in Barclay's presence the mellowness of years of exacting life, the mellowness of a veteran scarred by many wars in defense of his country; he was an old man who had distilled a rich philosophy from years of eventful living. He probably had read every book that had come into Liberia, and had a retentive and continuous memory. The laws of Liberia, its international problems, the native question, he knew in detail, with all their coloring of personalities and events, for he lived actively throughout most of the history of Liberia as a state. He discoursed with familiar knowledge on the activities of the various African societies, archeology, cultural problems, "air-flying," legal procedure in England and America, President Hoover's government by commissions. Although handicapped by partial deafness, he was able to follow issues before the commission with surprising comprehension, and made little or no use of the secretary provided him to compensate for this defect.

His first attitude was one of "cheerful noncooperation" on the matter of securing the first witness. His argument during the first days of discussion on testimony was, "There is nothing before the commission." He was disposed to defend the name of President King against any attack and to construe any unfavorable reference to the administration as disloyalty to the government. He raised objections to the definition of forced labor, maintaining that there would be no force so long as there was consent of the natives, however secured.

It was evident that he knew the history and details of much that was being discussed, but he offered no explanations except in defense. As the proceedings developed and as he sensed the fervor and persistence of charges, he dropped his defense; still later he showed surprise at the consistency of the revelations made; and finally he shook his hoary head in disgust. On one of his final objections, that natives were bringing to the commission matters which should have been carried to the appropriate departments of government, he was asked to assist a complaining native privately to get action on his grievance. Although it was a relatively small matter, Barclay discovered that it required him four days merely to get a hearing for the man. He saw the man intimidated and the case bandied between departments with no ultimate effective action taken. What he, with all his power and prestige, could not do for a native, it was clear to him that a native could not do for himself. The stern logic of the situation eventually overcame his emotional loyalties. With the air of an attorney who has exhausted every reasonable defense, he signed the full report of the commission without offering amendments. With characteristic courage and calm, Barclay faced the new future of Liberia.

Edwin Barclay, formerly secretary of state under King and later president of the republic, was a small quiet man of about forty-eight, sensitive and intellectual; before he entered actively into politics, he wrote poetry, and was always a lover of good work. His was the largest private law library in the country and he subscribed to the selected literature of an American book club. He smiled easily when conversing, and his expression could shift with incredible swiftness from an open, almost boyish smile, to a disconcerting seriousness. There was the barest suggestion of shyness, which frequently deceived strangers and guileless critics of official policy. The general opinion of the American and European colony was that he ranked next to President King in astuteness and acquaintance with the various and confused angles of the present Liberian situation. He lacked, however, the ability to make friends. Taciturn, seclusive, evasive of politics whenever possible, given to sudden piques, he was never a popular favorite, although he was regarded as a logical candidate by virtue of his important relations with government affairs over many years, his general shrewdness, and his intelligence. Fortunately for him, he managed to place himself on record as opposing practices noted in the recent charges against the government. One outstanding exception appears in certain early correspondence, revived and published by political opponents, which involved him and Vice-President Yancy in the shipment of native laborers to Fernando Poo. At this time he was a close friend of Mr. Yancy's; he had assisted in arranging for the education of Yancy's children in Monrovia, and had urged political promotions for Yancy. These relations, however, were broken off several years before the boy traffic reached its notorious proportions.

Barclay was criticized by some American-Liberians for taking an important part in the loan negotiations, and by natives for his part in the execution of a group of natives in carrying out instructions, as acting president, to stamp out the Leopard Society. This strange, ferocious society had killed and consumed hundreds of individuals, raided towns, and even, on occasion, had brought human flesh to the market for sale. At first, in the effort to check the outrages, Barclay tried sending out natives to locate the mainsprings of the movement, but when these investigators had tasted the flesh, they too became addicts. Finally, Barclay had the whole society rounded up, and some 600 were brought in, all of which could not be executed, naturally. Barclay picked the sixteen ring leaders and ordered them shot; some others he put in prison virtually for life. This action broke up the society.

There was some feeling on the part of the American colony, the fiscal group, particularly, that he was sensitive and prejudiced against White persons, making official relations difficult. An incident was related which helped to explain his attitude. Traveling in Europe a few years back, Barclay had decided to visit Monte Carlo for a period of recreation. He strolled into a gaming house to watch the play for high stakes, but took no part. An American White man, losing heavily at one of the tables, happened to see him and yelled, "Come around here, black boy, and stand behind me to give me luck." With his particular temperament, Barclay built up an attitude which he overgeneralized into bitterness toward all Whites. Because of his West Indian descent he was accused by American Blacks of opposing their immigration to Liberia. This was noted in numbers of published comments, and only later did he take pains to announce his changed attitude on this question. In his knowledge of the technical phases of government and international relations he was without peer.

This writer sought him out for a discussion of several general phases of Liberian problems; when he was told of the difficulty in getting literature about Liberia and asked why he did not set something down, he explained that a person in government had little time and could not well discuss politics and personalities without making political enemies unnecessarily. "The 'Old Man' [referring to his uncle ex-President Barclay] knows more about the history of Liberia," he said, "than perhaps anyone in the country." He had tried to get him to dictate his memoirs, or a story of the development of the country, or at least to save his speeches, "but the truth of the matter is, he is careless with his speeches once they are delivered." Some of his presidential addresses are preserved in the Department of State. President King indicated a desire to have all the presidential addresses bound and printed, but that involved money and there was none available for the purpose.

Commenting on other books about Liberia, he mentioned Reeves, whose *Black Republic* is an anathema in the state. Reeves, he said, was in Liberia in 1903–04. Many things he mentioned were doubtless true then, although he got them garbled from his only free sources of information— the traders on the waterfront. Sir Alfred Sharpe's introduction, he complained, was really the "unkindest cut of all," because it was written much later than the text of Reeves' book, when improvements had come naturally. President King also said that this gentleman had spent only three days in Monrovia on one occasion and three weeks on another, for the purpose of hunting in the Gola country not far from the Bay of Monrovia. He had never been in a Liberian home socially, Barclay claimed, and could have had no basis for his statement that girls were adopted to be made prostitutes for upper-class American-Liberians. Chiefs usually know some Liberian in good circumstances and they sent a child, as often a boy as a girl, to live with him to be educated, or at least to be given the benefit of exposure to civilization. This was usually accepted as a sacred trust and violations of this trust were rare. The chief assumed no responsibility for the child. He was fed, clothed, and sent to school; he frequently took the name of his new guardian and at times married into the group. Only the Golas, whose family ties were extraordinarily strong, went back to their native life.

One of Barclay's policies was that of basing governmental policy on a thorough and competent economic and anthropological survey, for which he preferred an American Black if it was possible to get one. The economic study would be valuable, he thought, because for one thing, it would determine what was in the country. This had been a controversial point on concessions; the concessionaires, being in ignorance of the country's resources, had to ask for enough to safeguard them from loss in the event of failure of their principal interest. Again, the ethnological data would have implications for control and development efforts. He proposed this scheme . to President King, and suggested $25,000 a year for five years. The president said it was a good idea but did nothing about it.

Another of his policies, which he hoped some day to see made a program, involved the final settling of the land question through a thorough surveying and reallotment of land to native communities—perhaps twenty-five acres to a family—in such a way that the land could not be taken back. As the natives developed from the communal arrangement, they could individually acquire title to their acres.

A. Momolu Massaquoi, postmaster general of Liberia under President King, formerly Liberian consul general at Hamburg, Germany, and defeated candidate for the presidency in 1931, was a link with the tortuous history not only of Liberia, but of Africa itself. A member of the Vai tribe, in his younger years he had been a paramount chief. The remarkable feat of spanning the chasm between a high rank in tribal society and a correspondingly high rank in the new society is unprecedented in Liberian history, nor has it since been achieved. One important force was his ready adaptability to European patterns of life and thought, and his command of the Vai language and writing system, which he was able to introduce to German students of African ethnology.

The process of adjustment to the dual cultures was not without its difficulties. The American commission of 1908, for example, recommended Massaquoi's removal from the interior where he had been serving as a native commissioner. By 1930, in his fifties, he had obtained, from residence in Europe, study, and administrative experience, a solid, even if new, social background against which to project his life. His attitude toward his tribe had developed into a detached interest and solicitude. He could speak dispassionately of the "basic culture of Africa," of African ethics and psychology, of the neglected value of the native institutions of the Devil bush, Porran, and Bondo societies; of the Suke, which is a highly spiritual society dealing entirely with spiritual matters, and is synonymous with the Greek *psyche*, in turn, no doubt, borrowed by the Greek mercenaries who frequented the Sudanese markets of North Africa during the glory of the Mellanese Empire. He had learned and associated himself spiritually with the history of Liberia, and spoke with reverence of the valor and sacrifices of "our founders, Elijah Johnson and Mathilda Newport." During a Liberian Independence Day celebration he was heard to deliver a forceful address on "The Struggling of Liberian Democracy," which was indistinguishable in point of view from that of any other American-Liberian. He was also heard proudly interpreting the ceremonies of a group of Mohammedan Vai priests to the president and, in the very session made possible by religious tolerance, he attempted to convince these Mohammedan priests that their religion was inferior to Christianity.

The Massaquoi family extends back into a romantic past—so far, in fact, that it can borrow without challenge from the glories of ancient Ethiopia. In the days of the Pharoahs, so runs the lore of this family, the people who inhabited the eastern and western banks of the Nile were the same as those who possessed the Sudan and Nigerian countries. The latter once constituted the great Ethiopian empire. When the Berbers were in their ascendancy, during the reign of Charlemagne, the House of Massaquoi arose in the ancient kingdom of Timbuctu. Their people were related to those families which ruled over the whole of the Sudan for thousands of years. Sometime around 12 or 14 A.D., the Berbers, Moor, Touaregs, and Tibbis, and all the tribes of the Sahara Desert confederated for the purpose of destroying the empire. After many wars, the houses of Massaquoi, Valinger, Kia Tamba, and Farhnbuley migrated westward. Kindred tribes to the east of Timbuctu moved eastward and established the kingdom which is now Victoria Nyanza Tancania.

The western branch was led on its westward trek by the Massaquois, surrounded by 1,000 cavalrymen. Farhnbuley was in the center, guarding the sacred vessels and the Ethiopian crown, and in the rear were women, the priests, and the baggage of the Mellestine Empire. They conquered tribes in their path; some of these tribes joined the conquering caravan. Eventually they reached the Musadu plains, and finding it good country they took possession and sat down. Branches of these people extended themselves further westward into Konoma, which is now Liberian territory. Here they encountered the Golas and Mendes, but having lost so many warriors on the long trek, they decided to make peace with these tribes. As they recovered their strength, they became the peacemakers between kings and tribes of the whole area.

When old King Peter, the doughty harasser of the first Liberian emmigrants, died, the Massaquoi were made trustees of King Peter's estate. It was thus to this family that Presidents Roberts and Benson appealed in some of their early tribal difficulties. (Here the lore begins to connect with recorded history.) King Peter's son, Jollah Finajay, challenged the estate and the Massaquois and Farhnbuleys, since to destroy King Peter's estate would invalidate the treaty agreement with the Colonization Society. To defend their position, arms were provided the Massaquois by the Liberian government. They acquitted themselves well. From this point dates the spiritual union of the Vais with the government of Liberia. At any rate, whether legend or fact, the story is sufficiently strong to survive un-challenged.

The year 1930 was one of unusual political excitement throughout Liberia, as preparations were made for another presidential election. The field, accordingly, was full of "dark horses," whispering their policies and criticisms and affecting a gravely noncommittal air. It was the good fortune of this writer to meet one such "dark horse," who in 1931 achieved the high office of vice-president.

Under the fire of unanswerable charges of malfeasance and incompetence, Governor Brooks of Maryland had been transferred to Bassa, and Governor Smith of Bassa, the "strong man" of country administration, had replaced him. Governor Smith was a huge man, weighing, it seemed, close to 300 pounds. Even so, he wore clothes too large for him, as if in desperation some Lilliputian tailor had cut a cloth large enough for any possible purpose, and arrived at the spacious proportions of a tent. With this vast but surprisingly nimble bulk went a small smooth head. A small brown hat of narrow brim and a soft collar propped up beneath the tie by a clasp of two gold bells as large as marbles, were also characteristic.

An impressive figure, despite his very small head, enormous feet and body, and quite mobile stomach, he would, when in serious discourse, wrinkle his brow painfully. Frequently he stressed his points by extending his body and sinking again violently into his chair with a sudden and violent impact.

Governor Smith's ideas of government, although crudely stated, were sensible and honest at the core. When he expressed them, his face took on an exaggerated aspect of acute righteousness, as if he were about to abandon the useless role of strong man and have a good cry. Nearly all that he said, although often grammatically incorrect, was aimed at a soundness which the country undoubtedly needed. He did not know, when I talked with him, which candidate's colors he would follow, and even hinted significantly that his own strength might conceivably be found an asset.

This is an awful condition (referring to the general political situation). Thousands and thousands of our people suffer from it. People are talking about the next president. I tell them it's too soon. The very words the president spoke to me when I had the conference with him when he told me he wanted me to come to Maryland. The last word he said was "Don't talk politics yet." He's a keen politician. I've come here. They needed a strong man. They're crying now, these little government crooks, saying times is hard. I just go on stopping up cracks. I say "What's the trouble, I hasn't done nothing." They say, "You know it cost money to live in this place." I just go on stopping up cracks. Yes, sir! They're squealing loud and I don't say nothing. Myself, I been here since February and not one cent I received from the government. I sent to my wife and got £150 then £120 more. It cost me £1 a day to live here. But I say, "My country first." I'll be dead and gone, but my country I wants to live. They say, "What! They trying to tear down our country?" I say, if you remove Vice-President Yancy, do that destroy the country? Or if you remove the president, do that destroy the country? Or, if you remove the whole cabinet, do that destroy it? No. It's time for a change. No more of this handing around offices in a little circle, just shifting the name of the office. I always say the man who follows President King got to be a strong man, and I ain't calling no names yet. Of course, there's Eddie Barclay. There ain't a shrewder man next to King, but that ain't settled yet. The man's got to be strong. We got to get a change from this little circle business. We don't need no more dictators. The Legislature ought to do the dictating like they used to do, I tell you, we had some strong ones once. The last of them went out before King. Strong men, old man Barclay will tell you. When he vetoed a bill once, they looked up and said "What!" and marched it back over his head quicker than that. They were sons of their fathers, these strong ones who founded the country. When legislation time came they didn't wait on no ship. They rolled up their pants and walked the beach that 250 miles to Monrovia. A boy carried a box for them and they set their own suitcase on their shoulders and marched on. When they met, presidents trembled. Now, if you get a strong man to represent you, you will be told—"No, not him, he thinks he's too smart. I want him (that little yes man who won't give nobody no trouble)." You know, in a way Faulkner was right. He wasn't fighting for himself so much as he was fighting corruption. In 1927, when he run for president against King he knowed there was crookedness. He applied to the courts, they wouldn't hear him. He applied to the legislature, they wouldn't hear him. He applied to the Supreme Court, they wouldn't hear him. Then, by God, he applied to the League of Nations.

16

The Slavery Issue

Slavery is that status in which any or all of the powers attaching to the right of ownership are exercised.
Anti-Slavery Convention of the League of Nations

All work or service which is exacted from any person under the menace of any penalty for its nonperformance and for which the worker does not offer himself voluntarily is forced labor.
Definition submitted by the International Labor Office

Throughout the recent history of Africa, imperialism and capitalist exploitation have proceeded hand in hand with civilizing agencies and an ever-increasing interest in the welfare of the backward peoples who have been the subject of this exploitation. In 1922, the Third Assembly of the League of Nations decided to include the question of slavery in its agenda. The ultimate concern was that of bringing about as soon as possible "the abolition of slavery in all its forms," and the inauguration of the necessary steps "to prevent compulsory labor from developing into conditions analogous to slavery." Liberia was a member of the League of Nations, as was Haiti, and a Haitian member, Dantes Bellegarde, was a member of the first Anti-Slavery Convention. Despite Britain's leadership for a number of years in these reforms, notably through Lord Lugard, it was only in 1927 that Sierra Leone, a British dependency, formally abolished domestic slavery within its territories. Following the discussion, new legislation was promulgated in other African colonies with respect to slavery and forced labor.

Important economic issues are necessarily involved in the competition set up between countries producing goods by unpaid forced labor, contract, or the familiar penal sanctions, and those producing goods by free wage earners. A great amount of the raw materials imported into Europe and America was produced by African labor under varied conditions of compulsion. The question, thus, became fundamental, and an effective economic arm supported the softer sentiments of humanity.

175

Throughout the deliberations of the Anti-Slavery Convention, there was conspicuous mention of both Abyssinia and Liberia. In the case of the latter, other forces entered to give it prominence. It was in itself a refuge for oppressed Blacks; it occupied a conspicuous position on the much traveled West Coast; and it had been subject to a great amount of publicity on its governmental policy and practice, which seemed to combine administrative incompetence and corruption with widespread forced labor, and with the survival of certain crass forms of domestic slavery. The suggestion that the Republic of Liberia clear its reputation of the charges came first from the United States, in keeping with its traditional policy of friendliness to Liberia. The American Minister's memorandum to the Liberian secretary of state, delivered on June 8, 1920, read in part:

> I am directed by the Secretary of State to advise Your Excellency that there have come to the attention of the Government of the United States from several sources reports bearing reliable evidence of authenticity which definitely indicate that existing conditions incident to the so-called "export" of labor from Liberia to Fernando Poo have resulted in the development of a system which seems hardly distinguishable from organized slave trade, and that in the enforcement of this system the service of the Liberian Frontier Force, and the services and influence of certain high government officials are constantly and systematically used.

In reply, the Liberian secretary of state wrote as follows:

> With regard to the specific allegations which have been made, I deem it my duty to record my government's solemn and categorical denial of the existence in the Republic of such labor conditions as would justify the characterization which has been applied to these conditions in your dispatch, and to declare that the government of the Republic will have no objection to this question being investigated on the spot by a competent, impartial and unprejudiced commission.

The first diplomatic blunder of the republic on the challenge regarding slavery and forced labor seems clearly to have been the decision to make a categorical denial of the existence of both these practices. Either these practices existed without being recognized, or it was naively expected that it would be sufficient for the government to enter an official denial and have it ended. In the first instance, they laid themselves open to the charge of stupidity; in the second, to the charge of mendacity.

There had always existed as part of the Constitution a provision against slavery, but this by itself did not influence the practice of domestic slavery which had been part of the social system of its aboriginal society for hundreds of years. Actually, this form of slavery was not in itself as oppressive as other forms of economic relationship involving the participation and profit of the civilized elements of the population. Historically, the slavery of the well-known *Uncle Tom's Cabin* type took on its most horrible aspect when it became a traffic exploited by civilized agencies. It was at this point of contact with the alien forces of exploitation in Liberia that tribal disorganization began, not so much on the old forms of domestic slavery as on the exploitation of its native labor, and threatened, through this heedless disorder, to disrupt both native and civilized societies. It is this unfortunate relationship with the native population, the development of which I have tried to set forth in the previous chapters, that constituted the shame of Liberia.

Sinoe County lies to the south of Monrovia, and will be remembered as the first settlement of American Blacks from Mississippi. It is entered by one of the most treacherous ports on the West Coast and a landing must be effected through vicious rocks and slashing breakers. It is the old Kru country, with its mountainous interior, in the hollow of which nestle numerous native villages.

In 1927 the district commissioner of this section was J.B. Watson, and the chief political figure of the whole area was the Honorable Samuel Ross. The selling of boys had been carried on sporadically in this section for many years, but only in the 1920s did it expand to the proportions of a traffic. Ross, who controlled this business under special executive sanction, built his barracoons at Blubarrow Point, commanded the Frontier Force, and from his headquarters in Greenville operated through the station of the district commissioner at Sikon in the interior. The confidential messenger for this effective combination was Quartermaster Edward Blackett, a cold, dull individual, capable of any crime so long as he had been ordered to commit it. The method of the raids was as follows: Ross would order the number of natives needed to complete a labor requisition. The district commissioner would send Blackett with soldiers into the villages to round up the number and to force them to collect from the communal granaries enough rice to serve them until they were taken aboard the ship, to tie them and lead them down to the coast under the prodding of the soldiers' whips and rifle butts. At first they were caught and led down to the coast on the pretense of selling rice for their tax money. But when the men failed to return to their homes and their people knew that they had been sent away, the old ruse no longer worked. It was necessary for the insensitive Blackett and his soldiers to capture the required numbers outright.

In September 1929, the quartermaster was ordered by District Commissioner Watson to make two raids, one for 350 men and another for 250, and deliver them to Samuel Ross in Greenville. Blackett caught 330 of the first order and the full 250 of the second, and carried them in. Let Blackett tell his story:

I was his District Quartermaster. While there, on the 21st of September 1927, I was ordered with some soldiers to go and have some men caught and carried down to Sinoe and turned over to Mr. Ross for shipment to Fernando Poo. That order was executed. I caught the men, carried them down to Sinoe and turned them over to Mr. Ross. That was the second trip. The first trip, District Commissioner Watson ordered me to go and get some men and carry them to Mr. Ross. I did so and collected 330 men and turned them over to Mr. Ross. Mr. Ross and I carried them on board ship. When I returned, then it was that he ordered me to collect the second set of boys, the number of which was 250. In this first set, District Commissioner Watson told the chiefs that he wanted so many boys to go to Fernando Poo as per the president's orders. Then I was sent to go and collect the laborers from the chiefs and to force any chief who failed to supply the laborers. I carried out his orders and turned the men over to Mr. Ross. Senator Roberts asked why are these men being sent to Fernando Poo. I replied that I was merely carrying out the orders of the district commissioner. On my way back, Mr. Ross sent the district commissioner £47 for the boys. My first orders I have with me here. When I turned the second set over to Mr. Ross, he placed them across the river [in the Blubarrow barracoons]. Then it was that Mr. Sherman asked me about the matter, but I told him that I was merely carrying out orders and that, if he wished to know anything, he should go to Mr. Ross.

Here Blackett produced a worn and soiled but authentic letter over the signature of Watson.

INTERIOR DEPARTMENT
LIBERIAN HINTERLAND

Tchien H.Q. Dist. No. 4.
September 21, 1927.

Reff: "Instruction"
Mr. Ed. H.A. Blackett
District Quarter-Master
District Number Four L.H.

Sir:

You are hereby ordered to proceed immediately with these soldiers upon the receipt of this letter, by the instruction of the Honorable Commissioner General John W. Cooper, of the Liberian Hinterland, R.L., down to Greenville, Sinoe, with as many men laborers as you possibly can, not exceeding 250, and there deliver them to Hon. Samuel A. Ross, for the purpose of being shipped to Fernando Poo, per order of his Excly., the President C.B. King; each man is to take with him one hamper of cleaned rice for his ration, and after the shipment, whatever is left you are to sell it out and report the cash here at this office on your return, to assist in paying off the staff.

Fail not: observing the above I remain,
Yours,
Faithfully, (Sgd) J.B. Watson
District Commissioner.

P.S. You are to make a general list of the names of the men shipped, and from each section they are from.

It so happened that on the occasion of the last of these deliveries, Postmaster General R.A. Sherman was in Sinoe inspecting the local postal service. He had come on a ship that was demonstrating a new ship-to-shore radio service. While he was still aboard, Ross appeared with a message for the secretary of state. It was to the effect that the Spanish steamer had not appeared and that some 300 boys were on hand; the expense of feeding them created a problem. Sherman sent the message, but when he went ashore he saw the group of natives huddled together in the compound under the guard of Blackett and his soldiers. The local postmaster, C.D. Majors, remarked that they had to be guarded by the soldiers until a steamer came because they did not want to be sent away. Sherman was advised to "keep his hands off" because Ross was too powerful for interference." Blackett himself was indignant over the meddling interference of the postmaster general. When Sherman asked, "Don't you know this is slavery of the worst sort?" Blackett replied, "That don't concern me. I know I'm over the boys, but I'm acting on orders, and I carries out my orders. You got no right to go over me to the men. If you want to talk to them, you ought to ask me."

When Ross appeared with a second set of messages of a grossly questionable nature and a casual bribe to make the request palatable, Sherman refused and wired the secretary of state and attorney general about the affair, referring to it as "slavery!" The attorney general replied that if the men were being sent against their will it was slave trading; but the men were sent, nevertheless. Sherman lost his job as postmaster as a consequence of his meddling, and the notorious Ross was appointed in his place. Moreover, the puny effort of the citizens of Greenville to have the practice stopped came swiftly to an end. They at first indicted Blackett, but failed to mention Ross. Then they quietly dropped the indictment of Blackett because it was so obvious that the responsible party was Ross. Both the young country attorney who tried to push the case and the county superintendent who was willing to investigate the matter found themselves suddenly out of jobs. District Commissioner Watson was advanced by appointment to the more desirable District No. 2 of the Liberian Hinterland.

Immediately after Yancy's inauguration as vice-president in 1928 he returned to Maryland County with new and bolder plans for the advancement of the section. The death of Ross had given him full command of the boy traffic. He called a meeting of all the chiefs of the section and addressed them: "I have just returned from Monrovia," he said, "and I have an order from the president that each paramount chief must furnish me men for

Fernando Poo. Now I want from each of you paramount chiefs sixty men. If you refuse, you must pay me the equivalent. To be specific, for each man less than sixty you will pay me £10. If you send neither the men nor the money, I will send soldiers to destroy your towns. If you doubt that I make this demand on the authority of the president, go to Monrovia and find out for yourself."

The chiefs were stunned by this bold, open demand. "Eh!" said one of them, "Since we begin we never see this thing. If anybody want to go to Gold Coast, they go themselves, never they sent by force." And still another cried: "This Fernando Poo, since we here been we no go. How, Mr. Yancy! Wedebo [sic] people you took there to punish them; plenty you send. 140 die there. What we done that you send we too?" But the wily old Jack Jarraca, who had bought this commission from Yancy, interrupted with crafty acquiescence: "Since you been instructed by the president, no one will refuse. Since the president has ordered it, it will be carried out."

Chief Jury of Picnicess was not yet satisfied. "Mr. Yancy," he protested, "we build road without pay or feeding; we pay taxes without commission. We bear this condition because here is our country, and yet the president say we must go to Fernando Poo? How can this be done? We cannot send people to Fernando Poo and to the road. Where we got such an amount of people?" But the vice-president was firm; he had spoken and he went home to await the results.

Old Chief Broh of Fernando Poo, sturdy, solemn, and wise, decided to put this extraordinary order to a test. He sent his messengers, Solomon N'Yapan and Nyantenee, to Monrovia to inquire of the president if he had given such destructive orders to his aide. At Grand Cess in Maryland County, Broh and his messengers recalled this experience. Solomon N'Yapan's rendering of the account could be readily verified by the reference to the recorded incidents in Monrovia.

We reach Monrovia 15th January, 1929. Our report had been sent to president, but president sent the same report to Secretary of the Interior, J.F. Cooper, to call us and ask us what confusion we brought from Maryland County to Monrovia. And then he sent his messengers to see us at Kru town [in Monrovia] where we stopped. Then we stated that the vice-president say that the president himself say that we should go to Fernando Poo. If we were unable to go, each of us paid ten pounds out of the sixty men which he required from the paramount chiefs. If not he will send soldiers to destroy the place. I told him Broh was very much afraid that his people would be destroyed, therefore we wanted to find out if you have given the vice-president the executive order from your Secretary Cooper's little secretary, typed same and sent it to the president.

Then the president sent a radio to Vice-President Yancy at Cape Palmas to come to Monrovia. We met in the Executive Mansion and president read our statement but do nothing about it.

We go back to Cape Palmas and the vice-president was very much annoyed that natives had been sent to Monrovia to tell the president. Then he sent soldiers by Captain Phillips to raid towns. Chief Broh was arrested. I was arrested. Forty-two men from town were carried to Cape Palmas to jail.

As the recital of Broh's troubles proceeded, there would be promptings by various members of the party who had been personally involved. With a nod, Broh would note its incorporation, adding a detail or relating it specifically to the thread of the incident as N'Yapan presented it. Sampson Coffer, one of the attendants of Broh, interposed this observation:

When the soldiers got into town, they tied our people with sticks behind their legs; flogged them, men and women, at the same time; killed our animals for their satisfaction, without any order from the chief or any of the sub-chiefs; they plundered us also, carrying goods from the town.

Broh's speaker then carried on the account:

We got to Cape Palmas tenth of May, 1929, at midnight. After we crossed the river, we were carried to the vice-president's yard and locked up as prisoners. Soldiers carried us. At daylight on the 4th of the month, we were carried to vice-president's farm and kept as prisoners.

When Vice-President Yancy got there, his first question to Chief Broh was, "And so it was you who sent Solomon N'Yapan and Nyantee to report me to president about the Fernando Poo matters. Now I got you in my hand and if I please, I can put you into this Spanish ship in the harbor and carry *you* to Fernando Poo. Or I can only give you to the soldiers to carry you to the barracks [at Barrabo], according to the president's order, while the other chiefs are here. But I will tell the soldiers on their way going that they may shoot you with their guns and they shall tell me upon returning that Broh die while we were going. I can simply write to the President that Paramount Chief Broh die by sickness and the President will say, "All right, that is the will of God." Do you know what secret matter I and the President decided in our private room before you sent my report to the President? Now, the President governs Monrovia and I govern Maryland County. Whatever I do here will simply tell the President that is all right and the President will accept it. But you don't know what you are doing yet: you are sending my name to my own countryman who is with me to be President of the Republic."

After this he tell Broh that he must be paid £272. before he can leave us alone from the soldiers. Then he turned his face around to the chiefs of Suehn, Topo, Barrabo, and Webbo and said: "You fellows, Broh had made you fools, therefore I will give you the same punishment which Broh received." And he fined them £200 each. After this had been done he released the chiefs. I do not know how many of all the people who died from the treatment of the soldiers but I know of Broh's: Mandoo, Keke, Doyalah, and Nimini, who died from the beating of the soldiers.

Broh sought a lawyer to protest the fine and Senator W.V.S. Tubman took the case, charging him a retainer's fee of £110. When the Government Council met in Cape Palmas, Tubman forgot to plead Broh's case. Said the old chief: "Many thanks to the Government Council, I will go to Monrovia and make my own appeal." He did, and several of the aggrieved chiefs went with him.

On December 20, 1929, they appeared before the president and talked with him in the presence of the secretary of the interior and the new superintendent of Maryland County, J.S. Smith. The president said: "Broh, go back to Maryland County. I will send the new secretary to see what is troubling you in Maryland County." Broh's speaker said: "Mr. President, you are the whole Republic. The people in Cape Palmas are giving us confusion and we have put our complaint before you and yet you tell us to return to Cape Palmas." The president said: "Do as I say. You need not say more. As I am now saying, your whole delegation will go back to Maryland County on the *Wadai* which will be here tomorrow. If your people do not go back on the *Wadai* and you are in town, I will put the soldiers on you and imprison you. Therefore each one will have to go." The natives were much frightened and when the *Wadai* came, they bought tickets and went home and sat down quietly.

The secretary of the interior made a tour of Maryland County and his confidential report to the president, which was never given to the public, included the following statement: "Mr. Yancy, when superintendent, had the practice of dividing the tribes over the question of paramount chieftancy. Whenever your Excellency would appoint one man, he would foster and support another man. . . . The natives had the impression that the vice-president has equal powers of the president. He could appoint and dismiss, deport and recall. The chiefs have been fined for making complaints to the president and they have been told by the vice-president, 'You are in my hands. Let President King come and deliver you out.'" But the president refused to act. Instead he permitted the vice-president to raid the sections of Suehn, Topo, Barrabo, and Webbo.

The total fines illegally collected from the chiefs of these four sections aggregated £94. The chief of the Barrabo people, who did not go with Broh to Monrovia, received as a reward favorable consideration on a long-standing land dispute against Broh's people, but in the end he had to pay £600.0.0 to the vice-president for this settlement.

Between 1920 and 1929 Broh was arrested sixteen times and had incurred fines aggregating £200, all of which he paid. He had asked for native schools in his section, for receipts for his hut taxes, and for a statement of the regulations by which they were expected to be ruled. On one occasion he was put in prison and fined £300 for saying: "Yancy likes money too much." He had been beaten by soldiers in the presence of his subjects. Their affection for him and his stubborn concern for their well-being held the respect of his people. The spirit of the old man could not be broken. The fines extorted from the chiefs in this Fernando Poo demand which failed, totaled £942.10.0 or about $9,500.00, exclusive of cattle and incidental fines of the other chiefs and of the large additional fines on the land issue. Some of this went to Superintendent Brooks, some to Senator Tubman, some to Lieutenant Phillips of the Frontier Force, and some to the district commissioner, but the bulk of it went to the vice-president, for his own coffers, and to be distributed among other essential officials in compensation for the privilege.

The account of the raid in Topo County is graphically told by Speaker Boryono Doco, who escaped the soldiers at the time Paramount Chief Gofa was arrested and carried to the barracks. He mentions the coming of the soldiers, the rounding up of the chief and the elders, and the first demands for men by the officer in charge.

After this he (Lieutenant Phillips) dismissed us; he said he was going to bathe and see about chop and ordered us to return to his quarters two o'clock after breakfast. At the appointed time all men of the town gathered in front of the zinc house he occupied, he ordered his soldiers to surround us on all sides; and when he was satisfied that all of the men were completely surrounded, he put this question to us: "Where is your Paramount Chief Gofa?" I arose and answered him that Gofa went to Monrovia. He asked me, "What is your name?" I said to him, "My name is Boryano Doco." Lieutenant Phillips then said he liked the man who would tell the truth. He raised his big rubber whip and began to flog me as hard as he could and when he was tired, he ordered the soldiers to throw me down and to beat me. The soldiers seized me, threw me down and began to beat me. After this severe beating, the soldiers put my foot between two pieces of hardwood and then tied the ends of the stick together, the tighter the ropes were drawn, the more the stick pressed into my flesh. I suffered awfully from this cruel treatment, the scar of the sore cut into my flesh by one of the sticks is right on my foot and I can show it to any person. I was not the only one who was flogged. The soldiers jumped into the crowd and beat the other men right and left and tied as many as they could and put them through the same torture. Afterward the Lieutenant put all of us into one house and locked us up at sunset. Yanfor and Magbe, the two eldest men of the tribe who are even older than Paramount Chief Gofa, were among the crowd; in fact the two men are owners of the country. We did not want them to sleep in confinement, so we went to Lieutenant Phillips and begged him to release them. He asked us to give him £10 if we did not want the old men to sleep in the guard house. The people gave Chief Gofa's speaker, M'ma Doe, £10 for the old men's release and he paid the money to Lieutenant Phillips. Upon the receipt of the £10.0.0 he released the two men.

After the release of the old men who are in the guard house are twenty-four men. On the following morning when Lieutenant Phillips and the soldiers were about to take us all to Harper as prisoners the people begged him to release me, they pointed out to him that being sick from the results of the severe flogging from his soldiers and himself, I might die on the way if he carried me to Harper, because the soldiers were most liable to beat me again on the journey. He agreed to release me, but asked the people to take me out of his hands, that is, they must bring something for my release. They gave him £7 but he refused to accept it, and demanded a cow, and said that he would carry me if it is not forthcoming. On hearing this the women began to cry and there was a great cry in the town. My family caught a grown cow with young one and gave it to Lieutenant Phillips and I was released.

He took the remaining twenty-three persons and moved off to Harper. The Lieutenant reached Harper very late in the night and gave the men to Vice President Yancy who sent them to his farm just before daybreak the next morning. The men were so severely flogged by the soldiers on the two day journey from our town to Harper that one of them, Kohkoh Jehleh by name, died from the effect of the beating two days after they reached the prison house at the Vice President's farm.

When the news of Jehleh's death reached us, my people, the Topo tribe, sent M'ma Doe as a special messenger to Vice President Yancy to find out what was the reason for the arrest of the men Lieutenant Phillips took to Harper and treated so cruelly that one was killed by beating. He said he sent and arrested the men because Paramount Chief Gofa of the Topo tribe went to Monrovia to report him to the President and that he would not release the remaining twenty-two men unless we sent him £100. We collected the £100 and gave it to the same M'ma Doe and Gebo Chea, and the two men carried the money and paid it to the Vice President. After the receipt of this money, he said to the two men, "I see this £100. I accept this amount as a fine for your Paramount Chief going to Monrovia. For this reason you must go and tell your people to send me another £100, before I release the prisoners." The two messengers returned to us with the news of the additional demands for money. We collected the second £100 and sent it to the Vice President by the same messengers. They paid the money to him and he released the men and sent them home by our messengers.

In spite of this, the report of the secretary of the interior was kept hidden, the raids and shipments of boys continued, and serious reprisals were taken upon all the natives who had dared report the outrages.

Further shipments of men were made by the vice-president eleven days after the report of the Commission of Inquiry had been presented to the government of Liberia. Soldiers of Nanakru in Sinoe, during September 1930, immediately after the departure of the Commission of Inquiry, raided villages, killing three women by flogging. Ex-Paramount Chief Glogba Togba, Subchief Tappi Togba, and paramount chief-elect Thomas Nimrod were arrested by soldiers, put in chains, and imprisoned: "You Kru people," they were told, "were glad when the commissioner was here and you reported us to them. Where are they now? Let them come and get you out of this trouble."

The mysterious orders under which these raids were being conducted in the interior of southern Liberia appeared in the case of Chief Choami of Kronrokeh and District Commissioner Carney Johnson. This commissioner was a native Gola, educated in Monrovia—a young man of frank, open personality who in his frankness had admitted many administrative irregularities. Chief Choami was under his jurisdiction. When first placed in this district, Johnson had advised the chiefs to resist the demands of the vice-president for laborers. Suddenly, however, he reversed his policy and became brutal in his efforts to force chiefs to produce more men for shipment. Choami told the story of one of the raids conducted by the district commissioner.

A demand had been made for a larger number of men than the section could supply, since most of their remaining young men were working on the public roads. Choami promised to send a few. Not satisfied, the commissioner confined the chief in their guard house. When the chief continued to refuse, soldiers were sent into his villages to take the number first demanded. As the soldiers approached, all the men of the town ran to the bush. The soldiers in reprisal caught their women, tied them, and subjected them to abuse throughout the night. The chief, from his confinement, hearing of the treatment of the women, appealed to the young men of the tribe to surrender so that the women might be released. His messengers, however, could find only old men and several subchiefs. Said Choami:

> The Chiefs and the old men said to the District Commissioner, "Is it possible for us to leave our wives and children to go to Fernando Poo? Fernando Poo is not a very good place to be; people die there frequently. If you want us to work on the road or at Firestone's, we will go, but not to Fernando Poo."

> "But you have to go to Fernando Poo. You did not give young men therefore you will have to go."

> Then the old men said, "Let us go and see if we can catch our young men, but Fernando Poo is a place where men die often and we do not want to go."

> Then he said, "If you all do not want to go then the Chief of every town must stay until men are found." Therefore chiefs returned to the guard room while the old men went to look for the boys. When he was coming out he met all the women who had been coming toward Nyaake to meet him, the king.

> The women said, "Since you left us yesterday, they put us in small house and if you had to go to the call of nature you had to be held by soldiers."

> The Chief said, "Let the women go."

> Soldiers said, "No. The D.C.'s orders must be obeyed."

> So he returned to the District Commissioner and said, "I go look for men and see how soldiers treat our women."

He said, "Well, if you don't want to go to Fernando Poo, you will be treated so. Tell the women to get their husbands from the bush or they will have to go."

They said, "All right. We will go, if our husbands said so."

When the soldiers came in the town to get the women, all ran. One woman ran fell in a ditch and broke her leg. Next morning he carried to the barracks 30 men.

"These boys that you want sent to Fernando Poo, will we get something from them as we get from the boys who go to Firestone's?"

He said, "It is none of your business and it is not mine to tell you. They are going for four to six months."

But since they went they have not come back, and it is more than six months now.

So afterwards at the expiration of six months, he went to the District Commissioner and said, "Where are the boys?"

"I will write to Yancy and what he says I will tell you!"

Commissioner Johnson verified this statement when the matter was brought to his attention and gave in explanation of his changed policy a letter from the president which had been presented to him in person by the vice-president. The letter itself was noncommittal but from his knowledge of methods of government he considered it wise to alter his policy immediately and radically, and this he did. This is the letter he received:

> This letter comes to advise you that I arrived in Cape Palmas on last week Wednesday and in leaving Monrovia the President handed me a letter bearing your address and of which he asked me to tender you this in person and not by proxy.
>
> In view of this fact I shall be pleased to have you come to Harper at an early date and thereby take receipt of same.

The official character of these raids was illustrated further in the following correspondence between the commander of the Barrabo Barracks and the vice-president.

> Barrabo Barracks,
> March 11, 1929.

Hon. Allen N. Yancy
Vice President, R.L.

Sir,

> Your letter through your Secretary was received yesterday, also a letter from the District Commissioner of this district touching on the matter of Fernando Poo Laborers.
>
> I am herewith sending the one squad of soldiers to the Superintendent and hope that they will be of good servicee to you both. Wish I had the time to

come along with these men to meet you; but the pressure of work demands my presence here for the time being.

With respect to the laborers from Fernando Poo, I shall urge the Station-master to get them to you as quickly as possible.

Hope you are well and enjoyed yourself while at Monrovia.

Wishing for you much success,
I am yours respectfully,

[signed] I. Whisnant
Captain, Liberian Frontier Force.

Barrabo
March 18, 1929.

Hon. Allen N. Yancy
Cape Palmas

Sir,

I am herewith sending some of the boys for Fernando Poo, and their names are as follows:

From Gbebo
1. Jim
2. Bestman
3. Blackman
4. John Peter
5. Mennah
6. Jacob
7. Moses
8. Pinco
9. Coffee
10. John Thomas
11. Samson
12. Josiah
13. Far Way
14. Money Sweet
15. John Toe
16. Sunday
17. Jack Spot
18. Myier
19. How For Do
20. Monrovia

Teampo
1. Charlie
2. Miller
3. Police Master
4. Martarday
5. Fine Glass

As the others come in I shall send them down to you. Expect others soon.

Yours respectfully,

[Signed] I. Whisnant
Acting District Commissioner,
District N. 5.

Harper, Cape Palmas,
1st April 1929.

Captain Isaac Whisnant, L.F.F.
Barrabo Section,

My dear Capt. Whisnant:

I am directed by Honourable Allen Yancy to inform you that out of the list of boys that the commissioner asked to be supplied, only twenty (20) were received from Gbebo.

The five (5) boys sent from Tienpoh came in the afternoon, and left the next morning, they have not been seen since.

Therefore, the boys which are to go to Fernando Poo from Gbebo are twenty in number only.

With sentiments and best wishes,

Yours faithfully,
[Signed] L.B. Andrews
Private Secretary

Camp King,
Barrabo,
April 1, 1929

Hon. Allen N. Yancy
Cape Palmas,

Sir,

I am herewith sending you twenty Fernando Poo boys from the Barrabo Section, and hope you will receive them correct.

There names are as follows:

1. Narkey	1. Kie (Headman)
2. Yenneh	2. Tom
3. Glay	3. Fasseh
4. Saudeh	4. Fyier
5. Tarkpah	5. Taumu
6. Sayee	6. Bodeor
7. Jaffah	7. Borway
8. Weah	8. Kusson
9. Toe No. 1	9. Marnee
10. Toe No. 2	10. Yenmah

These are all that can be gotten this trip. They are refusing to go and have to be pressed.

Yours faithfully,

[Signed] I. Whisnant
Captain, Liberian Frontier Force,
For the District Commissioner.

Camp King,
Barrabo,
April 6, 1929.

Hon. Allen N. Yancy,
Cape Palmas.

Sir,

With respect to the Fernando Poo boys, I have instructed the Station Master here to send for them. There are special places the Commissioner said that they should be gotten from, and Gbebe, Barrabo, Kiyedapo and Tienpo have sent theirs. Those from Twardo and Gleyo have not turned up yet. It is so very hard to get them from that end unless military force is used. But as they come in I shall send them to you.

I shall send in trace of the Tienpo boys who have deserted.

Respectfully yours,

[Signed] I. Whisnant,
Captain, Liberian Frontier Force,
For the District Commissioner.
Camp King

Barrabo,
April 8, 1929.

Hon. Allen N. Yancy
Cape Palmas

Sir,

I understand by the soldier who carried the Fernando Poo boys to you, that seven of them ran off. Please send me the names of them according to the list sent you. All of Chief Jodoflay's boys ran off the soldier reports.

Yours very respectfully,

[Signed] I. Whisnant
Captain, Liberian Frontier Force.

Camp King,
Barrabo
May 17th, 1929.

Hon. Allen N. Yancy

Dear Sir,

Yours of the 9th inst. received today. I am thankful to you for your appreciation of my cooperation with Superintendent Brooks.

Some time ago I received a letter from Supt. Brooks requesting soldiers to be stationed at the Camp for the purpose of road construction, and I immediately took the matter up with the Commanding Officer of the Liberian Frontier Force, as I have no authority to station men on out-station duty, and to do so instruction would necessarily come from Head Office. But up to the present my letter has not been answered. In the mean time should this authority be delayed much longer I shall repeat my letter. Am expecting something on the matter soon.

I have sent several sets of Fernando Poo boys to you from this district and do not know whether they reached you or not. Please let me know as soon as possible the number you have received.

Yours very respectfully,

[Signed] I. Whisnant,
Captain, Liberian Frontier Force.

The theory of the Fernando Poo shipments was that the men should remain away two years, receive half of their pay of £2. a month in Fernando Poo, and the other half through the Spanish consul when they returned to Liberia. In practice, those few who returned rarely brought anything with them, or received more than a pound or two on their return. Often they got nothing. Cases were noted of men who earned one pound for two years of work, and even as little as ten shilling for three years.

Apart from the Fernando Poo exportations, natives were kidnapped to be shipped to Libreville in the French Caboon. The most notorious case was that of 145 boys who were told by Alhaz Massaquoi that they were being recruited for the usual familiar coast labor, but who were taken instead to French Libreville and distributed among strange masters for long periods of service.

The contact between natives and irresponsible officials of the government provided opportunities in practically every division of public work touching them, for shameful excesses of abuse and exploitation. Chiefs were humiliated and abused in the presence of their subjects—flogged, fined, subjected to torture—and the natives themselves fared even worse at the hands of soldiers. Chief Wewe of Middletown, for example, was ordered to bring twenty men to assist on the building of the barracks at Pudukeh. Although he did not refuse, he was beaten before his people, thrown into prison for five weeks, and fined £3110. Soldiers had come into his town indiscriminately catching men. He sent one of his subchiefs, Hedo Wesh, to Harper to "find out" about it, but the chief and his subchief spent five weeks in prison for wanting to "find out."

Soldiers came to Rocktown demanding boys for road work, and the town chief, Teba, tried to get the number demanded. The soldiers, however, began flogging natives recklessly and amusing themselves by plucking out the long hairs of the chief's mustache. They also intimidated the chief with threats to burn his town—and they did, in 1916.

Chief Probone was short £8 on his hut tax; the superintendent paid the £8 and demanded a refund of £20 for his £8. The tribesmen were just cutting their farms and had no money. The chief was then thrown into jail and in addition to the £20, he had to pay out £15. for his release. This same chief, returning from a meeting with the commissioners at Garraway, was met on the road by a clerk from the office of the native commissioner at Grand Cess. Asked why he was out of his section, he explained that he had come at the call of the commissioners. After receiving a lecture about making complaints to foreigners, he was threatened with jail and finally fined the full amount of cash he was carrying. Needless to remark, the clerk had no authority to impose a fine and would not be expected to report it. Similarly, Paramount Chief Jury of Picniccess was taxed £100 for the simple privilege of rebuilding his town that had been destroyed, and £147 for his paramount chief's commission which legally carries no official cost.

In 1924, the governor of Maryland county sent word to the paramount chief of the Barrobo section that he must bring all hut taxes to him in Harper. The district commissioner at Webbo demanded of the chief that he bring these same taxes to Webbo. Still another commissioner for the Kru coast demanded that they be brought to Garraway, so that he could take them hurriedly to Cape Palmas. Perplexed, the paramount chief called together his subchiefs and fifteen of them went to Harper to inquire of the governor just where the taxes should be delivered. When they had assembled, the governor pondered a while, and shouted: "All chiefs from Barrobo arise and stand on one foot." The chiefs obeyed. Then the governor said, "Before you bring your foot down, each one of you must pay me £5." The chiefs, in their grotesque and eventually painful posture begged for time. They pleaded that they had not brought that amount of cash with them. The governor asked: "How many chiefs are left behind?" They told him three. Then he asked who was to bring the money down. Abraham Kine was selected. The governor then permitted them to bring down their feet and go home for the £5, a task they were glad enough to do. The three chiefs who had not posed the question of taxes were fined £12, and the governor went in person to the section to collect the money.

The Governor came up to Barrabo to Paramount Chief Karpeh's town. He said he came to see the country plus collect the amount of £12 from three chiefs. The money was paid. When he got to Paramount Chief Karpeh's town each of the chiefs going to shake hands with him, he demanded £1 cash, one hamper rice containing fifty-two pints, one nanny goat for soup. After having shaken hands he went back to Harper. The tax for which the chieftans had gone down was paid. Came another year. He started for Barrabo from Harper again to collect taxes for the year. When he reached Chief Doe's town, Tarke (Rocktown) the kola (greeting) that he gave to him that evening was a billy goat. In the morning the chief of the town gave him a bullock for soup, two fanahs of rice and he demanded that the taxes be paid. At the time each hut was 4/6 throughout the section and when he is giving the money the chief of the town gave him a cow. Then he passed on the Gropake, where the barracks are now. The chief of that town did likewise and his tax was paid. He passed on to extreme Barrabo, Gedoke. The Chief of Gedoke did the same. Then he passed on to Gbigo another section and tribe. What he done there we don't know. He returned back to P.C. Karpeh's town. Karpeh did likewise and his taxes were paid. Then he went on down to Harper.

Having gone down then he sent back an order to the P.C. of Barrabo that he must send him 150 laborers to work on the Government road leading from Harper to Plebo. Then when the laborers were done working on the road he sent all to his farm at Philadelphia and one at Kronroke, cutting sticks, etc. While laborers there they had to carry their own food and if it gave out they had to send back for more.

One Paramount Chief recited a bit of petty chicanery involving a gun permit, an incident characteristic of the dull witted acquisitiveness by which the spirit of the natives has been broken.

Liberian people come and tell us to give guns, to stop fighting each other, but we were not fighting each other, nor the Liberians, but they took guns and we gave them and Leopards come in Bath place in dark, came and grab one man, carried him in bush. Never saw that man. We have no gun to shoot to make them run. Superintendent say, "All right, I will give you some guns to protect yourselves. Pay £80. I will give you ten guns." We pay but he gave one gun. We ask for license to keep soldiers from taking it. He say, "Take it." Soldiers came and saw gun and reported to Superintendent and he fined us £40. Took gun and Yancy still has gun. Superintendent doing all these things to us, hurt us, but one thing he always tell us make us sorry—"When I tell you something, you try to cheat, refuse. Have you wings to fly in the air so I can't catch you, or is there anybody above me who can say, No?" This thing make us very sorry.

The case of the harrassed natives was well put by Yenipo speaking for Paramount Chief Nyan of Seuhun:

We live here in the world and many Liberian people control us. They who rule us are like a trap around a rat's neck. They are pressing us whenever they can. They come look for our chop. Then they say "we want money." We, too, give them money. After that these Liberians tell their other friends: "Here's a place to get money. We have some slaves from whom we can get everything." Then they bring fake report and find and then whatsoever they ask they compel the people to pay and they can't help it and pay at once. They beat them, force them to get it. Men and women run out of town into the bush when Liberian come. Paramount Chief send one man to Superintendent and ask "What cause this thing to happen to us?" "Do what my people tell you," he says. From this we can get little encouragement from the Superintendent. What shall we do? We think better try to make farm and not stay in town to pay tax, so we join farm matter. But when we try to make farm, as soon as we begin to do farm work they call us back to do this and that for the Government. The (native) King say, "Well, you Governor, you know that we can get no where to get tax except we depend on farm work. If I do not do farm work, where I get money to pay tax and fine."

The public road work, which began as a sound venture directed toward the opening up of trade routes to the interior, quickly degenerated under the hands of incompetent and dishonest officials into exploitation of the worst sort. It is a fact that labor has been impressed in numbers of African colonies for public work, but it has been recognized that unless closely safeguarded by policies of just and considerate treatment of natives, the ends of all the effort will be defeated. It is thus set forth, as a principle adhered to in the more advanced African countries, that labor shall not be impressed except in a general emergency; that the work must be of a public character; that there shall be a stipulated period during which such work is wholly inadmissible; that the labor must be paid for in terms of the current rates; that recruiting shall be done through the native chiefs; that the laborers shall be properly fed and housed; and that all fines shall be strictly accounted for.

The justification of the use of native labor in Liberia was assumed by the president when he announced his road scheme to a conference of chiefs at Suehun. The president said the roads must be built; the chiefs had little alternative but agreement. It is quite possible that some of them favored roads, and even the use of their men in building them, but it is just as certain that many of them did not, and that they made their view plain. The government policy of making and breaking paramount chiefs was of great importance in influencing the decision of some of the chiefs, particularly those who had received commissions from the government. Being neither interested in nor dependent on the wishes of the tribe, they could agree to anything. The sly-eyed old Chief Dade of Kakata in explaining his own position reflected the whole situation: "If you help someone to become big and you give him order he will take it. Therefore, I can refuse order from the President."

In carrying out the road programs, some 6,000 men were kept daily on the roads for a year. There were no engineers or surveyors. The surveying "method" involved a native's following a foot path through the bush with a line and a horn; when he reached the end of his line he would blow his horn, and the laborers would slash and dig their way to him. The stupendous waste of labor from this extremely inadequate procedure was most evident in the Harper Gbolobo road in Maryland (a stretch of twenty-five miles) which required 250 men daily for nine months of the year for over nine years.

The natives worked without pay. With the exception of one or two instances of a "dash" to the chief and paid labor group of less than 100 in

Monrovia, the natives got nothing for their labor. They were, however, in this broad exposure, at the mercy of the overseers on the matter of fines for tardiness, absence, improper work, sickness, or indeed any special whim of the overseer. They were not fed by the government, but were required to bring their own food or have it sent from their villages. They were not housed; such shelter as they had, they made from leaves and thatch of the surrounding forest. they had no tools save their own country hoes and cutlasses. There have been exceptions, when a small supply of tools was put into service in one section, but the natives paid for these as they wore out.

Roads have been cut out through the hills to a depth of ten to twenty feet; short country hoes and sticks were the sole implements and the dirt was carried away on baskets woven from palm leaves. Ill-treatment accompanied these handicaps; the natives complained vigorously and with good right. They paid an annual tax on each hut and were required to provide for the government monthly rations of rice and palm oil and free porterage for all officials. By regulation, the major of the Frontier Force, for example, was entitled to fifty free carriers throughout the interior; a captain was allowed thirty-two, the same as a district commissioner. In practice, any Liberian official, or citizen for that matter, could command as many natives as he required for free porterage. The natives fed the very Frontier Force soldiers who made their lives miserable, built barracks and compounds without pay, worked on the private farms of officials—all under conditions of nonpayment and ill-treatment.

> The natives cried: "We are working the road, and no tools. We ourselves furnish the tools. If we were furnishing the tools and get money that would be all right. Then they flog us when we tote loads. One man named Jimmie came from Bellayala to our town and asked for labourers; we got all the labourers except one. The first man that was here is our headman; I am the second. I told them to wait for me to go and get the boy; when I got half way the boys of the Commissioner caught me and took me to Jimmie, threw me down and beat me. Another brother of ours, they beat him until the blood came out."

A man from the Dey Country, which is in Montserrado County, complained:

> One time the Paramount Chief called us and told us the Government say we must open road, and we agreed. If they make it a Government duty we have to agree. The chief called all of us and said we must come so he can tell us the number of months Government wanted, and that the Government told him to get 135 labourers and they agreed. We got only five people in my town to send and we were able to send two men each week. When they got on the road they divided the road into sections. Every week when the men are ready to go

on the road I have to give them one cutlass each, one axe and one hoe. If I don't give them these things they fined them some times 2/- each. When they are ready to go on the road we have to give them 3/- each for food. When they divided the road they give the boys time to finish the work, if you do not finish it in that time you have to pay £10. When we asked the Paramount Chief to stop that he said they have to do it to finish the road quick. Sometimes if some of my people are sick and cannot go so they are fined. If you don't go you are fined 12/6d each week. If you send your boy and he does not go they send and arrest the town chief and put him on the road. When they go and arrest you the chief gives orders that they must tie you and they so do before they carry you to the Paramount Chief. If you do not pay they won't untie you until you pay, and you have to pawn your child or wife. I was not there I left my old man in the town; they forced him to work. He could not and I had to pawn my son to redeem the old man. If you send your boy on the road you have to feed him; otherwise they tie and whip you and send you on the road. All that I spent on the road for fines and feeding my boys on the road amounts to £24. That is for feeding. What they fine me is £18.0.2. Right now my son is in pawn for the same money.

These protests had the ring of desperation for they were made in the shadow not only of officials but of the impending reprisals by government soldiers.

The palaver which I bring is the road business. We are poor people, we have not got anything. The Government is our father, and when they bring some job in the country and ask us to work the job, they ought to make us satisfied to do the work, to pay us and feed us. The Government does not do anything like that. If the Government sends us on the road they must pay us and feed us. We are poor people and we must feed the people who go on the road. We cannot help it, we have to do it. After we feed the boys on the road sometimes they say how they don't come about six o'clock; if they are late they fine them, the same money we get for our food they take it. If the boys say they won't give up their food money they catch them and whip them. If they are sick and if they don't go on the road two weeks they catch us for not sending boys on the road and fine us and we have to pawn our children to pay the fine. After that the Paramount Chief in the country we have to tote him and tote the District Commissioner also. If they receive money from us, the little money we make on our farms, they won't allow us to eat our own rice. When the District Commissioner send for labourers and you refuse they catch the boys in the town and fine them. One of my boys who is here now with me they fined him 10/- on Saturday; he was to pay on Monday but he came down with me. Coffee and Kernels have no price now and they bring all these fines on us. Where are we to get the money to pay when we are not selling coffee. All my children is pawn now, and I have not got anything to pay fines.

From the Bassa section these bitter grievances came with little variation. The Bassas, frail people physically, seemed tragically destined for punishment because of the vehemence of their complaints. Nevertheless they complain and take whatever follows. Nowhere else in the sections visited were seen such general disfigurements of men. They were crippled, or had eyes punched out, or were in other ways maimed. Said one of them:

> The road started, and the people go. Mr. Cooper call all Bassa people. What you want us for? "Call you all for the road." If you say so, we hear. Bassa people plenty. If we must accept the road, we will accept it. Cooper say he don't care for the road. He say "You all go hang your head and 'gree for the road. The road we going to work is prisoners road. We say to the people that come for us, say, all right, if you say so, we must 'gree." We look behind us and see we got no backbone and we get scare. We started the road and worked for one week. After one week we say, we been working one week now, let us eat. The Government said, "You all look for your chop, the Government goin' feed you bye and bye." Up to today, bye and bye no come yet. Y'all no hear what Cooper say? He say clean roads. Well, what we going to do? We got no power. We sent two boys for one week. Sent these two boys, and the rain beat them and the sun got up before you work the road. We say rain stop us. Mr. Morris send messengers, they say "Where we chicken, where we rice, where palm oil? Today lost one day—you have lost six shillings." We take the same boys again and send them back. The boys say they must go quick. They had to go way from Mr. Morris's to the President's farm early in the morning, because when sun is up before they get there they say we done lost a day. If the boys don't be there when sun come up messenger done come. If three messengers come—twelve shillings. That day you done lost £1.0.0. If you got no money they put rope round your waist. After they done put rope 'round your waist, they catch chicken. They say they take chicken for chop money. I come here and got plenty things to tell you, but I scared.

In stumbling English these lamentations continued from the Kakata section. A native tried to make the case clear.

> I am town chief. They punish us too much. On this road construction work ever since the road started we have paid for all the labourers ourselves and in addition have to supply Kakata station with rice. When the town chiefs are called here the Government gives them no food. The rice belongs to the Government, they say. All this work is done by us for nothing. We have to buy our own tools and buckets and pots for the men to take on the road. Each village has to be taxed 5/- to buy the things. The villages are not all in one place; some are far away. Many of the men have to travel a long way to work. If a man is late he is whipped, and often fined 50 cents for the day. We see nothing good here; all is bad. Most of my people have gone away now, because there is nothing to eat.

The incentives were punishments which took ingenious turns—"smoked in the kitchen" and "No. 1 basket," for example. In the first instance, a refractory native was put up on the roof of one of the windowless native huts and a fire built under him. The discomfort of slow suffocation inevitably changed the victim's attitude toward work. The "No. 1. basket" was a favorite punishment for the natives and was likewise sport for the soldiers who oversaw the gangs. A double woven container with curled edges, about two feet in diameter and fifteen inches deep, with a concave bottom, constituted the basket. Normally, when filled, it required four men to carry it. For the recalcitrant laborer the basket was filled with dirt and stones, placed on the man's head, and given a spin. Or a man might be ordered to walk or turn around with it upon his head. It could break the neck or otherwise injure the spine, and there were many fatalities. In the Webbo section a native who had taken the name of Davis, developed a small rubber farm as early as 1924. District Commissioner Scott heard about the man, sent for him, and placed him under arrest for "stealing men from the road to work his farm." With his fifteen-year-old son the man was tied, beaten, and eventually put on the road with the taunt: "You think you are a White man, with a rubber farm, eh." The two were put through the "No. 1 basket" ordeal. The boy never recovered. Of eight men given the "basket treatment" at the same time, three died.

A result of this whole harsh policy, whether blindly pursued or no, has been the destruction of native morale, a stripping of the country of its manpower, the driving of natives across the Liberian border into French and British territory, and the loss on the part of the natives of the will to produce, even for themselves. They refuse to develop a surplus on the belief that it will be taken away from them; they fail, in their listlessness now, to produce even enough for their own needs, and "hungry time" is a time of suffering. They have abandoned their art, their gay festivities. They have lost faith in the justice and honesty of their rulers.

Such a state of affairs should unquestionably be of greater concern to Liberian than to the foreign critics of its internal policy.

17

Up-Country

The rainy season is a notoriously unfavorable time for interior travel on the African West Coast. Realization of this prompted the resignation of Dr. Meek, of Norway, the first League of Nations appointee to the Commission of Inquiry. His successor, Dr. Cuthbert Christy, a British subject of some forty years' experience in Africa with medical and hunting expeditions, convinced the league secretariat that travel at this season was at least possible, and in some respects preferable. And so it was decided that the trip would be tried. In Liberia, where the trails at best are vague and the method of transportation is exclusively head loading, such expeditions seldom are attempted.

This author was for his part without experience in the tropics, as was his able assistant, John F. Matheus of West Virginia. Otherwise, the climatic complications of torrential rains, countless swollen and bridgeless streams, and washed-out trails, would have registered more significantly at the outset. Planning the safari with a seasoned traveler was thus of incalculable value in preparing against the strange contingencies of the wooded depth back of the coast towns.

Importance had been attached from the beginning to the state of affairs of the country back of the coast towns. Only by such direct observation and conversations with natives in the setting of their own villages would it be possible to appraise the testimony heard in the formal sessions in Monrovia.

It must be confessed, however, that there was curiosity about the interior less specifically related to the inquiry at hand—about the influence of European culture and ideas upon native life in successive stages back from the coast; what elements they were absorbing, and what these alien materials and ideas were doing to their own social institutions, their work, and their art, for example. The journey, once begun, however, was soon crowded with the imperative clamor of natives voicing their fervent desire to find a way of peace with the new demands for hut taxes, government rice, road labor, carriers, plantation labor, export labor, customs charges, and head money.

The first objective of the commission was Kakata, in Pwessi county, about sixty miles back of Monrovia. It is a central point and easily accessible to tribes over a wide area of the north. Because of its location, the government had used it for its last general conference with chiefs of the interior. A series of roads connecting with the Du division of the Firestone Plantation make possible transportation by lorry through Careyburg, the president's summer home, to the Du. From this point on there were better trails.

The village itself was small. Once it was more prosperous, but the natives here, as at other points along the high trail to Zorzar, on the French border, had abandoned their old towns and built new villages deeper in the bush. The hand of the government was manifest in the wide, seldom-used marketplace, a military station, and commodious compound, within which was an enormous building of mud and thatch which served as quarters for the president of the republic. It was a curious blend of native construction and European conveniences, with its wood floors, *baraza*, garage, and chauffeurs' quarters, its wide verandas and sweeping thatch roofs. The Kakata school for natives (Booker T. Washington Institute) under American educational supervision was located here and had adopted, in its own buildings, this synthetic architectural design. Here also resided, in temporary seclusion, one of the most inexplicable characters in Liberia—Mrs. Dorothy Moll.

No one seemed to know who she was, why she had remained in Liberia for six or more years, or how she supported herself. She was a White woman of better than middle age, and American Mississippian by birth and a German by marriage. When President King was in Germany several years ago, Mrs. Moll managed to get herself introduced to his party. Later she came to Liberia. She was reputed to have been in the German secret service during World War I, to have been captured by the British, and saved from execution by her usefulness in revealing German intelligence. During her first year in Liberia she represented herself as the correspondent of the Associated Press, an assertion later found to be untrue. However, her influence with the president was enormous. With consummate energy and skill she inspired numerous intrigues, provoked jealousies, and sold her influence in securing high positions of government. On one occasion she represented herself to the president's aide-de-camp as an agent of the German consul, Mr. Hermanns, and offered him a most desirable dwelling on condition that he arrange certain favors. In turn, she offered Hermanns, from the president, certain government favors—also for a consideration. At still another time, the position of financial advisor was offered to the American agent of the Barber Line for $1,000. Later Mrs. Moll went to Fernando Poo, defended the Liberian policy of exportation, indulged in a few contracts, and remained on that island several months before returning to Liberia. She offered Spanish medals to district commissioners, sold intimate administration documents to the "opposition," and reported "opposition" gossip to the president. Finally, she retired to the house of the district commissioner of Kakata, from which point she sent out an article to the *African World* stating that the natives were happy and contented and advising the Firestone management that she was collecting data for the International Labor office. Kakata was a lonely retreat for an adventuress.

From the elevation of the compound where the commission took lodging, one could command a view of wide ranges of country. In the village a mile away, natives could be clearly seen moving about briskly. Beyond, one could glimpse groups of natives straggling single file as they came down from the hills toward the village. Shortly after the commission was settled in its lodgings, faint sounds of drums could be heard. A small group of forty or fifty natives drew together and moved toward the compound. The nearer they came, the more distinct and purposeful was the drumming. Finally the group moved into the compound enclosure.

Chief Dado, in a white gown, black felt Fedora hat, and country sandals, ambled along, his wizened old face twisted into a cunning grin; beside him was his speaker, Kolongey, deep-voiced and strong-headed. Heralding their approach with frantic singing and drumming were two natives dressed in blue European smocks, their stiff billed caps decorated with red braid, their khaki trousers rolled to the knees. Their drums were small and shaped like hourglasses, rounded and sloped from both ends toward the center; each end was covered with skin connected with strings. These drums were placed under the arm, and by pressing on the strings with the elbows, one could command a wide range of inflections. The natives beat these instruments in hectic rhythm for a period, then stopped and with fixed expressions repeated stretches of song. This was interspersed with dance movements consisting of quick shuffles and stamps, climaxed with grotesque hip movements.

Chief Dado seemed constantly amused by the performance, but Kolongey looked hard and impassive. Through his interpreter he explained that he had merely come to say "Good morning" and that he would come back the following day. Promptly the drumming began again, with the accompaniment of singing, and the party turned to leave. The night was heavy with the beating of drums. Across the opening, in the bush, flares moved slowly into town. Messengers appeared at the compound with news that many chiefs and natives were coming into the village for the council.

At daylight on the second morning, bands were still moving into the village, conversing noisily. Eventually a line formed and began to move. The natives filled the long road to the compound; they crowded into the *baraza* until there was no more room; they packed the floors and windows. The old chief wanted to have his say in the presence of his people. It was his business, he said, only to supply the men asked for; he did not go on the road. He could tell only what he saw, and, of course, nothing happens in one's village. The men screamed their disapproval of his evasions, thus revealing that he had no effective authority over them. In anger he retorted that the president, not they, had appointed him.

When the town chiefs and other natives began to discuss "'that road palaver what make we sick," abusing Dado in most vicious terms, the old codger merely sat back, his wizened face twisted into the same cunning grin, apparently satisfied to let them make their protests, as long as he had made the proper speech to be reported to the president.

These chiefs were men of good bearing and fine voices. Instinctive orators, they possessed all the postures, gestures, and intonations that go with the art of oratory. They spoke in Pwessis, each detail of emphasis mimicked by the truth of their assertions. Waving their hands they shouted: "Kakla ka mene?" (All you here, hear what I say is true?) And they would follow the reply, "Yeaa!" in a volume sufficient to crack the room.

On that night Dr. Christy was stricken with a strange and sudden illness later attributed to the organism cystomyacist. During the recent conference, several chiefs had developed symptoms similar to Dr. Christy's and had died. Some of these natives were known to have been in opposition to the government road program, and their deaths were regarded as convenient coincidences to the parleys. Commission members had been exceedingly careful on the matter of food, and had used, so far, only European bottled water. It was recalled that Colonel Davis had asked the quartermaster whether regulations on water were still observed, and he had been advised that they were. Thus, there was no explanation for Dr. Christy's peculiar attack. His eventual recovery was supported and hastened by fortunate emergency aid, together with his own extraordinary physical ruggedness.

District Commissioner Carter moved down from his station to his Kakata quarters. A pudgy, unctuous individual with bloodshot eyes, he talked with a heavily confidential air and dwelt at length on his love for his mother and sisters. Then he remarked, "We are both young men and when I saw you were not an elderly person, my heart was glad. If you don't work, they say you are lazy; if you do work and make a little something, they say you are stealing. What am I going to do?" At least it could be said that there had been work going on in his behalf, for despite a commissioner's salary of less than $100 a month, it had required several months to transfer his personal cattle and accumulated property when he moved from District 2 to District 1 .

Natives continued to arrive in town, some from as far away as "a five-day walk." Eight hundred were heard before the commission left the section. The first plans contemplated a route from southern Liberia through the interior of districts 4 and 5 following roughly the ragged line of the French border, from Webbo to Sanoquellah. Events were already bristling in the south, and there were murmurs of the danger of a native uprising if some measures were not taken to curb the abuses of officials. The southern end of the republic seemed a logical beginning for the expedition, since it offered the greatest chances of reaching promptly, or of being reached by, native chiefs of the larger settlements. Moreover, there were extreme restrictions of time on the interior visits. Accordingly the visitors took a steamer down the coast and reached Cape Palmas early in May.

Harper is the principal town of the South, and is the section colonized by the Maryland society. There is an interesting stipulation in the agreement between the Maryland colony and the government, to the effect that alternate lots of forty by sixty should be set apart for the society's use. The claim had never been made and the provision remained unaltered. A result was virtually the common exercise of "squatters'" privileges. The streets were not named, there had never been a census, no births nor deaths were recorded, the population of 500 or more Liberians lived on the government or by acting as middlemen for natives in trading on cassava, palm nuts, and rice. The settlement was delightfully located, however, and the view from the promotory was one of the most beautiful in the country, with its descent of about 200 yards to the ragged, rock-buttressed edge of the sea.

The commission took off from Cape Palmas with full field equipment. Crossing the Hofman River, the party followed a course up the beach in the direction of the old village of Rocktown. The hammocks, having been built for the rains, were heavily and awkwardly framed and covered with canvas. Four stalwart natives supported them on their heads. The jolting and the first shock of riding on men's heads proved less comfortable than walking.

For several days the rains had abated their violence, but heavy clouds hung overhead, introducing dreary speculation into every plan. Then suddenly the rains burst anew with dismaying completeness. The sea roared as if in madness; waves rolled like gigantic glass cylinders. No longer were there rain drops but continuous sheets of water that blurred the line between the ocean and the beach, obscuring the long line of porters with our water-soaked luggage.

On the third day out, the trail abruptly left the beach and turned inland. An hour or so of colorful but rain-soaked vegetation, and the elevated country appeared, then the town of Garraway. There the party settled. The whole morning was spent in search of a camp site. Most of the land was either low and swampy, or full of bush. Eventually good quarters were found with a civilized Grebo native, George Mooney, whose father had been "King of Garraway." Mooney's two-storied house was an interesting mixture of "civilized" and native moods and convenience. The first floor was used in part by his children, who had attended the Sierra Leone school and the local mission school of the A.M.E. Church. On the second floor were four rather good sleeping rooms not used by the family. In the rear, however, was a large native house, built in the characteristic conical shape, with mud walls, hard-packed floors, and long sweeping thatch roofs reaching nearly to the ground. Here the elder Mooney and his wife lived, contented in merely owning a "civilized" person's quarters and observing their children live in it. At times Mooney would appear fully dressed in European clothing and apparently comfortable; at other times he would appear in simple native gown without shoes, and in this garb he seemed equally at ease. Mooney was one of the first products of the Garraway Christian Mission school first established years ago under the direction of a Canadian woman. The station at the time of our visit was under the care of a woman graduate of Clark University who came to Liberia in 1905 under the African Methodist Episcopal Church.

Chiefs assembled from Garraway, Poo River, Niewie, Pitty, and Sodokeh. They came garbed in a ludicrous mixture of native and European clothing, which fell pitifully short of both standards of dress. The proud mark of the chief, a stiff silk hat, was either so small that it rocked, cradle fashion upon his head, or so large that it covered his ears, and constantly had be pushed up from his eyes. Some wore frock coats, much too large, over their skirts and bare feet; one was clothed in a footman's greatcoat with large ornate buttons. They were a group with a doubly saddened aspect, for their land, their authority, their pride, their "boys" had been taken away, not alone by government order (against which they were then complaining), but the devasting influence of coastal exposure.

On this part of the coast, the natives were aware of the prestige of "White men," and the designation, as applied, seemed to be more a cultural than a racial or color distinction, for they referred to Blacks of European culture as "White men." A subtle distinction was made between foreigners who had broken away for periods from their settings to work along the coast beyond Liberia. A Frenchman was a Frenchman; Spaniards and Portuguese were, in one Grebo dialect, *Seakobo,* or White Black "White men" with a cultural meaning is *Nye-plu.* The Englishman alone had a special designation, *Dobopu.* The name for a Black man was *Nye-Yidikapobo.* They appeared also to be utterly without race self-consciousness. There was no identification of themselves with Liberians on the basis of similar color, features, and ancestral origin. Tribal distinctions, however, are acute and war-provoking. But for this, the story of Africa would, no doubt, have been vastly different.

The rains continued at Garraway with brief respites. It was hard to conceive a dry earth, but it was necessary even so to visit the Webbo country. The group decided to separate so that Dr. Christy could return and rest for a brief period at the Cape, preparatory to an inland visit to Webbo later. This author would continue to Webbo country, taking a route through the Tienpo, Barrabo, Nyanbo, and Webbo sections, and rejoining Dr. Christy at the French border.

Poo River divides the Garraway section of the Grebos from the Poo River Krus; between the two tribes there has been enmity of long standing. It was necessary to pass through this country to reach Webbo. There had been, so far, no intimation of this hostility or of the imminence of an outbreak. It had merely appeared strange that Poo River porters were reluctant to cross the river for luggage to be relayed to the next point. One could not fail to note the ominous quiet of the natives and their elaborate preparations for some unexpressed fear.

Finally, porters from the town of Garraway came up and took the luggage to the river, loaded it in the canoes, and began crossing. Again, the un-engaged escort of these carriers seemed unnecessarily heavy, and in excite-ment they had left for me a canoe of disconcertingly frail proportions for the rapid current of the river. I followed in it, however, and observed expec-tant crowds on both banks of the river. Scarcely had I landed than my attention was drawn to two angry patches of natives tugging violently at the heavy hammocks.

A Garraway man was saying, "We are going to tote hammock." And a Poo River man replied, "Ah, you play, how you tote hammock when we have it." The Garraway natives challenged, "We show you." To which a Poo River native replied, "Try it and we beat you." "You beat us? You play again."

The taunts flew. And suddenly men began to push against each other with heavy thuds, while others tugged at one of the hammocks until it fell apart. Heated arguments sprang up along the shore. More Garraway men had crossed the river higher up and run down to this landing point. The fights spread. Men watching from the Garraway side across the river shouted that war had flared. The "buglers" of Poo River sounded the cry of trouble on their flutes and dispatched messengers to their warriors and the men on the rice farms. The drums began their agitated thumping. Before it could dawn upon me that this was actually a tribal fight, I was hopelessly and helplessly in the midst of it. Argument and appeals to reason and propriety were ludicrously out of place because they could not have been heard even if they could have been understood. A show of weapons would not have cowed them as much as it would have inflamed them with a more desperate fear. They drew blood; three men lay unconscious, staring upward with blank open eyes; more boats from Garraway brought men stripped for battle; the river was black with men swimming to the scene of combat. With the sensation of one attempting to empty the ocean with a bucket, I separated fighting groups.

Curiously, they allowed themselves to be cuffed about. But as soon as one group was separated, another one would rush viciously into combat. The old chiefs of both sides were there in a new role; some of them had been only a short while before in sober conference. Either they were powerless to stop the fight or they were quietly urging it on.

Our messenger, provided by the governor of Maryland as an escort, was, incidentally, an irritation of the worst sort to the natives and added to the confusion. He was of mixed Grebo and Kru origin, disliked by both sides. As a government messenger, he had developed obnoxious traits and was viciously uncivil to his half brothers when supported by any kind of authority, but he was a coward when alone. Several times I dragged him from a pile of angry natives who were pommeling him savagely. They promised faithfully to kill him when he returned, and would gladly have done so then, had I not been present. Thomas, the sleepy-eyed headman, whose only service so far had been trailing what he thought was the end of the safari, reaffirmed his uselessness by running to the next town and hiding there.

For two hours this struggle continued with increasing seriousness; separating fighting groups, and trying to prevent fresh boat loads from landing proved useless. George Mooney came over from the other side, and sensing, despite his tribal connection, the ineptness of this demonstration, tried to calm them but with little effect. His son, whom I suspected of being partly responsible for the scrap, had said, "If the Garraway men go back, it will be a serious reflection upon our bravery." It was a most unfitting moment for this tribal patriotism.

Finally, individual Poo River men were persuaded to take loads, and one by one got them away from the water. The women, young and old, were unrestrained in their encouragement of the men to fight. They danced around, beat their hands against their knees, and brought weapons to their sons and husbands.

Matheus led the first group of porters out of the village, while Mooney, with threats, pushed Garraway men into boats and shoved them in the direction of home. They floated about in the middle of the stream uncertainly.

There was one young man, handsome, magnificently proportioned, with a sullen but calmly courageous face, who looked on intently. I motioned him to a load. He drew away politely but firmly. Another native explained, "He warrior" and took the load himself. Seeing this, I suggested that he get me men for the other loads. This he did rather diffidently, half watching the men on the beach, all the while, and apparently eager for the encounter to reach that stage of finality which required his own professional skill.

The full loads were eventually headed out of town toward Grand Cess. Half a mile from the village appeared a group of breathless natives with gleaming cutlasses and poison-tipped spears, ready for battle. In response to the drum and flute call of trouble, they had run several miles. They would rush up to their brothers serving as carriers and touch them; then all would halt. Having their weapons, they repeated some lengthy martial ritual. One man would begin a chorus that sounded like a cross between an exalted chant and a college yell. At the end they relaxed. The flute player sounded: "Palaver finish," and they turned with their weapons to clatter along beside the carriers until the next excited group was met.

The Fishtown people are Grebos; the Garraway people are bush Grebos. Between Fishtown and Garraway is a small group, the Nemiah people, who have been involved for many years in land disputes with Half-Garraway. The Poo River people are said to have no close ethnic relation to the Garraway people, but are Krus, who migrated to the spot many years ago and probably long before the Webbo people settled on the land above them. They are related to the Krus above Grand Cess, but they speak a dialect which, though Kru at base, employs many Grebo words. The natives have been kept stirred on their land disputes by irresponsible officials of the government who have reaped personal profits from both sides. The same Poo River people, in their fight with the Webbo people in 1924, were fined for their part of the trouble. The Webbo people were also fined. It was at this time that the governor of Maryland insisted on borrowing money for them to pay the fine, and in turn demanded the first 500 men for Fernando Poo.

We reached the Bid Town of Poo River with about 300 noisy warriors. Gradually they dispersed and the real object of the journey could be resumed. After a pause, we crossed the river to the beach town of the Webbos. Chief Jeh made the long journey down to extend a welcome to his section. We met Karpeh, the headman of the first 500 Webbos carried away, and saw the point, strange to passing ships, where the steamer called, and where the town, in desperation, went aboard as hostages until the arrival of the boys from up-country.

It was an impoverished and broken village of just 157 huts, under a crafty chief. The labor of the men was divided between fishing and coast work, and there were more abandoned or widowed women with children than there were normal households. Even apart from these nonproductive widows, some thirteen persons of the households were hopelessly incapacitated through long sustained illness or deformity.

We moved on to Grand Cess, out of the Wedabo area, but the plan was to reenter it further inland, nearer its capitol. The native village of Grand Cess was an old and closely packed community. At the time, the streets were lined with native women who sat stripping the raffia palm fibers into *piassava*. They could get two shillings and sixpence for each fifty-six pounds at the trading store, and these accumulated shillings paid the taxes. It was Jack Jarraca's town. Deep in the village he had quartered himself in the first tin house in Grand Cess, built long before there had sprung up a civilized section. Jarraca was "ill with boils" and in his enforced absence from the councils, the town was actively debating means of relieving him of his chieftancy. However he was a wily fellow and let his medicine man guard his rights. When I talked to him, he was philosophical about native development in its new mold and put it most aptly:

> You see me? I be old. My arms not now strong. I have ears [he points]; I no hear good. I have eyes; I no see good. But my picin [children] that I born and raise, they have ears; they hear better. They have eyes; they see better. Look at Nebo [a civilized native]. You think when they know they don't tell we better thing to do. Look at this house. First tin house in Grand Cess. Here in 1888. Broken down and no good. Old. But look at that house on the hill with the tin flag pole. Ah! That better house. That Nebo's. That what I say.

While awaiting the arrival of chiefs at Grand Cess, it was possible to make some observations of the routine of life in this village set close against the sea. In this closely packed village of 727 households, the men directly responsible for the support of 110 of these households were away on the coast at work. Less than fifty families lived exclusively by fishing, although this was formerly a great fishing town. The number of households dependent on the community, as a result of the death or desertion of the men, was, it would seem, abnormally large—there were 116, or 16 percent. In seventeen of these cases several widows of the same man had been left in the same hut. The old people were supported by relatives or by the chief, and there were forty-three such nonproductive households. Less than a dozen lived by farming alone, and twenty-seven traded in *piassava*. According to the lore of the town, a curse was laid on farming many years ago, and since then the soil had refused to yield food:

> Our ground no bear good chop. Plant cassava, another year it get it some good cassava, before another time it be no get nothing. Our own country

people bring this trouble for we; spoil this country; spoil dem before me my mother it born me. Long time all dem old people been make some medicine and dem put him for ground inside bottom; then take one dem white man's plates and put him for inside the medicine for ground him bottom, before them talk, say, "The day when the white man's plate go grow for make some chop before this our ground go make some good chop for them when white man plant dem." [Or, in so many words, may this ground bear food when this white man's plate sprouts.]

Talk, say, "We no want chop for we country and we no get any money for buy some clothes for our women. We want our country to get white man thing. We want steamer for come to we country." It be so our country no get no chop from ground, but the white man done come now and bring him steamer; so it be now!

Although the community was reasonably prosperous, only a small proportion of the men could afford to buy more than one wife. Actually, only eighty-eight of the 578 men had more than one wife, and together they owned 157 women. The headman for coast laborers boasted the largest number of wives—he had seven.

After two days of waiting we saw that the chiefs began to arrive from the Sinoe country—Chief Jury of Picnicess, solemn-faced and gruff-voiced. Chief Nyan of Topo, wiry, old, and unprepossessing in the woman's raincoat of which he seemed so proud. He gave the impression of dullness until he began to speak, and then his face took on a fine fire and character. There came also Chief Yarn of Suehn; Speaker Bellor, representing Chief Jegbe of Barrabo and the venerable Chief Broh of Fernando Poo, whose stubborn rightfulness and unconquerable spirit had halted a bold crime against the natives of the section. These were the chiefs who had been assembled by the vice-president in his second wholesale demand for Fernando Poo men.

These chiefs had the bearing of leaders born to their role, and they moved with an unaffected dignity stripped of pomp. Their code of etiquette was full of subtle graces; meticulously, as day began, they came to say, "Good morning," and again at dusk to say, "Good night." Customs varied, but in this section the chiefs as a rule spoke through their speakers, or "prime ministers." At any point of narration, any one of them could interrupt to add or correct a detail. No address was begun without the express, "Chief say he thank you. He thank you very much." They talked gravely and with desperate defiance to warnings against voicing their complaints:

We are really born in this country. Our forefathers leave us here. Before some years gone by you people in America send some people called Liberians to control this place. When they come they met us with guns. They had no good houses, so we draw them to ourselves as our people. Then their children and our children play together as one people. Still we are in our country. Before you who sent them over here, you have them guns to fight against the natives. And they come to us and say, "Well, we have come to disarm you." But they got guns themselves. At that time when they come to disarm us, we pay no pool tax, no head money, no duty. So Europeans, when they brought cargo would give tobacco to natives for other things because we have our own land before they came. When they disarm us they draw from us whatever we got from the European. We have no tobacco, because the European traders say now we pay duty to the Liberian government and cannot pay the natives. After the disarming they came to us to pay the hut taxes. At time when Governor Brewer disarmed us; no one was giving trouble in the colony. Now all natives become slaves; because of this treatment. We wish to make statement, and if we got to die, all right.

The impression could not be escaped that natives in these villages near the coast, exposed to the contrast in the conditions of natives farther down the Gold Coast, had their restlessness magnified. A native man who had just returned to the town from the Gold Coast, after a three-year absence, was standing, hands akimbo, observing a half erected concrete building at the edge of the native village. His face was twisted into a heavy grimace of disgust: "I'm a tradesman. I wear tan and white shoes and eat at a hotel in Lagos. They told me they were building a great tower here and collected £6.0.0. I come back and see this thing. They call this thing the tower. If this wasn't my native land where my wife and child stay, I never come back. Look at the streets. They don't got none. No sewer. Nothing." This was, of course, expecting too much of Grand Cess, but it was the price of dominion.

After Grand Cess, our route led sharply inland, It seemed that it had been impossible to get anywhere without risking our luggage and more in getting across a river. The Grand Cess River was well worth remembering. It was bordered by a swamp impenetrable with mangroves and other tough and tangled vegetation. Over this, however, had been built a long and narrow bridge of poles, held together with rattan. The expanding waters had swept the bridge into a frail and uncertain string of poles. There was an hour of teetering along these poles over the swamps before the bridgeless river could be reached. Men with head loads performed most delicate feats of balancing, and all eventually crossed safely. One boy with a big box slipped, and executed one of the most perfect feats of balancing I have ever seen. He did not get excited or change the position of his head, but kept quick-stepping until he had found a secure footing. Such an exhibition of skill prompts the observation in contradiction of the reports of native laziness, that, so far as my experience went, there was no male, between fifteen and fifty, who could not pick up the regulation fifty-pound load and trot along with it on his head for three or four hours. My belief is that no constitutionally lazy person could ever acquire such resistance against fatigue.

The country was low bush, for the most part; the soil was sandy and spotted with tough aand useless vegetation. As we moved on, it became hilly, and in the depressions, small streams rushed over long grass. The men drank from all these streams, including those whose water was coffee-colored.

The approach to a village was always the same—a spraddle of rusty brown mounds like uniform stacks, and towering above, high into the air, a lonely cottonwood tree, and nearby, a patch of giant palm trees. Paths that had been faint, grew deeper and whiter as one approached. At the break of the spraddle a few of the huts crowded the range of view, mud smeared, chipped, and dirty; the thatched roofs were black from the escaping smoke of their ovens. Open doors revealed dark interiors with dull fires; women sat flat on the hard beaten dirt floors. Round porcelain or tin pans intended for decoration lined the rear wall of the houses. This was another gracious gesture; the larger the number of pans, the more prepared the householders were to welcome strangers.

Out of these huts poured curious children and adults who stood off for one moment, and the next were a part of the crowd dogging our steps. The old men were unfailingly polite in their manner, even though apparently bored with life in general. They waited patiently until all the luggage had been deposited, then they brought chairs for the visitors and for themselves, and solemnly approached to shake hands.

Chief Jeh, the most gracious of our hosts, dispensed with his internuncio and personally supervised plans for our comfort. He presented a goat as a "dash," helped locate a clearing for our camp, and actively managed the details of our sessions with his subchiefs.

The first night in Jeh's town, however, was disturbed. Tired and utterly worn down by an unusually long day of marching through difficult country, we slept early, only to be awakened suddenly by the excited shouts of men from the inside of their huts. It was most unusual, but in Jeh's town, I felt so completely secure that as soon as the shouting had ceased, I fell asleep again without investigating its cause. Sometime later there was a noisy and precipitous stampede through the ropes of my tent, which collapsed on one side, breaking my mosquito netting and frame. Retreating steps could be heard recklessly snapping through the bush. Still the village remained dark and heavily silent; there were no more shouts. I got my flashlight and went out to repair the damage to my tent. An inadvertent angle of the flashlight revealed a native moving stealthily between huts. I waited and he soon appeared with the message that Chief Jeh thought it best to abandon the tent and come into a more secure building. There were leopards in the town. Several women had been killed on their rice farms, a man had been attacked while bathing, a bullock had been dragged off. We decided to barricade and remain in the tent. Beyond the loss of a goat, nothing happened. The natives have been without guns since the general disarming in 1916, and they relied on special choral incantations to drive the leopards away.

Leopards visited the town on the following night and sent the cattle rushing madly off again. Only the occasional faint crunching of rough earth between the huts against the heavy silence of the night, however, marked the second visit.

The innate politeness of natives was here displayed at its best. Their ceremonies of welcome and their gestures of hospitality were full of charm and meaning. There were few young women it seemed, only girls and old women, and the old women were well used to toil. They wore only skirts; their flat, pendulous breasts were exposed. All the old men smoked the stemless clay pipes, familiar in the active trade with Europe. A special diversion of the men was snuff. Tobacco leaves were strung on fibre stems and charred over a fire, then ground in a small mortar and mixed with firewood ashes. This mixture, which they carried about in decorated shells, was sniffed with careless grace.

It seemed that there was an unusually large number of women with shaved heads. It developed that it was an expression of mourning, and indeed it could be observed that there were but few young men in evidence anywhere. A large proportion of the 757 huts within this village of Soloken, once so thickly populated, was vacant and crumbling from decay and inattention. In its better days, the town held no less than 2,500 persons. The present poulation by actual count was 651. For every 100 females there were but seventy males. Of these remaining households, I counted ninety-one from which men had been taken away by force, six years before, and had either died at Fernando Poo or for some other reason failed to return. This ragged remnant of a once large and prosperous tribe could well explain the trembling sadness in Jeh's voice as he talked about his people. Here and there, a cassava patch grew over a square mound of earth which had once supported a hut; there were many of these. Beneath the cotton-wood trees at the end of the village was the now abandoned site of a group of huts. There were no huts there when I saw it, nor had any been there for six years, but Jeh had been required to pay £6.0.0 a year in hut taxes for the villages that once stood there.

An hour's walk from Soloken is the town site of Kordor, hard hit by the raids. Forty-one huts had been inhabited. When the men were taken away, the families could not maintain themselves alone and they deserted the village. The rotting thatch and crumbling mud walls of the dwellings, the rampant vegetation, the toadstools, decaying bread-fruit everywhere, the reptiles scampering through the shells of the huts, all gave it the aspect of a city of the dead.

After all, the loss of a town, or even of a hut, entailed considerable labor and money, as money value went in a shilling-a-day economy. Communal labor built a hut, but the owner had to feed and entertain the labor and purchase the materials.

At Soloken there gathered the subchiefs: Zibo of Jalatuen, Martin of Gbanken, Key of Soloken, and Toklah of Julaken, who had been held in the Fernando Poo raids; returned "boys" from Libreville under the queer-eyed headman Biba; in fact, all the chief characters in the recent drama of the Webbos.

Hobbling through the crowd of elders and natives who packed the central area of the village was one figure that commanded attention above all the others. It was that of a gaunt old man, with absurdly jutting cheek-bones, deep hollows in his cheeks, and a chalked face resembling a ghastly caricature of death. He wore a beaver hat, frock coat, and loin cloth; from his silk hat there hung down, in a direct line over his nose, a stiff braid of hair. He was the old man who "owned the country." Of the members of the councils of the tribe over which he presided, only a few were permitted to enter his dwelling, and these might not turn their back on him when they left.

I had carried along a small field machine which recorded speech and music, temporarily, on wax discs. It had been intended first as a mechanical check on interpreters. The method of taking testimony and the prevailing custom of group narration, made this only casually necessary for that purpose. And so it was employed to register some of the quite extraordinary music of the section.

A few records had been made, and the old man with pardonable pride had sent to the rice farm for his daughter, Jua Jollica, who, he assured us, was a pleasing singer. She came, this Jua, strapping and strong, perfectly modeled, and wonderfully erect. As she crossed the compound, balancing a large earthen jug of water on her head, her easy, flowing grace made a picture with which one would identify as Africa, always.

However, for the recording Jua had carefully dressed, made herself late for effect, and finally approached through a long line of admirers, bathed and oiled, waving a cow's tail, and attired in an ancient pink, European chemise! She sang, a deep-throated baritone, and I recorded it in the dialect for the beauty of the music alone. I later learned that we had stumbled upon a quite fresh and pertinent legend. Loosely rendered it was "The Sad Story of the Webbo Women":

We were here when trouble came to our people
For this trouble Jeh was imprisoned and fined.
For this reason Yancy came to our country
He caught our husbands and our brothers,
Sailed them to Nana Poo
And there they die!
And there they die!

Tell us
Webbo women have no husbands
Yancy, why?
Webbo women have no lovers
Yancy, why?
Webbo women have no brothers
Yancy, why?
Mothers, fathers, sons have died,
Waiting for their return,
Yancy, why?

Jalabeh, Weze, Nego, Myerweah,
Where are you now?
It is better that you had remained here to die in war,
Where dying would be glorious
Where we could see your body,
Than to be lost and quiet in that far land of sickness and death.

From the town of Zokoke alone, 125 men had been taken and ninety-five of these had died before they could return.

The music in itself would bear elaborate study. It has a wealth of variety and markedly distinctive peculiarities. There was very little to suggest, to the layman, any dominant relationship to the characteristic music of the American Blacks, unless it be antiphony and the highly developed rhythm. Most of the songs were accompanied with percussion instruments. To an ear more accustomed to European music, the unvaried phrase repetition characteristic of so many of the songs became monotonous. But there were examples in which a countermelody was sung by one voice as ground motive to the principal melody of the rest of the chorus. Such was Jua's song.

The music seemed definitely to have a ceremonial value, and since ceremony was so definitely a part of life, it was a rare feature to hear the music in chorus, except by chance. There was, however, a type of minstrel song designed to eulogize the chiefs. Several of these songs were heard and they thrilled the audiences as much with their extravagant praises as with their musical significance. The singers faced the chiefs, who, at intervals, responded. The chief of a town in the Barrabo section was unfortunate in his choice of a singer. Her voice was not agreeable and her poetry evidently quite bad. The first response of the chief, although diffident and strained, was polite. As the singer grew worse, he made a response which threw the audience into a boisterous laughter. Having referred to her as the least mentionable part of a monkey, he advised her to stop singing.

We left Soloken for Kaaken in the Tienpo section. The rains, the never-ceasing rains, beat down relentlessly. The first day out there were some seventeen bridgeless streams to be crossed and two of these were deep rushing currents. Then we faced "high bush" and long hours of trailing beneath a dismal canopy of tangled rain-soaked forest, the black depths of which thundered now and then with the noise of falling trees. The rains had given new life to the vegetation, choking and obscuring the trails, making it necessary at times to send men ahead to cut a path. They swung their cutlasses with skill and with what seemed a great fondness for the feel and sound of snapping branches. The driver ants were on the march, and their line could be traced in the deep furrows across the trail. The beginning and end of this line have always escaped discovery, but, by some mysterious signal, they spread their millions for attack and give trouble to any animal incapable of keeping free from them.

The approach to a village in this section was marked by long lanes of graves, on the mounds of which were deposited clothing, vessels, and personal trinkets of the departed. Our hammock men, content to stride along burdenless through the thick forest, now requested that the hammock be mounted as maintenance of status for the burden bearer as well as the burden. The "exalted" of the earth do not walk, and hammock men too puny for their tasks were laughed at by the women. They began the "song of the hammock" with gleeful shouting.

The town chief of Kaaken was young and quite rigid in the matter of ceremonies. He sat in a line with the old men and the paramount chief until the whole load had been brought in. Then he came over, gravely shook hands, and went back. After a pause, the group moved over and brought their chairs to watch the setting up of the tent. The camp site in Kaaken was in the center of the town, a cleared, beaten-down space circled by the brown, dirty huts of the Tienpos. To the left was the inevitable drum house with its sharp-angled thatch roofs, jutting high, much higher than the rest. The hollowed logs which were the drums could be heard for miles—mellow, deep throbs of sound, as much a part of life as planting and storing the rice crops. Who was it that beat these could never be learned. But he was a master, drawing from these sound logs the very cadences of their curious speech. News of our visit was communicated and chiefs and natives from over a considerable area were summoned for a particular time.

The hearings were as stiff and as formal as all the rest of the ceremonies. Because of the rains, one session was held inside a large native house, which was more roomy than it appeared. The ceiling poles and matting had the deep brown and black color of polished mahogany. The floor, which was hard and smooth like cement, had been made with a special red clay secured from the road outside of town. Its cool, cementlike effect was produced by mixing it with charcoal and cow manure and beating it down with the hands.

The large number of children with open sores on their faces and bodies was conspicuous. All played together. Several of these children's faces were a mass of sores, but the children seemed to suffer no great discomfort. A favorite game was "soldiers catch men and beat them." Another game consisted of one chasing another with a rag until he succeeded in touching him with it. Another was hopping around a pole on one leg. Another, a sort of hockey, was played with a small rubber ball which was kicked with great dexterity. Still another was a tug of war over a stick.

Morning in a village was full of intimate touches of life. The men sheathed themselves completely in their heavily patterned *lappas*, and, unwashed and yawning, moved to the bushy edge of town to pass their morning water. They conversed in drowsy cadences in the shelter of the banana leaves. The women went off to another corner of the village. A boy with a wooden tray picked up the night's droppings of the cows with his hands, patting it in the tray and slinging off the sticky remnants from his hands. This manure was an essential ingredient for their cement-finished walls and floors. Little children were led out of the huts by their mothers and postured face to the well. The querulous cows began sniffing about, prying into every cranny. From the blackened thatch of the huts smoke began to rise. There was brief sweeping with a short bristling palm brush or with a spray of *piassava*. Girls with water jugs balanced on their heads appeared, depositing their burdens casually. The chill damp began to lift, the sun rushed out with an almost sudden spray, and another day was on.

Throughout the day there were the loud shrill voices of children, the cry of babies scarcely to be distinguished from the noise of hungry or harassed goats; the laughter of men and the droning conversation of women, through the thin walls of the huts; the sharp cackling of the crows high up in the cottonwood trees, the shrill chirp of crickets, the pounding of rice straws, the sifting of the grain, and far in the forest, the mournful cry of birds.

A lively beating of drums announced our approach to the Barrabo section. The paramount chief, Doe, had come from his capital at Tarea to the first town to meet us. A paralytic, he was brought out on a chair. Just about three years before, he had been suspected by his people of agreeing to the building of soldiers' barracks in the section, thus imposing upon them the enormous labor of clearing the forest and erecting these barracks. In addition, he was accused of maintaining the soldiers as long as the barracks remained. The tribe secretly administered a poison intended to kill him. Almost immediately they were convinced that his consent had been forced and their counteracting medicine spared his life, but paralyzed him. Their great retribution could be seen in the unbroken tenderness of their solicitude for him.

They had suffered deeply in this section. The soldiers took their women by force, and anything else they desired. With the men away on the roads and the women at the barracks, no one had planted farms this year, and as a result, there was no food. Native stewards for the commission could buy neither rice nor cassava.

At the meeting with the chiefs, we sat with the paramount chief, his speaker and interpreter, in the midst of the wide circle of men squatting on low stools. These old men represented, they said, the fifth generation of the Barrabo people in this place. The interpreter shouted, "Bateo!" (silence). After much exclamation he would give a heated sentence and repeat, "Bateo." To the "Bateo," the group responded with a short, sharp hum, or grunt, in remarkable unison, the intensity indicating the extent of agreement. As the narration proceeded, the grunts of assent were like the heavy throbbing of the earth. At the end, he exclaimed, "Batai," and everyone responded, "Batai," breaking the tension with laughing and chatting.

After our first meeting, we retired to our tent just outside the town gate. Suddenly there was a loud wailing in the village, which increased as it continued. A man had just died. A woman, the sister of this dead man's wife, ran out of the hut and threw herself upon her face with a terrible force. The wailing continued through the night. Runners were sent to inform the distant relatives and when they arrived the following morning, sweating up the hill to the town, they too were wailing loudly, very much in the fashion of old southern Black preachers. Someone was suspected of being responsible for the man's death, and people were saying: "You, now what you tried to do is done. You must be satisfied."

This was of some concern to us because our arrival corresponded so closely with the death of the man that we could well have been the subject of these broad hints. It was said that he was cleaning around the house, apparently in health, when our passenger had passed through the town three days before. It was explained by the speaker later that the man had been sick before but had more recently been beaten by soldiers looking for road workers.

Everywhere there was a shortage of food. I threw away a sandwich covered with ants. Three men ran after it. They said, "Ah, it good. I'm goin to keep it. It hungry time." And they consumed it, ants and all. At one sitting with the chiefs, the women stood around the rim of the crowd of men;

afterward they said that they wanted to be heard. Their speaker was a woman of about thirty-five, with a child on her back in the characteristic Kinja of the section—a woven seat with a matting looped above, to protect the child from rain and sun. She said in a ringing, clear voice:

> We stand here and listen to the men to see if they tell all. If they leave out anything, we tell it. They have told almost everything, but one thing we want to say. They took us women to the barracks against our will. Yes. They took us in groups of 200 and we were there for nine months. The soldiers used us as their wives, we who had husbands and children. They had guns and we could not protect ourselves and our husbands could not protect us. Now it is a country custom that when a woman conceives, she must prove her child [its paternity]. We have not been able to prove these children of the soldiers, and this has made much trouble for us at home, although we could not help ourselves, and the men who were there could not help us. It has been necessary for us to kill the children [before they were born]. We pray to have us stopped from having to go to the barracks.

There we had our greatest carrier trouble. All the young men of the town and sections nearby who were not out of the country were on the motor road. They brought up women for carriers. I demurred, but after losing a day, decided that if we were to get away at all, it would be necessary to allow the stronger women to take the lighter loads. There were fifteen women and fourteen men for the loads and sixteen hammock men. The men moved through the luggage, picking heavy loads for the women, saying that they were used to them, and the women agreed. For themselves, the men selected smaller burdens and pushed a pole through the ropes so that two of them could carry a load. Again to my surprise, the men were unabashed when I protested this division. Similarly, the women were not disturbed by a sense of unfairness.

Paramount Chief Doe, Speaker Weah, and the interpreter, Solomon Kine, followed us to Gropaka, the town near the Barrabo barracks. When we reached this town, the drums beat again, the men danced, the hammock men ran, and, shouting gaily, carried us around the town several times. A visit was made to the barracks, where we were met at the gate and admitted immediately. Captain Whisnant greeted us. An American by birth, he had come as a child to Liberia with his parents. He had just heard of our arrival and two officers were preparing to come down to extend an invitation to visit for a period at the barracks.

The place was well built and well policed. There were bungalows of excellent construction, and of a more fitting style of archicture than that of most buildings in the civilized towns. Captain Brewer, with his pleasing face and manner, had the appearance of any young collegian. I found it difficult to reconcile the charges against the Frontier Force with these agreeable faces. As Captain Whisnant escorted us out of the building to the veranda, he saw for the first time the chief and his party. His manner was immediately transformed into one of unpleasant patronage. His was the precise manner and intonation of the pre–Civil War southern White gentleman as he met his "darkies." I was amazed to see this pattern so faithfully and completely reproduced. Truly has it been said that race prejudice is least of all racial.

The honesty of these natives bears mention. I discovered back in Niwaken that I had not enough cash in shilling pieces for my needs. The chief provided a messenger whose name I never knew and whom I had seen once, only briefly. He carried my check for £40 to the nearest trading station (about five days' journey) and brought back the money intact to a village through which I planned to pass, and there he patiently waited until I arrived. Moreover, during the entire journey, not a single article was lost, although our tent was unguarded much of the time.

A new ceremony of welcome was encountered in the Nyanbo section. Natives brought kola nuts, palm nuts, salt, fresh water, two fowls, and a pan of rice. This gesture said: "We offer you what we eat; it is our hospitality." The stranger was expected to drink the water and eat the half of the kola nut handed by the host. The white salt was the symbol of friendship. On the following day, when the chiefs came to say, "Good morning," they presented a young bullock. We had to learn many things. When the first bullock had been presented, I had felt that it was an expression which they could not well afford, and returning it, asked for a fowl or eggs, instead. The gesture had offended. I learned also some of the subtleties of the ceremonies of welcome. Any stranger is given fresh water and allowed to rest before his business is asked. If it is wished that he move on soon, the natives will present cooked food; if they desire the guest to remain longer, they offer food to be cooked. On our trip, eight bullocks were presented.

An animal was butchered and after our selection of "meat for soup," it was offered to the town for a feast, which lasted long into the day. Some fifty or more families received the small portion of which they were traditionally entitled. One family, at all such divisions, got the skin, another the heart, another the entrails, and so on to the last scrap.

Paramount Chief Casar of Nyanbo, after a brief, polite recognition of our visit and thanks for stopping said, "You hear them say that they are afraid; that if we talk our town will be destroyed. It is true. This is likely. It is true that we are a small people and helpless before them, their soldiers and their guns." To which his followers responded, "*Ghanti.*" With an unexpected burst of voice, he continued, "Then let it be history for our children that the towns of the Nyanbo people were destroyed because they made known their trouble." And his followers screamed, "*Ghanti.*"

On the last stage of the journey to Webbo, our first stop was Wodoweka—a small town of the Nyanbos, whose chief was Chilebel. Drums were beaten as in the towns before and the women crowded around:

> *Our husbands are carried away—maybe dead*
> *We cannot hear*
> *We are all hungry*
> *We have but their hands to help us*
> *Nor any word, nor any money.*

Leaving Wodoweka we journeyed through rain, swampy land, steep hills, and high bush, toward Webbo. At Kronrokeh Dr. Christy rejoined the party. During the stop at Kronrokeh, Paramount Chief Choami gave an elaborate testimony which seemed to relieve him enormously.

We moved on to the rushing Cavalla River where a hollowed log canoe, large enough for twenty men and baggage, carried us down the stream to Gyidetarbo, a point near the southern division of the Firestone Plantation. The result of the Gyidetarbo visit was meeting more than 100 chiefs and subchiefs of eleven interior sections and hearing about 1,800 natives in their councils.

The merit of these cases was inescapable. But it was also clear that the Liberian situation would not be entirely ended if the interior natives had had no valid causes for complaint. This was brought home in the instance of one Grebo who was following what reason dictated as a straight course in the transition from primitive to civilized life. As a youth he had worked his way on a steamer to Germany as a purser's clerk; on his savings he had taken passage in steerage to Baltimore. Eventually he had found his way to Tuskegee Institute, where he remained four years. After his school years he had gone to Beloit, Wisconsin, and from there to Detroit, Michigan, where he worked in the Ford automobile plant. Finally under missionary auspices, he had returned to Liberia, bringing a sawmill with a capacity of 10,000 feet a day. In time the mill failed. The enterprising young Grebo had gone to work for Firestone at the Du Plantation, with Ohe Plenyano Welo, another returned native who had studied at Harvard and at the Union Theological Seminary. Because of his Grebo connection, Welo had been transferred to Cape Palmas. Difficulties had developed with the management and he had finally found himself out. Of native descent, he had taken advantage of a provision of the Firestone agreement to the effect that a native could claim a land reserve. He had thus secured 100 acres in Gyidetarbo adjoining the Firestone development. He now grew coffee, rice, cassava, cucumbers, okra, and onions, and made a fair living. But he was neither Liberian, native, nor American, nor was he able to exercise the prerogatives of a capitalist. He was simply "out." It was the plight of the self-reliant educated native who does not seek adjustment of his status in government employment.

When we finally reached Cape Palmas to take a steamer back to Monrovia we found ourselves marooned. Steamers were not calling at Monrovia; a yellow fever quarantine had been ordered. To reenter the city, we went to Junk and from this point inland by the Junk River to the Du, thence to Monrovia by land.

Our reception on the return was the most curious that we had experienced. There was a surprise of the most elaborate sort. The president and the secretary of state explained that there had been authentic rumors that all of us had been drowned, while crossing the bar at Sinoe, some days back. It was a relief to be able to demonstrate that the report had been "grossly exaggerated," but there was little comfort to be taken from the reflection that, despite the acceptance of the rumor as reliable, nothing had been done about it.

18

Bitter Canaan

It has been 127 years since the *Elizabeth* turned its prow eastward from America to begin a dreary exodus. For those dark thousands who sought a haven from oppression and the fullness of a promised land, it has been a bitter Canaan. As a vent for the Black population of America in a political emergency, it has proved completely abortive. As an experiment in independent statehood, it has been a consistent defeat. For, as a sovereign state, it has lacked capital, leaders, and that unchallengeable power which alone supports dominion. It has lived against a world of terrors—the terror of the superior strength of acquisitive nations, of the superior vitality of its aboriginal population, of the hovering shadow of tropic death, of the ironic fate of starvation in a land of plenty.

The slow inexorable wasting of the years has evolved a new ethic, a desperate rule of life, which has bluntly made those suffer who could not defend themselves and which has made wrong right when it could serve the vital ends of survival.

Successive generations have developed corrupt leaders, the machinery of government has been clogged with incompetence and vice; education has been neglected. They have lost the capacity for work, resisted reforms, and, in their extremity, turned the native population into virtual slaves.

These conditions have been everywhere evident. Yet it has been impossible to pass it by as the hopeless end of a high venture or to escape the haunting memory of its baffling problems. There is a question whether the Liberian element, in the absence of new immigration can, or should even hope to, resist eventual absorption into the aboriginal population. By the only light now, the soundest procedure seems to be to aid in the development of intelligent leaders from the natives, who will be capable of sharing responsibility for the conduct of government. The present situation in which any Liberian, however incompetent or vicious, can command precedence over a native of superior intelligence, places the premium on the wrong end and encourages that mental and physical slothfulness which distinguishes the mass of the Liberian population, young and old. It would be unwise to withdraw all resistance to the pressure of the aboriginal population, if that culture which the Liberians profess is to be reinforced. Western culture has already invaded Africa, and is a requisite of security in all new world relations. One of the most disastrous of Liberian policies has been that of encircling its feeble nucleus of culture so completely that it has resisted all reinforcement from without.

A new departure would involve prompt and radical revision of native policy, actual reorganization of the political division of the country, opening of its interior to trade and civilization, attention to sanitation, and the introduction of a fundamental educational policy for both Liberians and natives. Even so unsentimental a statesman as Bismarck has declared that "the nation that has the schools has the future," and Japan has demonstrated how effective education can be even in the reconstruction of a culture within an ordinary lifetime.

The responsible officials of this republic require more intimate exposure to the processes of government and of the welfare programs in more advanced countries. They have read very little and traveled even less. Where there has been travel, it has been an exalted affair of state, revealing only glamorous surfaces. These effects they have attempted to reproduce at home with little comprehension of their essential substance and meaning. Their youth, whose present ambition seems to be merely to excel in political cleverness, might well be soundly educated abroad and their services and newly instilled ideas utilized when they return.

The electoral system has been notoriously faulty and both consciously and unconsciously abused. There are laws enough for good government, but with virtually everyone sharing the traditional immunities of office, the laws can become meaningless, even for governing themselves. President Tubman became aware of this when he discharged several officials for malfeasance. The legislature refused to act and he was forced to take his case to the public press. Mere advice to greater efficiency and honesty would be insufficient. The tolerance so recently given to malfeasance in office, the ignorance of the interior on the part of officials, the general attitude toward the natives, the influence of family connections among executive officers, the lack among the people of means of education, the insularity of outlook—all leave grave doubts as to the possibility of improvement unless drastic revisions and renovations are made. A prompt beginning could be made in the reorganization and overhauling of the Department of the Interior. Among other things the all-important native situation demands redefining and restricting the duties of district commissioners; release of inefficient, dishonest, and resourceless district commissioners who are skilled only in means of extracting money from natives and devising means of punishment; a better scale of pay for district commissioners; thus making possible the securing of a better grade of official and of removing the temptation to inflict fines needlessly to meet regular expenses of maintaining headquarters; institution of a civil service for all important government posts; institution of a court of native appeals in the interior stations, of correlative rank with the district commissioner which would sympathetically examine the complaints of natives; prompt and adequate punishment of official dishonesty and cruelty; an exact outlining of procedure of Frontier Force soldiers and messengers in carrying out orders of the district commissioners; and finally, the employment, temporarily, of interior administrators with experience in successful and honest handling of native people.

The judiciary has been in a sad plight. There are no law schools or trained lawyers. The judges are not even required to be lawyers; they are poorly and irregularly paid, and organically dependent on the executive. The resulting situation of legal confusion and venality could not easily have been avoided. There is yet a chance that order and confidence in the courts can be restored through the use, for a period, of the services of a jurist of outstanding reputation who has no such intimate roots in the political situation. The same reorganization applies to native regulations, which so far have been scarcely more than spasmodic oracular outbursts by the president. Anthropology can aid native administrative policy by the study of aboriginal life and by charting the essential course of the cultural transition. The present Firestone agreement does not, on its purely developmental end, appear to impose hardship on the population, but is rather a source of income to the natives.

The country needs to know its own resources; it needs capital; it needs to keep step with the family of nations. Slavery, forced labor, and the compulsory shipments to Fernando Poo were abolished by proclamation. But this has not been and is not enough. These evils are rooted deeper in the unfortunate economy of the country. It is necessary that Liberia adjust itself to economic reorganization if the country is to survive. There must be trained agriculturists and artisans and, along with these, a restoration of the dignity of labor. The Liberian population appears to depend so completely on the government for support that where it fails there is no resource except the use, and too frequently misuse, of the native population either as free or poorly paid laborers. No satisfactory program of improvement is possible without a thorough review of this economy. With this, too, would go reduction of superfluous government offices, through raising standards of acceptance and combining of minor posts, and the introduction of civil service examinations.

In attempting these internal reforms, outside aid can be useful. Other countries have found it both expedient and profitable to enlist it. Here, however, the objection of Liberia has been most pronounced. Liberians have interpreted such aid as meaning White instruction and handling of their affairs, and they seemed to prefer their own inefficiency to efficient alien advice. Their reluctance has been justified all too frequently in the kinds of aid they have received. The important need, however, is sound, honest native administration, which might be secured through their own native administrators trained in other colonies, or through American Blacks who can share their outlook and concern for continued autonomy, or through American administrators under the safeguards and supervision of the United Nations.

The role of the United States in this mélange seems to be of the most embarrassing difficulty. The relationship between the two countries has been such as to permit the practices complained about to develop to a point which attracted the attention of Europe. Increased American control may mean the approach of imperialism in the country. The exigencies of World War II have drawn the two countries closer together and Liberia's economic center has shifted from Europe to America. United States experts are working out programs which touch most areas of the national life. This is being done with the approval and leadership of President Tubman, who appears to have envisaged the possible future of Liberia as an African state and to have the social courage to make the needed reforms. The task of reconstruction will be long and hard, involving a transformation of the national attitude; but for almost the first time in the country's history the material development of the country, basic to any sound growth, seems probable. The social progress of the natives in other parts of West Africa and the new experiences brought by the war to Liberian natives, have made inevitable the awakening of the aborigines. An intelligent, stable American policy, certainly now dictated by self-interest, can do much to guide and sustain current movements toward reform, if the middle course between imperialism and indifference is taken. America cannot escape its spiritual obligations to these exiles from its own institutions, even though their descendants have bowed down before strange idols in a Canaan stripped of illusions. It owes a corrective assistance through increased concern and through accentuated educational and economic enterprise. The fulfillment of this obligation must be tempered by a sympathetic understanding of the high aims of the republic, at times gravely obscured, not yet bright, but still burning.

Epilogue

An Interpretation of Charles S. Johnson's Life and Works

When Charles Spurgeon Johnson died suddenly in 1956 at the age of 63, he and his era were already slipping rapidly toward obscurity. His present marginal status in the annals of twentieth-century American history and indeed, more specifically, African American history, is the result of a tragic mixture of forces which afflict the lives of lesser known great men. His reserved personality resisted the status striving found among many of his contemporaries. He did not possess the charismatic leadership qualities that have attracted generations of cultural historians to Frederick Douglas, Booker T. Washington, and W.E.B. DuBois.

The greatness of a man (or of a woman for that matter) is defined better by tracing the significant others and events that shaped their lives and by reconstructing their activities in their contemporaneous world. From his father, the Reverend Charles H. Johnson, Charles S. Johnson developed an interest in race relations as a moral problem with socioeconomic and political consequences.[1] He left Bristol in his early teenage years, traveling to Richmond, Virginia. There he enrolled in the college his father helped to establish: Virginia Union University. He majored in sociology, served a brief stint in the army during World War I, and went on to the University of Chicago in 1917. The sociologist Robert E. Park, who had arrived at the University of Chicago earlier in 1913, quickly recognized Johnson's extraordinary research skills. Johnson had the capacity to store large quantities of quantitative data in his head and, at will, express their sociological meaning in innovative yet understandable terms. He also had unusual methodological and writing skills which enabled him to do first-rate observational and survey fieldwork. Robert E. Park, then president of the Chicago Urban League, appointed Johnson as the organization's first director of research and investigation in 1917. This was unusual, since Johnson was at the time only 24 years old.[2]

Although this position was to launch an incredibly fast-paced career for Johnson, it had an unfortunate consequence: he never received his Ph.D. in sociology. Nevertheless, his extraordinary accomplishments and recog-

227

nition of them by honorary degrees and other distinctions enabled him to be properly addressed as "Doctor" Johnson at least as early as 1929.

Park's appointment of Johnson as the Chicago Urban League's director of research and investigation could not have happened at a better time. In 1919, the Chicago race riot occurred. Influential citizens financed and organized the Chicago Race Relations Commission to investigate the causes of the riot and to recommend solutions. Park was chosen as the director of the investigation and Johnson as his assistant. But it was Johnson who did the data analysis and wrote over half of the lengthy report which was published as *The Negro in Chicago.*[3]

Johnson did not forget his contributions to the Chicago Race Relations Commission, but refined and extended the use of such investigatory bodies as social inventions. As the American representative to the 1930 International Commission on Inquiry into the Existence of Slavery and Forced Labor in the Republic of Liberia, he wrote the final report which greatly influenced American foreign policy toward Liberia up to World War II.

In the 1940s, he used his Fisk Institute on Race Relations and his Department of Race Relations as instruments for helping communities to conduct community-based race relations surveys and municipal race relations commissions. Certainly his effort to institutionalize metropolitan race relations commissions was not lost; the conflict-oriented 1960s renewed an interest in such investigatory bodies. Indeed, it would not be too far-fetched to say that the efforts of Johnson and his staff to expand the utility of race relations commissions helped to set the precedent for the National Advisory Commission on Civil Disorders.

In the early 1920s, Johnson left Chicago, moving his young family to New York City to work for the national office of the Urban League, where he served as director of research and investigations and editor of the organization's organ, *Opportunity.* As editor of *Opportunity,* Johnson published needed sociological interpretations of the rapidly changing demographics of the Black population. During his five-year term as editor he became the major patron saint of Black literary figures—members of the commonly called Harlem Renaissance. Many of them owed their first major publications and extensive public exposure to the *Opportunity* literary contests and the Urban League-sponsored dinners.[4]

Johnson's role as developer of Black talent did not cease when he became director of the Fisk University social science department in 1930. During the 1920s, his contacts with Julius Rosenwald, a patron of the Chicago Race Relations Commission, and with Rockefeller foundation officers while in New York, laid the groundwork for fellowship programs for African-Americans that he would help to administer in the 1930s and 1940s. Specifically, during that period of time, his important decision-making role at the Julius Rosenwald Fund and his influence on the Rockefeller foundations allowed him to direct the career development of scores of African-Americans in the fine arts, humanities, and social sciences. The impact of Johnson's interest in philanthropic foundations was manifest in the large number of Black Julius Rosenwald Fund and General Education Board fellows who became the first wave of African-American scholars and administrators in the post–World War II years' White universities and colleges.[5] Johnson was also instrumental in designing the Julius Rosenwald Fund Fellowship Program for White southerners; the U.S. government's Fulbright Fellowship Program; and the John Whitney Hay Fellowship Program for minorities.

Johnson's scholarly and consultant work, which he completed while serving in the Urban League and while at Fisk was, in the long run, effective in offering environmental race relations paradigms and intervention techniques. His 1930 book entitled *The Negro in American Civilization,* which he wrote for the 1928 National Interracial Conference, was the first post–World War I comprehensive statement on African Americans.[6] During the 1930s, his writings were mainly about Black social life in the South. In these studies, most particularly, *Shadow of the Plantation* and *Growing Up in the Black Belt,* Johnson used case materials and statistical data to portray how local economic, political, and social conditions shaped the developmental problems of Black life. In such analyses, he was most concerned with pointing out how environmental factors, such as plantation political economies, shaped Black institutions such as the family. He viewed these environmental factors and institutions as normal aspects of social life given the inherent strains due to race. His emphasis on normality rather than pathology in Black life set him apart from other Chicago-trained sociologists such as E. Franklin Frazier. Johnson, as it was argued earlier, was willing to use "caste" as an analytical tool for interpreting southern Black life more than other major race relations sociologists of his day.

In the 1940s, even after he became president of Fisk, Johnson continued to be a prolific scholar. In the early 1940s, he completed a monograph for Gunnar Myrdal's *An American Dilemma,* excerpts from which became the book's chapters on patterns of racial segregation.[7] The monograph was published as *Patterns of Negro Segregation.*[8] Like in previous years, but with more vigor, Johnson wrote on the economics of the Black experience and on Black education. As the first Black president of Fisk, Johnson became a major advocate for racial integration in public and higher education during the 1950s. True, his publications in major sociology journals virtually ceased during this period of time, but his speeches, special task reports, and personal correspondence are replete with sociological analyses of educational issues and general race relations concerns.[9]

Johnson's active participation in virtually every important agency, organization, and movement concerned with racial justice and race relations of his day gave him a powerful berth from which he dedicated his life to the eradication of racial inequality. His appointments to the 1930 international commission to Liberia, the United Nations, and to other international responsibilities assured a career which was influential in foreign as well as domestic affairs.

But, these statements are not meant to engage in the practice, let alone the ideology, of historical presentism. Johnson was by no means a raging radical or a rabid revolutionary. As much as he disdained racism, he believed in America and advocated conditional Black assimilation.[10] As Whites viewed him, he was a true believer in working within the civilities and structured White powers which were created. This is why they gave him access to their inner circles. His politeness, tact, and ironic sense of humor put them at ease as they pursued interracial cooperation at the expense of racial integration and more power-oriented solutions to racial inequality. He was not E. Franklin Frazier reminding them rudely about the pathology of White racism. Nor would he come out boldly like Carter G. Woodson, articulating how White philanthropy maintained the underdevelopment of Black education.[11] Whites were grateful that Johnson refused to violate the spirit of interracial cooperation or verbalize his anger in a "tactless" manner. Indeed, his conservative presentation of self angered not a few Black scholars and opinion leaders and delighted the White press. He found himself able to make major decisions about racial issues within the foundations and to a lesser extent, state sectors. He won great influence, directing the flow of research funds to Black researchers and Black institutions and fellowship funds earmarked for Blacks.

After Booker T. Washington's death in 1915, as race relations issues became more national and as ideals of interracial cooperation replaced more practical rural accommodationist philosophies, the financial elites enabled power and leadership to be transferred from the Czar of Tuskegee to the Sociology Professor at Fisk. The power Johnson obtained was never as comprehensive as in the case of Washington if only because the growing Black presence was becoming more complex, it was nonetheless particularly pervasive in the areas of education and research.[12]

Political, economic, legal, and demographic shifts in White/Black relations decreased the relevance of Washington's racial accommodation stance and turned it against him. So it was with Johnson and the dominant interracial cooperation paradigm of his day. World War II and its immediate aftermath forged the material conditions and demands for a racially

integrated labor force and mass consumer culture; "interracial cooperation" was seen for what it was—a way of advocating racial justice in theory
without tampering too much with biracial social structure in practice.
Eventually it too became obsolete as a race relations strategy. The progressive erosion of Jim Crow education in the courts beginning in the latter
1930s exacerbated this growing irrelevance of interracial cooperation and
its advocates.[13]

A content analysis of the speeches Johnson gave and the papers he wrote
in the late 1940s and 1950s, reveal his growing weariness with mounting
White liberal resistance toward the fulfillment of racial integration. He
commented on the irony of this liberal White resistance, which was a
disillusioning contradiction to what they professed to be their goal.[14] But,
the "always tomorrow" philosophy of interracial cooperation for liberals
who turned neoconservative was a stalling tactic, not a genuine hope for a
future racially integrated society.

The political, economic, and sociocultural changes, both domestically
and internationally, which began to alter American race relations disinte-
grated Johnson's power base. Johnson's advocacy of interracial cooperation
became increasingly out of step in an era in which more aggressive stances
against Jim Crow were becoming dominant, such as the Montgomery boy-
cott and the initial sit-in movement during the 1950s and early 1960s.

His gifts of persuasion were ineffective in the face of the emergence of
White resistance to racial integration and foundation subsidization of that
movement. Johnson's ineffectiveness was most apparent in his inability to
stop foundation sector support for the Southern Educational Reporting
Service (SERS) which was stealing his idea of an information clear-
inghouse to monitor school desegregation problems in the South. As well,
the SER's governing board was dominated by White segregationists hostile
to a significant Black input. For all Johnson's persuasive powers, which
worked so well in previous years, he did not prevail in this case. This
incident soured Johnson's optimism about future racial betterment. It was
also an indication of how out of touch he was becoming with inner circles
of foundation politics.[15] During the late 1940s and early 1950s, the retirement and/or death of foundation officers Johnson had known for years
resulted in the emergence of administrators who only knew Johnson
slightly. Also, new foundations such as the National Science Foundation
and the Ford Foundation had their networks which included younger Black
consultants.[16]

Why did Johnson become disappointed with the neoconservatism of
interracial cooperation advocatess and the "new racism" in the 1950s? Was
it because he was such an assimilationist that he felt betrayed by his liberal
compatriots? Or did he feel, perhaps, that all his efforts in playing a role

which was contrary to his true racial orientation came to naught? Those who adhere to the first argument base their facts on public knowledge about Johnson—his writings, speeches, and what contemporaries observed about him in meetings and conversations. As a master of civilities and as a reserved person, Johnson remained aloof from most of his contemporaries. His extraordinarily busy schedule, which went from 8 a.m. through the midnight hours for years, prevented him from developing a wide circle of intimate friends. These factors led many of his contemporaries to presume wrongly that he was arrogant, deceitful, and lacked a sense of humor.

His efforts to protect his privacy perhaps had a more important reason for him: he harbored a critical racial attitude he was not willing to let many persons see despite his accommodative public persona. It was more expedient, so he thought, to engage as much as possible in interracial activities as a kind of diplomatic strategy. He did not believe that the strategy was all that sound. (Indeed, given his deep disdain for paternalism, it is no wonder he was afflicted with migrain headaches in the course of his work with Whites, whose advocacy of racial justice was sincere and acceptance of real racial integration virtually nonexistent.)

Johnson's value of privacy is apparent in the paucity of materials in his voluminous papers which reveal his real thoughts on race relations. We can only get to this issue by turning to recently opened archives of persons with whom Johnson corresponded and to institutions with which he was affiliated. It is only then that Johnson's subtle and critical racial attitude surfaces. Johnson expressed his critical racial attitude mostly through other people. Like Booker T. Washington, Johnson learned how to remain saintly in the eyes of White elites while at the same time doing battle with them through sponsoring and befriending Whites and Blacks bold enough to lash out. Given the climate of Johnson's time, which was only minutely better than Washington's, it was necessary for powerful Black leaders and scholars with conservative personalities and philosophies (but who were indignant over the atrocities of racism) to indulge in such duplicity, and not always consciously.[17]

In the 1920s, as *Opportunity* editor, Johnson encouraged E. Franklin Frazier, then working in Atlanta, to submit critical commentaries on race relations, often under a pseudonym. His admiration for Frazier's uncompromising stance is expressed quite clearly in the correspondence. Johnson assisted Frazier's efforts to gain admission to Chicago through his informal ties with the Chicago faculty and with the Laura Spelman Rockefeller memorial. He helped Frazier get his first major post-doctoral grant to continue the line of Black family research and gave him his first position as a professional sociologist at Fisk University. It was only after the early

1930s, after Frazier had left Fisk feeling stifled by the more conservative impression-management of Johnson, did the two men draw apart. Sometimes Johnson spoke by endorsing the views of an outspoken opinion leader such as Edwin R. Embree.[18] Johnson and Embree met in the 1920s. The two gravitated toward high-brow decision-making circles in New York concerned with the changing racial situations in the United States. During those years Johnson was at the National Urban League and Embree was an officer of the Rockefeller Foundation. Instrumental in bringing the men together at conferences and organizations was the Laura Spelman Rockefeller memorial. Examples were the 1927 Negro Problems Conference, the National Interracial Committee of 1928, and the Social Science Research Council's Interracial Relations Advisory Committee. In each of these organizational settings, Embree could not help, but he was dazzled by Johnson's statistical and sociological abilities. Also, Johnson was a modest man who did not do battle with Embree's well-fed ego. Johnson, in his usual quiet way, was probably much impressed by Embree's willingness to learn about race relations and to say what was on his mind even when it put his prestige on the line. Opposites often attract and, especially after 1935, Embree considered Johnson to be his best friend and evidence indicates the feeling was mutual.[19]

Embree became president of the reorganized Julius Rosenwald Fund in 1928. He called on Johnson to develop the foundation's race relations funding targets and policies. The most important recommendation Johnson made was that the Rosenwald Fund establish a fellowship program to develop Black talent. Embree appointed Johnson as a trustee in 1934. The result was a powerful clique which, together with Will Alexander, ran the affairs of the foundation. Embree, Johnson, and Alexander directed the foundation's fellowship program, organized a regional development plan which was incorporated into New Deal policy circles, and established the Division on Race Relations in the 1940s. Johnson's Fisk Social Science Department and the Institute on Race Relations were the major targets for Rosenwald funds for race relations research and fellowships. In many senses, Embree made Fisk a field laboratory for Rosenwald Fund activities in race relations.[20]

Embree was first as much a product of his environment as was Johnson. His racial attitudes were shaped by his renowned grandfather, John Fee, the abolitionist who founded Berea College in the hills of Kentucky. For years, Embree boasted of how Grandfather Fee's abolitionist stand on the slavery question and his childhood experiences with different races gave him a sympathetic view about the problems of Blacks and native Americans.[21] But his ideas were still quite paternalistic when he became president of the

Julius Rosenwald Fund in 1928. Like other progressive White liberals of his day, Embree believed that as much should be done within the confines of a biracial society as possible. This was not due to the need to expand deserved charity to Blacks but because the urbanizing Black population posed a threat to Whites unless they were given resources to develop their own effective leadership and viable institutions.

Embree began to change his mind as he increasingly moved into the orbits of Charles S. Johnson and liberal organizations dedicated to going beyond interracial cooperation and advocating racial integration. The extensive correspondence in the Julius Rosenwald Fund Archives reveals the growing dependency of Embree and other fund officers on Johnson for data to develop controversial race relations stances in the 1940s and 1950s. Additionally, in the 1940s, when Embree evolved into a racial integration advocate, Johnson's Institute for Race Relations conference series became his forum for voicing his newly found stance. Once, his statements were so critical of segregation that the White press ostracized him for days. Given the deep respect Embree had for Johnson, and his awareness of Johnson's sensitive position, more than likely he solicited Johnson's approval of the speech before making it.

As Embree liberalized his thinking, the race relations organizations he helped to establish became a safety net for Johnson. This was essential since, as the 1940s progressed, Johnson became increasingly impatient with the emerging White resistance to the racial changes wrought by World War II. While E. Franklin Frazier, St. Claire Drake, Horace Cayton, and other social scientists published work during that decade highlighting patterns of racial assimilation and accommodation, Johnson developed paradigms of racial conflict with a powerful futuristic component. He organized an Institute for Race Relations newsletter, *Monthly Trends*, which discussed the volatile racial climate of the war years and their aftermath. *Monthly Trends* was financed through the American Race Relations Council. This organization, established by Embree's foundation, was staffed with integration-oriented liberals who defended Johnson from potentially dangerous White criticism that arose from the remarks he made in *Monthly Trends*. If it were not for this protection, it is doubtful that the cautious Johnson would have dared to be so overtly bold.

Notes

1. Charles H. Johnson to Charles S. Johnson correspondence, in possession of Mrs. Patricia Clifford.
2. John H. Stanfield, *Philanthropy and Jim Crow in American Social Science.* Westport, CT: Greenwood Press, 1985.
3. Ibid.

4. David L. Lewis, *When Harlem Was in Vogue.* New York: Oxford University Press.

5. See lists of Black Rosenwald fellows in Edwin R. Embree and Julia Waxman, *Investment in People.* New York: Harper Brothers, 1949.

6. Charles S. Johnson, *The Negro in American Civilization.* New York, 1930.

7. Gunnar Myrdal, *An American Dilemma.* New York: Harper Brothers, 1944.

8. Charles S. Johnson, *Patterns of Negro Segregation.* New York: Harper Brothers, 1943.

9. For an overview on Johnson's presidency years, see Patrick Gilpin, "Charles S. Johnson: An Intellectual Biography," Ph.D. dissertation, Vanderbilt University, 1973, pp. 570-644. Gilpin fails to analyze systematically Johnson's sociological thought during his presidency years as revealed in his conference papers, speeches, and journal and newspaper articles.

10. Willis D. Weatherford, and Charles S. Johnson, *Race Relations: Adjustment of Whites and Negroes in the United States,* Boston: D.C. Heath and Company, 1934; Charles S. Johnson, *Shadow of the Plantation,* Chicago: University of Chicago Press, 1934.

11. E. Franklin Frazier, "The Pathology of Race Prejudice," *Forum,* 70 (June 1927): 856-62; Carter Woodson, *The Miseducation of the Negro,* Washington, D.C.: The Associated Publishers, Inc., 1936.

12. Butler A. Jones, "The Tradition of Sociology Teaching in Black Colleges: The Unheralded Professionals," in *Black Sociologists: Historical and Contemporary Perspectives,* ed. James E. Blackwell and Morris Janowitz. Chicago: University of Chicago Press, 1975.

13. Morton Sosna, *Search for the Silent South.* New York: Columbia University Press, 1977.

14. For Johnson's slightly earlier criticisms of the neoconservatism of White liberals, see Charles S. Johnson, "What the Negro Wants," by Rufford W. Logan, *American Sociological Review,* 11 (1946): 244-45.

15. Patrick Gilpin, *Charles S. Johnson: An Intellectual Biography,* pp. 600-603.

16. Samuel M. Nabrit interview, December 1982.

17. See Raymond L. Hall's insightful analysis of Washington's dual role allocation in *Black Separatism in the United States.* Hanover, NH: The University Press of New England, 1978, pp. 38-57.

18. John H. Stanfield, *Philanthropy and Jim Crow in American Social Science.* Westport: Greenwood Press, in press. Shortly after Embree's death, a close friend of his wrote to Johnson: "Ever since Edwin's shocking death I have wanted to write to you because I believe you and I were closest friends and writing to you may somewhat lessen the grief of not being able to write to him. Since the death of Clarence Day I know of no man in Edwin's wide acquaintance who has held so sure a spot in his affections and in his esteem as you have" (Helen Dean Miles to Charles S. Johnson, 4 March 1950, Charles S. Johnson Special Collection). Johnson responded: "Under the weight of the sudden passing of Edwin Embree who was so much a part of both of us, about the only vent that is possible is that of talking to one another about him. It has been difficult to get reorganized after such an impact" (Charles S. Johnson to Helen Dean Miles, 13 March 1950, CSJ).

19. John H. Stanfield, *Philanthopy and Jim Crow in American Social Science.* Westport: Greenwood Press, in press.

20. Ibid.

21. Patrick Gilpin, *Charles S. Johnson: An Intellectual Biography.*

Appendix: Ten Men

Chavis Pinewine[1]

There was a long road and on it walked ten men. Nine of these men looked very much alike, except for minor differences as to size, eye color, and cranial shape. They moved along at different paces despite the fact that their hands were free and their heads bare and erect. The tenth man, however, was strangely and somewhat embarrassingly encumbered. His arms were strapped to his body just above the elbow, and on his head was fixed a huge and bulging basket full of stones of diverse sizes. So strange was he, indeed, that he was the subject of much discussion among the others. They called him the stone-head man, and for purposes of contrast they called themselves the meat-head men.

The stone-head man could walk, talk the same language, think the same thoughts, feel the same quality of emotion, and was going the same way, but he could not reach the basket of stones on his head however much he strained. In fact, his awkward efforts tended to distract the others from their enjoyment of the landscape and their contemplation of the beauty of nature and the goodness of God.

One of them said, "Why is that stone-head boy going along here with us? We are meat-heads. Observe the close affinity between those stones and his head; they are a part of it by nature's own decree and God's unchallengeable creation. It is clear as day that he was created to carry these stones for us in order that we might hold our heads erect, move our arms freely, and glorify the earth about us." The stone-head man, observing around him no common impulse to do anything about his odd emcumbrance, and seeing no other road, groaned softly, grinned mirthlessly and tried to blow the salty streams of sweat away from his eyes.

There was a general comment on this from several of his companions. One said, "How naturally he carries himself. Those stones aren't heavy for him; see him grin. How hard and white his teeth are. Hear him humming to himself. It sounds like music that our great meat-head masters forgot to compose. Let's make him sing out loud. It will be entertaining and will prove that those stones are not heavy."

The stone-head man sang out loud, but he used double words so that he could protect his own unseen spirit and still keep tolerance for himself in the company of the meat-heads. For his arms were tied and there was no other road for him.

By and by a third man said, "We've been walking along here together for a long time and we can't get rid of stone-head. After all it probably isn't his fault that he has all of those stones on his head. They way he weaves and jerks at times, some of those stones might fall out of that basket and hurt us. Of course, I'm not suggesting that we unstrap his arms; he might throw all of the stones away; or even at us. When he's not singing we don't know what he's thinking. I'll go up to the basket and take out one of the stones— just one, a little one. He might not know what to do with himself if we removed a big one too suddenly, or more than one or two small ones. Then, too, we have to be careful about some of our friends who think the time is not yet ripe to remove any of them. If they had their way they would probably climb up on top of the basket. Some of them don't have any stones on their heads and their arms aren't tied and they aren't moving any faster than old stone-head. But they'd get mighty sore if we let stone-head move any faster."

That was a noble and courageous speech. The stone-head man relaxes as much as possible in order to discern with proper appreciation the difference in his load. The kindly meat-head man who had spoken, with some risk to his popularity, donned his gloves and after much deliberation selected a tiny pebble and tossed it ostentatiously to the side of the road. There was a low murmur of approval as this was done, despite the fact that it was against the status quo. It was called noblesse oblige, humanitarian gesture, a Christ-like act. He became thereafter a protector, guardian and interpreter of the stone-head man, to be consulted on all matters having to do with the latter's condition. It was unsafe for the stone-head man thereafter to say that his feet were tired or that he was thirsty or that the straps were chaffing or that he needed food. The protector was consulted in all such delicate matters, to save the stone-head man from attacks for insolence and the meat-heads from the shock of any discernible change in their relationship with him.

The canonization of the kindly man who threw away one of the stone-head's little stones eventually aroused another whose real profession was kindliness and humanitarianism, for he was the leader of a great religious institution. It occurred to him while pondering the problem of social untouchability, given Scriptural dramatization in the story of Jesus and the woman of Samaria. In a flood of new conviction he decided to organize the benevolence and Christian spirit demonstrated by the kindly man without any obvious disaster to himself. He began a movement on behalf of Christian brotherhood. Once a year all the meat-head men were to gather around the stone-head man, shake his hand, pray with him, and let him sing. There was to be nothing about this calculated to stir the stone-head to wild idealistic dreams. He would still keep his straps and stones, but he would be permitted to forget himself for a day in contemplating with his meat-head fellow Christians a future life where there would probably be no baskets, stones, or straps because no one quite knew how God planned to handle these problems—once He had to deal with them in his own bright mansions.

The stone-head man thanked his reverend brother, praised him for his sterling qualities, his moral leadership, his tireless battling for the Lord, and used florid double words in a tense and torpid prayer. The meat-head men, after their wave of righteousness, returned to their positions with relief and a sense of having done all that was expedient to bring the Kingdom of God on earth.

The stone-head man, although he almost always had to speak through his protector and get his messages the same way, was aware of the endless discussions of his status and his stones and the speculations about what he was thinking. He was reasonably well prepared for the scientific spirit when it presented itself in the person of another of his fellow travelers. He was going to be studied scientifically for the answers, by one who had no patience with preachers, missionaries, and other sentimentalists. The objective student asked him his age, had him hop on one foot, measured his head with shining calipers, tested the tensile strength of his bonds, counted the stones without disturbing their position, checked his vitamin deficiency, compared his walking speed and manual dexterity with that of his unencumbered brothers, and came to the conclusion that (1) his arms were pinioned, (2) there were stones on his head, and (c) this was just the way things were and it was not the business of the objective student to do anything about it. If things were that way there must have been a reason, and since they had been that way so long the reason must be valid. These findings were recorded with precision, down to the last coefficient of correlation, and placed in a book.

The stone-head man had no comment on these findings, but also no especial respect for the erudition so neatly embalmed in the literature. As time went on he was getting more and more wearied and peeved about his stones and straps, and ever so often, he would show more interest in jostling some of the stones out of the basket than in their static color and configuration. He was warned, however, that to talk about his straps would sound dangerously like agitation, and meat-head folks would not stand for that. He would set himself back miles, because he would alienate the kind gentleman who picked out the pebble, the minister who held every year a meeting around him, and the student who spent days right up against him, feeling the shape of the stones, photographing the calluses on his head and describing his awkward gait.

But every so often he would disturb his fellow travelers with something that sounded like muttering, and he lost interest in singing, even in a double tongue. He would mill around, getting in the way of his nearest companions, silently and sometimes sullenly exhibiting his basket of stones, or, on a chance of shaking some off, he would cut ridiculous capers. He would spurt ahead to get closer to the un–stone conscious men who knew he was somewhere in the rear, but who had not been faced with the practical issue of head stones and arm bands and who, as a consequence, felt very superior on this matter.

Then there came upon all the travelers a period of food scarcity and depression. The stone-head man was not an utter stranger to this condition and he speculated hopefully that hunger might bring a new preoccupation for his companions. There was great fear and despair on the high road and, when certain doom for all of them seemed just ahead, another voice spoke up, saying: "We are all in the same sinkhole, brothers, and it doesn't help any trying to find somebody to blame it on. It will add something to the effort to get out if we take some of those stones off that fellow's head and slip his belt a bit." There was a great roar of protest. "If we slip that belt," said one, "none of us will be safe. We may be poor and hungry, but it is better this way than having that ambling, sweating stone-head fellow think-ing he's as good as we are. How else can we know that we are superior if you remove those very necessary measures of restraint and give him the same chance at things. He couldn't beat any of us at the game, of course, but he might, and there's no need of taking chances by disturbing our amicable relations. We'll handle our own problems in our own way, and we resent your outside meddling. It's unconstitutional."

And so the neighbors of the stone-head man, still in panic over their own condition and afraid to be utterly defiant of a stern injunction, came to-gether and rearranged the stones in the basket, camouflaging some of them blue and some gray, so that from a distance it seemed that there were fewer stones. In the nervous rearrangement some of the stones fell off and the stone-head man grinned, but said nothing, even when stray stones fell on the toes of the frightened handlers. After the stones had fallen and the belt had slipped because hunger had thinned the body of the stone-head man, the kindly man who had tossed off the first stone said, "See, we have stepped up our benevolence and our tolerance." The stone-head man knew that it required too much energy either to replace the stones or to tighten the straps again, and he praised the meat-head men for their impelling sense of justice and fair play, and promised to work harder and not boast about the way things slipped.

The party was still a bit exhausted from its long period of depression when it encountered across its path a thick-chested, cropped-haired, strutting phalanx calling themselves "prime meat-heads." This was very ominous and something had to be done about it, for the prime meat-heads were serious and out to make the ordinary meat-heads work for them. It took all the fun out of having a stone-head man around, and they counselled for war. In the precipitous huddle, the stone-head caught up, alternately arguing and swelling with pride. He learned all the speeches and trailed along to all the rallies, holding out his hands now more boldly, demanding that he be untied so that he might work and fight. Eventually his basket was lifted from his head to his shoulders and one of his arms was released. He was then able to remove some of the stones himself. Whenever he slipped off another stone he shouted "Democracy!" so loud it was embarrassing to the others when they tried to pick it up and put it back, for they were also shouting "Democracy!" and "Down with the prime meat-heads!"

By and by one of the meat-heads who had been quietly brooding throughout most of the journey and who all along had been baffled and unimpressed by the various proposals, ventured a remark. He said, "Brothers, the timid and partial measures you have been proposing do not make sense to me. Brother Stone-head seems to me to be very much like the rest of us except that he has his arm still fettered and a miserable load on his back which we can easily remove completely if we only would. Why use half measures, evasions, and excuses? Why not free him completely? We shall then have no need to find excuses for his disposition. His untrammeled spirit can free us of the need for self-deception, and his labor can help us build a great new world."

There followed a deep and ominous silence for the proposal was a brazen one and without precedent in history. The resentments that flooded to the surface did not make vocal replies that sounded either rational or moral. Finally, one of them said, "Pay no attention to that wild-eyed radical. He is trying to destroy our way of life. He is a Communist! He is against the church! He is trying to undermine our form of government! He would make a mockery of our sacred Constitution!"

Having thus properly accused and condemned the proponent of full freedom, they fell upon him and stoned him. The following day they called a conference to discuss the proper working for a charter of freedom for other and more comfortably remote areas of the world.

Notes

1. Charles S. Johnson wrote at least one critical critique of White/Black relations under the fictitious name "Chavis Pinewine": "Ten Men." Evidence in the Johnson Papers suggests that "Ten Men" was written sometime in the late 1930s or the early 1940s. Whether or not the essay was ever published and if so, where, is an issue of ongoing research by the editor.

Bibliography
(From Johnson's Bibliographic Notes)

Books

Alexander, Archibald. (1846). *A History of Colonization on the Western Coast of Africa*. Philadelphia: W.S. Martien

Alexander, William T. (1887). *History of the Colored Race in America*. Kansas City, Mo: Palmetto Publishing Co.

Anderson, Benjamin. (1870). *Narrative of a Journey to Musardu, the Capitol of the Western Mandingoes*. New York: S.W. Green.

Ashmun, Jehudi. (1822). *Memoir of the Life and Character of the Rev. Samuel Bacon, A.M.* Washington, D.C.: Jacob Gideon, Jr.

———. (1826). *History of the American Colony in Liberia*. Washington, D.C.: Way & Gideon.

Bacon, Ephraim. (1824). *Abstract of a Journal Kept by Ephraim Bacon, assistant agent of the United States, to Africa*. Philadelphia: Clark & Raser, printers.

Baker, James Loring. (1860). *Slavery*. Philadelphia: John A. Norton.

Benezet, Anthony. (1788). *Some Historical Account of Guinea, its situation, produce and the general disposition of its inhabitants*. London: J. Phillips.

Blyden, Edward Wilmot. (1869). *Liberia: Past, Present, and Future. Address delivered on July 28, 1866, on Mount Lebanon, Syria, at the celebration of the 19th anniversary of the independence of Liberia, held by American missionaries and other citizens of the United States residing in Syria*. Washington, D.C.: McGill & Witherow.

———. Lewis, T.D.D. and Dwight, T. (1871). *The People of Africa*. New York: Anson D.F. Randolph & Co.

Boone, Clinton Caldwell. (1929). *Liberia as I Know It*. Richmond, Va.: The Author.

Brown, George S. (1849). *Abridged Journal Containing a Brief Account of the Life, Trials, and Travels of G.S. Brown*. Troy, N.Y.: Prescott & Wilson.

Brown, George William. (1941). *The Economic History of Liberia*. Washington, D.C.: The Associated Publishers, Inc.

Buell, Raymond Leslie. (1928). *The Native Problem in Africa*. 2 vols. New York: MacMillan Co.

_____. (1929). *International Relations.* New York: Henry Holt & Co.
_____. (1947). *Liberia: A Century of Survival.* African Handbook 7. Philadelphia: University of Pennsylvania Press.
Cendrars, Blaise. (1927). *The African Saga.* New York: Payson & Clarke.
Coffin, Joshua. (1860). *Slave Insurrections: An Account of Some of the Principal.* New York: American Anti-Slavery Society.
Cowan, Alexander M. (1858). *Liberia, as I found it, in 1858.* Frankfort, Ky.: A.G. Hodges.
Crummell, Alexander. (1862). *Future of Africa: Addresses, Sermons, etc., Delivered in the Republic of Liberia.* New York: Charles Scribner.
Davis, Harold Palmer. (1929). *Black Democracy: The Story of Haiti.* New York: Longmans, Green, & Co.
Davis, Jackson, Thomas M. Campbell and Margaret Wrong. (1945). *Africa Advancing.* New York: Friendship Press.
De la Rue, Sidney. (1930). *The Land of the Pepper Bird.* New York, London: G.P. Putnam's Sons.
Dosson, J.J. (July 1915). *Liberia: Her Origin, Rise and Destiny.* (An oration) Harper, Maryland County.
Durrant, Robert Ernest. (1924). *Liberia.* (A report) Monrovia: African International Corporation. [catalogued under: African International Corporation]
Ellis, George Washington. (1914). *Negro Culture in West Africa.* New York: Neale Publishing Co.
Faulkner, R.P. (1910). *The United States and Liberia. American Journal of International Law,* 4. New York: Baker Voorhis & Co.
Firestone, Harvey Samuel. (1926). *Men and Rubber.* New York: Doubleday, Page & Co.
Fitzgerald, Walter. (1940). *Africa.* London: Methuen.
Foote, Andrew Hull. (1854). *Africa and the American Flag.* New York, London: D. Appleton & Co.
Freeman, Frederick. (1837). *A Plea for Africa.* Philadelphia: J. Whethem.
Frobenius, Leo. (1913). *The Voice of Africa.* 2 vols. London: Hutchinson & Co.
Furbay, Elizabeth Jane Dearmin. (1943). *Top Hats and Tom-Toms.* Chicago, New York: Ziff-Davis Publishing Co.
Goddard, Thomas Nelson. (1925). *The Handbook of Sierre Leone.* London: Grant Richards.
Goldenweiser, Alexander A. (1922). *Early Civilizations.* New York: Alfred A. Knopf.
Gurley, Ralph Randolph. (1933). *Life of Jehudi Ashmun.* Washington, D.C.: James E. Dunn.
Harrison, Hubert H. (1920). *When Africa Awakens.* New York: Perro Press.
Hayman, Arthur Ingram and Harold Preece. (1943). *Lighting Up Liberia.* New York: Creative Age Press.
Heard, William Henry. (1898). *The Bright Side of African Life.* AME Publishing House.

Hoyt, William B. (1952). *Land of Hope*. Hartford: H.J. Fox & W.B. Hoyt.

Innes, William. (1831). *Liberia or the Early History and Signal Preservation of the American Colony of Free Negroes on the Coast of Africa*. Edinburgh: Waugh & Innes.

Jay, William. (1835). *American Colonization and American Anti-Slavery Societies*. New York: Leavitt, Lord, & Co.

Johnston, Sir Harry Hamilton. (1906). *Liberia*. 2 vols. London: Hutchinson & Co.

Jore, Leonce. (1912). *La République de Liberia*. Paris: Librairie de la Société Recueil Sirey.

Kahn, Morton Charles. (1931). *Djuka: The Bush Negroes of Dutch Guiana*. New York: Viking Press.

Karnga, Abayomi. (1926). *History of Liberia*. Liverpool: D.H. Tyte.

Kennedy, John Pendleton. (1843). *Report on African Colonization*. House Report, No. 283, 27th Congress, 3d. session. Washington, D.C.: Gales & Seaton.

Kingsley, Mary Henrietta. (1901). *West African Studies*. New York: Macmillan Co.

Latrobe, John Hazelhurst Boneval (1880). *Liberia: Its Origin, Rise, Progress, and Results*. Washington, D.C.: American Colonization Society.

Lewis, Ethelreda. (1928). *The Boys' Trader Horn*. New York: Simon and Schuster.

Lugard, The Right Hon. Sir Frederick Dealtry. (1926). *The Dual Mandate in British Tropical Africa*. London: William Blackwood & Sons.

Lugenbeel, James Washington. (1906). *Sketches of Liberia*. Washington, D.C.: C. Alexander (1850).

Matthews, John. (1788). *A Voyage to the River Sierra Leone on the Coast of Africa*. London: B. White & Sons.

Maugham, Reginald Charles Fulke. (1920). *The Republic of Liberia*. London: George Allen & Co.

McPherson, J.H.T. (1891). *History of Liberia*. Studies in Historical and Political Science, ed. Herbert B. Adams. Baltimore: Johns Hopkins University Press.

Migeod, Frederick William Hugh. (1927). *A View of Sierra Leone*. New York: Brentanos.

Mills, Lady Dorothy. (1926). *Through Liberia*. London: Duckworth.

Moon, Parker Thomas. (1930). *Imperialism and World Politics*. New York: Macmillan Co.

Phillips, Hilton Alonzo. (1946). *Liberia's Place in Africa's Sun*. New York: The Hobson Book Press.

Sibley, James L., and D. Westermann. (1928). *Liberia: Old and New*. Garden City, NY: Doubleday, Doran & Co., Inc.

Stockwell, George S. (1868). *The Republic of Liberia*. New York: A.S. Barnes.

Strong, Richard Pearson. (ed.) (1930). *The African Republic of Liberia and the Belgian Congo.* Harvard African Expedition, 1926-27.

Williams, George Washington. (1882). *History of the Negro Race in America.* New York: G.P. Putnam's Sons.

Yancy, Ernest Jerome. (1934). *Historical Lights of Liberia's Yesterday and Today.* Xenia, O: The Aldine Publishing Co.

Young, James Capers. (1934). *Liberia Rediscovered.* Garden City, NY: Doubleday, Doran and Co., Inc.

Periodicals

Furbay, John Hawey. (May 1940). "Light on Liberia." *Living Age:* 358, 204.

———. (June 1940). "Liberia Fails as Negro Haven." *Living Age:* 358, 459-63.

Hanson, Earl Parker. (February 1947). "The United States Invades Africa." *Harper's Magazine:* 170-77.

Hogue, Dock. (1945). "Liberian Road." *Atlantic Monthly* 175 May, June: 75-78.

Holbrook, Stewart H. (February 1946). "Prophet Jehudi." *American Merdury* 175: 214-19.

Villard, Henry S. (1941). "Liberia: Link in Democracy's Lifeline." *Christian Science Monitor Weekly Magazine:* Oct 4:3

———. (September 15, 1943). "American Relations with Africa." *Vital Speeches* 9: 722-25.

———. (March 1943). "War Comes to the Negro Republic." *Travel* 80: 16-19.

References

Africa and Its Explorations as Told by Its Explorers. Vol. 2. London: Sampson Low.

African Republic of Liberia and the Belgian Congo. Vols. 1, 2. Cambridge: Harvard University Press.

Alexander, Archibald. (1846). *A History of Colonization on the Western Coast of Africa.* Philadelphia: W.S. Martien.

Annual Reports. American Society for Colonizing the Free People of Color of the United States.

Crummell, Rev. Alexander. (1862). *The Future of Africa.* New York: Charles Scribner.

De la Rue, Sidney. (1930). *The Land of the Pepper Bird.* New York, London: G.P. Putnam's Sons.

Fitzgerald, Walter. (1940). *Africa.* London: Methuen.

Foote, Andrew Hull. (1854). *Africa and the American Flag.* New York, London: D. Appleton & Co.

Great Britain, Secretary of State for Foreign Affairs (December 1930–May 1934). Papers concerning affairs in Liberia.

Handbooks of Liberia (1940). Published by authority.

Heard, William Henry. (1898). *The Bright Side of African Life*. AME Publishing House.

Johnston, Sir Harry Hamilton. (1906). *Liberia*. London: Hutchinson & Co.

Lugenbeel, James Washington. (1853). *Sketches of Liberia*. Washington, D.C.: C. Alexander

McPherson, J.H.T. (1891). *History of Liberia*. Vol. 9. John Hopkins University Studies in Historical and Political Science, ed. Herbert B. Adams.

Peace Handbooks (1920). Vol. 20: *Spanish and Italian Possessions: Independent States*. No. 130: *Liberia*.

Sibley, James L., and D. Westermann. (1928). *Liberia: Old and New*.

Stockwell, George S. (1968). *The Republic of Liberia*. New York: A.S. Barnes

Strong, Richard Pearson. (ed.) (1930). *The African Republic of Liberia and the Belgian Congo*. Vol. 1. Harvard African Expedition, 1926-27.

U.S. Department of State. Vol. 1. *Report on Slavery in Liberia* (1931). *Documents Relating to the Plan of Assistance Proposed by the League of Nations* (1933).

Williams, George Washington. (1882). *History of the Negro Race in America*. New York: G.P. Putnam's Sons.

Young James Capers. (1934). *Liberia Rediscovered*. Garden City, NY: Doubleday, Doran and Co., Inc.

Index

249